WALKS IN THE WORLD

WALKS IN THE WORLD

REPRESENTATION AND EXPERIENCE
IN MODERN AMERICAN POETRY

Roger Gilbert

PRINCETON UNIVERSITY PRESS

PRINCETON, NEW JERSEY

PUBLISHED BY PRINCETON UNIVERSITY PRESS, 41 WILLIAM STREET,
PRINCETON, NEW JERSEY 08540
IN THE UNITED KINGDOM: PRINCETON UNIVERSITY PRESS, OXFORD

LIBRARY OF CONGRESS CATALOGING-IN-PUBLICATION DATA
GILBERT, ROGER, 1960–
WALKS IN THE WORLD : REPRESENTATION AND EXPERIENCE IN
MODERN AMERICAN POETRY / ROGER GILBERT.
P.   CM.
INCLUDES BIBLIOGRAPHICAL REFERENCES AND INDEX.
ISBN 0-691-06858-5
1. AMERICAN POETRY—20TH CENTURY—HISTORY AND CRITICISM.
2. WALKING IN LITERATURE.   I. TITLE.
PS310.W34G55   1991   811'.509355—dc20   90-47797   CIP

THIS BOOK HAS BEEN COMPOSED IN LINOTRON BASKERVILLE

PRINTED IN THE UNITED STATES OF AMERICA BY
PRINCETON UNIVERSITY PRESS,
PRINCETON, NEW JERSEY

1   3   5   7   9   10   8   6   4   2

In my room, the world is beyond my understanding;
But when I walk I see that it consists of three or four hills and a cloud.

Wallace Stevens, "Of the Surface of Things"

CONTENTS

PREFACE AND ACKNOWLEDGMENTS

AS MY TWO-TIERED title is meant to suggest, this book has a double focus, both on a particular kind of poem and on the larger aesthetic and theoretical issues that it raises. The walk poem, as I call it, is a poetic genre that has not been widely recognized despite its long history: instances of it tend to be lumped together with topographical or descriptive poetry, although it differs from those modes in significant ways. This genre achieves special prominence in the twentieth century, where it becomes a versatile and responsive medium for a wide variety of poetic projects. My primary goal is to examine some of these projects as they display themselves in the walk poem, and to consider why the genre seems so peculiarly suited to the more radical aims and assumptions of modern American poetics.

My secondary focus is on the larger issue of poetic representation, particularly as it applies itself to immediate experience. In an age when traditional forms of mimesis seem to become ever more problematic, how can poems represent ordinary experience with the kind of fullness and immediacy that our sensibility still seems to demand? And how can a poem that purports to be no more than a record of experience justify itself as a *poem*, rather than a piece of versified journalism? These questions form the larger theoretical background against which my study of the walk poem is framed.

In writing this book I have received support and encouragement from many people, and I am especially grateful to those who managed to take my topic seriously despite its patent eccentricity. Chief among those who reassured me as to the project's validity are John Hollander, who directed the dissertation on which this book is based, and Geoffrey Hartman, whom I also enlisted as a director at a time when I planned to cover eighteenth-century and Romantic walk poems more extensively than I have. Both of them kept up my morale and helped me negotiate the treacherous and often diverging paths of research, writing, and job hunting. The manuscript was read in part or in whole at various stages by A. R. Ammons, Harold Bloom, David Bromwich, Joel Porte, and Thomas Whitaker, all of whom offered valuable suggestions; I'm especially grateful to the two readers solicited by Princeton University Press, John Burt and Lee Edelman, for their detailed and thoughtful comments.

I am also grateful to the following people for various forms of advice and assistance: Marie Borroff, Cynthia Chase, my parents Sandra and Elliot Gilbert, John Guillory, David Lehman, J. Hillis Miller, and William Pritchard. Many other teachers, friends, and colleagues at Yale and Cornell contributed to this book in ways impossible to document. I wish to thank the Whiting Foundation for a fellowship that was of great help in completing this book. Bob Brown at Princeton University Press has been a supportive and friendly editor; I owe him a great debt for soliciting the manuscript, which I was convinced still needed years of work. Judith Adler was a diligent, perceptive copy editor; many others at the Press have lent their talents to my book as well, and I thank them all.

Thanks are also due to the following publishers for granting permission to quote long portions of their books: Alfred A Knopf Inc., from *The Collected Poems of Frank O'Hara*, copyright (c) 1971 by Maureen Granville-Smith, Administratrix of the Estate of Frank O'Hara; from *The Collected Poems of Wallace Stevens*, copyright (c) 1954 by Wallace Stevens. Doubleday, a division of Bantam, Doubleday, Dell Publishing Group, Inc., from *The Collected Poems of Theodore Roethke*: "The Waking," copyright (c) 1953 by Theodore Roethke; "A Field of Light," copyright (c) 1948 by The Tiger's Eye; "A Walk in Late Summer," copyright (c) 1957 by Theodore Roethke. Farrar, Straus & Giroux, Inc., from Elizabeth Bishop, *The Complete Poems*, copyright (c) 1975, 1978 by Elizabeth Bishop; copyright (c) 1979, 1983 by Alice Helen Methfessel. New Directions Publishing Corporation, from William Carlos Williams, *Paterson*, copyright (c) 1946 by William Carlos Williams; from William Carlos Williams, *Collected Poems Volume II 1939–1962*, copyright (c) 1954 by William Carlos Williams; from Gary Snyder, *The Back Country*, copyright (c) 1960 by Gary Snyder. W. W. Norton and Company, from A. R. Ammons, *The Selected Poems, 1951–1977*, copyright (c) 1977, 1975, 1974, 1972, 1971, 1970, 1966, 1965, 1964, 1955 by A. R. Ammons. North Point Press, from Gary Snyder, *Riprap*, copyright (c) 1965 by Gary Snyder. University Press of New England, from James Wright, *Collected Poems*, copyright (c) 1961. Viking Press, Inc., from John Ashbery, *Self-Portrait in a Convex Mirror*, copyright (c) 1975 by John Ashbery; from John Ashbery, *Houseboat Days*, copyright (c) 1977 by John Ashbery.

And finally I must thank my two chief walking companions: my wife Gina Campbell, without whose receptive but skeptical readings, ongoing conversation, and tolerance for soliloquizing I could not have written this study; and my son Valentine, without whose ceaseless distractions and invitations to the playground I could probably have finished it sooner, but with a woefully impoverished sense of the world's allure, its way of calling us to walk in it.

WALKS IN THE WORLD

INTRODUCTION

A WALK IS A POEM, A POEM IS A WALK

Walk, sb. 1. An act or spell of walking or going on foot from place to place; *esp.* a short journey on foot taken for exercise or pleasure.

Poem. 1. "The work of a poet, a metrical composition" (J.); a composition of words, expressing facts, thoughts, or feelings in poetical form; a piece of poetry. 2. *fig.* Something (other than a composition of words) of a nature or quality akin or likened to that of poetry.

(Adapted from *Oxford English Dictionary*)

S INCE ANCIENT TIMES, poetry and walking have seemed to go hand in hand. From Theocritus and Horace, Dante and Petrarch, Spenser and Milton to the present, poets have represented themselves as walkers, figures wandering in a landscape and translating their movement into poetry. More concretely, many poets, including Milton, Wordsworth, and Stevens, have preferred to compose while walking, finding in the rhythm of their own bodies a kind of metronome for the rhythm of their poems. It is as noun rather than verb, however, that the word "walk" reveals its deepest affinities with the poem. As a brief excursion directed toward no practical goal but undertaken purely for the pleasures of movement, reflection, and aesthetic perception, the walk closely resembles the modality of the lyric poem, which also can be said to lack the kind of teleological element encountered in prose writing, be it narrative or expository. Thus Babette Deutsch writes that "the one [prose] resembles a man walking toward a definite goal; the other is like a man surrendering himself to contemplation, or to the experience of walking for its own sake."[1] Like walks, poems can be seen as exploratory movements that remain uncommitted to any particular goal or outcome beyond movement itself. Both walk and poem therefore offer especially pure instances of the aesthetic, conceived as the negation of practical or end-directed activity.

More recently the poet A. R. Ammons has declared in a brief essay that "A Poem *Is* a Walk" (italics mine). Ammons's title recalls some of Stevens's more deliberately outrageous *Adagia*, such as, "A poem is a pheasant," "A poem is a meteor," "A poem is a cafe." But where Stevens is playfully metaphorical, Ammons is more intently analogical.

He sees a profound affinity between the form and function of walk and poem, and he does not hesitate to posit it as "a reasonably secure identity":

> What justification is there for comparing a poem with a walk rather than with something else? I take the walk to be the externalization of an interior seeking, so that the analogy is first of all between the external and the internal. Poets not only do a lot of walking but talk about it in their poems: "I wandered lonely as a cloud," "Now I out walking," "Out walking in the frozen swamp one grey day." There are countless examples, and many of them suggest that both the real and the fictive walk are the externalizations of an inward seeking. The walk magnified is the journey, and probably no figure has been used more often than the journey for both the structure and the concern of an interior seeking.[2]

Ammons is here primarily concerned with the analogical relation between poem and walk, and I will consider his analysis of this relation in more detail later on; but he also recognizes that poets have perennially exploited this resemblance by writing poems *about* actual walks. His examples, from Wordsworth and Frost, give only the barest hint of the walk poem's diversity as a genre. As he acknowledges, "countless examples" could be cited: Spenser's "Prothalamion," Milton's "L'Allegro" and "Il Penseroso," Cowper's *The Task*, Schiller's "Der Spaziergang," and many poems by Wordsworth and Clare, to name only the most prominent earlier instances. These and many other poems are in the simplest sense accounts of particular walks, but all of them reach toward a more intimate relation between poem and walk than the word "account" suggests. Indeed the central aim of the walk poem as a genre may be said to consist in a desire to erase the difference between text and experience, to assert and sustain an absolute coincidence of language and bodily sensation. In this study I will concentrate on twentieth-century American versions of the walk, because it is here that we find the most radical coalescence of poetic form and experiential matter. Ammons's own walk poem, "Corsons Inlet," gives a spectacular illustration of how the very shape of the poem may be molded to follow the fluid contours of the walk. It will be my primary contention that, as both experience and literary form, the walk uniquely answers the various and often incompatible impulses to redefine and remake poetic representation that have guided American poets over the past century.

A Walk Is a Poem

Since Emerson, it has been one of the primary assumptions of American poets that all of experience itself constitutes a form of poetry.

Nothing more clearly distinguishes American poetics from its European counterparts than this insistent redefinition of the poem as already immanent in the phenomenal world, to be transcribed by the poet sufficiently gifted to apprehend it.[3] No longer is the poem dictated by a celestial muse; instead it is manifested in the very hum of the senses, in the mere consciousness of reality. Certainly such a view has its British precursors, most especially in the poems and prefaces of Wordsworth. But the strain of Wordsworthianism that insists on the hallowing of the commonplace did not take hold in England as it did in America, perhaps because British aesthetics demanded a more exalted conception of the poetic. It remained for nineteenth-century American writers like Emerson, Thoreau, Whitman, and even lesser figures like Bryant and Whittier, to explore the ramifications of Wordsworth's theory and practice more fully.

One consequence of the notion that ordinary experience is in itself poetic appears in the convergence of poetry and journalism. Thus the line between journalistic prose on the one hand and poetry (or prose poetry) on the other becomes less and less distinct as American literary history continues. Emerson, Thoreau, and Whitman were all faithful journal keepers, and all drew extensively on their journals in their more canonical writing (as Wordsworth had drawn on Dorothy's). As an open-ended, literal record of daily life, the journal may be said to come closest to the latent poetry of experience, setting it down without the kind of shaping and selection that written poems generally employ. Yet it is precisely for this reason that the journal comes to embody a major threat to the project of American poetry. For if poetry and journalism merge entirely, poetry must give up its heightened aesthetic aura and its claims to canonical status. The central dilemma for American poets, then, takes shape as the problem of how to sustain the identity between experience and poetry while still maintaining the privileged status of the poem.

This problem becomes most acute, perhaps, in those longer American poems that model themselves directly on the journal, aspiring to absolute coextensiveness with the continuum of experience. Such works as Lowell's *Notebook*, Ginsberg's *The Fall of America*, Creeley's *A Day Book*, Snyder's *Mountains and Rivers Without End*, and Ammons's *Snow Poems* present themselves as literal transcripts of an extended period of time, absorbing all the minutiae of travel, meals, and trivial incidents with apparent ease. Their form is that of an endless printout or graph, an analogy that Ammons amusingly literalizes in his long *Tape for the Turn of the Year*, which he composed at the typewriter on a roll of adding machine tape. Such poems carry toward its furthest logical extreme the peculiarly American belief that everything in experience counts, has its place in the poem. But by doing so, they risk condemn-

ing themselves to the worst of fates: unreadability. For the more fully
the poem assumes the dimensions of experience, the more it threatens
to take on the diffuseness and opacity of experience as well. In its most
radical form, the American poetics of experience asymptotically approaches a point where the very rationale for the written poem collapses, and we are left with an endless skein of recorded living, a text
too massive to enter. At this hypothetical point of convergence, the
poem becomes like Lewis Carroll's map drawn on a scale of one to
one—where can one unfold it? When can one read it?[4]

In order to avoid the dangers of open-ended journalistic form that
arise from the poeticization of experience, American poets need to
find ways to write *poems*, self-contained literary artifacts that can sustain
repeated readings; yet they must do so without forsaking their sense
that poetry in its raw state is evenly distributed throughout experience.
The walk offers an ideal solution to this problem, because it makes possible a form of closure already latent in experience itself, not arbitrarily imposed from without. A walk is a kind of frame, within which experience takes on a more intensely aesthetic quality. It thus allows poets
to preserve a distinction between the special status of the poem and
the continuity of experience without having to go outside the realm of
the daily. We might venture the following formula: the walk is to experience as the poem is to poetry. In other words, if experience is a kind
of poetry, that is, an aesthetically charged *medium*, a walk is a kind of
poem, possessed of the formal unity and lyric concentration that characterize a successful art object. In their efforts to tap the latent poetry
of experience, American poets can employ the walk as a way of bestowing closure and intensity on their poems while still remaining faithful
to the texture of ordinary life. Within the boundaries of the walk,
there is room for the ongoing and contingent blend of thought, perception and encounter that makes up the fabric of everyday experience; yet these casual elements are rigorously contained and busy deline-
ated by the frame of the walk, whose presence signals a heightened attention to the particulars of time and place.

Standing Still and Walking

I now want to briefly contrast the walk poem with some related poetic
genres, in order to clarify further how the peculiar features of the walk
as experience find their correlatives in the poem. I have chiefly in
mind the Romantic genre first defined by M. H. Abrams in his classic
article "Style and Structure in the Greater Romantic Lyric." Like the
walk poem, the greater Romantic lyric is firmly located in time and

space, and moves between description of an outer landscape and reflections prompted by that landscape. Here is Abrams's initial characterization of the genre:

> They present a determinate speaker in a particularized, and usually a localized, outdoor setting, whom we overhear as he carries on, in a fluent vernacular which rises easily to a more formal speech, a sustained colloquy, sometimes with himself or with the outer scene, but more frequently with a silent human auditor, present or absent. The speaker begins with a description of the landscape; an aspect or change of aspect in the landscape evokes a varied but integral process of memory, thought, anticipation, and feeling which remains closely intervolved with the outer scene. In the course of this meditation the lyric speaker achieves an insight, faces up to a tragic loss, comes to a moral decision, or resolves an emotional problem. Often the poem rounds upon itself to end where it began, at the outer scene, but with an altered mood and deepened understanding which is the result of the intervening meditation.[5]

Abrams credits Coleridge with the invention of this genre, which was only subsequently taken up by Wordsworth in "Tintern Abbey"; and the form is indeed Coleridgean rather than Wordsworthian, reflecting a more detached, hermeneutic relation to the physical world than Wordsworth customarily displays. The descriptive and meditative parts of the poem are clearly separated; the poem's structure is a movement from description to meditation and then back, what Abrams calls an "out-in-out process." This kind of poem is not primarily descriptive in purpose, however; as Abrams says, "the description is structurally subordinate to the meditation, and the meditation is sustained, continuous, and highly serious."[6] The kind of poem Abrams describes, then, most fully represented by Coleridge's "The Eolian Harp," "Frost at Midnight," "Fears in Solitude," and "Dejection: An Ode," is essentially a meditative poem grounding itself in a particular landscape. The landscape provides both the subject of the framing description and the stimulus to meditation, but the poem's basic movement is an inward one.

Abrams contrasts this kind of poem with what he calls the "local poem," an eighteenth-century genre that he cites as the main progenitor of the greater Romantic lyric. Where the local or topographical poem differs from the later genre, according to Abrams, is in the absence of a centrally placed meditation; instead "the order of the thoughts is the sequence in which the natural objects are observed; the poet surveys a prospect, or climbs a hill, or undertakes a tour, or follows the course of a stream, and he introduces memories and ideas intermittently, as the descriptive occasion offers." The sequentiality which Abrams finds characteristic of the local poem reaches its apex in the walk poem, in which sequence becomes a function of spatial movement rather than the more arbitrary analysis of a landscape into parts. As in the local poem, the walk poem does not generally include a distinct meditative phase set off from the surrounding descriptive passages; instead, description and reflection are more continuously interwoven than in the Coleridgean form that Abrams discusses. The somewhat static "out-in-out" structure of the greater Romantic lyric is replaced by a more fluid mixture of perception and thought, less rigorously organized but more mimetic of the fugitive operations of consciousness.

The walk poem differs from both the standard local poem and the greater Romantic lyric in one crucial respect: it takes as its subject not a landscape, an essentially static entity, but an experience. It is thus *transcriptive* rather than descriptive. The distinction is an important one for my purposes; where *de*scription or writing *of* suggests the linguistic representation of something fixed and spatial, *trans*cription, writing across or "taking down," implies the carrying into language of something fluid and temporal, as when one transcribes speech or music. Though sequentiality plays a part in the local poem, as Abrams notes, sequence generally remains subservient to the sense of the place or landscape as a whole, a spatial totality. And similarly, while the meditative section of a greater Romantic lyric may give the impression "of the casual movement of a relaxed mind, retrospect reveals the whole to have been firmly organized around an emotional issue pressing for resolution."[7] Both these related genres are therefore essentially spatial in form, centering on either an external or internal object which remains outside the flux of experience. The walk poem, by contrast, takes this flux as its true subject, and in transcribing it assumes a radically temporal form.

This modal difference between the two genres stems from the obvious fact that in the greater Romantic lyric the speaker stays in one place, whereas in the walk poem he is in continual motion. While this may seem a banally literal point, it has important structural implications for the two modes. As Abrams observes, the central meditation in a greater Romantic lyric unfolds autonomously, propelled by its own inner logic, while the "order of thoughts" in a local poem is determined by the order in which objects are observed. When the speaker is walking, the parallel currents of thoughts and phenomena become still more intricately braided; because new objects are continually coming into view, thought itself must remain plastic and responsive, always ready to shift direction as the moment may prompt. Samuel Johnson, in a *Rambler* dedicated to the idea that "very few men know how to take a walk," offers an elegant account of this receptive mode of consciousness:

> There are animals that borrow their colour from the neighbouring body, and, consequently, vary their hue as they happen to change their place. In like manner it ought to be the endeavour of every man to derive his reflections from the objects about him; for it is to no purpose that he alters his position, if his attention continues fixed to the same point. The mind should be kept open to the access of every new idea, and so far disengaged from the predominance of particular thoughts, as easily to accommodate itself to occasional entertainment.[8]

With Johnson's help we can begin to see a fundamental difference between the modes of thought at work in the two genres. The Coleridgean landscape-meditation, as Abrams notes, ultimately derives from the seventeenth-century meditative tradition in which the poet contemplates some fixed object, taking it as an emblem of spiritual truths. Coleridge too tends to view the landscape as an organic analogue, or more simply a metaphor, for some inner condition. But as the passage from Johnson suggests, the walk poem approaches the external world metonymically rather than metaphorically, finding in the succession of phenomena a series of associative stimuli rather than a single coherent trope of spirit. Indeed Johnson implies that the walk defeats solipsism by forcing the mind to change continually in accordance with the shifting landscape.

This metonymic component of the walk poem virtually insures that the poet will be unable to maintain the totalizing, spatial perspective characteristic of the greater Romantic lyric. But while this means that closure will always be more tenuous in the walk poem, it also means that the poem will remain truer to the temporal character of experience, the pure successiveness that governs human life. Discussing what he calls "a new kind of reflective poem, the contemporary poem of travel" (as exemplified for him by Thomas Kinsella, Philip Larkin, and W. S. Graham), Calvin Bedient eloquently describes the way such poems heighten our awareness of time, in terms directly transferable to the narrower genre of the walk poem:

> Like certain earlier poems—Gray's "Eton Ode," for instance, or Wordsworth's "Tintern Abbey"—these face a solitary consciousness towards place and time yet do not, as it were, sit still, are not even ostensibly at rest, but move through the world, continually stimulated to new observations, reactions, associations. Cast through space, these poems bring a flutter to the tentativeness of consciousness, which they heighten. They ride on motion the way, and at the same time as, the mind floats on duration.

Informed by our contemporary hypersensitivity to the moment, they say that life is only here and now, and fleeting, a thing that *cannot* stand still; and more, that space is as unfathomably deep as time, is time's body, but at least outside ourselves, both mercifully and cruelly outside. The poems increase the sense of exposure to existence as actual travel renews and magnifies the sensation of living.[9]

Bedient recognizes how bodily motion synchronizes space and time, allowing each to be experienced in terms of the other. Such experience comes closer to the Heraclitean and Einsteinian sense of reality as flux that has come to dominate Western thought in the last century than does the more static meditative posture of the greater Romantic lyric. If the latter genre tends toward the kind of Platonic, transcendental vision we associate with Coleridge, the walk poem (and Bedient's poem of travel) tends to emphasize process in all its manifestations, both mental and physical.

Walking and Thinking

Walking and thinking are, of course, closely associated in the Western tradition. From Parmenides's "road of discourse" to Heidegger's "Weg zum Sprache," walking has been a key trope for the progress of thought.[10] More literally, we know that philosophical activity has often been linked with the walk's leisurely movement; the legend of the Peripatetic school codified this connection, while Plato's *Phaedrus* provides a particularly clear instance of the walk as scene of philosophy.[11] Rousseau's *Rêveries d'un promeneur solitaire* represents the Romantic culmination of the belief that philosophical reflection finds its ideal occasion in the walk. The fact that Rousseau chooses to divide his book into numbered "Promenades" (rather than, say, "Essais" or "Rêveries") emphasizes the occasional character of his meditations; and indeed at key moments in the work certain incidents of the walk obtrude themselves, interrupting Rousseau's train of thought and forcing it in new directions.[12]

The poet's walk is also undertaken as much for meditation as for observation; the rhythm of the walk ideally produces an easy and harmonious alternation between thought and perception, self-consciousness and the consciousness of a world beyond the self. In his recent study, *The Walk: Notes on a Romantic Image*, Jeffrey Robinson beautifully captures the fluid transactions that the walk elicits:

> The walk is an occasion of limited vulnerability. I offer myself to unpredictable occurrences and impingements. The world flows past my body,

which may block, pleasurably or uncomfortably, some sudden cometary intrusion and create a *situation*. But mostly I can modulate the immediacy of random intrusions for the sake of encouraging, unimpeded, the "inner life." Raising the stakes, the walk implies a mixture or an alternation of committed responses and disinterested reflection, or the world on a walk engenders the mental polarity of critical thinking all the way to wonderment. The walker observes things from a distance, and if the power of the object is in some way too compelling, he by definition detaches himself from it by walking on. Yet the walker is in experience, feels and thinks in his movement through time and space, and is reaching out (or can) to the world in time.[13]

As Robinson makes clear, the walker's thinking differs from the philosopher's in that it always takes place within the context of the walk. The particulars of time, place, weather, and landscape continually inform the walker's consciousness, stimulating thoughts and associations which might not otherwise have arisen. A kind of fluid oscillation between external objects and inward ideas and images may ensue, one whose very rapidity blurs the borderline between physical and mental experience. The walk poem is thus ideally situated to register the subtle impingements of a world, a setting, upon the apparently autonomous process of thinking. It is in the intricate dialectic between perception and reflection that the walk poem finds its center; as a genre it emphasizes the ineluctable dependency of the general on the particular, the abstract on the circumstantial. Thinking is shown to be not a mastering of experience but a product of it, circumscribed by the temporal and spatial limitations of the body itself.

The temporality of thought and consciousness is especially underscored by the walk poem. Such forms as the essay or treatise may appear entirely spatial in organization, masking the inherently temporal nature of discursive thought. But by coordinating thinking with the real-time action of the walk, the walk poem restores a temporal dimension to philosophical reflection, allowing us to observe its fugitive motions, false starts, sudden leaps, and to see them all the more clearly because they are set against the literal movements of the body through space. Thought ceases to be wholly cognitive, directed toward some final object of knowledge, and becomes instead a process of wandering as wayward and impulsive as the walk itself. Within the frame of the walk, thinking is as much an aesthetic activity as looking, a mode of play rather than work.

As a form of experience, then, the walk is able to subsume functions of consciousness as different as perception and reflection; its temporal rhythm allows for their continual interplay, while containing both within a larger experiential context. The critic John Elder, prefacing a discussion of Wordsworth, describes the way walking integrates inner and outer worlds:

> Just as the wasteland and the wilderness are reconciled through earth's circuit of soil-building decay, the landscape and imagination may be united through the process of walking. The mind's flicker of attention from the earth to its own associations seems on one level to have an inescapably binary quality. But mental sunlight and clouds are also borne out under a larger sky in the meandering circuit of the poet's walk. Walking becomes an emblem of wholeness, comprehending both the person's conscious steps and pauses and the path beneath his rising and falling feet.[14]

Whether such wholeness is organic or synthetic, it embraces a range of mental activity not ordinarily present at one time. The walk thus serves as an epitome of a temporal mode of consciousness at once open to its surroundings and aware of its own workings. The poet can use the walk to examine and represent the area in which mind and world interact most closely, losing hard-edged definition as they modify each other by turns and at once.

Scene and Process

Let me now try to situate the walk poem more specifically within the field of twentieth-century American poetics, and particularly in relation to two central strains that might be called the processive and the scenic. Process has of course long been a primary motif in American poetry, particularly as a means of subsuming poetic form and both physical and mental reality. Poets as diverse as Stevens, Pound, Frost, Williams, and Ammons have defined the poem as an action rather than an object, possessing "the form of a motion" (to quote the phrase from Williams's "The Wind Rises" that also serves as the subtitle of Ammons's long poem *Sphere*).[15] Clearly such a kinetic model of the poem finds special fulfillment in the rendering of a walk, itself a motion possessed of a definite form. Curiously, however, the poet who committed himself most vocally to the notion of process as form did not himself write directly in the genre. I have in mind Charles Olson, who, in his famous essay "Projective Verse" and in many other polemical pieces, aggressively championed Whitehead's concept of process as both a model of reality and a paradigm for the poem.[16] No one has more forcefully argued for the kinetic nature of successful poetry than Olson; his insistence in both theory and practice on reinventing syntax so that it more accurately reflects the flow of language and appearance gives only one measure of the radicality of his stance.[17]

Yet while Olson and his Black Mountain associates often invoke walking as a metaphor for the poem, they seldom if ever turn to the actual walk as poetic material.[18] This avoidance of the walk poem reflects a more general resistance to the kind of representation that the genre seems to involve (although in fact, as we shall see, the walk poem can accommodate a wide range of representational strategies). For all his emphasis on the importance of place and its particulars, Olson is rarely able to represent those particulars with the experiential immediacy of a Williams or an O'Hara, because his radical conception of process ultimately undermines representation itself. For Olson the poem must record the very process that brings it into being; hence his obsessive emphasis on the twin stimuli of breath and typewriter, which he claims together regulate the rhythms of the poem. Taken to this extreme, kinesis supplants mimesis entirely.[19] If the poem is to embody the process of its own creation, it cannot reflect or transcribe any other, more worldly process, since that would be to deny the primary reality of the moment in which the poem is written; the obvious analogy here is to Jackson Pollock's Action painting, which must likewise disown all figuration. Thus Olson's poems remain tied to the scene of their composition, whereas a typical walk poem seeks to bypass that scene altogether by behaving as though it had come into being simultaneously with the walk that it recounts.

To be sure, Olson's poems do in fact vigorously engage the world, both in the localized form of Gloucester, Massachusetts, and in its broadest geographical and historical sweep. Yet they do so not mimetically, but didactically; Olson generally assumes a panoptic point of view that lies outside and above experience. Indeed, the Maximus persona can be viewed precisely as a means of dissociating the prophetic seer of Gloucester, whose gaze takes in not only its topography but its history at a glance, from the actual resident walking its streets. Such a perspective, based on omniscience rather than experience, enables Olson to maintain the primacy of the compositional moment, since it gives him unlimited access to the world without imprisoning him in a specific experiential context.[20] Thus the poem is free to follow the impulsive thrusts of its own internal momentum, unrestricted by external circumstances. The risk, of course, is precisely the kind of solipsistic immersion in one's own thought for which Dr. Johnson recommends the walk as antidote. When the poem is so cut off from direct experience that its only context is the typewriter, then process becomes an endless act of self-indulgence, a perpetuation of pure ego. At its best Olson's work escapes this trap, but too often it succumbs to the temptation of a process imagined as wholly autonomous, without the informing pressures of immediate experience.

At the opposite extreme from Olsonian projective verse, we find what Charles Altieri has labeled the "scenic mode," a strain of poetry that he argues achieved increasing prominence in the 60s and 70s. Altieri associates this mode most closely with poets of the so-called Deep Image school, like Robert Bly, James Wright, William Stafford, and others; but he traces its influence far beyond this group, seeing it as a dominant and enervating presence in contemporary poetry. His description of the typical scenic poem may initially lead us to suspect that it is merely an updated version of Abrams's greater Romantic lyric:

> The work places a reticent, plain-speaking, and self-reflective speaker within a narratively presented scene evoking a sense of loss. Then the poet tries to resolve the loss in a moment of emotional poignance or wry acceptance that renders the entire lyric event an evocative metaphor for some general sense of mystery about the human condition.[21]

The scenic lyric, as Altieri here describes it, shares the greater Romantic lyric's strong consciousness of landscape and its push toward emotional resolution; what it lacks is an extended meditative movement: "There is virtually never any sustained act of formal, dialectical thinking or any elaborate, artificial construction that cannot be imagined as taking place in, or at least extending from, settings in naturalistically conceived scenes." For Altieri, it is the exclusion of extended thought that marks the essential failure of the mode, its inability to do more than point beyond itself to the ineffable.

One may wish to temper the harshness of Altieri's critique while granting that in its purest form the scenic lyric does indeed represent a dangerously weakened conception of poetry. Altieri centers his attack on the mode's naturalism, which he views as a naively simple form of mimesis that cannot adequately address complex thematic issues. One might modify this position by noting that the typical Deep Image poem takes stasis rather than process as its goal, seeking to embody a stillness that remains outside language and experience. Hence it is usually unable to incorporate the kind of wandering, temporally extended thinking that I have associated with the walk. Instead, thought takes the form of epiphanic insights emerging suddenly and inexplicably from scenic perceptions, as in Wright's famous "Lying in a Hammock at William Duffy's Farm in Pine Island, Minnesota":

> Over my head, I see the bronze butterfly,
> Asleep on the black trunk,

Blowing like a leaf in green shadow.
Down the ravine behind the empty house,
The cowbells follow one another
Into the distances of the afternoon.
To my right,
In a field of sunlight between two pines,
The droppings of last year's horses
Blaze up into golden stones.
I lean back, as the evening darkens and comes on.
A chicken hawk floats over, looking for home.
I have wasted my life.[22]

One may admire this poem as a successful and moving embodiment of the edges of articulate consciousness confronting a mute world, while still feeling that its ostentatious closure verges on sentimentality. Indeed such a poem suggests that in contemporary verse the sentimental consists precisely in the foreclosing of continued thinking through the emphatic use of emotive language at poem's end. It is perhaps not wholly insignificant that the poem's title informs us of the speaker's bodily stasis; that posture seems to mirror the essential passivity of the poem's consciousness, its reluctance to move discursively or reflectively among the images it registers. Even the last line presents itself less as a thought than as a simple fact arising directly from the phenomena of the landscape.

Altieri may be too quick to condemn the mimetic aspect of the scenic mode as the source of its weakness; after all, American poetry has always located itself in particular landscapes with present-tense immediacy, from "Song of Myself" to "Burnt Norton," "Credences of Summer," and "The Pisan Cantos." But where those poems remain open to process, allowing mind to flow through and modify the representation of landscape, the scenic poem tends to distrust the workings of discursive thought, and so tries to minimize the speaker's intrusion on the scene. The result at its worst is like a Coleridgean landscape poem stripped to its bare bones, capable of expressing little more than a vague sense of depth and mystery.

Both the poetry of process and the poetry of scene, then, taken to their furthest limits, reach dead ends: in one case a solipsistic immersion in the composing (or typing) self, in the other a virtual erasure of self in the face of a landscape perceived as ineffably other. I take the walk poem to represent a form capable of reconciling these two projects, rendering them mutually supportive rather than rigidly opposed. The walk poem unites kinesis and mimesis, process and scene, mind and landscape, time and space, in such a way as to avoid or defuse the dangers associated with each of these elements in isolation. It thus constitutes a tenuous compromise between opposing poetic projects. As such it necessarily violates the purity of each project; Olson would no doubt reject a walk poem as an inadequate embodiment of process, just as a scenic poet might accuse a walk poem of obtruding itself too aggressively on the landscape. But it is a measure of the strength of the genre that so many walk poems can sustain their hybrid status and remain vital to readers, while specimens of "purer" modes survive chiefly as period pieces, exemplary products of a movement or school rather than successful poems in their own right.

World and Body

As I have noted, Olson's Projectivism places great emphasis on the experience of the body at the moment of composition; breathing, typing, and other bodily sensations all contribute to the process of the poem. Olson later developed the concept of "Proprioception" to further underscore the importance of "the 'body' itself as, by movement of its own tissues, giving the data of, depth."[23] This sense of the body as source and center is of course wholly in keeping with what we have seen to be the self-generating character of Olsonian poetry; the poem becomes an extrusion, almost literally a bodily product, rather than a registering of anything in the world outside the body. Conversely, Altieri's scenic mode might be said to seek a dissolution or forgetting of the body in the face of a world that completely excludes the human.[24] As my stationing of it between these two possibilities should already suggest, the walk poem displays a double orientation, toward both world *and* body. Because the body is in continual, muscular action it remains an importunate reality in the poem; but by the same token the body's motion heightens the presence of the world by bringing new elements of it into view at each moment. The walk thus serves to foreground the reciprocity of world and body as together they enter and inform consciousness.

For both philosophers and poets, the term "world" signifies not simply a collection of discrete objects, but an elemental ground that subsumes all particular places and entities. Thus Stevens writes in his *Adagia*: "The most beautiful thing in the world is, of course, the world itself."[25] Martin Heidegger makes essentially the same point, though without Stevens's aesthetic inflection, in *Being and Time*. For Heidegger the structural priority of the world is expressed by the concept of "worldhood," which refers not to the world as an objective entity, but to the existential condition of being-in-the-world. Arguing against the Cartesian model of subject and object, which assumes a cogito essentially isolated from the world, tentatively probing into it from within a sealed chamber, Heidegger insists that the subject is always already *in* the world, that no other condition is possible, and that the notion of subjectivity as an autonomous sphere is a philosophical fiction:

> When Dasein directs itself towards something and grasps it, it does not somehow first get out of an inner sphere in which it has been proximally encapsulated, but its primary kind of Being is such that it is always "outside" alongside entities which it encounters and which belong to a world already discovered. . . . And furthermore, the perceiving of what is known is not a process of returning with one's booty to the "cabinet" of consciousness after one has gone out and grasped it; even in perceiving, retaining, and preserving, the Dasein which knows *remains outside*, and it does so *as Dasein.*[26]

For Heidegger, then, the world is a constitutive element of Dasein or human existence, one that cannot simply be left behind at will. His use of the spatial term "outside" to designate the self's ineluctable placement in the world may suggest why the walk is able to disclose the fact of "worldhood" with special force. What for Heidegger represents a universal condition becomes in the walk poem a concrete circumstance, dramatizing the sense in which life is always "outside" itself, in the midst of a world.

As a literary form, the walk poem displays its ties to the world most clearly in moments that appear to resist strictly realistic norms of mimesis. In a trenchant discussion of romance, Fredric Jameson borrows Heidegger's concept of worldhood to help distinguish romance modes of representation from those of realism:

> A first specification of romance would . . . be achieved if we could account for the way in which, in contrast to realism, its inner-worldly objects such as landscape or village, forest or mansion—mere temporary stopping places on the lumbering coach or express-train itinerary of realistic representation—are somehow transformed into folds in space, into discontinuous pockets of homogenous time and of heightened symbolic closure, such that they become tangible analoga or perceptual vehicles for *world* in its larger phenomenological sense. . . . [R]omance is precisely that form in which the *worldness* of *world* reveals or manifests itself, in which, in other words, *world* in the technical sense of the transcendental horizon of our experience becomes visible.[27]

Jameson's rather scornful metaphor of the "express-train itinerary of realistic representation" might appear to assimilate the mobility of the walk poem with realism rather than romance; the latter mode creates what he calls "folds in space," essentially static settings capable of taking on a totalizing function. I would suggest, however, that the walk poem typically moves *between* the linear, sequential relation to the world of realism and the epiphanic one of romance, in which "world-ness" as such becomes visible. For all their realistic accounting of objects, particulars, and "stopping places," walk poems almost invariably include what might be called a romance moment, characterized by a nonphenomenal apprehension of space as unity rather than extension. Such moments serve to bring a fragile sense of wholeness out of the myriad details of the walk, allowing the world to be experienced in its own right, as the element of constancy underlying the walk's shifting phenomena. Yet because of their context within the ongoing temporality of the walk, these moments tend to be more provisional and contingent than more traditional epiphanies, from Wordsworth's "spots of time" to Eliot's "timeless moments"; they are experienced as brief pauses or intervals, after which linearity and flux take over once more. Realism and romance thus represent another polarity that the walk poem seeks to span, through its fluid modulations from dense particularity to symbolic unity, from the world as plural to the world as singular.

It is the bodily nature of the walk that allows it to approach the world more intimately than do other forms of experience. The walk does not seek to transcend experience, to attain an objective, theoretical knowledge of the world; instead it remains caught up in movement, in the "equipment" of paths and roads, in the muscular activity of walking. Yet this activity has no practical goal; it seeks only to perpetuate the movement of walking itself, and to continually bring new objects into view. The walker remains *in* the world, actively engaged with it, but also is constantly looking *at* it as it passes; the world is both something to be negotiated and something to be perceived. (Unsurprisingly, poems about driving or riding on buses or trains tend to keep the world at a greater distance; it is no longer a kinesthetic, tactile presence, but a movie swishing by under glass. This dreamlike quality lends itself to its own special themes and effects, of course, as in Bishop's wonderful bus poem "The Moose," or Ashbery's "Melodic Trains.")

Poets and critics have often pointed to the role the body plays in mediating between consciousness and the world.[28] Paul Valery, in his essay "Poetry and Abstract Thought," gives a celebrated account of an ordinary walk that turns into a kind of rhythmic poem:

> As I went along the street where I live, I was suddenly *gripped* by a rhythm which took possession of me and soon gave me the impression of some force outside myself. It was as though someone else were making use of my *living-machine.* Then another rhythm overtook and combined with the first, and certain strange *transverse* relations were set up between these two principles (I am explaining myself as best I can). They combined the

movement of my walking legs and some kind of song I was murmuring, or rather which was being murmured *through me.* . . . Notice that everything I have said, or tried to say, happened in relation to what we call the *External World*, what we call *Our Body*, and what we call *Our Mind*, and requires a kind of vague collaboration between these three great powers.[29]

The triangular relationship Valery describes between world, mind, and body, as activated by his walk through the street, produces the experience of momentary possession that serves as his instance of the poetic state of mind, as opposed to the mere labor of composition. Characteristically, Valery emphasizes the purely formal, almost mathematical character of the walk; for him the walk becomes a poem not by virtue of the external phenomena it encounters, but through the inner logic of its rhythms. Yet those rhythms, he tells us, are inextricably linked to the physical engagement of those "three great powers," mind, body, and world. The body in motion acts as a kind of membrane between mind and world, registering in its very muscles the subtle "transverse" rhythms passing between them.

More recently Tony Hiss has written about how the experience of walking through certain places, like Grand Central Terminal or Central Park, can demonstrate our capacity for what he calls "simultaneous perception," the ability to be aware of many phenomena at once: "simultaneous perception, putting at our disposal an even-handed, instantaneous, and outward-looking flow of attention, can act like a sixth sense organ."[30] Such expanded attention, Hiss argues, fundamentally alters the way we view ourselves in relation to the world:

> Ordinarily, we seem to be completely separate from everything and everyone in our surroundings, and our sense of external things (if not of other people) is that they are waiting around until we can find something for them to do. At moments when the boundaries flow together, perhaps even disappear, a different sense emerges. Walking through a landscape, we have the sense that the plants and animals around us have purposes of their own. At the same time, our sense of ourselves now has more to do with noticing how we are connected to the people and things around us—as part of a family, a crowd, a community, a species, the biosphere.

The walker's bodily engagement with the world, requiring as it does a continuous stream of data for navigational purposes, in fact permits this sense of connection to emerge more fully than in mere passive looking. All the senses are brought into play, and together they allow the world to be experienced as a complex system of which we are a part, not simply as a succession of discrete objects.[31]

Once this awareness of worldhood starts to be achieved, the relation between body and world can take on a highly erotic dimension. In effect the world as place or setting gives way to what John Crowe Ransom has called "the world's body," a sense of the world as a living, sexual whole inviting a lover's tender explorations.[32] For many poets the walk becomes just such an act of love, though one that must always end with a measure of frustration. In a lyrical essay entitled *The Open Street* (originally intended for *A Walker in the City* but published as a separate booklet), Alfred Kazin movingly describes the desire for such a union that motivates his walks:

> Walking I am unbound, and find that precious unity of life and imagination, that silent outgoing of self, which is so easy to lose, but which at high moments seems to start up again from the deepest rhythms of my own body. How often have I had this longing for an infinite walk—of going unimpeded, until the movement of my body as I walked fell into the flight of streets under my feet—until I in my body and the world in its skin of earth were blended into a single act of knowing![33]

The walk in its most openly Romantic phase pursues just such a quasi-sexual merging of body and world; and while this merging can never be literally achieved, the walk may be said to allow a more intimate contact between the two than virtually any other form of experience. In its mixture of direct physical engagement and relaxed, aesthetic awareness, the walk serves as an ideal vehicle for the poet who wishes to evoke the world in both its seductive beauty and its obstinate solidity.

This sexual dimension of the walk naturally raises questions of gender, both the world's and the walker's. Insofar as "world" is to be identified with "earth," it has traditionally been gendered as female, though neither equation is automatic or self-justifying. Jeffrey Robinson poses the question of the walker's gender directly: "Do women write about their walks differently than men? one inevitably asks. Do they, more basically, walk differently?"[34] He offers a tentative answer based on a few passages from Marge Piercy, Gretel Erlich, and Dorothy Wordsworth. For women, he argues,

> the walk envisions the body, the mind, and the world not as well-bounded entities (perhaps hostile to one another) but as a gradient that signifies well-being. . . . As the [female] walker crosses the line, or blurs the line, of land and water, she creates a vision of a return to the sources of life. Air becomes earth, or rock, and water, engulfing and penetrating, deadly and life-giving. When they *lie down*, female walkers extend the walker's vision into the ecstatic realm of rebirth through the conscious welcoming of the body as a source of knowing, or relationship and touch as the way of being. (pp. 48–50)

As commentary on Piercy and Wordsworth, this account may well be accurate; as general theory, however, it seems to me far too dependent on the sentimental notion that the female mind and body are some-how closer to nature than the male. The finest walk poem by a woman that I know, Bishop's "The End of March," portrays the landscape pre-cisely as hostile rather than nurturing. The particular relation to the world that a poet projects surely depends as much on individual per-sonality as on gender.

My own interest in the poetics of the walk as genre, as distinct from Robinson's interest in the thematics of the walk as image, leads me to ask a slightly different question about gender and walk poems: Why is the genre one that women seem to write around, or on the edges of? Certainly there are many poems by women that engage the walk at some level—Plath's "Berck-Plage," Moore's "An Octopus," Lowell's "Patterns," Dickinson's "I started early," Rich's "Upper Broadway"—but with very few exceptions (most notably Bishop's poem), none of these takes the walk itself as its primary subject, instead focusing on some in-cident, object, or emotion for which the walk provides a convenient frame: a funeral, a glacier, the death of a lover, the sea, a sense of being "halfborn." In other words, most women poets do not seem to use the walk the way men do, as a means of connecting disparate kinds of experience, preferring instead to build their poems around a single experiential center.

I can only speculate briefly and inconclusively as to why this should be so. It may be that the dialectic of mind and world which the walk poem starts from has to presuppose an essentially *universal* conscious-ness—universal in the sense of basic, normative, not specially marked or distinguished. This lack of marking then frees the mind to engage the world directly, without having to reflect on its own specificity. Women poets, of course, as well as poets belonging to highly marked ethnic groups, do not tend to assume such universality as readily as white men, whose culture positions them as normative. Instead, they often require narrative or descriptive occasions that permit them to ac-knowledge and reflect on gender or ethnicity as constitutive elements of their own consciousness. The walk may *contain* such occasions, but it rarely is one itself, since, as I have suggested, it tends to move toward a sense of the world as a totality, rather than as a field of differences. For all its emphasis on particularity and contingency, the walk poem ulti-mately extends the Romantic tradition of universalized consciousness confronting a totalized world; and as such it is a genre whose primary practitioners have inevitably been white men. Whether this will con-tinue to be so is another matter, not only because women and ethnic poets have begun to appropriate canonical forms more aggressively, but because white male poets themselves can no longer take their own universality quite so much for granted. Indeed, it may be that the walk poem itself will not survive current changes in our cultural self-awareness. It is also possible, however, that it will simply adapt to new, more inclusive notions of universal consciousness.

The Cry of Its Occasion

Thus far I have spoken of the walk as a kind of subject matter, characterized by such traits as mobility, reflectiveness, and an orientation towards the world. The term "subject," however, implies a certain distance between the poem and the experience it records which the walk poem habitually strives to abolish. A better word for the walk in its relation to the poem, I would suggest, is "occasion." There exists, of course, a whole tradition of what is called "occasional poetry," but in common usage the term has come to refer chiefly to poems written for or upon some highly *formal* occasion, such as a birthday, wedding, funeral, or coronation. I have in mind a much simpler sense of the word "occasion," perhaps best expressed by its use as a verb: the walk *occasions* the poem. What difference does it make to say that the walk is the poem's occasion rather than simply its subject? Undoubtedly the crucial distinction is that an occasion belongs to the order of reality, of actual experience, whereas a subject may be entirely fictive. Because the poem's occasion is perceived by the reader as real, as having in a sense *produced* the poem, the poem itself becomes no more than an extension or consequence of the occasion it records, a part of the same essential activity. This is not to say, of course, that a poem may not fictionalize its own occasion; ultimately the difference between subject and occasion is not ontological but grammatical. The occasional poem behaves *as though* it were a direct response to lived experience, and it is this behavior that matters, not the historical or fictive status of the occasion itself.

The special relationship between poem and occasion is memorably described by Wallace Stevens in a famous canto from "An Ordinary Evening in New Haven":

> The poem is the cry of its occasion,
> Part of the res itself and not about it.
> The poet speaks the poem as it is,
>
> Not as it was: part of the reverberation
> Of a windy night as it is, when the marble statues
> Are like newspapers blown by the wind. He speaks
>
> By sight and insight as they are. There is no
> Tomorrow for him. The wind will have passed by,
> The statues will have gone back to be things about.[35]

I will offer a fuller commentary on these lines in the context of the poem as a whole in my second chapter; for now let me simply draw out their implications for the walk poem as a genre. As I have suggested, and as Stevens affirms, the notion of the poem as rooted in its occasion works to overcome the gap between representation and subject; the poem becomes "part of the res itself and not about it," with "res" denoting not a physical object or setting but the occasion, the experiential moment out of which the poem springs. The poem is not "about" this moment, that is, it does not describe or represent it mimetically; rather, it is an extension or product of the occasion, a "cry" issuing directly from experience. Clearly such a conception of the poem bears a strong resemblance to Charles Olson's theory of projective verse; where Stevens differs from Olson is in his elision of the scene of composition, which for Olson constitutes the poem's only true occasion. Where Olson brackets worldly experience so as to capture the rhythms of writing itself, epitomized by breath and typewriter, Stevens portrays the poem not as an act of writing but as an utterance, a cry. He thus is able to locate the poem in the world, amid the "reverberations of a windy night," external phenomena whose presence is registered by the poet's speech (as the word "re*verb*erations" suggests).

The notion of the poem as spontaneous utterance can only be a fiction, of course, since a poem is first and foremost a text. But it is a fiction central to the walk poem as a genre. In its purest form, the walk poem presents itself not as a written record of a walk, composed after the fact, but as a linguistic event occurring simultaneously with the walk itself, and therefore absolutely coextensive with it. In effect the walk poem denies the distance and difference inherent in writing, striving for the intimate participation in an occasion that is possible only in speech. This claim to simultaneity is most clearly set forth by the walk poem's habitual use of the present tense; as Stevens says, "the poet speaks the poem as it is, not as it was." This grammatical device is an instance of deixis, the use of language to point directly to "the situation of utterance," which Jonathan Culler has identified as a key element of lyric poetry in general; other examples often found in walk poems include demonstrative pronouns and articles like "this" and "these", and adverbs of time and place like "here" and "now."[36] Where Culler emphasizes the purely conventional and fictive nature of deictics in the standard lyric, the way they force readers to construct a "fictional situation of discourse" that can assume "a thematic function," in the walk poem these elements take on a more purely literal force, insisting on the poem's immersion in an occasion presented as experiential fact.

Yet the insistence on simultaneity, on the poem as cry of its occasion, creates a dilemma for the poet. For if the poem rejects representation too categorically, how can the reader reconstruct the occasion that gives rise to it? As Stevens recognizes, the original moment of utterance will pass by, and "the statues will have gone back to be things about." Like the statues, the poem must pass from participation to representation, "of" to "about", if it is to survive its own occasion and become intelligible to its readers. Thus while the poet may seem to insist on the unmediated presence of the poem's occasion, he must nonetheless *describe* that occasion if it is to assume any recognizable presence for the reader. The tension between these two grammatical modes, between cry and description, is at the heart of the walk poem, which has to both assert its simultaneity with the walk as present occurrence, and to re-present that occurrence to the reader. Wittgenstein usefully analyzes this grammatical tension in a section of his *Philosophical Investigations*:

> I look at an animal and am asked: "What do you see?" I answer: "A rabbit".—I see a landscape; suddenly a rabbit runs past. I exclaim "A rabbit!"
>
> Both things, both the report and the exclamation, are expressions of perception and of visual experience. But the exclamation is so in a different sense from the report: it is forced from us.—It is related to experience as a cry is to pain.[37]

Clearly the mode of utterance toward which the walk poem aspires is that which Wittgenstein here calls "exclamation," a spontaneous naming that arises in response to a particular occasion. Interestingly, Wittgenstein likens such utterance to a cry, Stevens's term, but more specifically to a cry of pain. The resemblance between exclamation and cry, however, as Wittgenstein presents it, is one of analogy rather than identity. An important difference remains, one that allows us to see how a poem can act as both the cry of its occasion and a description of that occasion. The cry of pain is pure expression, an inarticulate response to an inner state; whereas the exclamation, though in part an expression of excitement or surprise, serves also as a rudimentary description or naming of the object that inspired it. In fact the two utterances Wittgenstein contrasts, the report and the exclamation, differ externally only in their end punctuation; the real difference is grammatical. Where the first is a detached observation, the second is causally linked to the phenomenon it names. Walk poems are generally modeled on the exclamation rather than the report, insofar as they tend to present themselves as arising in direct response to the immediate stimuli of the walk.

Of course a simple cry of "A rabbit!" is very different from the extended, often syntactically elaborate descriptions one finds in many walk poems. Genuine exclamations may occur there, but they are too limited in their descriptive capacity to serve as sufficient representations of the poem's occasion. Wittgenstein concisely formulates the grammatical principle behind the walk poem: "A cry is not a description. But there are transitions."[38] It is precisely in the transitional space between cry and description that the walk poem locates its discourse. A sense of spontaneous utterance flowing directly from its occasional context must be balanced by a more deliberately mimetic or representational use of language, meticulously evoking phenomenal appearances for the benefit of readers who are themselves divorced from the poem's occasion. Thus the poem can assert its direct participation in its occasion while still making that occasion available to the reader. This double grammar may ultimately deconstruct the poem's claim to be "part of the res itself and not about it"; but poetry thrives on illusion, and it is the special achievement of the walk poem to create the illusion of a present occasion with almost phenomenal immediacy.

Before I leave the topic of occasionality, I must note one further complication in the link between poem and occasion that has been elegantly expressed by James Merrill in an interview with David Kalstone:

> We've all written poems that imitate a plausible sequence of events. "I go out" for a walk and find these beautiful daffodils or this dead songbird and have the following feelings. But, for better or worse, that walk is in fact taken—or Yannina is visited—by a writer in hopes of finding something to write about. Then you have not simply imitated or recollected experience, but experience in the light of a projected emotion, like a beam into which what you encounter will seem to have strayed. The poem and its occasion will have created one another.[39]

Merrill gives a neat Wildean twist to Stevens's dictum: if the poem is the cry of its occasion, the occasion is also the cry of the poem, a kind of retroactive echo. This insight in no way undermines the principle of occasionality; it merely extends it, by recognizing that the relationship is a reciprocal one. Poets do not take walks for exercise, but for poems, and so the walk is from the start invested with desire and potential. The poem's cry thus issues from the convergence of poetic desire and an occasion that answers this desire. As Merrill's own illustrations suggest, the walk is perhaps the classic instance of an occasion expressly sought in the interests of a poem, in part because it is both easily initiated and largely unpredictable in its content.

A Poem Is a Walk

The kind of intimate bond with its occasion that walk poems set out to achieve is facilitated by a number of formal resemblances between poem and walk. I want to return now to A. R. Ammons's essay "A Poem Is a Walk" in order to begin discussing these resemblances in detail. As

I have already noted, Ammons's stated concern is with the walk as a paradigm for poetry in general; but his list of affinities between poem and walk help us to see how those poems that specifically take the literal experience of a walk as their occasion are themselves *shaped* by the walk. The form of the walk becomes the form of the poem: it is just this coalescence of form and matter that has made the walk so attractive a subject for poets at certain moments in literary history.

Ammons announces that he will explore four basic resemblances between poems and walks. The first of these returns us to the centrality of the body:

> How does a poem resemble a walk? First, each makes use of the whole body, involvement is total, both mind and body. You can't take a walk without feet and legs, without a circulatory system, a guidance and co-ordinating system, without eyes, ears, desire, will, need: the total person. This observation is important not only for what it includes but for what it rules out: as with a walk, a poem is not simply a mental activity; it has body, rhythm, feeling, sound, and mind, conscious and subconscious. The pace at which a poet walks (and thinks), his natural breath-length, the line he pursues, whether forthright and straight or weaving and meditative, his whole "air," whether of aimlessness or purpose—all these things and many more figure into the "physiology" of the poem he writes.[40]

Like the walk, Ammons suggests, the poem unites all the functions of human life—those of the body, both motor and perceptual, and those of the mind, both emotional and cognitive. Clearly Ammons would reject any conception of the poem as a work of intellect alone. For him, as for other poets, the poem has a strong bodily component, one that is most clearly reflected in the many prosodic terms derived from the act of walking: feet, iamb, enjambment, and less technical concepts like that of pace. All of these suggest that the verbal rhythms of the poem are intimately associated with bodily movement. Especially in a language as heavily accented as English, it is difficult to ignore the purely muscular aspect of poetic meter, the way in which each stress arises from or elicits a slight surge in the motor centers. Even in reading a poem silently, then, the body is engaged at a kinesthetic level, much as it is when listening to music.[41]

What allies such minimal motor activity more firmly with walking is the linearity of both. Ammons explicitly puns on the term "line," contrasting the "straight" with the "weaving," and so literalizing the analogy between the poetic line and the line or route traced by a walk. Of course in a purely visual sense the analogy is imperfect; a poem consists not of a single continuous line but of a series of sharply divided lines, hardly a pattern that the typical walk follows. Yet the convention of the line break, while it may seem to weaken the overt spatial resemblance between poem and walk, is in fact a further sign of the poem's deeper affinity with the walk. Unlike prose writing, whose "line" can indeed be thought of as continuous insofar as its breaks are determined purely by the accidents of typography, verse, especially free verse, foregrounds *choice* as an ongoing determinant of form. Just as a true walk does not have its course mapped out in advance, but chooses its direction at each moment, so the poem must continually choose where and how it will move down the page. Not only the length of each line, but the nature of the break itself, whether end-stopped or enjambed, affects this sense of variable movement. Walk poets are thus able to evoke in the very spacing of the verse the rhythm of a trajectory punctuated by choice, pausing in one place or leaping ahead as the moment dictates.

Ammons's next analogy is somewhat more problematic, and I will not be able to pursue its implications fully just yet:

> A second resemblance is that every walk is unreproducible, as is every poem. Even if you walk exactly the same route every time—as with a sonnet—the events along the route cannot be imagined to be the same from day to day, as the poet's health, sight, his anticipations, moods, fears, thoughts cannot be the same. There are no two identical sonnets or villanelles. If there were, we would not know how to keep the extra one; it would have no separate existence. If a poem is each time new, then it is necessarily an act of discovery, a chance taken, a chance that may lead to fulfillment or disaster. The poet exposes himself to the risk. All that has been said about poetry, all that he has learned about poetry, is only a partial assurance.

Ammons's point here may at first seem perverse. Surely part of the essence of a poem is that it *is* reproducible, that is, it can be reread, duplicated, printed, reprinted, whereas a given walk can be experienced only once and by only one person. I will consider this crucial difference later; for now let me simply clarify Ammons's point by rephrasing it. The poet can only *write* a given poem once, then he must abandon it and move on. Every new poem is thus wholly new, an adventure or "act of discovery" that cannot rely on past successes to guarantee its own. Both walk and poem create themselves as they go along.

With his third analogy, Ammons shows us how the larger structure of a poem can mirror that of a walk:

> The third resemblance between poems and walks is that each turns, one or more times, and eventually *re*turns. It's conceivable that a poem could take out and go through incident after incident without ever return-

ing, merely ending in the poet's return to dust. But most poems and most walks return. I have already quoted the first line from Frost's "The Wood-Pile." Now, here are the first three lines:

> Out walking in the frozen swamp one grey day,
> I paused and said, "I will turn back from here.
> No, I will go on farther—and we shall see."

The poet is moving outward seeking the point from which he will turn back. In "The Wood-Pile" there is no return: return is implied. The poet goes farther and farther into the swamp until he finds by accident the point of illumination with which he closes the poem.

But the turns and returns or implied returns give shape to the walk and to the poem. With the first step, the number of shapes the walk might take is infinite, but then the walk begins to "define" itself as it goes along, though freedom remains total with each step: any tempting side-road can be turned into on impulse, or any wild patch of woods can be explored. The pattern of the walk is to come true, is to be recognized, discovered. The pattern, when discovered, may be found to apply to the whole walk, or only a segment of the walk may prove to have contour and therefore suggestion and shape. From previous knowledge of the terrain, inner and outer, the poet may have before the walk an inkling of a possible contour. Taking the walk then would be searching out or confirming, giving actuality to, a previous intuition.

Like the walk, the poem unfolds temporally, moving through a series of phases, turning from one path to another, ultimately reaching a point at which it can either stop or turn back. Both poem and walk are thus primarily sequential in structure, a fact that allows the walk poem to assume the precise contours of the walk it records with ease. Things are encountered in a particular sequence, and this sequence is then incorporated in the poem as a constitutive element of *its* structure. At the level of the sentence, this sequential character often expresses itself through strongly paratactic constructions, in which clauses are strung together without subordination. Indeed, parataxis might be said to govern the larger sequences of walk poems as well, since these tend to lack the kind of logical or causal links that require hypotactic, heavily subordinated structures for expression.

Sequence, however, is not the same as pattern, Ammons's word for a large ordering shape that brings a sense of wholeness and closure to both poem and walk. Discussing sequential structure in her book *Poetic Closure*, Barbara Herrnstein Smith argues that poems whose organization is primarily temporal or successive must depend on other elements for closure, such as theme or narrative: "To mention only one of the most familiar possibilites: where a poem narrates the successive stages of a search or pilgrimage, the end will coincide with the poet's discovery of his object or arrival at his destination."[42] The walk, of course, generally lacks such narrative overdetermination; one moment follows another without the kind of causal unity found in fictional plots. This is not to say, however, that the walk lacks a narrative *shape*, only traditional narrative content. The formal logic of a walk, and by extension of a walk poem, is impeccable: it begins with a setting out, proceeds to a certain point at which a turn is made, and ends with a return. Not every poem follows this movement exactly; as Ammons's example from Frost indicates, some end with the attainment of a privileged point without bothering to retrace the path home. But every walk poem contains the rudiments of a classic formal structure: inception, anticipation, attainment or frustration, and return. Indeed, it could be argued that a walk, as represented in poetry, is simply a quest writ small. What the walker quests for, however, is not some place or object known in advance and taken as a goal; rather, as Ammons suggests, the walker quests for the walk itself, for the "pattern" that will give the walk a sense of fulfillment. More specifically, as in "The Wood-Pile," the walker quests for a point from which he can turn back without feeling that he has abandoned his quest. The discovery of that point also provides the basis for closure in the poem, lending it a shape that seems organic rather than arbitrary.

Ammons's final analogy between walk and poem takes us back to the purely motor or kinetic aspect of both:

> The fourth resemblance has to do with the motion common to poems and walks. The motion may be lumbering, clipped, wavering, tripping, mechanical, dance-like, awkward, stag gering, slow, etc. But the motion occurs only in the body of the walker or in the body of the words. It can't be extracted and contemplated. It is non-reproducible and non-logical. It can't be translated into another body. There is only one way to know it and that is to enter it.

I have already discussed some of the ways in which a poem, like a walk, may be said to move across and down the page. From the prosodic motion of feet and lines, to the syntactic motion of words and sentences, to larger semantic movements among thoughts and images, poems are capable of evoking kinesis at many levels. Charles Olson's previously noted commitment to kinesis as poetic principle led him to develop a technique he called "composition by field"; and while his own practice of it for the most part excludes any mimesis of actual movement, the style lends itself readily to the walk poem, by creating a more flexible analogy between the landscape of the walk and the typographical "field" of the poem.[43] In his prosodic handbook *Rhyme's Reason*, John Hollander offers an entertaining example of such imitative form, one that reads almost like a verse translation of Ammons's essay:

And to be able to wander, free
          (in a wide field, as it were)
verse can amble about
   on a kind of nature walk
      the lines following no
    usual path, for
    then the poem might seem
    to have wandered into
another kind of meter's backyard
          but
            sometimes
         seeming
          to map out the syntax
            sometimes
       seeming to do almost the
         opposite,
   this kind of meandering verse can
          even
oddly
      come upon a flower
      of familiar rhythm
         a sight for sore
  ears, or encounter
      a bit later
on,
     once again a patch of
     trochees growing somewhere
         (like an old song)
          and
    take one by the
       stem
  and
    break
  it
   off[44]

Hollander here wittily illustrates the most extreme attempt to provide a prosodic correlative for the experiential form of the walk. (Ammons's walk poem "Corsons Inlet" makes use of just this kind of form, and may be Hollander's model here.) Although this mode does not become prevalent until the later twentieth century, and even then fails to make major inroads, Hollander's example helps us to see the potential analogy between the form of any poem, however regular, and a walk. Like a walk, a poem proceeds through both time and space, pausing here and there to examine some point, hurrying along elsewhere to reach some object seen in the distance. The regulation of tempo, the syntactic evocation of event and perception, the forward motion implied by verse rhythms, all contribute to the walk poem's formal mimesis of its subject.

Paradoxically, then, the walk bestows on the poem both a sense of freedom and a sense of containment. Within the bounds of the poem, a kind of wandering is possible, an exploratory movement from place to place, topic to topic, which is not governed by any rigid causal or teleological structure. Yet the bounds of the poem are clearly marked, coinciding as they do with the beginning and ending of the walk. The walk poem thus represents a compromise between closed and open forms, to invoke the polemical distinction that has divided American poets in recent years. Just as the walker's freedom is limited and enclosed by the walk itself, so the walk poem displays a strict yet seemingly natural closure, while remaining continually open to the promptings of the moment, both discursive and phenomenal. Once the formal identity between poem and walk has been established, the poem, like the walk, can stand apart as an autonomous, organically unified piece of experience, possessing the integrity of a process with a beginning, middle, and ending, while at the same time embracing the full range of thought, feeling, and perception found in ordinary experience.

A Poem Is Not a Walk

As a genre, then, the walk poem rests on a double analogy. Insofar as a poem is itself a kind of walk, the task of representing an actual walk in language can take advantage of all the formal resemblances that Ammons describes. Conversely, insofar as a walk is itself a kind of poem, that is, a way of framing or marking off a stretch of time and space which confers upon it a heightened aesthetic value, one can say that the poem need only reproduce those qualities already inherent in the walk itself in order to subsume the experiential and the poetic.

Yet there remains an overwhelming difference between the walk and the poem, one which prevents a simple translation of experience into language from being sufficient for the perpetuation of the walk as art. Simply put, this is the difference in ontology, in the most basic modes of being which walk and poem embody. A walk is ephemeral, an experience situated in time and passing out of existence as soon as it is completed. A poem is a permanent artifact, a text that remains outside of time in its virtual essence, and that can be exactly reproduced as often as desired. A particular walk is therefore only one of a potentially infinite series of similar experiences, and this fact gives it a peculiar status that distinguishes it decisively from a poem. A walk, it might be said, is a disposable aesthetic experience, used once and then lost to oblivion—unless, of course, it is made into a poem. Yet the very process of making the walk into a poem must take into account this essential disposability and in some way negate it, since a disposable poem is almost a contradiction in terms. For a poem to succeed, it must in some way assert and sustain a claim to be worthy of rereading, of permanence as an artifact. Never easy, the advancement of such a claim becomes especially difficult when the poem appears to be no more than the record of an experience that is ordinary, ephemeral, and, by its nature, not unique, but merely one out of countless similar experiences. Why should *this* walk be preserved, reproduced, reexperienced in verbal form over and over, rather than some other, equally pleasant walk?

We might at this point recall Baudelaire's definition of modernity as "the ephemeral, the fugitive, the contingent, the half of art whose other half is the eternal and the immutable."[45] For Baudelaire the great achievement of "the painter of modern life," exemplified for him by Constantin Guys, is "to distill the eternal from the transitory." Baudelaire is of course speaking of visual art, which may be said to reach toward the timeless by virtue of its immobility. In the case of the walk poem, which attempts to render the contingent succession or flux of phenomena in its temporal dimension, such "distillation" becomes more problematic. As much as Baudelaire values the contingent and ephemeral in art, his own poetry seldom approaches the mode of the walk poem, precisely because his temperament inclines him to seek out the eternal or timeless within the press of sensations. The typical walk poem achieves a more precarious balance between transience and permanence. Much of the power of a successful walk poem comes from our appreciation of how little contingency has been given up in the name of art. That we nonetheless recognize in it some element of permanence, something that can compel our continued interest and bring us back to the poem in the future, attests to the skill with which the poet has invested his walk with value without distilling away all that connects it to our ordinary, fugitive experience of the world.

The walk poem, then, must walk a fine line between journalism and poetry. I have already discussed the importance of the journal as source and model for American poets; just as important is the poet's ability to maintain some *distance* from journalistic norms. A journal entry differs from a poem not merely as prose from verse. Where the conventions of the journal allow for considerable repetition, and for each entry's subordination to the ongoing record, a poem is generally written as an independent work, to be valued for its unique qualities and contents. A successful poem possesses an aesthetic aura, to use Benjamin's trope, that the most eloquent journal entry lacks. The difference may in the end be a purely generic one, stemming from the greater mystique attached to the poem in our culture. Yet the difference is no less vital for being conventional. More than any other kind of text, the poem is aimed at posterity rather than (or in addition to) an immediate readership. It must therefore demonstrate its singularity, since the canon has little room for redundancies.[46] As I have suggested, the walk poem by its nature asserts its continuity with daily experience, and so works against its own canonization. In fact, it is paradoxically the genre's very *resistance* to canonical norms that has in part been responsible for its success. By coming so close to the continuities and repetitions of journalism, the walk poem seems almost to cancel its own status as poem in the interests of fidelity to experience. Of course, a saving distance has ultimately to be kept, and it is the agility with which the poem keeps that distance while dallying at the brink that provokes much of our admiration.

One measure of the walk poem's placement on the representational continuum between journalism and poetry is the extent to which it permits or resists repetition as a genre. In other words, how many walk poems can one poet write? As I have noted, a walk is defined in part by its repeatability as an experience. Not that one can take the *same* walk more than once, since, as Ammons tells us, every walk is unreproducible; but for that very reason it becomes necessary for the walker to keep taking new walks. Given this potential infinitude of walks, however, each different, each equally valuable, why cannot the poet write an infinite number of walk poems, with each one being equally worthy of our attention? Clearly, repeatability is one property of the walk that is not readily transferable to the poem. Again this dissymmetry can be traced to the fact that a walk is ephemeral, a poem permanent. A poem can and must be reread; to insist on writing a new poem for every new walk would be to deny the ontological difference between the two.

Yet while no poet has carried the analogy between walk and poem quite so far, there are many poets who have written more than one walk poem. Even when a poet's attempts at the genre number in the single digits, certain problems begin to arise. A single walk poem can claim a place for itself in a poet's canon purely as an anomaly, a temporary break with more conventional modes and subjects. But the moment a poet offers more than one such poem, we must begin to look for principles of individuation. Actual walks may be interchangeable, in the sense that while they differ in their exact content they can easily blur together in memory. But poems aspiring to canonical status have to prove themselves unique in order to justify their preservation. Thus poets who compose several walk poems must find ways to counter the tendency of real walks to look alike, while still remaining faithful to the repetitive, closely woven texture of experience.

For this reason poets who begin by writing "pure" walk poems often find themselves deviating more and more from the genre as they continue to pursue it. Wordsworth, for example, begins his career with "An Evening Walk," a paradigmatic instance of the genre, varies it by magnifying the scale in "Descriptive Sketches," and gradually moves away from the walk poem in its purest state by introducing the essentially narrative device of a central incident or encounter in "Poems on the Naming of Places," "Nutting," "I Wander'd Lonely as a Cloud," "Resolution and Independence," and many episodes from *The Prelude.* The obtrusion of incident in his later poems gives each a unique center, thus permitting it to be distinguished from the rest in memory; yet by the same token it carries him away from the walk as a continuum, and toward his privileging of "spots of time" that stand apart from the fabric of experience. In effect the walk ceases to be a subject in its own right, instead serving as a background or occasion for a particular "spot." We can trace Wordsworth's gradual recognition of the need for individuation in some of his early manuscript fragments, particularly two that begin "Sweet was the walk along the narrow lane" and "How sweet the walk along the woody steep."[47] Here the formulaic openings betray the essential sameness of the two sketches, despite the total difference in the settings that they record. Faced with this evidence, Wordsworth undoubtedly realized that he could not keep writing in the mode of "An Evening Walk" if he wanted his poems to survive as individual works.

That realization seems to have eluded John Clare, who perhaps lacked some of Wordsworth's canonical ambition. Clare wrote dozens of walk poems; they vary primarily in setting, season, and minute detail.[48] Charming as they often are, however, no one of them truly sets itself apart from the rest. Indeed, the kind of formulaic opening line that for Wordsworth represented an impasse to be broken becomes for Clare simply a stylistic convention; again and again his descriptive poems begin with such phrases as "How sweet," "How pleasant," "I love to," etc. Unfortunately, experiential and aesthetic value do not always converge; Clare's repeated insistence on the value of the experiences he records fails to confer an equivalent value on the poems. It is hardly surprising, then, that he is remembered instead for the more focused description of "Badger" and the tortured lyricism of "I Am." More so than those of most other poets, Clare's walk poems constitute a kind of versified nature journal, a potentially endless series of inventories that ultimately fail to rise above their journalistic motives. They represent an extreme instance of the dangers of repetition that beset any poet who hopes to use experience as the material of his art.

Development of the Genre

Unlike such well-defined genres as the pastoral, the epic, and the ode, the walk poem has seldom been recognized as such, at least not until recently. This creates a difficulty in speaking of it *as* a genre: does a particular kind of poem constitute a genre if it has not been pointed out, labeled and defined? Certainly the walk poem lacks a degree of formal self-awareness that other genres possess; yet the very term "walk," especially when present in a poem's title, acts as a kind of generic marker, implicitly acknowledging the poem's relation to previous poems of the same kind. As Alastair Fowler has recently emphasized, genres are not essences but traditions, lines of historical descent and transformation. Fowler's term for the process by which a genre is revised and transformed is "modulation," and the concept is a useful one for appreciating the generic status of the walk poem.[49] Not itself a classical genre recognized by criticism, the walk poem developed out of a number of already established genres. It cannot, however, be strictly termed a "subgenre," since that would imply the existence of a broader genre within which the walk poem could be comfortably situated. In fact no such larger genre exists; the relation of the walk poem to existing genres is rather that of a mutation, an outgrowth which essentially alters the form and matter of its matrix. Moreover, the walk poem represents the convergence of a number of different genres and modes, rather than the natural transformation of a single genre.[50] Indeed, the generic identity of the walk poem can only be fully described by the *history* of the walk poem, since it is only there that we can see all the generic strands that make it up.

The earliest literary walk occurs quite literally in the beginning; that is, in Genesis. I refer, of course, to Yahweh's walk "in the garden at the breezy time of day," during which he discovers Adam and Eve's primal transgression.[51] Interestingly, although this walk is associated with the natural beauty and comfort of Eden, it is God rather than man who experiences it; even in its earliest form the walk seems to take its identity in contrast to more purposeful activities, in this case that of the Creation itself. Adam and Eve, one might speculate, are incapable of taking a walk because their lives contain nothing but leisure to begin with; the particular sense of *bounded* freedom that the walk embodies can have no meaning for them until they fall into lives of labor and hardship.

To be sure, God's walk in Genesis is not a walk *poem*, only a passing reference. More direct precursors to the genre can be found in Greek and Roman poetry: in the pastoral idylls of Theocritus, with their evocations of leisure and casual perception (particularly Idyll *VII*, which recounts a short journey to a festival); in the *Sermones* or satires of Horace, especially *I.5*, a long and detailed description of a trip to Brundisium, and *I.9*, in which Horace attempts to rid himself of a boorish pest while walking in the marketplace; and in Virgil's *Georgics*, whose instructional rhetoric conceals its true aim, to describe meticulously and vividly the appearances of the countryside, often from a directly experiential point of view. All of these works and the genres they initiate contribute important representational elements to the walk poem as it emerges definitively in the eighteenth century; but none of them truly approaches its characteristic blend of perception and meditation, placing greater emphasis on narrative or didactic elements than on individual consciousness.

Another generic constituent of the walk poem is the use of physical movement as a structural principle. This device can be traced as far back as the "wandering" section of *The Odyssey*, in which various encounters occur purely on the basis of spatial and temporal contingency, rather than through firmer narrative connections. The journey remains a prominent structural device in poetry well into the Renaissance and beyond, taking many forms: the voyage, the quest, the descent to the underworld, and so on. Of these, the most relevant to the formation of the walk poem is the pilgrimage, because it comes closest to the essentially plotless character of the walk. The pilgrim differs from the quester in that he is essentially passive; indeed his primary activity is precisely that of *passing*, rather than confronting, overcoming, and so on. Early poems of pilgrimage, most notably Dante's *Commedia*, are primarily allegorical in nature, and thus divorced from the realm of direct experience that the walk poem inhabits; yet despite its visionary content, Dante's epic is *structured* very similarly to a walk poem, as a series of sights or phenomena together with reflections on them, bound together through their spatial and temporal contiguity.

It is Chaucer who naturalizes the pilgrimage in *The Canterbury Tales*, carrying it from the realm of allegory to that of empirical experience.

While the frame may be subordinate to the tales themselves, it possesses an immediacy and verisimilitude, especially in its depiction of time and movement, that make it another precursor to the walk poem. The walk poem emerges most directly, however, from a slightly different, though related, medieval convention, that of the waking frame for the dream-vision. In Middle English poems such as *Pearl*, *Piers Plowman*, and *The Legend of Good Women*, the protagonist is first introduced walking in a naturalistic landscape before he falls asleep and receives his vision. As in *The Canterbury Tales*, the frame remains a subordinate element of the work, serving mainly as a foil for the vision that follows; yet it constitutes a significant development insofar as it opens the way for more sustained representations of walklike experience. Indeed the frame becomes progressively more extended, until in Chaucer's *Legend of Good Women* it has expanded to include a meditation on the relative merits of books and outdoor experience, a paean to the daisy, and not one but two walks, the second of which is dreamed yet described in lucid detail. Chaucer's poem thus stands on the threshold beyond which the walk can be represented for its own sake, not as a frame for a more visionary experience.

That threshold is finally crossed in the Renaissance. Spenser's "Prothalamion" might be viewed as the first walk poem, although in certain respects it has more in common with the medieval dream-vision. The walk's occasion is established with confessional frankness; Spenser has evidently not received preferment at court, and so he walks to ease his depression:

> Calm was the day, and through the trembling air
> Sweet-breathing Zephyrus did softly play—
> A gentle spirit, that lightly did delay
> Hot Titan's beams, which then did glister fair;
> When I (whom sullen care,
> Through discontent of my long fruitless stay
> In princes' court, and expectation vain
> Of idle hopes, which still do fly away
> Like empty shadows, did afflict my brain)
> Walk'd forth to ease my pain
> Along the shore of silver-streaming Thames[.][52]

While walking beside the Thames, he witnesses an elaborate procession of swans and nymphs, intended to represent a double marriage soon to take place at court. Clearly there is a kind of allegorical or visionary cast to this spectacle; yet Spenser gives us no explicit transition from the initial realism of the walk to a different state of consciousness, as in a dream-vision. The walk and the vision are presented as continuous rather than discrete, and so the poem can never really be said to leave the walk behind, although it quickly moves to a different level of representation.

It remains for Milton, in "L'Allegro" and "Il Penseroso," to execute the definitive turn from the visionary to the experiential. In these two poems one could say that the earlier relationship between frame and vision has been reversed; now it is the frame that hosts the visionary figures of Mirth and Melancholy, while the bodies of the poems are given over to extended representations of ordinary experience at its two affective poles. "L'Allegro" in particular displays the paratactic accumulation of realistic detail that marks the walk poem:

> Some time walking not unseen
> By Hedgerow Elms, on Hillocks green,
>
> . . . .
>
> While the Plowman near at hand,
> Whistles o'er the Furrow'd Land,
> And the Milkmaid singeth blith,
> And the Mower whets his scythe,
> And every Shepherd tells his tale
> Under the Hawthorn in the dale.
> Straight mine eye hath caught new pleasures
> Whilst the landscape round it measures,
> Russet Lawns and Fallows Gray,
> Where the nibbling flocks do stray;
> Mountains on whose barren breast
> The laboring clouds do often rest;
> Meadows trim and Daisies pied,
> Shallow Brooks, and Rivers wide.[53]

By contrast "Il Penseroso" shows the walker in his more meditative and introspective phase:

> I walk unseen
> On the dry smooth-shaven Green,
> To behold the wand'ring Moon,
> Riding near her highest noon,
> Like one that had been led astray
> Through the Heav'n's wide pathless way[.][54]

Both poems served as influential models for later walk poems, and indeed it might be said that as a genre the walk poem typically attempts to unite the two, blending the perceptual riches of "L'Allegro" with the intense self-consciousness of "Il Penseroso."

If Spenser and Milton provide initial paradigms for the English walk poem, its immediate generic matrix is the topographical poem, a form that becomes increasingly popular from the later seventeenth century on. As its name suggests, the topographical poem emphasizes setting or locale over experience; thus the poems are almost always named after the place they describe, since that is their true subject. Yet as the genre evolves, more and more prominence is given to the role of the spectator, and a gradual shift begins to take place from the representation of landscape to the representation of an *experience* of landscape. One manifestation of this shift can be seen in the way movement is represented. In early topographical poems like Drayton's massive *Poly-olbion*, movement is entirely discursive in nature; the poem "moves" from one scene to another purely at the level of topic, although it often invokes physical transportation as a trope for this movement (a device probably inherited from Virgil's *Georgics*, which also speaks of its subject as a kind of "field" to be discursively covered by the poem). Later topographical poems begin to literalize this kind of movement, presenting it as bodily rather than cognitive. Such a modulation is perhaps most clearly visible in Marvell's "Upon Appleton House," which belongs to that subgenre of the topographical poem known as the country house poem. After describing the house and its history, and praising its owner Lord Fairfax, Marvell turns his attention from the house to its grounds: "And now to the abyss I pass / Of that unfathomable grass" (ll. 369–370).[55] Here the transition is ambiguous; the verb "pass" might describe either a discursive or a physical movement. Later stanzas, however, increasingly represent Marvell's tour of the grounds as experiential: "But I, retiring from the flood, / Take sanctuary in the wood;" "Then as I careless on the bed / Of gelid strawberries do tread" (ll. 481–482, 529–530). "Upon Appleton House" might thus be said to illustrate internally the historical shift from the topographical poem, whose subject is conceived as independent of any observer, to the walk poem, in which the subject is not the place but the poet's singular experience of it.

That shift is yet more plainly visible in two poems by the minor eighteenth-century poet John Dyer. Dyer's best-known poem, "Grongar Hill," is a conscious successor to Sir John Denham's famous "Coopers Hill," which established another subgenre of the topographical poem, the hill or prospect poem. Denham's poem represents a transitional point in the development of the topographical genre; the speaker's physical placement on the hill is acknowledged, but only in terms of the movement of his eye as it roves about the scene. Dyer originally composed his imitation of Denham, "Grongar Hill," as an irregular Pindaric ode, and in this form it only contains traces of the kind of experiential perspective that culminates in the walk poem. The emphasis, as in most topographical poems, is on description of, praise for, and meditation upon the place itself. After composing this initial version, however, Dyer wrote another poem set in the same locale, but patterned after Milton's "L'Allegro" in meter and style. This poem, "The Country Walk," can fairly be called the first true specimen of the walk poem, exhibiting all the characteristic features of the genre: a fluid blending of perception and reflection, an evocative rendering of movement, a generous selection of particulars, and a use of the present tense that implies the total coincidence of poem and walk:

> And now into the fields I go,
> Where thousand flaming flowers glow;
> And ev'ry neighb'ring hedge I greet,
> With honeysuckles smelling sweet.
> Now o'er the daisy meads I stray,
> And meet with, as I pace my way,
> Sweetly shining on the eye,
> A riv'let, gliding smoothly by;
> Which shows with what an easy tide
> The moments of the happy glide.[56]

Dyer's success with this poem led him to revise "Grongar Hill" radically, casting it in octosyllabics and placing much greater emphasis on the observer's movement through the landscape.[57] In effect the two versions of "Grongar Hill" represent the before and after states of a focal shift in descriptive poetry, from place to experience. If the revised version of "Grongar Hill" has received more praise both in Dyer's time and our own than "The Country Walk," it is doubtless because of its greater polish; but "The Country Walk" is the poem that most clearly signals the emergence of a new genre.

To be sure, Dyer's adoption of "L'Allegro"'s tripping octosyllabics limits his capacity for extended meditation; both "The Country Walk" and "Grongar Hill" tend in their reflective moments toward aphorism. It is not until blank verse has been firmly established as a medium for descriptive poetry that the walk poem can fully incorporate the representation of thought as an ongoing process within its mimetic field. Here the generic matrix is not the topographical poem but the georgic, which underwent a wide revival in eighteenth century England. James Thomson's *The Seasons*, the first section of which was published in 1726, the same year as "Grongar Hill," had a tremendous influence on poetic fashions for the rest of the century. The poem is clearly modeled on Virgil's *Georgics*, both in its four-book format and in its generalized descriptions of nature, although it displays none of Virgil's didactic emphasis on labor. Thomson's blank verse permits close attention to natural detail, yet the landscape of the poem completely lacks the specificity of those found in topographical poems; appearances and objects are generic, described in terms of seasonal patterns rather than particular settings. Nonetheless, the poem's richly expansive descriptions and its ability to weave moral reflections into them served as a model for many later poems; Dyer himself wrote an unsuccessful georgic called *The Fleece*.

In order to deal more closely with particularized experience than Thomson does, however, the English georgic has to undergo an important modification, in which the chief catalyst is a version of satire.[58] Paralleling the revival of the georgic, and indeed anticipating it, is the emergence of the mock-georgic, a cousin to the better-known mock-epic. Here Swift may be cited as the chief originator, in poems like "Description of a City Shower" and "Description of the Morning"; but it is John Gay who develops the form most fully, in his *Rural Sports* and *Trivia*. The latter in particular is relevant for our purposes, since it is subtitled "The Art of Walking the Streets of London." In its careful enumeration of the sights, sounds, and petty inconveniences that walkers may encounter, the poem may be said to look back to Horace's *Satires*, whose attention to the minute fabric of daily experience serves as one major progenitor of the walk poem. If *Trivia* is not finally a true walk poem, this is because, like Virgil's *Georgics*, it presents itself as didactic rather than descriptive in function, offering useful advice to the would-be walker: "Through Winter Streets to steer your Course aright, /How to walk clean by Day, and safe by Night, /... / I sing."[59] Yet its satiric character enables it to assimilate the materials of common experience much more fully than do the serious georgics of Virgil and Thomson.

The final stage in the georgic's modification by satire comes with William Cowper's *The Task*. A descriptive and meditative poem in six books, *The Task* is heavily influenced by *The Seasons*, and in turn greatly influenced Wordsworth and Coleridge. Three of its six books are long, ruminative accounts of walks in the country, in which nature is described entirely from the walker's perspective, as it is not in Thomson. From a generic point of view the most interesting feature of the poem, and the one that may be responsible for its more experiential texture, is its opening frame, in which the poet reluctantly accedes to a young lady's request that he produce a descriptive poem about a sofa. The first hundred or so lines of the poem are given to this subject, treating it with the kind of humorous solemnity and lofty rhetoric that characterize the mock-epic and mock-georgic. From here, however, Cowper quickly modulates into the leisurely descriptions of outdoor experience and related reflections that dominate the remainder of the poem. The last two books, "The Winter Morning Walk" and "The Winter Walk at Noon," offer the purest examples of walk poetry, although passages of it are scattered throughout the poem:

> The vault is blue
> Without a cloud, and white without a speck
> The dazzling splendour of the scene below.
> Again the harmony comes o'er the vale;
> And through the trees I view th'embattled tow'r
> Whence all the music. I again perceive
> The soothing influence of the wafted strains,
> And settle in soft musings as I tread
> The walk, still verdant, under oaks and elms,
> Whose outspread branches overarch the glade.[60]

I would suggest that it is precisely because Cowper begins the poem *as though* it were to be a mock-georgic that he is then able to overcome the generality of the Thomsonian georgic and offer instead a representation of direct experience. The satiric element deflates the georgic's claim to universal knowledge, locating it more firmly in a specific time and place, and within the closed sphere of an individual consciousness.

Cowper's use of blank verse and a longer form allows him to achieve far greater meditative complexity than Dyer, although by the same token he loses much of the exuberance of perception and movement that make Dyer's poems so winning. The meditative aspect of the walk reaches its culmination in the late eighteenth century, in Schiller's "Der Spaziergang" and Rousseau's prose *Rêveries d'un promeneur solitaire*. These works use the walk primarily as a vehicle for moral and philosophical reflection rather than scenic description. In England the meditative walk that Cowper pioneers receives its fullest development in Wordsworth's *The Excursion*, though in a form that moves outside the consciousness of the poet and instead presents itself as a dialogue among several travelers. The poem's philosophical utterances are assigned to individual speakers, while its descriptive passages belong to the narrative frame; as a result, thought and perception are kept strictly separated, rather than freely intermixing as they do in solitary walk poems.

It is in Wordsworth's early poem, "An Evening Walk," that the purely descriptive walk poem reaches a kind of fulfillment. Commentators have repeatedly pointed to the conventionality of this poem, its indebtedness to the rhetoric of eighteenth-century descriptive verse; and indeed it shows little of the mature Wordsworth's bare diction and affinity for the sublime.[61] Yet in terms of the generic history of the walk poem, "An Evening Walk" marks a significant development. Its break with prior walk poems is most clearly evident in its title; where Dyer and Cowper both use the definite article ("*The* Country Walk," "*The* Winter Morning Walk"), Wordsworth uses the indefinite article. While this may seem a trivial change, it has far-reaching consequences for the poetic representation of experience. One effect of the definite article is to imply that the noun has a representative status, referring not to a single object but to an entire category. In both Dyer's and Cowper's poems, the walks described are intended to stand for all walks of a certain kind, that kind being specified by the adjectives in the titles. But by shifting from the definite to the indefinite article, Wordsworth fundamentally alters the implied relation between poem and experience. Now the poem claims to represent only a single evening walk, not a class of walks. As a result the poem gains sharply in specificity, in the evoked sense of a singular, unreproducible experience. This heightened immediacy is perhaps most clearly evident in the poem's persistent emphasis on sounds, which can be said to possess a temporal definition that visual phenomena lack, and so help to increase our impression of the moment's particularity:

> The song of mountain-streams, unheard by day,
> Now hardly heard, beguiles my homeward way.
> Air listens, like the sleeping water, still,
> To catch the spiritual music of the hill,
> Broke only by the slow clock tolling deep,
> Or shout that wakes the ferry-man from sleep[.][62]

At the same time, however, the whole problem of repetition starts to enter, since to speak of *an* evening walk suggests that there can also be *another* evening walk. I have already discussed the way Wordsworth combats the tendency of his own poetic grammar to generate endless repetitions; ultimately his refinement of the walk poem forces him to move away from the genre, toward the more episodic mode of his mature poetry. Nonetheless, he remains loyal throughout his career to the basic lineaments of the walk poem, which can, I think, be described as the generative form for virtually all of his poetry. His descriptive poems, ballads, meditations, and occasional lyrics all arise from the matrix of the walk; and even his autobiographical poem *The Prelude*, like the medieval dream-vision, is framed by a walk, while returning again and again in its narrative to remembered walks.[63] Indeed it is precisely because the walk is so central to Wordsworth's experiential subject matter that he is led to vary and dilute the walk poem as a genre, since pure repetition would lead to aesthetic disaster, as it did for Clare.

Wordsworth can only continue to draw on the walk as experience by abandoning or modifying the walk as form.

Wordsworth is not, of course, the only Romantic poet to write walk poems. I have touched on Clare already, who can be seen as a "naive" version of Wordsworth, blithely continuing to write endless poems in the same mode regardless of the consequences for the poems themselves. Coleridge, on the other hand, tends to avoid the genre, as my earlier discussion of Abrams's "greater Romantic lyric" might suggest. The closest he comes to it is in "This Lime-Tree Bower My Prison," which is revealing precisely because it describes a walk from which Coleridge is himself absent, having injured his foot and remained behind. We might speculate that Coleridge favors a static position in his poems because he is generally interested in defining the precise boundaries between mind and world, whereas Wordsworth tends to dissolve those boundaries in movement so as to facilitate the great marriage he prophesies in the "Recluse" fragment. Coleridge's poetry exemplifies a mode of thought for which the walk is inimical, analytic where the latter is associative, metaphoric where the latter is metonymic. Surprisingly perhaps, it is Blake among the first generation of Romantics who joins Wordsworth in producing a true specimen of the walk poem; his "With happiness stretchd across the hills," composed as part of a letter to Thomas Butts, is a curious blend of natural description and Blakean mythography, in which phenomenal particulars such as a thistle and the sun are transformed by the poet's "double vision" into figures from the prophetic books.[64]

As the different cases of Wordsworth and Clare show, the walk poem arrives at something of an impasse in the early nineteenth century, in which the alternatives appear to be either repetition or modification. It should therefore come as no surprise to find the genre declining in prominence throughout the remainder of the century, in England at least. Poems like Shelley's "Alastor," Keats's "I Stood Tiptoe," Browning's "By the Fireside" and "The Englishman in Italy," and Arnold's "Resignation," "A Summer Night," and "Epilogue to Lessing's Laocoon" all derive in part from the walk poem as it is transmitted by Wordsworth from the eighteenth century; but all inject other narrative and thematic elements that effectively displace the poem's focus from the walk itself. ("Alastor" in particular can be viewed as a rather savage parody and repudiation of the walk poem, in which the scenic particulars stubbornly block thought and imagination rather than giving it material to work on.) Other scattered instances can be found by Barrett Browning ("A Sea-Side Walk"), Hopkins ("Hurrahing in Harvest"), Meredith ("The Night-Walk"), Wilde ("Magdalen Walks"), and certain minor poets, but the genre more or less dies out in England as the century progresses, to be revived only much later in the twentieth century, under the influence of both American poetry and the renewal of interest in Wordsworth. (The so-called Georgian school may also have contributed to a revival, but only in an archaicizing way.) It could be argued, of course, that the genre had already begun to die out in Wordsworth's own writing; the threat of repetition that led him away from the walk poem in its purest form may also have been responsible for the genre's decline among nineteenth-century British poets, who tended to prize originality and uniqueness more than the poets of the eighteenth century. But it is also in the mid-nineteenth century that the walk poem migrates to America, where it eventually enjoys wider popularity than it has ever known before.

Whitman and Thoreau

Near the beginning of this introduction I tried to suggest something of why the walk poem was to find its most congenial setting in the United States. Not only does the rougher, less cultivated landscape of nineteenth-century America lend itself to the kind of close descriptive treatment developed in eighteenth century English poetry, but the very attitude toward experience that American writers hold leads them to take up with new vigor the mode of representation that in England effectively ends with Wordsworth. Indeed it could be argued that Wordsworth's most faithful poetic disciples are not Keats and Shelley, but Americans like Bryant and Whittier; at least, they are closer to Wordsworth in overt style and matter than their British cousins. At a deeper level, of course, Wordsworthianism passes through Emerson to Whitman and Thoreau. I want to consider the way each of these last two figures in particular translates the walk poem into his own form and idiom, since between them they lay the ground for the genre's subsequent flourishing in the twentieth century.

I have claimed that American poetic theory is distinguished by its radical identification of experience and poetry. Both Whitman and Thoreau act on such an identification, but in markedly different ways. Of the two, Whitman is of course far more deeply committed to poetry per se, as a specific verbal medium. Despite his occasional poetic output, Thoreau is essentially a prose writer, his primary form being that of the journal. Yet Thoreau's influence on later American poets has been almost as great as Whitman's, so that it will not do to exclude him from an account of poetic representation on purely formal grounds. Moreover his habit of interpolating original passages of verse in his prose works suggests that for him writing is a continuum that spans the extremes of prose and poetry, though tending at any given moment more towards one or the other. Thus we can fairly juxtapose Thoreau and Whitman as practitioners of poetic writing, if not of verse.

What the two men share, as I have intimated, is a sense that experience is charged with immanent aesthetic value, and that merely in transcribing what he sees and hears the writer can capture and preserve this value for others. It is in their methods of transcription that they differ most sharply. Whitman's catalogs and Thoreau's accounts of natural objects may superficially resemble one another, but in one crucial respect they are radically opposed—namely in their representation of time. Whitman's poems rarely locate themselves within a specific moment, as Wordsworth's usually do; instead they tend to station themselves *above* experience, surveying all of it simultaneously. Thus his catalogs are not experiential but panoptic, ranging over a wide expanse of material drawn from the poet's accumulated knowledge of the world. This insistence on seeing everything at once, as if from an omniscient perspective, is in keeping with the prophetic stance Whitman habitually assumes in his poems. Whitman's poetic persona is not generally that of an individual man immersed in his own private experience, but rather that of a *singer*, hence his poems obey the temporality of utterance or song rather than that of experience. The primary action in his poetry is the speech act "I sing," which draws all of the particular events and phenomena he enumerates into its field, canceling their temporal specificity and instead subsuming them within the pure present of speech. (This present, it should be noted, differs from the present tense that characterizes the walk poem, in that it implies a transcendence of rather than an immersion in linear time.)

Thoreau, by contrast, rigorously observes the temporal limitations of experience, recording each day's phenomena as they occur, and seldom moving into the synoptic time of Whitman's catalogs (although he frequently shifts into the mode of Emersonian aphorism, which makes no claim to be mimetic). This method can of course be attributed to the centrality of the journal for Thoreau's practice. Aside from the simple fact that the thirty-nine-volume journal constitutes Thoreau's longest production by far, its importance lies in its use as a source or quarry for virtually all his more finished writings. Moreover, the chronological organization of the journal serves as a paradigm for Thoreau's travel books, each of which roots its descriptions in the context of lived time; *A Week on the Concord and Merrimack Rivers* is most schematic in this respect, assigning a chapter to each of the seven days spent on the trip. Even *Walden*, Thoreau's most canonical work and the one that departs furthest from journalistic format, explicitly confines itself to a two-year period, and while parts of the book deal with ongoing events and experiences in a synoptic way, its most memorable descriptive passages are given to specific occasions: the walk to Baker Farm, the battle of the ants, the thawing bank, and so on.

Whitman and Thoreau might thus be seen as polarizing the functions of Wordsworthian representation, with its emphasis on particulars. In Whitman, such representation is pushed toward the condition of pure song or lyric, while in Thoreau it is given the status of journalism, a day-by-day accounting of experience. Naturally this split has a decisive effect on the two men's use of the walk as material. Both present themselves as incessant walkers; but where Thoreau's walks, as meticulously recorded in his journal, are a series of individual experiences, each with its own interest as an encounter with the natural world, Whitman prefers to represent his movement in the world as *walking*, an open-ended, ongoing process without the closure and specificity of a walk. Thus in "Song of Myself" he declares, "I tramp a perpetual journey," while refusing to situate that journey in time and space.

We can see this difference most clearly in two works that approach the walk poem from opposite directions: Whitman's "Song of the Open Road" and Thoreau's "A Winter Walk." Whitman's poem, as its title suggests, is primarily lyric rather than descriptive in aim. When it deals in particular phenomena, it does so in the mode of apostrophe— "You flagg'd walks of the cities! you strong curbs at the edges!"[65]—a typical strategy of Whitman's for establishing his own performative authority over the object world. Again, Whitman does not represent his walk as a succession of moments or points along the way, but as a kind of self-declared omnipresence: "From this hour I ordain myself loos'd of limits and imaginary lines." Whitman's emphasis here, as throughout his poetry, is on the power of his own voice to raise him above circumstance and limitation. He ends with a prolonged invitation to the reader to accompany him, punctuated by cries of "Allons!"—a gesture that once more seems to deny the experiential limits of the walk.

Thoreau's "A Winter Walk" is an essay that he published in *The Dial*, under Emerson's editorship. While its style is not that of the journals, being more formal and consciously literary, it shares their keen awareness of time as a succession of individual moments, each of which has its own salient qualities. Where the journals are open-ended and cumulative, however, treating each day's walk as only the latest in an infinite series, "A Winter Walk" claims a more representative status for itself. While its title makes use of the Wordsworthian indefinite article, thus suggesting that the walk is a specific and singular one, the seasonal context allows Thoreau to deal in recurrent phenomena, and so to enlarge the walk's field of reference from a single occasion to a time of year. (Thoreau's other walk essay, "A Walk to Wachussetts," concerns itself more with place than with season, but here too the specification of a context, in this case topographical, allows the piece to refer beyond its occasion to an essayistic "topic.") As a self-contained piece of writing intended for publication, "A Winter Walk" necessarily departs from the purely contingent mode of the journals; the transcription of occasional particulars has to be balanced by a more generalized representation of time and place in order to justify the work's status as essay. Thus "A Winter Walk" shows Thoreau consciously transforming the matter of his journals into a more canonical form, a process that ultimately leads him to *Walden*. Nevertheless, "A Winter Walk" is very far from the prophetic range and depth of Thoreau's masterpiece, being primarily descriptive in intent. Only in his late essay "Walking" does Thoreau convert the raw material of his walks into something like the philosophical poetry of *Walden*, and then at the cost of the integrity of individual walks, as the title's gerundive form suggests; here Thoreau joins Whitman as a transcendental walker rather than a taker of walks.

Neither of these works is a true walk poem, "Song of the Open Road" because of its resistance to temporal and spatial limits, "A Winter Walk" because of its journalistic prose. But for later poets interested in writing poems about walks, Whitman and Thoreau mark two extreme possibilities that demand to be negotiated. In short, subsequent poets must find a way to inhabit the middle ground between Whitman's barbaric yawp and Thoreau's journalism. At one end, experience all but vanishes as a temporally differentiated medium; at the other, poetry subsides into the prosaic transcription of daily minutiae. The challenge for twentieth-century Americans who want to explore the possible relations between poem and walk is in effect to put Whitman and Thoreau together, to combine the lyric intensity and scope of the former with the experiential particularity of the latter. In the chapters that follow, I will examine some of the ways later poets have found to balance the demands of poem and walk so that the two coalesce into a volatile whole.

I

ROBERT FROST: THE WALK AS PARABLE

ROBERT FROST is the first American poet in the twentieth century to explore the formal possibilities of the walk poem. From his first volume, *A Boy's Will*, to his last, *In the Clearing*, Frost exhibits a special fondness for ambulatory plots, and this is not simply due to his preference for rural settings and subject matter. Although he was conscious of his affinity with Georgian poets like Edward Thomas, for whom the countryside presented an inexhaustible source of picturesque objects for representation, Frost is never simply concerned with landscape per se. His true origins are American, and while Emerson may ultimately have influenced him more profoundly, Thoreau provided his most immediate model. (By contrast he shows little interest in or influence from Whitman, whose transcendental stance with regard to ordinary experience may have seemed to Frost to touch on what he himself feared most, the state of "formlessness.")

Many of Frost's lyrics read like versified Thoreau; they are factual records of daily experience, moments in the life of a subsistence farmer and inveterate walker. Yet they are, after all, *poems*, whereas Thoreau's characteristic production is the journal entry, a form to which even his more finished works show their debt. How do Frost's poems differ from Thoreau's prose? At what point do they cross the line between journalism and poetry? That line, we have seen, has much to do with the canonical ambitions of a piece of writing. For Thoreau the journalist, the amassing of experience in verbal form is an end in itself; no single walk or passage is meant to stand alone, for each is part of an ongoing whole coextensive with experience. But Frost is a poet, and his concern is with the creation of aesthetic constructs that will reward repeated scrutiny. His aim is thus not simply to reproduce experience but to transform it into something compact, singular, and lasting: in short, a poem. Each poem must therefore constitute a unique artifact, not one of hundreds of similar accounts whose value lies in their exhaustive transcription of daily particulars. (In shaping his journals into books, of course, Thoreau shows a similar concern for bringing to his raw experience the singularity of art, as attested to by Frost's frequent citation of *Walden* as his favorite poem.)[1]

Frost is thus faced with the problem of translating a Thoreauvian attention to the minute fabric of experience into a form capable of the concentration and permanence that we expect of a poem. His solution is the parable, or rather a strange hybrid of anecdote and parable that he made peculiarly his own. Frost's best poems exhibit an uncanny ability to locate themselves precisely on the border between literal and figurative modes of representation. The parable is his favorite trope because it displays just this ambiguous status. Parables are generally less transparent than allegories, lacking the one-to-one correspondence between image and concept that characterizes allegorical figuration; yet they nevertheless insist on a level of interpretation that transcends the literal. They present themselves as simultaneously literal and figurative, rather than purely one or the other. By taking up the representational strategy of parable, then, Frost's poems are able to fuse description and revelation, fact and figure, so that they are virtually indistinguishable. Seldom do we question the literality of his images, their origin in actual experience; and yet over and over they assume a parabolic dimension that lifts them above the experiential, enabling them to participate in a higher "wisdom" that for Frost constitutes the true aim of poetry. Like Thoreau in his treatment of Walden Pond, Frost seeks to imbue his images with thematic resonance without robbing them of their brute substantiality, their thing-ness.

For Frost the walk offers an especially good basis for parable, because its form seems to mirror the kind of thematic or parabolic movement he favors. Like his poetic heir A. R. Ammons, Frost tends to conceptualize poems in terms of walks. Here, for example, are some passages from his famous essay "The Figure a Poem Makes":

> No one can really hold that the ecstasy should be static and stand still in one place. It begins in delight, it inclines to the impulse, it assumes direction with the first line laid down, it runs a course of lucky events, and ends in a clarification of life. . . .
>
> Step by step the wonder of unexpected supply keeps growing. The impressions most useful to my purpose seem always those I was unaware of and so made no note of at the time when taken, and the conclusion is come that like giants we are always hurling experience ahead of us to pave the future with against the day when we may want to strike a line of purpose across it for somewhere. The line will have the more charm for not being mechanically straight. We enjoy the straight crookedness of a good walking stick. [. . .]
>
> Scholars get theirs [knowledge] with conscientious thoroughness along projected lines of logic; poets theirs cavalierly and as it happens in and out of books. They stick to nothing deliberately, but let what will stick to them like burrs where they walk in the fields.[2]

It should be evident that the idea of the walk informs much of Frost's meditation on the nature of the poem. The analogy is a buried one, not an explicit equation as in Ammons's essay, but it is no less significant for that. Like a walk, a poem is an act of exploration, a dynamic process that unfolds "step by step" and eventually finds itself in some new, unforeseen "place." It occurs without a plan, moves impulsively, and may take many detours before arriving at its destination. Although this account of the poem seems to emphasize composition rather than the finished work, Frost refuses to differentiate between process and product; for him the value of a poem lies in its ability to reenact the impulsive movements that brought it into being. Thus each reader relives the initial process on each reading. The poem preserves a movement without freezing or fixing it in amber.

As with Ammons, this figure of the poem as movement has a tendency to become literal in Frost's own poetry. Because Frost conceives of the poem as an exploratory process, his poems are especially receptive to the walk as a kind of governing plot. In effect the walk enables him to externalize the deep structure present to one degree or another in all his lyrics. Thus for Frost the walk poem is not simply a container to be filled with description and meditation, random thoughts and perceptions bound together only by their copresence within the frame of the walk. Rather, the walk functions in his poetry as a parable of enlightenment, beginning in delight and ending in wisdom, in a "clarification of life" that gives us "a momentary stay against confusion" (*Prose*, p. 18). Frost departs from purely descriptive walk poems by insisting that the walk is not merely aesthetic but cognitive, a finding of new knowledge. In this way he moves beyond the Wordsworthian impasse, the realization that any walk can be made into a poem and that therefore any given walk poem is merely one of thousands of potential poems, with no special claim to uniqueness. What makes Frost's walk poems unique are the insights they generate, the clarifications they achieve. Thought and experience are more closely knit than in previous walk poems; the walk and the process of discovery form a single whole.

For this reason Frost's walk poems generally lack the dense accumulation of particulars that characterize previous instances of the genre. He is interested less in evoking the experience in its entirety than in distilling its wisdom, the special story or parable it tells. For the most part they are quite short, often composed in stanzas rather than flowing blank verse like Wordsworth's. This insistence on lyricism, through compression and emphatic prosody, is a way of asserting the distance between the experience in its raw, unprocessed state and the poem it occasions. Scrupulously selective, he includes only those details that in some way contribute to the deeper movement from delight to wisdom that each poem maps out. As parable, the walk embodies its own meaning. That meaning or wisdom is never baldly signaled or openly stated;

rather, it inheres in the walk itself, in the succession of images, the walker's movement from the familiar to the strange.

. . . . .

Frost's earliest walk poem is also arguably his purest, since it is the only one that labels itself as a walk in its title. Nonetheless, "A Late Walk" is not representative of Frost's mature manner. Little of anything that can be called wisdom is brought forward; the parabolic dimension that comes to play so prominent a role in Frost's later poetry is here but a faint whisper. Instead we are given a series of decorative, melancholy tableaux:

> When I go up through the mowing field,
>   The headless aftermath,
> Smooth-laid like thatch with the heavy dew,
>   Half-closes the garden path.
>
> And when I come to the garden ground,
>   The whir of sober birds
> Up from the tangle of withered weeds
>   Is sadder than any words.
>
> A tree beside the wall stands bare,
>   But a leaf that lingered brown,
> Disturbed, I doubt not, by my thought,
>   Comes softly rattling down.
>
> I end not far from my going forth
>   By picking the faded blue
> Of the last remaining aster flower
>   To carry again to you.[3]

The poem is most notable for the lack of any internal logic connecting the images into a coherent movement. Instead they are united as similarly wistful expressions of a mood projected by the speaker onto the landscape; indeed when it was first published in *A Boy's Will*, the poem bore a gloss that read "He courts the autumnal mood." This sense of a willfully melancholy youth trapped within his own sensibility dominates the poem, and prevents any movement towards genuine insight or apprehension from occurring. The lack of movement is clearly acknowledged in the final stanza. "I end not far from my setting forth"—this applies to the poem as well as the walk, since the speaker remains caught up in the autumnal mood with which he began the poem. He has stayed within a closed space, a "garden ground"; he has not ventured beyond the confines of either his familiar terrain or his solipsistic consciousness.

Despite this lack of real movement, however, "A Late Walk" almost uncannily foreshadows the imagistic and thematic concerns of Frost's later walk poems, albeit in a vague, unrealized form. What appears as a sentimental mannerism here—the projection of human affect onto nature, what Ruskin named "the pathetic fallacy"—will become one of Frost's chief preoccupations, one he never fails to frame with a high degree of irony and self-consciousness. It could be argued that the addition of the gloss, "He courts the autumnal mood," is an attempt precisely to ironize the poem, to acknowledge the speaker's solipsism and in some minimal way to reflect upon it. If so, however, it only serves to distance us from the poem itself and the sensibility it depicts; we are not given the continuous movement towards self-awareness of a single mind that will be so characteristic of Frost's later poems, only a formal split between an ironic and a sentimental consciousness.

I want to call particular attention to the second stanza, since bird imagery will come to be a kind of trademark for Frost, serving as a recurrent symbol for the attempt to find a human voice in nature. "One had to be versed in country things / Not to believe the phoebes wept"—evidently this speaker is not so "versed," since he has no compunctions about finding the "whir of sober birds . . . sadder than any words." The poem's most blatant instance of projection occurs in the next stanza, when the speaker indulges his belief in the power of mind over matter: "a leaf that lingered brown, / Disturbed, I doubt not, by my thought, / Comes softly rattling down." Again it could be said that the phrase "I doubt not" carries a certain irony, since it admits the possibility of skepticism in the very act of denying it. Yet the tone is too indeterminate to sustain such a reading definitively; Frost has yet to master the tonal subtleties that will eventually be the pillar of his art.

Perhaps the most striking premonition of Frost's later walk poems, though again one that remains entirely latent, comes in the final stanza, when the speaker picks "the last remaining aster flower /To carry again to you." Aster, of course, means star, and while the image is a buried one it directly anticipates the closural function of stars in a number of Frost's later poems. There the star represents an alternative to the humanized nature represented most often by birds; here the aster flower simply adumbrates the dominant mood of lateness and regret, without providing a new perspective on the landscape. It is as though the speaker lacked the power to perceive the star within the flower, the hidden emblem of a higher vision free from delusive projections of self.

To a remarkable extent, then, "A Late Walk" contains all the key elements of Frost's later walk poems, while failing to assemble them into a thematically cohesive whole. In its evocation of mood rather than movement it remains embryonic; Frost has not yet learned to use the sequential juxtaposition of images for cognitive ends. The beauty of this principle is that it disguises deliberate substitution as mere succession; that is, it avoids the overt didacticism of a "turn" from one attitude to another by presenting what is on the surface a mere temporal sequence, but which on closer examination proves to be a deeper movement—in Frost's terms a movement from delight to wisdom, or as I would translate it, from play to knowledge.

We can observe this principle at work in two poems from Frost's second volume, *North of Boston*. "The Wood-Pile" and "Good Hours" are very different poems in both tone and form; yet I would suggest that they manifest the same essential structure, a progress from playful communion with an animate landscape to a more sober and detached enlightenment. Frost himself chose to juxtapose these poems in assembling the volume; "Good Hours" was printed at the end of the book in italics as a kind of epilogue immediately following "The Wood-Pile." In my reading I will follow Frost's own ordering, first considering "The Wood-Pile"'s chilly excursion, then its somewhat lighter revision in "Good Hours."

"The Wood-Pile" is written in the flexible and unobtrusive blank verse that dominates *North of Boston*. Most of the other poems that employ it, however, are dramatic monologues or narratives with a heavy proportion of dialogue; there it supplies a fluid medium for the capturing of those speech rhythms or "sentence sounds" that so fascinate Frost. "The Wood-Pile" has a more solemnly meditative sound; unlike the conversational blank verse poem "Mending Wall," which opens the volume, its language is pitched slightly above the idiomatic, lending it an almost Wordsworthian dignity. Its rhythm is not that of casual speech, but of a measured exploration of the self and its terrain, at once a physical and an inner foray.

"The Wood-Pile" immediately differentiates itself from "A Late Walk" by opening with an explicit moment of choice:

> Out walking in the frozen swamp one gray day,
> I paused and said "I will turn back from here.
> No, I will go farther—and we shall see."

(Poetry, p. 101)

Unlike the speaker in "A Late Walk," this walker chooses to go *beyond* the point at which it seems natural to turn back, in a gesture that Richard Poirier, following Frost who himself follows Thoreau, aptly calls "extra-vagance," with its root sense of "wandering beyond limits."[4] This movement of transgressing the boundaries of the familiar, of en-

tering into strange and possibly dangerous territory, recurs throughout Frost's poetry, always suggesting not a desire for escape so much
as a desire for distance, for a kind of lucidly alienated perspective
on one's home ground. By willfully continuing his walk despite his instinct to turn back, Frost explicitly hopes to "see"—that is, to *know*
something that is unavailable within the confines of familiar or domestic space.

The very surface of this ground is precarious—"The hard snow held
me, save where now and then / One foot went through"—suggesting
the dangers that attend any movement out of bounds. (Already the
analogy between walk and poem is being played on in the word "foot,"
whose sudden displacement coincides with a spondee that similarly interrupts the poem's metrical progress.) Just such a vertiginous caving
in of one's accustomed ground will be the ultimate outcome of this
walk, though in no literal sense. The onset of this dislocation is signaled by the absence of landmarks:

> The view was all in lines
> Straight up and down of tall slim trees
> Too much alike to mark or name a place by
> So as to say for certain I was here
> Or somewhere else: I was just far from home.

Although we are not told so explicitly, one of the disturbing implications of these lines is that the speaker is lost. He can only define this
"place" negatively: it is "far from home," but otherwise it is nameless.
As is so frequently the case in Frost, the literal situation here seems to
resonate with a kind of parabolic meaning without ever becoming
openly allegorical. This wood is not the "selva oscura" of the *Inferno*,
yet at the same time the language Frost employs suggests that it is
more than an aggregation of trees: it is the very antithesis of "home,"
of the place in which the speaker knows himself and his surroundings.
In its barren linearity the landscape takes on a kind of abstraction, and
we can hardly avoid associating the image of black lines on a white
ground with that of a text. There is nothing legible about this scene,
however, since the crucial signifying element of language, difference,
is absent: the trees are "too much alike to mark or name a place by."

Yet even here, in this abstract, angular landscape, Frost manages to
find an anthropomorphic presence:

> A small bird flew before me. He was careful
> To put a tree between us when he lighted,
> And say no word to tell me who he was
> Who was so foolish as to think what *he* thought.
> He thought that I was after him for a feather—

The white one in his tail; like one who takes
Everything said as personal to himself.
One flight out sideways would have undeceived him.

Surely Frost means us to feel the strain in this rather too Disney-like attempt at personification. Unlike the humanized birds of Poe, Whitman, and Hardy, this bird is not invested with tragic dignity; rather, his
motives are assumed to be absurdly literal. We can speculate that the
elaborate fiction of the bird's paranoia is meant to account first of all
for his disturbing silence: he would "say no word to tell me who he
was." Curiously, by characterizing the bird's silence as an absence of
speech the narrator manages to posit the *potential* for a human utterance emanating from this inhuman landscape; he can thus reassure
himself that its muteness is circumstantial, not essential.

In imagining the bird's thoughts, however, the speaker does not
truly deceive himself; unlike the speaker of "A Late Walk," he does not
say "I doubt not." He knows he is playing with the bird, attributing
more consciousness to it than it actually possesses. Yet the bird's fear is
presumably real enough (although it may also be a projection of the
speaker's own paranoia, as Richard Poirier suggests).[5] It is only
through metaphor and simile that Frost turns the bird into a homely
human type: "Like one who takes /Everything said as personal to himself." Beyond this overt figure of speech, the very notion that the bird
fears for its tailfeather rather than its life is essentially metaphorical, a
reduction of the bird's survival instinct to a kind of anxious vanity,
thereby substituting an amusing fiction for the more sober facts of nature. For Frost, of course, metaphor is the supreme form of play, a way
of indulging the imagination without entirely losing sight of reality.
Here metaphor helps Frost to domesticate an alien and elusive presence, providing him with a kind of companionship where otherwise he
might feel too helplessly alone; but it is difficult to say precisely how
far the speaker lets the metaphor carry him from the truth of his situation, his solitude in a place that is "far from home."

Reality breaks into the poem in the form of the pile of wood that
seems, grammatically as well as visually, to appear from nowhere: "And
then there was a pile of wood." The unceremonious words "And then"
seem to represent this transition as pure succession, not the kind of dialectical turn commonly introduced by the Stevensian "And yet"; but
the effect is nonetheless a decisive shift in the poem's imaginative
course. Similarly, Frost's use of the phrase "there was" rather than "I
saw" emphasizes the sudden obtrusion of the wood-pile, the way it
thrusts itself upon the speaker's consciousness almost against his will.
It thus provides a striking instance of the kind of discovery essential to
Frost's lyric program: "It is but a trick poem and no poem at all if the

best of it was thought of first and saved for the last" (*Prose*, p. 2). Like the walker, the poet cannot know in advance what he will find; it is the element of surprise that validates the poem. Here the wood-pile disrupts the speaker's comforting fantasy of companionship and makes him aware of his own isolation. In its starkness and inanimacy it contrasts sharply with the bird, who disappears behind it as though unable to exist in the same frame.

At first all the speaker can do is describe it meticulously, as though still startled by its brute factuality:

> It was a cord of maple, cut and split
> And piled—and measured, four by four by eight.
> And not another like it could I see.
> No runner tracks in this year's snow looped near it.
> And it was older sure than this year's cutting,
> Or even last year's or the year's before.
> The wood was gray and the bark warping off it
> And the pile somewhat sunken. Clematis
> Had wound strings round and round it like a bundle.
> What held it though on one side was a tree
> Still growing, and on one a stake and prop,
> These latter about to fall.

Like the speaker of the poem, the wood-pile seems strangely out of place. Indeed, though it is a product of human labor, intended for a human dwelling, its presence in the swamp serves as an ironic reminder of the scene's estrangement, its distance from home. The very fact that it has been standing so long, and that the stake and prop which hold it up are about to fall, suggests that not only space but time as well have come between it and whatever home it was meant to warm. As a kind of mute signifier, the wood-pile might be seen as the landscape-text's first and only "word," a difference created by the human act of displacing the lines that are the scene's basic constituents, shifting them from a vertical to an horizontal position.

In reading this word, Frost at first resorts to the same strategy he used in confronting the bird: he invents a fiction to explain an absence. In the case of the bird the absence was his lack of speech; here it is the absence of the wood-pile's maker, and of any sign that he had made use of his work:

>   I thought that only
> Someone who lived in turning to fresh tasks
> Could so forget his handiwork on which
> He spent himself, the labor of his ax,
> And leave it there far from a useful fireplace

To warm the frozen swamp as best it could
With the slow smokeless burning of decay.

Just as he posited the bird's paranoia to account for his lack of speech, so the speaker now posits a kind of vigorous amnesia to explain the wood-pile's presence in the swamp. The words "I thought," however, alert us that this image of the absentminded woodsman is not to be taken as fact; it is a conjecture, and while not an implausible one it is no more rooted in reality than the far more fantastic notion of the bird protecting its white tailfeather. Critics have taken the poem's ending as an unambiguous affirmation of human labor and the happy forgetfulness of "turning to fresh tasks"; but to do so they themselves must forget that this vision is entirely hypothetical.[6] In fact it is not difficult to supply a more likely explanation for the wood-pile's abandonment, one more in keeping with Frost's poetry as a whole: useful objects are abandoned because the person to whom they are of use no longer exists. By imagining a prolific energy of life responsible for this singularly lifeless object, the speaker evades the darker possibility of the woodsman's death; once more he chooses to let his imagination distract him from his solitude.

A passage from Hawthorne's *The Blithedale Romance* may lurk in the background here; if so, it confirms the buried suggestion that the wood-pile's maker is dead:

In my haste, I stumbled over a heap of logs and sticks that had been cut for firewood, a great while ago, by some former possessor of the soil, and piled up square, in order to be carted or sledded away to the farm-house. But, being forgotten, they had lain there, perhaps fifty years, and possibly much longer; until, by the accumulation of moss, and the leaves falling over them and decaying there, from autumn to autumn, a green mound was formed, in which the softened outline of the wood-pile was still perceptible. In the fitful mood that then swayed my mind, I found something strangely affecting in this simple circumstance. I imagined the long-dead woodman, and his long-dead wife and children, coming out of their chill graves, and essaying to make a fire with this heap of mossy fuel![7]

If this is a kind of pre-text for Frost's poem, as would appear to be the case, then his revision of it has centered on the speaker's sensibility; he is no longer gloomily attuned to the wood-pile's implications, but instead valiantly tries to imagine life rather than death as the cause for its abandonment. Thus an ironic tension is introduced, where Hawthorne gives us a simple convergence of mood and object.

One may well ask whether the speaker has progressed at all by the end of the poem. Although Frost the poet may intend us to recognize the inadequacy of the speaker's response to the wood-pile, we cannot dissociate him completely from the voice of the poem; it is not, after all, a dramatic monologue, and while it is filled with ironies at the speaker's expense, Frost's mastery of tone allows us to read the poem as the self-subverting utterance of a consciousness at once deluded by play and aware of its own delusions. If the poem had ended with the woodsman, this complexity would be lost; as it stands, the last three lines of the poem take us back to the wood-pile itself, leaving behind the cheerful image of the laborer, and demonstrate a starker understanding of the object. There is a grim irony in the notion of the wood-pile "warming" the swamp in its decay. The total absence of domestic comforts is made all the more apparent by the attempt to see the wood-pile fulfilling its destined function in so pathetically futile a way. Indeed, we should recall that the swamp is "frozen," and that the speaker has by now been cold a long time, so that the wood-pile has a very real, bodily significance for him; it is a potential source of heat, though one that cannot be used because, like the speaker, it is "far from a useful fireplace."

The highly Frostian vision conveyed by the final line is of decay as a gradual, inexorable process, one that produces no warmth, no smoke, only a slow absorption back into nature. The wood-pile becomes a small-scale version of the statue in Shelley's "Ozymandias," an artifact which in its stubborn survival points to human mortality, and in its gradual decay points to the mortality of human works. (Indeed the poem's closing cadence, together with the use of the word "decay," seems a furtive echo of the close of Shelley's poem: "Round the decay / Of that colossal wreck, boundless and bare / The lone and level sands stretch far away.")[8] The poem ends, then, with a wisdom that transcends the speaker's playful speculations about bird and woods-man; he finally confronts the absence of the human from the scene in all its intractable blankness. Ironically his "extra-vagant" journey away from the domestic and familiar has only returned him to a vision of domesticity that cruelly exposes its delusiveness. He has had to walk away from his own home, into the frozen swamp, in order to recognize the fragility of everything home stands for: life, warmth, labor. His domesticating imagination finally yields before the stubborn reality of the wood-pile, which tells him that his own house must also decay and fall.

Before leaving "The Wood-Pile," I think it is useful to consider the relevance and the necessity of its form. Why is it a walk poem? Could it exist in another shape? Thematically, of course, the walk is important in that it carries the speaker into the bleak, unfamiliar space where estranged vision is possible. But just as important is the walk's formal structure, in particular the principle of successiveness that I referred to earlier. Unlike other lyrics such as "Hyla Brook," "The Oven Bird," or "Mowing," in which Frost confines himself to his titular subject, "The

Wood-Pile" is not simply about the wood-pile; rather, it is about the movement *toward* the wood-pile, a movement that includes the landscape and, most prominently, the bird. In a sense it is the transition from bird to wood-pile that is at the heart of the poem. By moving from an animate to an inanimate object, Frost arrives at a recognition of the landscape's silence and inanimacy that cannot be imaginatively deferred, and that ultimately points to death. As I have noted, this movement is not presented as a rhetorical "turn"; rather, it belongs to the poem's temporal plot or diegesis. Wisdom seems to emerge of itself, without the poet's conscious participation, and as a result we are given the tonal complexity of the speaker's resistance to the woodpile's meaning, a resistance that finally only strengthens the impact of that meaning. A truth has been *arrived* at, one all the more authentic for its having forced itself upon the speaker despite his infatuation with play. The poem fulfills the speaker's initial prediction that "we shall see," but in a way that dramatizes the intractability of genuine knowledge, its complete opposition to human will and desire. In Poirier's words the poem presents "a reductive process by which possibilities of metaphor—of finding some reassuring resemblances—are gradually disposed of."[9] It is of the essence of this process that it move from bird to wood-pile, since the difference between these objects is finally the difference between life and death. The sequential or temporal dimension of the poem is thus integral to the kind of knowledge it attains, a wisdom won from the jaws of delight.

In its placement in *North of Boston*, "Good Hours" seems intended as a deliberate sequel to "The Wood-Pile," one that recasts the previous poem in a different form, and in an utterly different mood. Jaunty where "The Wood-Pile" is brooding, "Good Hours" nonetheless presents the same basic pattern of a movement away from home that exposes the true nature of home more fully:

> I had for my winter evening walk—
> No one at all with whom to talk,
> But I had the cottages in a row
> Up to their shining eyes in snow.
>
> And I thought I had the folk within:
> I had the sound of a violin;
> I had a glimpse through curtain laces
> Of youthful forms and youthful faces.

(Poetry, p. 102)

Once again the speaker is walking through a winter landscape, and this alone is a significant fact, since it implies that his motives are unlike those of a person walking in springtime; he is interested not in

flowers, but in the kind of knowledge that can only be had by testing
the limits of one's terrain. Like the speaker in "The Wood-Pile," this
walker is alone—he has "no one at all with whom to talk"—yet he lets
his imagination supply him with company. This time his companion is
not a bird, but the houses themselves, which are explicitly personified
in the line "Up to their shining eyes in snow." The eyes are of course
windows; again the speaker is playfully projecting an excess of consciousness onto the landscape by means of metaphor. The repeated
emphasis on the verb construction "I had" lays stress on the peculiar
nature of this "having," which emerges as a deeply inward, imaginative
mode of possession.

In the next stanza Frost turns from the houses to the "folk within,"
who are also imagined to be accompanying the speaker on his walk. As
in "The Wood-Pile," the tenuous, conjectural status of the inhabitants
is signaled by the phrase "I thought," a phrase which for Frost usually
amounts to a covert denial of what has been asserted. What, after all,
does the speaker "have" here? He has glimpses through curtains,
sounds of music—stray impressions that create a congenial atmosphere, but impressions only. In effect the metaphor of "having" substitutes for the more expected verbs of perception: seeing, hearing.
Again it is only through play that Frost converts these impressions into
the more substantial "company" of his walk.

The speaker's actual isolation is confirmed in the next stanza, when
he outwalks the houses and reaches a place not unlike the deserted
swamp of "The Wood-Pile":

> I had such company outward bound.
> I went till there were no cottages found.
> I turned and repented, but coming back
> I saw no window but that was black.

The uninhabited void, it seems, was his destination all along; as pleasant and companionable as the cottages may have seemed, the speaker
was bent on leaving them behind, on traveling "outward," away from
the familiar and the domestic. The seriousness of this intent is indi-
cated by the word "repented," which implies that the speaker's initial
resolve was to continue and not to turn back; at the same time, the
word carries a sense of guilt, as though in leaving the houses behind
the speaker felt he had somehow betrayed them. Indeed there is a still
subtler hint in the word "but" that the speaker's action has actually
caused the blackening of the windows, and that his repentance has
come too late to save them. The imaginative weight of this deed becomes clear when we recall that the windows were formerly "shining
eyes"; the speaker has in effect killed them, destroying the signs of life
that had previously provided him with companionship.

What does it mean to say that the speaker has "killed" the houses? Obviously there is no literal connection between his passing beyond the houses and the extinction of their lights. But we should note that metaphor itself has also disappeared; the houses are no longer personified, the windows have stopped being eyes and reverted to their purely physical identity. In leaving the houses behind, then, the speaker has also abandoned the fiction of companionship itself; he has been forced to assume a more literal mode of vision. Like the wood-pile, the houses have turned into lifeless physical objects that poignantly express the fragility of human dwellings and of human life. Here, however, there is a more willful element in the speaker's turn to the literal; he has brought this change on himself by walking out into the uninhabited void, and by carrying the void back with him.

"Good Hours" differs from "The Wood-Pile" also in the tone of its ending. The final stanza has none of the sober majesty of "The Wood-Pile"'s closing line; it seems to show little more than a cheerful disrespect for the stodgy habits of the villagers:

> Over the snow my creaking feet
> Disturbed the slumbering village street
> Like profanation, by your leave,
> At ten o'clock of a winter eve.

Yet even here the speaker remains an outsider, alone with only the sounds of his own footsteps for company, now unaccompanied by violin. His use of the weighty term "profanation" for this noise (immediately deflated by the slightly insolent and homely "by your leave," as though the speaker had to ask our permission to use such a Latinate word) subtly reinforces the sense that he has returned to a dead place, from which the living have vanished and in which the houses are corpses. The dark knowledge of "The Wood-Pile"'s close has been transmuted into a wry, joking awareness of the perilousness of our illusions of home and community. Having once achieved the perspective of an outsider, the speaker cannot return to the same friendly place he left; once again the landscape confronts him with his own solitude.

The poem's title tells us that these have been "Good Hours," and so they may well be; but if the first hour, outward bound, is good because of its cozy sense of community, the second hour, coming home, is good because it leads to a barer, starker vision that corrects the imaginative excesses of the first. The cottages do not have eyes, and the speaker does not "have" the people in them: this is the simple but vital truth that emerges from both the walk and the poem. Where "The Wood-Pile" centers on the uninhabited swamp and the single artifact the speaker finds there, "Good Hours" follows the walker back from the outer darkness, and discovers the consequences of such an excursion for his perception of home itself. In effect the houses *become* the wood-pile; the implicit synecdoche that identified the wood-pile with home is reversed, and we are shown that home, as represented both by the village in which the speaker lives and by the individual houses that resemble his own, is itself little more than a pile of wood, a physical object without a soul.

As poems of "extra-vagance," both "The Wood-Pile" and "Good Hours" show Frost wandering beyond the limits of home ground; yet unlike Thoreau, who can lose himself in the nonhuman, Frost is never able to leave home behind entirely. Instead he moves to a vantage point from which home appears in a stark, denuded form, stripped of the cheerful pathos that had previously clung to it. Frost's tone, however, remains willfully homey, despite his apprehension of the void that surrounds and inhabits the home. Unlike Stevens, he is more interested in seeing nothing that is not there than the nothing that is. As Poirier says,

> For Frost's lonely walkers, far from "home," nothing can come from such nothing, and they therefore must try to speak again and in such a way as to make known an ordinary human presence. Frost in this mood is bleaker than Stevens. He resists the transcendental willingness to disentangle the self from the ties of "home" and from any responsibility to domesticate whatever might be encountered while one is "extra-vagant."[10]

In short, "extravagance," the will to walk out into the frozen swamp, brings not transcendental freedom but renewed responsibility. The special knowledge Frost achieves in walking keeps forcing him back home, although home itself can never be the same. His refusal to give himself over to Emersonian transcendentalism or Hardyesque fatalism, his persistently colloquial voice and anecdotal manner, indicate that for Frost the walk is a circuit, not a one-way trip. It is the movement of return that validates the knowledge achieved; only by coming back from the swamp, back to the familiar world of home and village streets, can he confirm what he has learned, while leaving room for new forays into the wilderness.

. . . . .

Both "The Wood-Pile" and "Good Hours" present the walker in the act of discovering the true nature of home. In both poems the speaker begins by imaginatively supplying himself with a kind of domestic companionship even as he wanders away from humanity. The recognition that home is subject to death and decay is therefore presented as an in-

terruption or obtrusion, an insight forced on the speaker against his
will. But as Frost became older, he naturally began to represent knowledge less as discovery than as confirmation. As this change occurs, his
depiction of the walk also changes, becoming more static, less sequential. That shift is visible in another poem about nocturnal perambula-
tions, the well-known "Acquainted with the Night." Like "Good
Hours," this poem is about the sense of isolation and outsideness that
the speaker attains simply by staying up later than everyone else. It is
one of Frost's rare city poems, and perhaps for this reason its tone is
rather different from his usual rustic manner. Indeed it may at times
seem reminiscent of Eliot, particularly in its repeated use of the "I
have" construction, recalling such Prufrockian lines as "I have gone at
dusk through narrow streets / And watched the smoke that rises from
the pipes / Of lonely men in shirt sleeves, leaning out of windows."[11]
Such grammar dispels the kind of precise sequential focus that the earlier poems display, instead creating a repetitive space in which constancy rather than change is emphasized.

Nonetheless, "Acquainted with the Night" has a number of elements
in common with "The Wood-Pile" and "Good Hours." As in "Good
Hours," the speaker makes a point of "outwalk[ing] the furthest city
light," leaving behind the human markers and habitations that create a
sense of community, and faring into a lonelier kind of landscape. And
again his solitude is underscored by the sound of his own footsteps,
which here enter his consciousness only when he stops making them.
Most significantly, we are given a new version of the dialectic between
companionship and detachment, one that makes use of terms developed more fully in other poems:

> When far away an interrupted cry
> Came over houses from another street,
>
> But not to call me back or say good-by;
> And further still at an unearthly height,
> One luminary clock against the sky
>
> Proclaimed the time was neither wrong nor right.
> I have been one acquainted with the night.
>
> (*Poetry*, p. 255)

The speaker's casual denial that the cry is addressed to him contrasts
with the projections made by the speakers in "The Wood-Pile" and
"Good Hours"; perhaps because this poem lacks Frost's characteristic
playfulness he is never tempted to construct a fiction of companionship. Instead his labor is wholly negative, revealing a more austere sensibility than we have previously seen.

In the next line the image of the "luminary clock" seems to offer an alternative to the "interrupted cry." It too "proclaims," yet its utterance is impersonal, directed to no one in particular. As critics have pointed out, this clock is undoubtedly the moon, a fact reinforced by the burial of "lunar" in "luminary." Thus its face is blank, and can tell us only that the time is neither wrong nor right. A kind of detached neutrality, an impassiveness that can be achieved only from an "unearthly height," is the reward of the speaker's acquaintance with the night. Unlike the walkers in "The Wood-Pile" and "Good Hours," he is disenchanted from the start, and so we are not given a movement from play to wisdom, only a static portrait of alienation. The very grammar of the opening line portrays the self as a constant, fixed entity, "*one* acquainted with the night" (italics mine); the speaker is not undergoing a process of self-transformation in the course of the walk, but is simply confirming his initial sense of solitude. The poem's essential stasis is emphasized by the repetition of its first line as its last, thereby framing the intervening lines as an elaboration of a single sentence. This lack of true progression can be ascribed to the poem's synoptic temporality; its events all take place in the timeless space of "the night," and so do not possess the kind of narrative specificity we have seen in Frost's other walk poems.

Yet although its speaker, like the speaker in "A Late Walk," does not move beyond his initial expression of self-pity, the poem itself contains a succession of images, most saliently the cry and the moon, which do imply a dialectical movement. The turn from a human or humanized voice to an "unearthly" celestial object, be it moon or star, becomes an important motif in Frost's poetry, most prominently displayed in two poems that bear close comparison, "Looking for a Sunset Bird in Winter" and "Come In." In both these poems a walker turns his gaze from a bird to a star, and in so doing he crosses over to a new, colder mode of vision. Yet the speaker's relationship to bird and star is significantly different in the two poems, and provides a measure of how Frost's later poetry departs from the exploratory paradigm set forth in "The Figure a Poem Makes."

"Looking for a Sunset Bird in Winter" appeared in *New Hampshire*, Frost's fourth volume, and in form it resembles "The Wood-Pile" and "Good Hours." As in those poems, the speaker is brought against his will to a new perspective, although here he is confronted not with an image of decay and abandonment but rather, as in "Acquainted with the Night," with an image of lofty detachment. He is on his way home when he sees something: "I thought I saw a bird alight." Again the words "I thought" warn us as to the nature of this perception. The speaker remembers a bird with an "angelic" voice that he heard in summer; but now, even though he goes twice around the tree, he can see nothing but a single leaf. The voice or song he desires is not there; only his own nostalgic imagination has led him to expect the bird.

In the beautiful closing stanza, however, the speaker receives a kind of compensatory vision:

> A brush had left a crooked stroke
> Of what was either cloud or smoke
> From north to south across the blue;
> A piercing little star was through.

(*Poetry*, p. 233)

Unlike the closing images in many of Frost's poems, this last image is genuinely a surprise; nothing in the title prepares us for it. The poem dramatizes the process of coming upon something inadvertently, while looking for something else—a process, as we know, central to Frost's conception of poetry. Yet there is a curious relationship between this little star and the object of the speaker's search, summed up in the word "piercing," which can be used to describe both a sound, like a bird song, and an appearance. (The pun is reinforced by the apparent displacement of "piercing" from its position as a verb—"A little star was piercing through"—to its more ambiguous adjectival position.) The reference to the brush suggests that this image is another kind of aesthetic reward, though in a different medium from the song. The seasonal setting of the poem may help to explain the substitution of star for bird; in this wintry landscape a star is a more appropriate object of vision, colder and more distant, less subject to imaginative distortion.[12]

As the fourth stanza tells us, the speaker in some measure shares the star's perspective: "From my advantage on a hill." Like the moon in "Acquainted with the Night," the star is a figure for a kind of vision, one that remains poised above desire and gazes impassively at human suffering. Increasingly Frost will turn to emblems for such a stance, choosing to celebrate his own victory over mutability rather than to mourn its effect on others. His exhortation to "Take Something Like a Star" may be seen as his response to the tragic discoveries presented in early poems like "The Wood-Pile," and critics have complained that in his later poetry Frost at times too easily dismisses the reality of pain and loss, finding repose in a cold, smug detachment. Yet one might say that it is precisely the measure of Frost's sensitivity to pain that he must find refuge in the stars.

From this point of view "Come In" offers an illuminating contrast to "Looking for a Sunset Bird in Winter." Published some twenty years later, it revises the earlier poem's outing by showing the speaker as now impervious to a bird's melodic invitation:

Far in the pillared dark
Thrush music went—
Almost like a call to come in
To the dark and lament.

But no, I was out for stars:
I would not come in.
I meant not even if asked,
And I hadn't been.

(Poetry, p. 334)

Where the bird in "Looking for a Sunset Bird in Winter" was wholly a creation of the speaker's desire, here it is an assertive reality, demanding the speaker's imaginative participation. But this time he is out for stars, not birds, and refuses even to toy with the notion that the bird's song is a "call to come in" and join the bird in lamentation. As in "Acquainted with the Night," the speaker remains undeceived from the start, and as a result "Come In" is also essentially static; that is, it does not dramatize the speaker in the process of changing his mind. Certainly the last line makes a powerful gesture of rejection, but there is little sign in the poem that he is at any point truly tempted by the bird's call. The effect is rather of a decisive reaffirmation of his continuing commitment to stars. The hardening of Frost's sensibility is evident in the loss of the fluidity and dynamism that enabled him to write the kind of poem he describes in "The Figure a Poem Makes," one that "unfolds by surprise." To put it another way, the walk is no longer organic to the poem; because the walkers in "Acquainted with the Night" and "Come In" have already chosen stars over birds, detachment over involvement, they have nowhere to go. "No one can really hold that the ecstasy should be static and stand still in one place," Frost writes; yet the poems of his later years *do* stand still in one place, appropriating as they do the fixed perspective of a star.

It is not until Frost's last great poem, "Directive," that he manages to reconcile the desire to write a poem that moves *toward* wisdom or "clarification" with his mature stance as one who has already achieved the wisdom of detachment. His solution is an ingenious one; the poem is written in the second person, in the voice of a guide. Thus it is the reader who enacts the process of moving from play to knowledge, while Frost himself maintains the perspective of an all-knowing sage. The walk described in the poem is a walk *we* are being asked to take, and while we may assume that our guide has covered this route himself, he evidently has no further need for it. "Directive" is thus like a late version of "The Wood-Pile" in which the speaker has retired from the scene to oversee the initiation of new walkers.

The poem's famous opening lines establish the coordinates and goal of the walk we are being sent on:

> Back out of all this now too much for us,
> Back in a time made simple by the loss
> Of detail, burned, dissolved, and broken off
> Like graveyard marble sculpture in the weather,
> There is a house that is no more a house
> Upon a farm that is no more a farm
> And in a town that is no more a town.
>
> (*Poetry*, p. 377)

Much has been said about the intricate syntactical ambiguities these lines present: should we read the first line, for example, as an imperative or a prepositional clause? And should the word "now" be taken as a substantive rather than an adverb? We are indeed being urged to "back out" of the "now" of present history, to embark on a journey into the past; yet even the status of this apparently "simple" time is uncertain, for its simplicity seems to be a function of erosion, rather than an inherent property of an earlier era. Indeed the very point of our excursion into this landscape may be to undermine nostalgia, as another version of the sentimentalizing pathos that Frost backs away from in his earlier poems. The simile "like graveyard marble sculpture" hints that not simply attrition but death is the precondition for the kind of bare clarity of outline the poem is leading us to, recalling the image of the woodpile that survives its maker. The series of riddling phrases that begin "There is a house that is no more a house" further confuse our understanding of time. Had Frost written "There *was* a house that is no more a house" the ambiguity would be dispelled; as it is we cannot tell whether we are being directed into a past moment imagined as present, or to a present site haunted by its past. We only know that the poem is leading us to a place in which present and past, life and death, being and nonbeing intersect.

The first part of the poem's itinerary abounds in the kind of playful personification also found in "The Wood-Pile" and "Good Hours," suggesting an initial phase of imaginative projection that must eventually yield to a more sober apprehension. But where the speakers in the earlier poems confined their personifying to relatively small objects, a bird and a row of houses, Frost here magnifies this impulse to include the landscape as a whole:

> The road there, if you'll let a guide direct you
> Who only has at heart your getting lost,
> May seem as if it should have been a quarry—
> Great monolithic knees the former town

> Long since gave up pretense of keeping covered.
> And there's a story in a book about it:
> Besides the wear of iron wagon wheels
> The ledges show lines ruled southeast northwest,
> The chisel work of an enormous Glacier
> That braced his feet against the Arctic Pole.
> You must not mind a certain coolness from him
> Still said to haunt this side of Panther Mountain.

Vast forces of nature are tamed and domesticated by the poet's imagination, and geological histories of the region are turned into storybooks. As in "The Wood-Pile," there is an element of forced playfulness here that seems to call attention to its own excess; the almost cartoonlike portrayal of the quarry's knees and the glacier's feet, representing feminine culture and masculine nature (a typically American realignment of the traditional gender associations), creates an effect of Rabelaisian unreality which I think is meant to put us on our guard. What these fantastic figures hide is the essential destructiveness of this landscape, its tendency to wear away both at itself and whatever human community seeks to tame it. Once more Frost invents a humanized companion (the glacier is referred to as "him") to disguise his, or rather our, solitude in a barren landscape; and once more this gesture can be perceived as a defensive strategy for staving off tragic knowledge.

Frost is never more artful than in this part of the poem. The cleverness, the arch tone, the overelaborated conceits, all I think are *meant* to trouble the reader, to start us of our own accord towards the poem's ultimate destination, which is the antithesis of such distracted play.[13] As if to move us gradually towards our goal, Frost allows the landscape to darken slowly, permitting more ominous details to enter one by one:

> Nor need you mind the serial ordeal
> Of being watched from forty cellar holes
> As if by eye pairs out of forty firkins.
> As for the woods' excitement over you
> That sends light rustle rushes to their leaves,
> Charge that to upstart inexperience.
> Where were they all not twenty years ago?
> They think too much of having shaded out
> A few old pecker-fretted apple trees.
> Make yourself up a cheering song of how
> Someone's road home from work this once was,
> Who may be just ahead of you on foot
> Or creaking with a buggy load of grain.

The word "ordeal," with its overtones of quest-romance, flippantly points us to the true nature of this walk. It is a quest because, unlike the walker in "The Wood-Pile," we know that there is a goal ahead, the "house that is no more a house." At this point, however, only our guide knows why the house is a suitable object of our quest. Unlike us, Frost knows what is to come; having traveled this path many times before, he can no longer be surprised by what he finds. Yet he can still conduct us there in such a way that the full impact of discovery is maintained. To this end he distracts us with jokes, similes, garrulous tales, all meant to offset the stark knowledge to come.

Again there is a touch of imaginative projection in the reference to the forty "eye pairs," perhaps recalling the "houses up to their shining eyes in snow" of "Good Hours"; but even without the simile we are still "being watched from forty cellar holes," so that rhetorically only the firkins are overtly fictional (perhaps inspired by Ali Baba's forty thieves hidden in their barrels). The use of the simile deflects the walker's deeper fears and uncertainties about the landscape's inhabitants by turning to explicit figurations; yet the literal sense of being watched remains. More importantly, the image of the cellar holes looks forward to the single ruined house that we are seeking, a cellar hole somehow different from the rest, more isolated and more tragic.

Another blatant projection comes with the "woods' excitement over you," as Frost again offers a complete narrative to account for their humanized behavior. Now, however, the personification has the landscape responding directly to the walker's presence (we may recall the leaf that falls in "A Late Walk," "disturbed, I doubt not, by my thought"). Here of course Frost's tone remains wryly self-conscious; but the story he tells about the trees gives an oblique indication of the landscape's true history. They are "upstarts" because they are young; they think well of themselves because they grew tall enough to block the sun from an apple orchard, thus killing it. The implicit scenario, as throughout the poem, is of nature overwhelming culture, obliterating the products of human labor with frightening ease. The apple trees belonged to someone's farm, and we should remember that Frost himself wrote of apple picking with great authority. (The epithet "pecker-fretted" may provide a hint as to why the orchard was originally abandoned.) The speaker's playful characterization of the woods, then, is another shrugging off of tragedy, an attempt to portray nature as responsive to the humans whom in reality it overwhelms.

Frost's deadly encouragements reach a climax in his advice to "make yourself up a cheering song of how / Someone's road home from work this once was." At last the motivations behind his jangling rhetoric become apparent: he, like us, is in urgent need of cheering. Indeed the first part of the poem has been nothing other than a "cheering song," made up to animate a landscape whose truth is too painful to face. The fact that the song we are instructed to make up only brings us closer to the landscape's history of ruin is an irony in keeping with what has gone before. The cheerful vision of the laborer "who may be just ahead of you" is very much a reminiscence of the forgetful wood-cutter in "The Wood-Pile," a human figure imagined as full of life when in fact the scene before us tells only of his death.

Why does Frost go through the motions of making fictions, endow-ing a landscape with life when he is only too aware of its desolation? There is something almost sadistic or taunting in the way he seems to offer comfort and reassurance while actually showing us the evidence of human failure at every turn. I would suggest that he is mocking his former self as much as us, the persona of "The Wood-Pile," the senti-mentalist of "A Late Walk." He gives us a kind of savage parody of the playful imagination that has been his metier for more than forty years, the mainstay of Frost the whimsical old New England sage. If we miss the irony in this part of the poem, we cannot adequately confront the massive repudiation carried out in the poem's closing section, in which we are made to gaze steadily and remorselessly at an emblem of decay far more devastating than the wood-pile.

The poem's final movement begins as we reach "the height / Of country where two village cultures faded / Into each other." A crucial difference between this walk and the walk in "The Wood-Pile" is that here we are moving *upward*, toward a summit, a vantage point. This topographical revision is in large measure responsible for the salva-tional cadence of the poem's ending. Before that saving movement can take place, however, we must be brought to witness the scene of de-struction in all its sorrow. We are not greatly moved, perhaps, to hear of how the two village cultures are now lost; loss on the scale of culture is difficult to connect with human suffering. But as we are told to "make ourselves at home," the scale shrinks down to the domestic. For it is precisely a home that we have been brought to see.

Even here, Frost brings us to our goal by degrees:

> First there's the children's house of make believe,
> Some shattered dishes underneath a pine,
> The playthings in the playhouse of the children.
> Weep for what little things could make them glad.

In the relationship between the playhouse and the house in earnest, Frost brilliantly epitomizes the central movement of the poem as a whole. It is difficult to avoid associating the "children's house of make believe" with all the fiction making and projection of the poem's first half; and the repeated emphasis on "play" in "the playthings in the playhouse" further underscores the relation between children's toys and that higher form of play called poetry.[14] But the dishes are shattered, and this surely suggests that the poem's play is also at an end, its cheerful fictions broken. We weep for the little things that made them glad because we know they will never make us glad again, and because we recognize how fragile and inadequate a shield such playthings provide before the destructive forces of time and nature.

And so we turn from the children's house of make believe to

> the house that is no more a house,
> But only a belilaced cellar hole,
> Now slowly closing like a dent in dough.
> This was no playhouse but a house in earnest.

The implicit riddle asked at the beginning of the poem—"when is a house not a house?"—is answered here: when all that is left of it is the cellar hole, the original excavation on which it was built. The image of this hole "slowly closing like a dent in dough" simultaneously captures the lost sense of domesticity associated with the baking of bread, and the slow, inexorable process of decay evoked so memorably at the end of "The Wood-Pile." (Frost's source for this image is probably *Walden*, the chapter entitled "Former Inhabitants": "These cellar dents are all that is left where once were the stir and bustle of human life.") In the next line the phrase "a house in earnest" poignantly summons up all the serious, simple needs and wishes that the house once contained and partly satisfied. But the house and its inhabitants are gone, and we are faced with the ruins of their labors slowly blending back into nature. (We should recall that when this poem was written Frost had already buried his wife and two of his children, so that his own "house" had quite literally returned to the earth.)

Yet "Directive," unlike "The Wood-Pile," does not end with the image of a rotting human artifact. We have still not attained our goal:

> Your destination and your destiny's
> A brook that was the water of the house,
> Cold as a spring as yet so near its source,
> Too lofty and original to rage.
> (We know the valley streams that when aroused
> Will leave their tatters hung on barb and thorn.)

The house too, it seems, has only been a byway, part of the ordeal rather than the reward. It is the brook that has been our destination all along. Yet why bring us this far to see a brook? The answer lies, I think, in the *relation* between the brook and the house. As in Frost's other walk poems, meaning arises here from the succession of images, the movement from playhouse to house to brook. This sequence plots a deeper imaginative movement that begins by shucking off the playful defenses indulged in during the first part of the poem, confronts the bare evidence of human transience, and finally finds refuge in the lofty perspective Frost associates elsewhere with stars. This brook is not just a brook, but a figure for a kind of vision and a kind of poetry.[15] It is cold because it is near its source; translated into human terms, we could say that coldness, apparent indifference to human suffering, actually comes from being close to the sources of life, the natural forces that both create and destroy it. The line "too lofty and original to rage" is even more suggestive. Once more impassivity is imaged as height, as a starlike distance from worldly affairs. From this unearthly vantage point, as in "Acquainted with the Night," "the time is neither wrong nor right." The brook's loftiness, then, suggests a refusal to pass judgment on life, a refusal to rage at it for taking away all that it gives us. The parenthetical lines about the valley streams that "when aroused / Will leave their tatters hung on barb and thorn" can be taken to represent both the self-lacerating effects of indiscriminate rage against our given condition, and the very forces that provoke such rage.

Even here, at the poem's climax, an element of playfulness intrudes as the poet offers us the "broken drinking goblet like the Grail," again an allusion to quest-romance. (There is also a touch of personification in the reference to the old cedar's "instep arch," recalling the glacier's "feet" earlier.) Frost's awareness that these playful elements have been smuggled in illicitly is expressed when he tells us "I stole the goblet from the children's playhouse," thus implying that it too is only a prop or toy. Yet in the end it seems we cannot do without such toys, without the leaky vessels of metaphor and parable, although the true goal of our quest is the water itself, emblem of a perfect and inhuman lucidity:

> Here are your waters and your watering place.
> Drink and be whole again beyond confusion.

By drinking this cold water we may attain what Frost says is the aim of all his poems, "a clarification of life—not necessarily a great clarification such as sects and cults are built on, but a momentary stay against confusion" (*Prose*, p. 2). The costs of such a clarification are great, however; notice the way the word "whole" in the last line echoes the cellar "hole" that the house has become. Such wholeness requires that we empty ourselves of all our illusions, fictions, toys—except of course the one toy we keep to drink from. The cold wisdom Frost's poems attain can never be wholly purified of play, of the trappings of domesticity; rather, it is only *through* such play that knowledge can be held and tasted. Yet knowledge for Frost is always knowledge of that which shatters play, home, companionship, leaving us alone in an empty place, beyond confusion.

"Directive" differs from "The Wood-Pile" in that it takes us beyond the contemplation of decay, to the contemplation of the power of contemplation itself. The poem ends on a celebratory note, but what it celebrates is the ability to see the worst that can befall us without flinching. It is for this reason that the poem's trajectory up the mountain is significant; whereas the walker in "The Wood-Pile" travels outward, into darkness, in "Directive" we move up, attaining a height from which the landscape can be viewed in its totality. As an old man who has seen his own house fall, Frost may have felt he *had* seen everything, the fated end of every house and every human. Having attained the glacial cold of detachment himself, he becomes a guide in "Directive," ushering the less experienced through the landscape he has already traversed, ending at the water where each pilgrim will learn clarity and acceptance.

Poems like "The Wood-Pile" and "Directive" bring a new thematic weight to the walk poem. Frost reinvents the genre by building on the formal analogy between poem and walk; both travel from the familiar, the domestic, the human to a renewed sense of contingency and mortality. In Frost's hands the walk becomes a parable for the way the mind comes to knowledge, by encountering realities that resist its domesticating impulse. Thus the walk serves him as a vehicle for charting inner movements, adjustments in perspective, the temporal process of discovery and understanding. His primary goal is not description but what he calls "wisdom," and so each poem narrows itself around some image embodying an insight; facts that may originate in experience are infused with parabolic significance, losing their status as mere data. Yet the way in which wisdom is attained is as important to Frost as the nature of wisdom itself, so that his best poems are never simply statements. Poems like "The Wood-Pile" and "Directive" use the structure of the walk, with its rhythmic principles of movement, succession, and arrival, to illustrate the way wisdom can suddenly emerge in the midst of play, startling us into sadness and understanding.

II

WALLACE STEVENS: THE WALK AS OCCASION

"AN ORDINARY EVENING in New Haven," Stevens's last long masterpiece, does not look like a walk poem. Unlike Frost's poems, it lacks a clear-cut narrative frame, the kind of anecdotal preamble we get in a poem like "The Wood-Pile": "Out walking in the frozen swamp one gray day." Such an introduction generally serves to establish the walk as formal container, but Stevens eschews the grammar of narrative entirely. The poem's organization is not mimetic but discursive; the sequence of thirty-one eighteen-line cantos corresponds to no literal temporality, but rather to a flow of meditative thought. Indeed, as does so much of his poetry, "An Ordinary Evening in New Haven" scrupulously avoids the pronoun "I," thus eliminating any hint of the directly experiential. Yet although its language and structure so thoroughly resist the kind of first-person narrative characteristic of most walk poems, "An Ordinary Evening" represents a major culmination of the genre, one that carries to a new level of sophistication the walk poem's meditative tendencies. The idea of the walk informs virtually every section of the poem, but Stevens refuses to *represent* his walk in any conventional manner. The walk is present in the poem not as its "subject," something to be rendered or translated into language, but rather as its *occasion*, the experience out of which the poem seems to arise and of which it is itself a part.

This crucial distinction is clearly set forth in two key lines occurring in consecutive cantos of the poem. The first is the well-known declaration that "The poem is the cry of its occasion" (XII). I have already discussed the implications of this statement in my introduction, but in order to apply it to the poem we need to juxtapose it with another line from the succeeding canto: "He skips the journalism of subjects" (XIII). Together these phrases outline an entire polemic, directed against mimetic ideas of representation and toward a more dynamic conception of the ties between poetry and experience. We may speculate that one of the targets of this polemic is none other than Robert Frost, with whom Stevens carried on an uneasy rivalry. In a famous exchange at Key West, Stevens is reported to have told Frost, "Your trouble, Robert, is that you write on subjects"; to which Frost retorted, "Your trouble, Wallace, is that you write on bric-a-brac."[1] Frost's quick rejoinder has generally attracted more attention as a succinct if unfair caricature of

Stevens's style; but I think Stevens's initial accusation is both more serious and more revealing. What does it mean to "write on subjects," and
how might this be viewed pejoratively?

As in all poetic polemics, of course, Stevens's charge is really an anxious defense of his own practice against the challenge of an alternative
way. Frost's parables necessarily treat experience as a source of "subjects," in the sense of images that can be infused with significance without losing their solidity. Where Frost locates wisdom outside the play
of consciousness, in the recognition of external necessity, Stevens insists on the continuity between reflection and understanding. For him
the play of imagination is not a toy to be broken by confrontation with
the real, but the very medium within which reality can be approached.
He is therefore less interested in investing specific "subjects" with
meaning than in perpetuating the motion of mind as it reflects on experience.

Yet while Stevens's poetry generally resists what he pejoratively terms
"the journalism of subjects," the merely accurate notation of time and
place, his thematic emphasis throughout his career is on the innate
value of immediate experience. A tension arises, then, between Stevens's methods and his beliefs. How can the value of ordinary experience be affirmed without descending to journalism? In his later poetry
Stevens confronts this problem by developing a new mode of meditative poetry, one that acknowledges immediate circumstances without
slavishly transcribing them. Frostian description must at all costs be
avoided, since it has the effect of subordinating meditation to anecdote, the act of mind to the development of a "subject." Helen
Vendler has remarked on the shift to a more occasional mode in such
late poems as "Credences of Summer" and "The Auroras of Autumn":
"No previous long poem in Stevens' collections had ever placed a lyric
speaker firmly in a landscape of the present moment. . . . To fix the attention on the present is not at all a new idea in Stevens' verse; what is
new is the expression of the idea in the present tense, in the actual
scene, in the poetry of 'this' and 'here' and 'now.' "[2] The emergence
of what Vendler calls a "temporarily topographical poetry" in Stevens's
late work signals a new attention to the occasion of poetic utterance,
not as a subject to be represented but as a scene for meditation. Both
"Credences of Summer" and "The Auroras of Autumn" take specific
experiences of landscape as their occasion, and while both poems
move away from those occasions as they unfold, a sense of experiential
context continues to inform their language and imagery, giving them
far more dramatic and sensual immediacy than Stevens's earlier poems
display.

But it is "An Ordinary Evening in New Haven" that conveys the
strongest sense of its occasion, which is directly named only in the

poem's title. There is a special reason for the poem's heightened occasionality; in genesis it was, in fact, an occasional poem in the accepted
sense, that is, a poem written not on but *for* a specific occasion. That occasion was the sesquicentennial meeting of the Connecticut Academy
of Arts and Sciences in New Haven, in the autumn of 1949.[3] Stevens
was asked to contribute a commemorative poem to be read at the meeting; understandably reluctant to write a poem singing the glory of the
Connecticut Academy of Arts and Sciences, he instead agreed to *dedi-
cate* a poem to the Academy. Louis Martz recalls a conversation with
Stevens about the poem's composition:

> "I wanted to have something that would relate to the poem's occasion but
> not directly. So I just fixed on this idea of a poem about a walk in New
> Haven, but then branching out." He said it really got so far away from the
> base that New Haven hardly appears in it. "It's only the title, really, but,"
> he said, "that's the way things happen with me. I start with a concrete
> thing, and it tends to become so generalized that it isn't any longer a
> local place. I think that puzzles some people."[4]

The poem therefore has not one but two occasions, one past and
the other future, although the two moments share a single location.
First there is the "walk in New Haven" that supplies the central situation from which the poem branches out; and secondly there is the
meeting at which the poem is to be read, also in New Haven. Of these
two senses of the word "occasion," clearly the first is intended in the
line "The poem is the cry of its occasion"; certainly Stevens did not
view this poem as the "cry" of the sesquicentennial meeting of the Connecticut Academy of Arts and Sciences. Indeed, the poem's title may
be intended to distinguish the thoroughly unremarkable evening that
inspires the poem from the ceremonial occasion on which it was to be
read, perhaps implying that the true occasions of poetry are precisely
the ordinary ones. Although Stevens seems to deny the influence of
the occasion in speaking with Martz, he exaggerates considerably when
he says that "New Haven hardly appears in it." In fact New Haven, or
the poet's experience of New Haven, is an almost constant presence in
the poem, but not as the poem's putative "subject."[5] Rather, the poet's
walk through the city becomes a testing ground for his speculations
about the nature of reality. By rooting his meditation in experience,
Stevens forces himself to remain open to the world in all its stubbornly
empirical existence; thought must be tempered by perception, not allowed to proliferate in its own rarefied atmosphere.

The poem's title, with its indefinite article, implies that the evening
invoked is one out of many, selected as representative rather than
unique. It may be, of course, that Stevens did not have a specific evening in mind, but merely constructed an amalgam of ordinary evenings

as he wrote (although details of season and weather remain consistent throughout the poem). Whether or not a single walk in New Haven lies behind it, however, the poem explicitly *organizes* itself around what appears to be a particular occasion. As it happens, we know that Stevens visited New Haven often, and for somewhat surprising reasons. The following exchange with the poet was taken down by the critic Frank Jones, who was at the time a young scholar and poet paying homage to the great man:

"I often get away to New Haven for a weekend—find it a good place to relax, entertain myself."
"You mean you actually find New Haven a relief from Hartford?" I am incredulous, having inhabited New Haven for a year.
"Why, yes."
"Strange. That's just the way I feel about Hartford."
"There! That shows how silly it is, really. A state of mind." [6]

Jones's incredulity is understandable to anyone familiar with New Haven; but as a poet Stevens is attracted as much to poverty and tawdriness as to lushness and fecundity. Hence New Haven offers him a choice setting for meditation on the commonplace, on reality unadorned by art. It has the further advantage of not being Hartford, that is, not being completely familiar, possessing the slight strangeness that facilitates clear vision. As Harold Bloom writes, "New Haven is simply any city that is not home, a city that unsettles the self just enough so that it is startled into meditation, but close enough to home so that the meditation keeps contact always with the commonplace."[7]

The exchange quoted above, however, also makes clear that for Stevens New Haven is a state of mind, a place of and in the mind. And it is with delineating the precise provinces of mind and world, or, in Stevens's favored terms, imagination and reality, as they intersect on an ordinary evening in New Haven, that the poem is primarily concerned. How much of New Haven, as perceived by a poet walking its streets on a windy evening, is real, and how much is unreal? This is the question the poem asks over and over, and it keeps returning to experience for an answer, testing its hypotheses against the remembered sensations and impressions of that windy night. The poem's ultimate solution lies in a redefinition of "reality" itself, so as to include the incessant motion and change of subjective experience. Such a solution only emerges, however, after a long and sinuous meditation on the occasion as it is refracted through the many prisms that make up the poem's thirty-one cantos.

The poem's opening canto establishes both the theme and the form of the work as a whole:

The eye's plain version is a thing apart,
The vulgate of experience. Of this
A few words, an and yet, and yet, and yet—

As part of the never-ending meditation,
Part of the question that is a giant himself:
Of what is this house composed if not of the sun,

These houses, these difficult objects, dilapidate
Appearances of what appearances,
Words, lines, not meanings, not communications,

Dark things without a double after all,
Unless a second giant kills the first—
A recent imagining of reality,

Much like a new resemblance of the sun,
Down-pouring, up-springing and inevitable,
A larger poem for a larger audience,

As if the crude collops came together as one,
A mythological form, a festival sphere,
A great bosom, beard and being, alive with age.[8]

The poem opens with a statement of axiomatic simplicity and generality, although even here certain dialectical subtleties begin to appear.
We are told that "The eye's plain version is a thing apart"—but apart
from what? From the distorting impositions of mind? Or from the full
complexity of the real? The next phrase only heightens this ambiguity
in the nature of seeing: the vulgate of experience may denote a common, vernacular way of knowing the world, free from the pretensions
of what Stevens elsewhere calls "the imagination's Latin"; on the other
hand, it may be precisely a Latin Vulgate, a translation of a more original and authentic text into a language that is itself removed from the
vernacular.[9] The play on "vulgate" leads us to suspect that the "eye's
plain version" may not be so plain, and moreover to recognize that it is
a *version*, a translation rather than the thing itself. Already, then, Stevens is stressing the doubleness of mere perception; it is at once the
common ground of experience and an abstraction from experience.
In a sense the entire poem germinates from this split; throughout its
length it oscillates between asserting the necessity of "the eye's plain
version" and its inadequacy as an account of reality.

It is not surprising, then, that Stevens immediately alerts us to the incessant qualification of this initial proposition that will ensue. In so
doing he calls attention to the form the poem will take, which is not ar-
gumentative but dialectical, a potentially infinite series of refinements

and corrections, each responding to its predecessor, never attaining a point beyond which no further qualification is possible. Indeed Stevens openly announces that the poem is essentially incomplete, since it is only a fragment, a "*part* of the never-ending meditation" (italics mine). Because the meditation itself cannot end, the poem's closure must finally be arbitrary, a cutting off of a process that can have no intrinsic point of completion.[10]

This admission that the poem is only a "part" of an endless whole points us to an important difference between Stevens's use of the walk as formal paradigm and Frost's. Where for Frost the walk takes on an essentially narrative or parabolic shape, bringing the poet to a point at which a discovery is made and a clarification achieved, for Stevens the walk is more open-ended; the energies of thought are evenly distributed, so that at each moment the faculties of contemplation are fully engaged. To put it another way, where Frost focuses on what might be called the macro-structure of the walk, its broad lineaments of excursion and return, Stevens is more interested in portraying its microstructure, its finer blendings of perception and reflection. The very rhythm of meditation as Stevens describes it resembles the rhythm of a walk, in which one step follows another without any cumulative or teleological progress being made. Indeed one might find in the phrase "and yet, and yet, and yet" a model of the poem's structure that makes the analogy with walking quite apparent. If we take each "and yet" to stand for a canto of the poem, we can see its basic rhythm as a sequence of repeated iambs: 1   2, 1   2, 1   2. What is important to note about this pattern is that it contains two distinct kinds of movement. There is first the movement from "and" to "yet," a relatively smooth syntactical transition; but there is also the movement from "yet" to "and," whose more disjunctive nature is marked by the comma that stands between the two words. In terms of the poem, this means that there is both a movement *within* individual cantos, a kind of gliding motion of gradual qualification or revision, generally taking the form of incrementally modified appositional phrases; and a much more disjunctive movement *between* cantos, a sudden leap from one thought or image to another, often with no evident transition whatsoever.[11] These two kinds of movement, gliding and leaping, are equally central to the poem's larger itinerary, and together may be said to constitute its distinctive meditative gait.

The remainder of the opening canto goes on to elaborate the two basic positions between which the poem will oscillate. These are imaged by Stevens as two giants locked in mortal combat; and the entire poem might be seen as their struggle, except that this hardly describes the measured, stately, calm style of the work even at its most dialectically intense. We could gloss these giants in Freudian terms by calling them the reality principle and the pleasure principle, or the impulse to see reality in its barest, most impoverished state, and the impulse to reshape reality imaginatively so as to make it responsive to one's desires (although certainly Freud's valorization of these terms differs sharply from Stevens's).[12] The first giant, we are told, is a question, and indeed Freud describes the reality principle as a kind of compulsive questioning of appearances, or "reality-testing." But typically for Stevens, what begins as interrogation shades appositionally into assertion. "Of what is this house composed if not of the sun" sounds like a rhetorical question, but even if it is we still must determine what it means for the house to be composed of the sun. In Yeatsian symbology the sun is cognate with the reality principle, but for Stevens it is a much more dialectical image, often pointing us to the area in which the real and the imaginary meet and overlap (as in the beautiful stanza from *Notes Toward a Supreme Fiction* beginning "My house has changed a little in the sun" [*Palm*, p. 212]).

In any case, the canto's grammar shifts between the second and third tercets and the question begins to answer itself, while at the same time there is a shift from the singular demonstrative article "this" to the plural "these." The shift in articles points to a crucial alteration in the status of the "house" that is the ostensible object of Stevens's inquiry. In the singular "this house" is clearly a metaphor, perhaps for the physical world as a whole, perhaps for the closed space defined by the limits of a single mind's perceptual capacities. But in revising "this house" to "these houses," Stevens decisively literalizes the image. Suddenly we are *in* New Haven, among the difficult objects and dilapidate appearances that surround the walker. The demonstrative pronoun becomes a mark of presence, a gesture that forestalls description by pointing directly to the thing itself.[13] Unlike Frost, who describes the woodpile meticulously and in so doing turns it into a kind of emblem, Stevens wishes to preserve the brute factuality of New Haven, since it is this very quality of givenness that his poem seeks to understand. He therefore treats New Haven and his walk in it as a kind of assumed body of data to be referred to deictically as needed. The lack of any descriptive, pictorial view of the scene reinforces its experiential status; it is the unrepresented raw material out of which the poet's meditation arises. In effect Stevens reverses the emphasis of his earlier poem "Description without Place," giving us instead a powerful sense of place without description.

The opaque literality of these objects is made plain when we are told that they are "Words, lines, not meanings, not communications, // Dark things without a double after all." In semiotic terms they are signifiers without signifieds, or, to gloss the enigmatic eighth line, appearances in which nothing appears. This vision of reality as surface without depth is too barren for a sensibility like Stevens's to tolerate for long, and the rest of the poem devotes itself to modifying it, bringing it into a more humanly acceptable form. Indeed the first qualifying gesture occurs in the next line, beginning not with "and yet" but "Unless." Here we are introduced to the second giant, the arch-nemesis of the first, who succumbs to his rival in the hypothetical scenario that follows. I have called this second giant the pleasure principle, and Stevens gives a remarkably clear definition of that Freudian concept in the phrase "a recent imagining of reality." The imagining must be recent because it must respond to present desires, and it must be an imagining *of* reality because it must substitute *for* reality in its dilapidated state, just as "a new resemblance of the sun" (always Stevens's favorite object for reimagining) must replace the sun itself.

The last five lines of the canto, as Harold Bloom points out, quite openly evoke the manner and aims of Walt Whitman, whom Bloom has taught us to see as Stevens's single most important precursor.[14] Yet the floodlike rhetoric of "a larger poem for a larger audience" sits uncomfortably with Stevens, who is well aware of the elite status of his own audience; and so I think we must view this projected victory of the second giant over the first as a false prospectus of the poem's plot. In fact the poem never does take on the totalized, rounded form of a sphere, much as Stevens might have liked it to; its form is far more tentative and open-ended. To put it another way, the second, Whitmanian giant does not kill the first; instead the two engage in an intricate and surprisingly affectionate dance in which each takes the lead by turns.

In canto II the second giant is given the distinct advantage:

> Suppose these houses are composed of ourselves,
> So that they become an impalpable town, full of
> Impalpable bells, transparencies of sound,
>
> Sounding in transparent dwellings of the self,
> Impalpable habitations that seem to move
> In the movement of the colors of the mind[.]

I would argue that this canto represents a deliberate overreaction on Stevens's part to the threatening dominance of the reality principle in the first canto. His awareness of the essential grossness of this solipsistic vision is signalled by the word "Suppose"; the canto is explicitly presented as mere hypothesis, unfounded on intuition or insight. Having swung so far towards the dilapidation of reality in the first canto, he now keeps his balance by swinging correctively towards the opposite extreme of Emersonian idealism, in which external reality becomes a mere projection of the self, thereby adopting the position of his own early walker Hoon, who chants "I was the world in which I walked, and what I saw / Or heard or felt came not but from myself" ("Tea at the Palaz of Hoon,"*Palm*, p. 55).

This oscillating movement is gradually refined as the poem proceeds, until it is no longer a violent teetering between equally stark extremes, but a rapid and subtle motion among finely drawn nuances—in the words of the poem, an "immobile flickering." For now, however, Stevens must temporarily commit himself to an overly broad delineation of his themes, establishing as a polarity what will eventually become a continuous spectrum. In the second canto the brute factuality of New Haven is left behind entirely; we are poised in a sense "Without regard to time or where we are," wholly divorced from occasion. Even here, however, a gliding movement away from the canto's initial position occurs; where Stevens begins by suggesting that the houses are composed of ourselves, and move in the colors of the mind, by the fifth tercet the sun has been readmitted as a possible constituent: "in colors *whether* of the sun / *Or* mind" (italics mine).

This movement is continued in the next canto, which acts to further qualify the preceding canto's solipsistic confusion of mind and reality. Where canto II had found in the mind's projection on the scene evidence of "the enduring, visionary love," canto III substitutes for this love the more rigorous concept of desire; and in so doing it acknowledges the critical function of reality in providing the raw material that prompts desire:

> The point of vision and desire are the same.
> It is to the hero of midnight that we pray
> On a hill of stones to make beau mont thereof.
>
> If it is misery that infuriates our love,
> If the black of night stands glistening on beau mont,
> Then, ancientest saint ablaze with ancientest truth,
>
> Say next to holiness is the will thereto,
> And next to love is the desire for love,
> The desire for its celestial ease in the heart,
>
> Which nothing can frustrate, that most secure,
> Unlike love in possession of that which was
> To be possessed and is. But this cannot
>
> Possess. It is desire, set deep in the eye,
> Behind all actual seeing, in the actual scene,
> In the street, in a room, on a carpet or a wall,
>
> Always in emptiness that would be filled,
> In denial that cannot contain its blood,
> A porcelain, as yet in the bats thereof.

Where the previous canto seemed to portray a mode of consciousness in which the pleasure principle was constantly fulfilled, this canto offers a more reflective awareness of the dependence of pleasure on desire, which in turn depends on lack. "The point of vision and desire are the same": the visionary impulse that transformed the city in canto II is the same as desire because the vision must be desired in order to be seen. This desire for transformation necessarily begins with the real, the "hill of stones" that we pray will be translated into "beau mont."

The recognition that reality in its very misery provides the starting point for vision permits Stevens to revalue the terms of his argument; in effect, the first giant is seen to be necessary to the second giant's very existence. Indeed, in lines 8 to 12 Stevens accomplishes a remarkable inversion of the traditional hierarchy that places love over desire. At first we are told that the desire for love is "next to" love, presumably just below it in worth; but by way of the pronoun "Which" in line 10, whose antecedent could be either love or desire, he carries us smoothly to a sense of desire's superiority. It is desire, we learn, that nothing can frustrate, that is most secure, precisely because it "cannot / Possess." Clearly Stevens has a special sense of "desire" in mind, since normally it and not love is defined in terms of possession. Here desire appears to denote a kind of perception—it is "set deep in the eye"— yet at the same time it is not simply "the eye's plain version," because it is stationed "*Behind* all actual seeing" (italics mine). It is a consciousness not of what the scene is but of what it is not, of its essential emptiness. Stevens values such a consciousness because it allows us a sharper sense of the mind's powers; visionary love, as in canto II, moves too quickly toward fulfillment, toward the possession of what it projects, and so loses all sense of the boundaries between itself and reality. But desire avoids such confusion; it perceives the emptiness for what it is, but also sees its possible redemption: "A porcelain, as yet in the bats thereof." Desire stays with the bats, the unfinished clay or raw material, without shaping it into a porcelain, because it knows it can achieve a greater pleasure by maintaining the distinction between the two. As in Freud, the pleasure principle is brought into conformity with the reality principle so as to purchase a surer, more lasting satisfaction.

The next three cantos continue to explore the mutually sustaining relations of reality and desire, "plain things" and "illusion," "common earth" and "moonlit majesty," at moments seeming to favor one pole over the other, but always moving toward a vision of their ultimate interdependency. This movement culminates in the famous canto VI, which opens "Reality is the beginning not the end, / Naked Alpha, not the hierophant Omega," elaborating the relation as that of an infant and an ornate but "twisted" lord. Much has been written about this canto, and so I will pass over it, in part because I have little to add to the existing commentary, but also because I find the poem to be at its weakest when it analyzes its central antithesis schematically rather than exploring it dialectically. Viewed as a spatial opposition, the reality and pleasure principles become abstractions; it is only when Stevens engages himself emotionally with one or the other by turns that they come to life. The poem's strength lies in its rendering of ambivalence from within, and this strength is dissipated when Stevens attempts to stand back and view both sides at once.

The first six cantos of the poem thus establish its central dialectic, while beginning to suggest the ways in which the two terms interpenetrate and modify one another. Thus far the poem's empirical base has remained fairly remote, invoked largely through phrases that combine substantive vagueness with deictic precision: "these houses, these dilapidate appearances." In the next seven cantos, however, the poem's occasion clearly emerges as the ground of its meditations. It is here that the walk itself comes into focus, lending experiential immediacy to the poet's ruminations. Reality ceases to be a theoretical abstraction, and instead takes on the concrete identity of a particular city on a particular evening, as viewed by a man walking through its streets and musing on what he sees.

It should be noted that a fairly accurate sense of the city's topography emerges in these cantos. Indeed, I think we can locate Stevens quite precisely in relation to the city's central landmarks. The "hotel" referred to in canto IX is surely the Taft, at one time New Haven's most prestigious. This would place Stevens squarely at the junction between the Yale campus and the church-strewn New Haven green, a surmise confirmed by the opening of canto VII: "In the presence of such chapels and such schools." One might say that the triangular relation between hotel, church, and academy literalizes the discursive "space" of the poem itself, which situates itself at the intersection of the commonplace, the religious, and the theoretical. This kind of speculation is not wholly trivial; in a poem that explicitly bases itself within a particular landscape, it is obviously important that we know the makeup of that landscape. It is significant, for example, that Stevens, or the observer within the poem, stands at a point from which he can see both ornate Gothic structures and modern office buildings and storefronts, since this contrast can be said to embody the relation between "naked Alpha" and "hierophant Omega," a relation central to the poem as a whole.

Indeed just this architectural contrast is the subject of canto VII:

> In the presence of such chapels and such schools,
> The impoverished architects appear to be
> Much richer, more fecund, sportive and alive.

The objects tingle and the spectator moves
With the objects. But the spectator also moves
With lesser things, with things exteriorized

Out of rigid realists. It is as if
Men turning into things, as comedy,
Stood, dressed in antic symbols, to display

The truth about themselves, having lost, as things,
That power to conceal they had as men,
Not merely as to depth but as to height

As well, not merely as to the commonplace
But, also, as to their miraculous,
Conceptions of new mornings of new worlds,

The tips of cock-cry pinked out pastily,
As that which was incredible becomes,
In misted contours, credible day again.

As Helen Vendler has pointed out, this canto is founded on the peculiar relationship between architects and the works they create.[15] Buildings become part of the world as other works of art do not; hence they supply a useful measure of the distance between the self and reality, partaking as they do of both. Gothic buildings, like those of the Yale campus (which are in fact conscious parodies of Oxbridge Gothicism, a fact that may inform Stevens's sense of their essentially comic character), seem to possess an inherent fecundity, a decorative exuberance or sportiveness, that stands in sharp contrast to their "impoverished" creators. Yet this landscape also contains "lesser things . . . things exteriorized / Out of rigid realists." Presumably these rigid realists are modern architects responsible for plain, functional buildings, "lesser" not necessarily in size but in imaginative energy. Having established a distinction between realistic and fecund architecture, however, Stevens proceeds to blur it in the lines that follow. Both kinds of building can be seen as "men turning into things," since both "display / The truth about" the men who made them, their secret dispositions toward either plainness or sportiveness. Yet the phrase "dressed in antic symbols" would seem to refer only to the Gothic buildings, since the plain buildings, like naked Alpha, are not dressed at all. Characteristically, Stevens first introduces an avatar of the reality / imagination polarity, then subtly tips the balance toward the imaginative without appearing to make an explicit *choice* between them.

This covert favoring of the Gothic mode becomes more evident in the last two tercets. The syntax of these lines is obscure, but the gesture they make is apparent: "not merely as to the commonplace, / But, also, as to their miraculous." Again we are being guided to the visionary aspect of New Haven's architecture; indeed the next line openly echoes Revelation: "Conceptions of new mornings of new worlds." A marvelous impressionist rendering of the appearance and effect of Gothic spires follows: "The tips of cock-cry pinked out pastily." Yet having seemed to reject the "lesser" forms of plain buildings in favor of the miraculous, Stevens beautifully returns us to reality in the last lines: "As that which was incredible becomes, / In misted contours, credible day again." The trope of morning, at first apocalyptic, now signals the return of "credible day," in which the most extravagant objects take on a bluntness and solidity that proclaims their physical being. Reality finally subsumes even the Gothic.

Canto VII, then, traces an extremely mobile series of reactions to New Haven's architecture, in which Stevens begins by noting the fecundity of the Gothic, turns to the products of "rigid realists," is pulled back in the direction of the Gothic, and finally ends with a larger, less rigid, more comprehensive view of reality. Movement itself is thematized in this canto, in the second tercet: "The objects tingle and the spectator moves / With the objects." These lines may simply evoke the mobile perspective of a walker strolling among the city's buildings, or they may point to the more inward kind of movement that the canto itself maps out. In any case, the emphasis on moving *with* the objects is crucial to the poem's ultimate redefinition of reality as dynamic rather than static; this conception of a movement that includes both subject and object eventually provides Stevens with the means to escape the poem's pervasive dualism, and to reach a point of rest beyond oscillation.

Canto VIII does not transcend dualism, but it substitutes for Cartesian dualism the dualism of the sexes. This is perhaps the most passionate canto of the poem, touching a thematic strain of openly sexual desire for a kind of female world-spirit that is perhaps more familiar from poems by Williams like "A Marriage Ritual" and parts of *Paterson*, although it is by no means absent from the rest of Stevens's oeuvre.[16] The deeply personal tone of this declaration of love for the real is enhanced by Stevens's turn to the first person plural, which dominates the next three cantos as well. "We" is as close as Stevens gets to "I" in this poem, or indeed in most of his poetry (the major exception being the great climactic cantos of *Notes*). But while "we" certainly remains an evasion of "I," and in some respects is farther from the solitary ego than the representations of selfhood Stevens offers under the guise of "he" or "one," it shares with "I" the crucial element of identification between speaking voice and grammatical subject. This use of the first person makes possible not only a heightened lyricism but a stronger sense of the experiential; hence it is not surprising that the turn to "we" coincides with a more direct treatment of the poem's occasion.

The central trope of the canto is the subtle and evocative one of breath as conversation:

> We fling ourselves, constantly longing, on this form.
> We descend to the street and inhale a breath of air
> To our sepulchral hollows. Love of the real
>
> Is soft in three-four cornered fragrances
> From five-six cornered leaves, and green, the signal
> To the lover, and blue, as of a secret place
>
> In the anonymous color of the universe.
> Our breath is like a desperate element
> That we must calm, the origin of a mother tongue
>
> With which to speak to her, the capable
> In the midst of foreignness, the syllable
> Of recognition, avowal, impassioned cry,
>
> The cry that contains its converse in itself,
> In which looks and feelings mingle and are part
> As a quick answer modifies a question,
>
> Not wholly spoken in a conversation between
> Two bodies disembodied in their talk,
> Too fragile, too immediate for any speech.

In this canto, desire is no longer the rather abstract conception of canto III; it has become wholly bodily, despite the fact that its object remains "disembodied." But in the beautiful figuration of breathing as a mode of both communication and intercourse, Stevens succeeds in evoking a kind of physical consummation of this desire. Significantly the tryst takes place only after we have descended to the street; as is the case throughout the poem, we must stand outside human enclosures to confront the world. It is there that the "love of the real" is excited, amid fragrances and leaves, green growths and blue air.[17]

Although reality is explicitly given the female role in this canto, we should note that it is the speaker whose "sepulchral hollows" are filled by the "health of air" that is her most intimate gift, perhaps compensating for his overly aggressive stance in the first line. The desperate element of breath becomes a language, a primal word expressing recognition, avowal, and passion all at once, as in a single cry. The word "cry," which has already appeared in canto IV, is a key term here, and its referent will be magnified in canto XII from breath to poem, suggesting that the poem itself is born of a similar response to the real. Even as breath, this cry starts to take on a dialogical complexity, since it "contains its converse in itself," punningly preparing for the word "conversation" in the last tercet. The very immediacy of the real precludes any language beyond that of breath; at the same time the sense of reality as a female presence is so fragile, so precarious, that to speak would destroy it. In transfiguring the automatic activity of breathing, the canto offers a moving vision of the tenuous, intangible satisfactions the lover of the real may receive, while convincing us that they *are* satisfactions, however disembodied.

Canto IX is a less sensual testament to the attractions of the real:

> We keep coming back and coming back
> To the real: to the hotel instead of the hymns
> That fall upon it out of the wind. We seek
>
> The poem of pure reality, untouched
> By trope or deviation, straight to the word,
> Straight to the transfixing object, to the object
>
> At the exactest point at which it is itself,
> Transfixing by being purely what it is,
> A view of New Haven, say, through the certain eye,
>
> The eye made clear of uncertainty, with the sight
> Of simple seeing, without reflection. We seek
> Nothing beyond reality. Within it,
>
> Everything, the spirit's alchemicana
> Included, the spirit that goes roundabout
> And through included, not merely the visible,
>
> The solid, but the movable, the moment,
> The coming on of feasts and the habits of saints,
> The pattern of the heavens and high, night air.

This canto offers perhaps the starkest instance of the poem's overarching strategy: to overcome dualism by redefining reality so that it includes the incessant motion of both world and mind. Thus the passage proceeds from formulations based on exclusion—"the hotel *instead of* the hymns," "*untouched* by trope or deviation," "*without* reflection"(italics mine)—to the inclusive formulations of the last two tercets. At first reality seems to refuse both the transcendent and the figurative; as in canto I, the object is wholly literal, "untouched by trope." Yet even in this bare, literal form, reality is still a "poem," exerting a

mysterious aesthetic allure: "Transfixing by being purely what it is."
The impulse to find a redeeming poetic dimension in even the plainest of appearances is an important strain in the poem, but one that invariably yields to a more aggressive version of the pleasure principle
that compulsively tropes reality into more fluid and transcendent
forms. To see New Haven through an eye made clear of uncertainty
and reflection is to give up too much of the self, so that Stevens's repeated insistence that "We seek / Nothing beyond reality" comes to
sound like a weak protestation, at least until "the spirit's alchemicana"
has been readmitted. More significant than the inclusion of the self in
reality, I think, is the renewed emphasis on movement: it is "the spirit
that goes roundabout / And through" that is included; and similarly
"the visible, / The solid" gives way to "the movable, the moment." Even
the religious imagery excluded in the first tercet is allowed to return in
an incipient mode: "The coming on of feasts and the habits of saints, /
The pattern of the heavens and the high night air." We seem to be
above the hotel again, with the hymns that fall upon it out of the wind,
although now these have become part of the spirit's alchemicana, aspects of experience rather than of a transcendent order.

   As though aware that he has allowed himself to mount too far above
the hotel of reality, Stevens begins the next canto with an explicit repri-
mand:

> It is fatal in the moon and empty there.
> But, here, allons. The enigmatical
> Beauty of each beautiful enigma
>
> Becomes amassed in a total double-thing.
> We do not know what is real and what is not.
> We say of the moon, it is haunted by the man
>
> Of bronze whose mind was made up and who, therefore, died.
> We are not men of bronze and we are not dead.
> His spirit is imprisoned in constant change.
>
> But ours is not imprisoned. It resides
> In a permanence composed of impermanence,
> In a faithfulness as against the lunar light,
>
> So that morning and evening are like promises kept,
> So that the approaching sun and its arrival,
> Its evening feast and the following festival,
>
> This faithfulness of reality, this mode,
> This tendance and venerable holding-in
> Make gay the hallucinations in surfaces.

The celestial sublime which closed the previous canto is both fatal and empty: fatal in its fixed pattern of cyclical change, empty in its distance from phenomenal reality. With the next line Stevens decisively returns us to New Haven, in a phrase that cannot help but recall Walt Whitman at his most ebullient: "But, here, allons." "Allons" is, of course, the near-refrain of "Song of the Open Road," a poem that takes the walk as an occasion for the expansive gestures of inclusion and transcendence that Whitman performs throughout *Leaves of Grass.* By invoking it here Stevens may be attempting to impart a similar expansiveness to his own walk, which remains, however, far more rooted in time and place than Whitman's; Whitman, after all, does not locate himself geographically as Stevens does.

Certainly the particulars of the scene have taken on a new depth and mystery, recalling Whitman's declaration "I believe that much unseen is also here."[18] "The enigmatical / Beauty of each beautiful enigma" is a surprising chiasmus that conveys the reciprocal relation of surface and depth in giving the object-world its mysterious allure. In canto I the objects of the city were "dark things without a double after all," but now they have become "amassed in a total double-thing" in which "we do not know what is real and what is not." The anxious desire to distinguish between real and unreal that dominated the previous canto is gone, however, and as a result a new and more persuasive sense of the opulence of appearances emerges. This opulence is set against the barrenness of the moon, and a subtle distinction is drawn between its imprisonment "in constant change" and the freedom of our spirit, which inhabits "a permanence composed of impermanence": that is, between the empty repetitions of lunar change and the underlying permanence of a world in which nothing is permanent, and which therefore allows for novelty and creation. The moon's "man of bronze" is incapable of true change, and hence he is dead; bronze for Stevens generally connotes a state of cold fixity, as when at the close of "The Sense of the Sleight-of-Hand Man" he speaks of the life that "is fluent in the wintriest bronze" (*Palm*, p. 168).

The canto ends with the difficult but moving concept of "This faithfulness of reality," a faithfulness that seems to combine repetition and reticence, while transcending the moon's deterministic cycles. To say that "morning and evening are like promises kept" suggests an element of uncertainty that redeems them from mere repetition. The sun's "evening feast and the following festival" take us back to the "coming on of feasts" at the end of canto IX, but now the feasts inhere in the diurnal cycle itself. The last two lines return to the motif of the object world's "enigmatical beauty," which now seems to depend on its "venerable holding-in" of its own being or essence. We may be reminded of the great closing passage of "Crossing Brooklyn Ferry," when Whitman addresses the "dumb beautiful ministers" of the object-world and declares that "Not you any more shall be able to foil us, or withhold yourselves from us."[19] Where Whitman envisages an apocalyptic transformation in which essences and appearances henceforth coincide, Stevens praises the world's opacity as a source of aesthetic pleasure. It is just this reticence, faithful because both venerable and familiar, that "Make[s] gay the hallucinations in surfaces." The very obscurity of the depths permits the surfaces to receive our own playful projections; hallucination, the inability to distinguish real from unreal, has become a source of gaiety rather than anxiety.

Canto XI offers a more openly visionary account of the walk:

> In the metaphysical streets of the physical town
> We remember the lion of Juda and we save
> The phrase . . . Say of each lion of the spirit
>
> It is a cat of a sleek transparency
> That shines with a nocturnal shine alone.
> The great cat must stand potent in the sun.
>
> The phrase grows weak. The fact takes up the strength
> Of the phrase. It contrives the self-same evocations
> And Juda becomes New Haven or else must.

The doubleness that had become a compound whose elements could not be distinguished in canto X is now separated out into "the metaphysical streets" and "the physical town," suggesting that Stevens is no longer fully content with beautiful enigmas, but is again restlessly searching for the line that divides real and unreal. Clearly it is for use in a poem—presumably *this* poem—that Stevens saves the phrase "the lion of Juda"; but in the context of an ordinary evening in New Haven he quickly becomes aware that this lion is too much a "lion of the spirit," suited to a more visionary poem than the one his walk occasions. (Stevens may again be recalling Whitman here, who speaks in "Song of Myself" of "Walking the old hills of Judaea with the beautiful gentle God by my side.")[20] The fact that it "shines with a nocturnal shine alone" allies it with the rejected moon of canto X; and after that canto's celebration of the solar cycle we are not surprised to hear that "the great cat must stand potent in the sun." It is important to recognize that the lion is not being banished, only translated into a form more compatible with the light of day. As phrase alone the lion must inevitably grow weak; only when it resides in the immediacy of fact can it survive. But how can so visionary a beast walk the streets of so ordinary a city? Clearly Stevens is demanding a more internalized form of sublimity, one that can preserve the lion's majesty while staying close to the plain reality of New Haven. The lion thus represents the persistence of the sublime even in the tawdriest of settings.

The second half of the canto essentially repeats the scenario of the first half in the third person singular, while attempting to give a clearer sense of what imaginative forms may suffice as replacements for such overt fictions as the lion of Juda:

> In the metaphysical streets, the profoundest forms
> Go with the walker subtly walking there.
> These he destroys with wafts of wakening,
>
> Free from their majesty and yet in need
> Of majesty, of an invincible clou,
> A minimum of making in the mind,
>
> A verity of the most veracious men,
> The propounding of four seasons and twelve months,
> The brilliancy at the central of the earth.

Presumably the lion of Juda was an instance of the "profoundest forms" that accompany the walker; now, however, those forms are destroyed, in a more radical gesture than the lion's transplantation from Juda to New Haven. What destroys the forms are the wafts of wakening that return the walker to his actual setting, and this wakening is seen both as freedom and as poverty or neediness. In the absence of visionary forms, the walker in reality must find a more minimal kind of majesty, a fiction the size of a nail yet as securely held in place. Such a fiction is represented by the calendar itself, a human construct that begins with the flux of reality, while bringing to it the stately divisions of a pageant. More moving though less precise, it is represented by the idea of a central "brilliancy," a primal beauty that stands at the origin of earth's particular beauties. These fictions are examples of the minimal makings permitted within the real, adding majesty to it without leaving it behind for such wholly visionary realms as Juda or the moon.

Having introduced the notion of a making that originates in reality, Stevens is at last ready for the grand theoretical pronouncement of canto XII, which definitively anchors the poem in its occasional context:

> The poem is the cry of its occasion,
> Part of the res itself and not about it.
> The poet speaks the poem as it is,
>
> Not as it was: part of the reverberation
> Of a windy night as it is, when the marble statues
> Are like newspapers blown by the wind. He speaks

By sight and insight as they are. There is no
Tomorrow for him. The wind will have passed by,
The statues will have gone back to be things about.

The mobile and the immobile flickering
In the area between is and was are leaves,
Leaves burnished in autumnal burnished trees

And leaves in whirlings in the gutters, whirlings
Around and away, resembling the presence of thought,
Resembling the presences of thoughts, as if,

In the end, in the whole psychology, the self,
The town, the weather, in a casual litter,
Together, said words of the world are the life of the world.

As polemic this directs itself against both mimetic and visionary theories of poetry: the poem is not about its occasion, but neither can it escape that occasion. The difficult relation between poem and occasion is expressed by the preposition "of," with its perennial ambiguities. Does the occasion *produce* the cry? Or is the occasion in some sense "cried" by the poem? More centrally, the cry is "of" its occasion in the sense that we say someone is of their time and place; it is *part* of its occasion, standing for it not as metaphor but as synecdoche. In this sense the poem must be seen as an act or event, as much a part of its place and moment as any other event; indeed the image of the blown newspapers suggests that it participates in that banal class of ephemera we call "current events." We should note the peculiarity of the term "res" here, which has a much richer constellation of meanings than the more usual "thing itself." In part Stevens undoubtedly chooses the Latin term because it is the etymological root of the poem's central thematic word, "reality." (The use of Latin also recalls the poem's initial evocation of "the vulgate of experience"; once again Stevens seems to imply that our plain perceptions of reality are already a translation of it into a more abstract language.) But "res" also refers to a wide range of human commodities, including both cities and subject matter.[21] As part of the res itself, then, the poem becomes part of the city in which it originates, part of New Haven on a windy night.

But this insistence on the continuity between poem and occasion is severely qualified as the canto proceeds. Only as utterance or "cry" can the poem be said to take part in its occasion; as text or, in the canto's image, statue, the poem inevitably becomes a "thing about." "The poet *speaks* the poem as it is" (italics mine): here "speaks" is a trope for "composes," not a reference to Stevens's recitation of the poem at the Connecticut Academy (which was reportedly inaudible). In the pure present of composition, objects as fixed and timeless as marble statues become caught up in the flow of time; in linguistic terms, text gives way to utterance, a mode of expression tied ineluctably to the moment of its production. For the poet wholly engaged in his poem there is no tomorrow, no future point from which the poem can be viewed as a completed whole. Yet that future *will* come, and when it does, when the wind of utterance has passed by, the poem will have hardened into a marmoreal text, a referential icon that is no longer a part of its occasion, only about it. This point would seem to undermine the canto's initial characterization of the poem as a cry inseparable from its occasion; but the contradiction is a typical one for American poets, who tend to conceive of poems as both texts and utterances, objects and actions. In the end, Stevens recognizes, the poem must be both of *and* about, both cry and representation.

The last half of the canto expresses this doubleness by uniting images of voice and text in the extraordinary figure of leaves being whirled away by the wind. I must demur from Bloom's Shelleyan reading of these lines as a despairing call for help in the face of destruction.[22] Although Shelley is certainly in the background, the canto's emphasis is on life rather than death, as the last line makes clear. The canto does not express despair so much as an existential commitment to an absolute present that is always disappearing into the past. The "area between is and was" is the transitional zone in which presence flickers into absence, cry into text, yet it is not an avatar of death; rather, it is the very motion of life, of "always cresting into one's present," to quote the beautiful phrase of Stevens's admirer John Ashbery.[23] The leaves, like the newspapers and like Shelley's "dead thoughts," are texts, words that once sprang directly from the poet's consciousness but now lie detached, blown about in a "casual litter" that unites self, town, and weather. Yet this litter of words is "the life of the world" because in whirling around and away it makes room for new words, new thoughts, new cries. Ultimately, then, this image of transience does not threaten the self, which remains as a fixed point of origin, always able to add new words to the accumulated litter.

If canto XII provides the theoretical basis for a poetics of the occasional, canto XIII represents the occasion more directly, giving us the clearest image in the poem of the walk as meditation:

> The ephebe is solitary in his walk.
> He skips the journalism of subjects, seeks out
> The perquisites of sanctity, enjoys
>
> A strong mind in a weak neighborhood and is
> A serious man without the serious,
> Inactive in his singular respect.

He is neither priest nor proctor at low eve,
Under the birds, among the perilous owls,
In the big X of the returning primitive.

It is a fresh spiritual that he defines,
A coldness in a long, too-constant warmth,
A thing on the side of a house, not deep in a cloud,

A difficulty that we predicate:
The difficulty of the visible
To the nations of the clear invisible,

The actual landscape with its actual horns
Of baker and butcher blowing, as if to hear,
Hear hard, gets at an essential integrity.

The shift from first person plural to third person singular, "we" to "he," partly begun in the previous two cantos, is now fully accomplished. The "we" of cantos VIII–X has become the solitary "ephebe," a figure familiar from *Notes*, where he represented the student of poetry being instructed by Stevens. Now, however, it seems clear that Stevens himself is the ephebe, reflecting the less authoritative tone of "An Ordinary Evening." By moving from first to third person Stevens distances himself from the rendered consciousness of the poem, but he also makes a contraction from plural to singular, a move necessary to this canto's meditation on the solitary mind confronting the actual landscape.

The ephebe's walk is not directed toward the observation of particulars; we are told that "He skips the journalism of subjects," which I have already suggested means he bypasses a Frostian focus on discrete objects, and turns directly to "The perquisites of sanctity." Yet sanctity is not readily at hand in these surroundings; the gap between the ephebe's consciousness and his setting is expressed by the phrase "a strong mind in a weak neighborhood." This line can be taken as a revision of the concluding formulation from "The Auroras of Autumn," "an unhappy people in a happy world," where in the terms of the poem "unhappy" means "afraid," and "happy" means "innocent." Now the terms of this contrast between mind and world have been decisively altered, reflecting the more relaxed and confident mood of "An Ordinary Evening." This strong mind finds no match in its neighborhood, but that does not prevent the poet from taking a narcissistic pleasure in his own strength. The notion of strength is next refined into that of "seriousness": he is "A serious man without the serious." The term "serious" is a complex one in the poem, ultimately being identified with the "commonplace" (canto XVII); here, however, the ephebe's seriousness is defined in opposition to the commonplace world through which he moves.

In the next tercet Stevens rejects both the religious and the academic as modes of sanctity: "He is neither priest nor proctor at low eve." Both priest and proctor seek their spiritual truths "deep in a cloud," in the transcendences of God and metaphysics respectively. But the ephebe opts for a colder, more immanent spirituality based on the difficulty of appearances, "a thing on the side of a house." The predicated "difficulty of the visible" recalls the "difficult objects" of canto I, although now this difficulty is set against the "nations of the clear invisible," presumably nations populated entirely by priests and proctors. The difficulty of visible objects seems to lie in their blankness, their unwillingness to declare themselves; but in the last tercet a kind of aggressive listening is proposed that "gets at an essential integrity." The shift from sight to hearing is always significant in Stevens; here it signals a more strenuous mode of perception capable of overcoming the opacity of the landscape and arriving at its deep nature. "Integrity" here may mean "honesty" as well as "unity"; finally what matters most about the world, and what hearing seems better equipped than seeing to discern, is its simple self-identity, which precludes both falseness and fragmentation. This difficult candor is what endears the world to the walker, making it a fit object not just for perception but for love.

The germ of this canto, and indeed of "An Ordinary Evening" as a whole, may lie in the second section of Stevens's early poem "A Thought Revolved":

> The poet striding among the cigar stores,
> Ryan's lunch, hatters, insurance and medicines,
> Denies that abstraction is a vice except
> To the fatuous. These are his infernal walls,
> A space of stone, of inexplicable base
> And peaks outsoaring possible adjectives.
> One man, the idea of man, that is the space,
> The true abstract in which he promenades.
>
> (*Palm*, p. 131)

This passage contrasts with "An Ordinary Evening" in a number of ways, perhaps most obviously in its more particularized account of the scene in which the poet walks. Stevens's cataloging of shops and offices has the effect of emphasizing the triviality of the neighborhood, enforcing a more absolute gap between the poet in his abstraction and the "inexplicable base" of given reality. At this point in his career Stevens is moving toward the myth of Major Man as a kind of heroic

abstraction wholly divorced from time and place, and so he is less interested in the possible sublimity of the phenomenal world. By the time
of "An Ordinary Evening," however, a subtle change has taken place
in Stevens's representation of the poet walking in reality. To begin
with, he is far less willing to name the elements of the scene even in a
random sampling, since that would comport with "the journalism of
subjects." At the same time, however, the rigid distinction between
common reality and the mind's constructions has become softer, more
fluid; Stevens is now able to identify his "fresh spiritual" with "a thing
on the side of a house." The visible and the invisible have become
interfused, and so the poet no longer walks through the actual landscape with eyes averted, intent only on the abstract space of his idea.
His energies are redirected toward the world in all its weakness and
opacity, seeking out the essential integrity that underlies its dilapidate
appearances.

"An Ordinary Evening in New Haven" thus epitomizes Stevens's late
swing toward the eye's plain version, after a lifetime of celebrating the
imagination's ornate one. His aim throughout the poem is to stay true
to the occasion, to New Haven and its empirical solidity, while finding
a place within it for the kind of imaginative activity that had previously
led him to construct supreme fictions. Cantos vii–xiii represent this
quest most directly; here the poem's occasion comes to the forefront.
From this point on, however, the poem's sense of occasional immediacy begins to diminish. Vendler notes a gradual detachment from an
initial "immersion in the scene" in "Credences of Summer," and the
same kind of movement occurs in "An Ordinary Evening," as Stevens
turns from the direct sensory data of the walk to more fictive modes reminiscent of *Notes Toward a Supreme Fiction.*[24] Fables, personae like Professor Eucalyptus, aphorisms, and tableaux all carry the poem away
from its experiential base; yet that base never entirely fades from view.
Indeed it could be said that the very title of the poem acts as a kind
of anchor, tying even the most visionary cantos to the solid ground of
occasion.

There is in fact a simple narrative explanation for the relative dimi-
nution of the occasion in the second half of the poem; despite his
diffidence about representing experience directly, Stevens plots a fairly
consistent spatial and temporal course as the poem unfolds. After the
introductory movement of the first six cantos, in which New Haven is
invoked from a distance, we are given seven cantos that are clearly set
in the midst of the city. In most of them the time appears to be early
evening ("low eve"—xiii), although there are a few references to morning and day as well. We might speculate that Stevens chooses evening
as the time of his walk because it heightens his sense of standing on a

threshold between seeing and imagining; this is the hour when the eye's plain version begins to give way to dream, hallucination, and fiction. Indeed that threshold is effectively crossed after canto XIII, as fictive modes come to dominate the remainder of the poem. Experientially, cantos XIV–XXIV seem to locate themselves *above* the street, in a room (perhaps the hotel room Stevens stayed in); this is made clear by references to the room itself in XIV and XX, the water-spout in XV, and the window in XVIII. Moreover the time appears to be later, "after dark" (XXIII), and the weather has changed from the blustery wind of XII to the "repugnant rain" of XV, perhaps suggesting why the walk had to be cut short.

All this may seem trivial, especially given Stevens's overt rejection of the "journalism of subjects," but in fact time and place always play a key role in determining the particular relationship between self and world in this poem. It is surely significant, for example, that after the poem moves indoors the nameless "ephebe" of XIII, more or less directly identified with the poet, gives way to the comic persona of Professor Eucalyptus, whose scholarly bent keeps him from engaging fully with the world. Like the Canon Aspirin in *Notes*, Professor Eucalyptus parodies Stevens's own enterprise in the poem, "not so much mocking it as repeating it in a coarser tone."[25] Both figures carry Stevens's secular quest into the realm of orthodoxy, literalizing it in a way that exposes it to skepticism. Professor Eucalyptus's search for "God in the object" is doomed not only because he substitutes an hypostasis for the more fluid spirituality Stevens seeks to define, but because "He sits in his room," thus precluding the immediacy and mobility of perspective that in this poem mark an authentic relation to the world.

Yet as the poem proceeds this interior perspective starts to take on an authority of its own, allowing a more austere vision of the real to emerge, in which the manifold particulars of day are reduced to "a bough in the electric light /And exhalations in the eaves, so little / To indicate the total leaflessness" (XVI). Now the whirling leaves that acted as a sign of life in XII have vanished (or been metamorphosed orthographically into "eaves"), and we are left with a single bare branch visible in the street light as the only exemplar of what lies outside the room. The gaiety and sensuality that characterized the phenomenal world in the walk cantos are here replaced by a barren, starkly reductive view of "the dilapidation of dilapidations," a condition of poverty that goes beyond the "dilapidate appearances" of canto I to touch a more fundamental plainness, what Stevens describes in XVII as "The dominant blank, the unapproachable." Even in this reduced, leafless state, however, New Haven remains an insistent presence in the poem, one that may yet be redeemed as a true source of poetry.

This movement of the poem culminates in cantos xx and xxi, as the possibility of a solipsistic withdrawal from the world in its poverty is once more entertained:

> The imaginative transcripts were like clouds,
> Today; and the transcripts of feeling, impossible
> To distinguish. The town was a residuum,
>
> A neuter shedding shapes in an absolute.
> Yet the transcripts of it when it was blue remain;
> And the shapes that it took in feeling, the persons that
>
> It became, the nameless, flitting characters—
> These actors still walk in a twilight muttering lines.
> It may be that they mingle, clouds and men, in the air
>
> Or street or about the corners of a man,
> Who sits thinking in the corners of a room.
> In this chamber the pure sphere escapes the impure,
>
> Because the thinker himself escapes. And yet
> To have evaded clouds and men leaves him
> A naked being with a naked will
>
> And everything to make. He may evade
> Even his own will and in his nakedness
> Inhabit the hypnosis of that sphere.

This canto explicitly locates itself late in the day, as the poet considers the "transcripts" of his experience of New Haven, comparing these to his more objective sense of the town as "a neuter shedding shapes in an absolute." By this definition reality is a blank or neutral substance endlessly sloughing off its phenomenal appearances, like the serpent in canto I of "The Auroras of Autumn." Yet this severely abstract knowledge of reality, the knowledge of the thinker in his room, cannot wholly supplant "the transcripts of it when it was blue," as made by the walker in the streets; shape, color, and feeling persist in his memory, however rigorously he may pursue the dominant blank. The last three tercets give us an almost muscular sense of the thinker's effort to abstract himself from experience, to inhabit a sphere of pure thought, entirely sealed off from the pressures of time, place, and occasion.

The burden of canto xxi is that such evasion is impossible. Stevens skillfully modulates from the end of xx to the beginning of xxi by means of the word "may," whose meaning subtly shifts in the process. The thinker in his room "*may* evade / Even his own will" (italics mine); here the "may" would seem to indicate an available option. Canto xxi opens with the terse sentence "But he may not," which has to be para-phrased "he cannot" rather than "he might not," as becomes clear in the next line when Stevens himself shifts to the former: "he cannot evade / The will of necessity." Now the very possibility of such evasion is being denied, as the poet once more emphasizes the ineluctability of the world. After describing necessity as a "Romanza out of the black shepherd's isle," Stevens returns us to the empirical scene:

> Close to the senses there lies another isle
> And there the senses give and nothing take,
>
> The opposite of Cythere, an isolation
> At the centre, the object of the will, this place,
> The things around—the alternate romanza
>
> Out of the surfaces, the windows, the walls,
> The bricks grown brittle in time's poverty,
> The clear. A celestial mode is paramount,
>
> If only in the branches sweeping in the rain:
> The two romanzas, the distant and the near,
> Are a single voice in the boo-ha of the wind.

Through the trope of the isle Stevens now manages to reconceive sense experience as enrichment rather than impoverishment, giving rather than taking; and in so doing he confers a new value on the real, which is once more invoked by deixis—"this place, / The things around." The very room, its windows, walls, and bricks, have taken on a heightened immediacy; and even the bare branches, which earlier indi-cated "the total leaflessness," now participate in a "celestial mode," a sublimity that inheres in the actual. Once more the wind serves as a unifying agent, sweeping together the "two romanzas" of transcen-dence and immanence, and giving them "a single voice." The poem seems to have temporarily reconciled the claims of inside and outside, room and world, thought and perception, although the truce is a pre-carious one.

As the poem moves toward its end, it gradually disengages itself from both walk and room, assuming a less clearly situated point of view from which to reflect on New Haven as synecdoche for reality. Canto XXVI opens with a reference to a walk, but one that appears to be set in the country rather than the city, and perhaps in a different season as well:

> How facilely the purple blotches fell
> On the walk, purple and blue, and red and gold,
> Blooming and beaming and voluming colors out.

This pastoral walk is remembered as a carnivalesque riot of color lacking form and definition, a shower of impressionist blotches. Such experience, Stevens implies, makes the world all too easy to love; deeper and more intimate is the love that recognizes the poverty of the beloved:

> But, here, the inamorata, without distance
> And thereby lost, and naked or in rags,
> Shrunk in the poverty of being close,
>
> Touches, as one hand touches another hand,
> Or as a voice that, speaking without form,
> Gritting in the ear, whispers human repose.

Walking in New Haven on a windy evening in late autumn ensures that one's love of the real is genuine, not skin-deep. Earlier in the canto the earth was "*seen* as inamorata" (italics mine); here touch and hearing establish a closer relationship to the world, one not falsified by natural beauty, but grounded in the pathos of mere presence.

After the Eucalyptian aphorisms of xxvii, the elaborated syllogism of xxviii, and the fable of the lands of lemon and elm trees in xxix, the poem's penultimate canto returns to the leafless landscape one more time, and finds in it a last vision of the "fresh spiritual" that the poem has been seeking to define:

> The last leaf that is going to fall has fallen.
> The robins are là-bas, the squirrels, in tree-caves,
> Huddle together in the knowledge of squirrels.
>
> The wind has blown the silence of summer away.
> It buzzes beyond the horizon or in the ground:
> In mud under ponds, where the sky used to be reflected.
>
> The barrenness that appears is an exposing.
> It is not part of what is absent, a halt
> For farewells, a sad hanging on for remembrances.
>
> It is a coming on and a coming forth.
> The pines that were fans and fragrances emerge,
> Staked solidly in a gusty grappling with rocks.
>
> The glass of the air becomes an element—
> It was something imagined that has been washed away.
> A clearness has returned. It stands restored.
>
> It is not an empty clearness, a bottomless sight.
> It is a visibility of thought,
> In which hundreds of eyes, in one mind, see at once.

With its short declarative sentences and its uncanny clarity, this canto approaches the manner of Stevens's final lyrics. As in those poems, the plainest, most naked version of reality is shown to be more presence than absence. The canto's central thought is expressed grammatically, through the use of gerunds, verbs acting as nouns. Even this still, clear scene is infused with a kind of movement, the movement of "exposing," of "coming on" and "coming forth," of "grappling." The essentially dynamic character of reality has been uncovered by the barrenness of winter.

But if the landscape is more visible in this newly restored clearness, so is thought itself. "A visibility of thought" is a difficult concept, but it is clearly crucial to Stevens's ultimate reconciliation of the spiritual and the visible. The startling image in the last line of "hundreds of eyes, in one mind" refers most literally to the squirrels in the trees, but it also evokes a more internalized mode of perception that can see and think at once. Each eye is a thought that mediates reality, and together they form a consciousness in which perception and reflection are no longer separate functions. Thinking becomes seeing, seeing thinking; this is the "fresh spiritual" the ephebe has sought, an ideal that Stevens continued to explore in the last poems he wrote.

The poem's final canto provides a satisfying if necessarily arbitrary closure to its "never-ending meditation":

> The less legible meanings of sounds, the little reds
> Not often realized, the lighter words
> In the heavy drum of speech, the inner men
>
> Behind the outer shields, the sheets of music
> In the strokes of thunder, dead candles at the window
> When day comes, fire-foams in the motions of the sea,
>
> Flickings from finikin to fine finikin
> And the general fidget from busts of Constantine
> To photographs of the late president, Mr. Blank,
>
> These are the edgings and inchings of final form,
> The swarming activities of the formulae
> Of statement, directly and indirectly getting at,
>
> Like an evening evoking the spectrum of violet,
> A philosopher practicing scales on his piano,
> A woman writing a note and tearing it up.
>
> It is not in the premise that reality
> Is a solid. It may be a shade that traverses
> A dust, a force that traverses a shade.

This marvelously vivid catalog gives us a last exuberant instance of Stevens's gliding technique, a kind of movement thematized in the canto as the "edgings and inchings of final form." It begins with a series of images that evoke the poem's major project of refinement, of arriving at less legible meanings, lighter words, subtler nuances within the broad play of reality and imagination. The phrase "dead candles at the window when day comes," for example, beautifully captures the persistence of nocturnal imaginings like the lion of Juda into the light of day, where they no longer seem credible. Stevens values this ability to see the remnants of the night by day because it allows for a more complex sense of the relation between opposites; ultimately he needs a vision in which opposing principles are not mutually exclusive, in which the first and second giant can peacefully coexist.

The image of "fire-foams in the motions of the sea" carries us from the theme of nuance to the theme of motion which dominates the remainder of the canto. "Flickings from finikin to fine finikin" recalls the "mobile and immobile flickering" of canto XII, but now the flickings become part of the continual process of refinement, of moving toward ever subtler versions of the truth. Such incremental movements are all finally avatars of the poem's own discursive movement, its "swarming activities of the formulae / Of statement, directly and indirectly getting at." These lines perfectly characterize the poem's tentative, provisional formulations and incessant qualifications, its rhythm of "and yet, and yet, and yet." No "final form" or summation can be possible, because the world is itself in constant motion. Discourse can only mime the becoming of reality, not fix it in a formula.

The three images of the poem's penultimate tercet offer three alternative tropes for the poem itself. "An evening evoking the spectrum of violet" refers most directly to the poem's titular occasion; as metaphor the "spectrum of violet" substitutes a continuum in which no clear boundaries can be discerned for the poem's earlier polarities—first and second giant, Alpha and Omega, real and unreal, and so forth. This metaphor implies that the poem has only explored various nuances of violet, not distilled any primary, absolute colors, because it has remained within the context of an actual evening and its misty evocations. If it has touched on the abstractions of philosophy, it has been in the manner of "A philosopher practicing scales at the piano," not attempting to make a final, definitive statement but merely exercising the faculties of thought through continual motion, continual activity. Perhaps the most satisfying image for the poem is that of "A woman writing a note and tearing it up." Not only does this capture the poem's endless qualification and retraction of its own formulations, it points to the essentially amorous nature of Stevens's relation to the world. His constant tearing up and rewriting of his notes on reality stems finally from his love of the real, and his desire to express that love without idealization or distortion.

The final tercet is a famous statement of the Whiteheadian conception of reality as process. In its appearance of logical hypothesizing, it presents a final qualification of the poem's entire argument. The "premise" is presumably the poem's opening statement, "The eye's plain version is a thing apart," of which the whole poem has been saying "and yet, and yet, and yet." This last "and yet" does not discard the premise, but merely refines it by showing what it does *not* imply. The poem has been moving steadily toward the recognition that reality is not a solid but a fluid; even here, however, Stevens does not forego the tentativeness of "It may." Unlike *Notes* and "A Primitive Like an Orb," this poem does not end with a resounding "That's it," since such a gesture would betray its whole spirit. The final propositions are offered as alternative possibilities, not definitive truths.

The poem comes to rest on the resonant yet strangely arid images of "a shade that traverses / A dust, a force that traverses a shade." These have been interpreted as roughly equivalent figures of traversal conveying an almost Einsteinian sense of reality as energy rather than matter. Yet such accounts miss both the difference between the two phrases and their crucial relation to the poem's occasion. "A shade that traverses a dust," while clearly engaging traditional tropes for spirit and matter, is in fact a purely experiential image, based on the act of looking down while walking and seeing one's shadow move along the ground. This image provides a rich symbol for the ineluctable imposition of subjectivity upon the object-world. The shade moves because the walker does, representing his consciousness moving across the field of external objects, covering a different segment of it at each moment. Thus it is the relation *between* static dust and mobile shade that constitutes reality. Yet this vision, although it includes consciousness within reality, is finally too limited for Stevens; and so the image is recast into the less phenomenal, more abstract phrase "a force that traverses a shade." All subject/object dualisms must in the end give way to a vision of force, of power—presumably the power of the mind *over* its world. Stevens's essential romanticism could be satisfied with nothing less, and although he couches this final trope of power in apparently impersonal terms, it brings the poem to a characteristically strong if muted cadence.[26]

The relation between these final two images thus encapsulates the broader movement of the poem as a whole, from the immediate occasion in all its concreteness to a more abstract vision of reality. The poem itself can be described as a "traversal," a lateral movement from point to point that never arrives at a definitive place of rest.[27] In this sense the very epistemology of the poem is informed by the act of walking; the essential aimlessness of the walk is mirrored by the poem's incremental motion as it covers the same thematic ground over and over, refining and qualifying but never exhausting. Stevens's walk lacks the firm narrative design of Frost's walks, which culminate in an explicit moment of discovery; but at the same time it can better display the ongoing nature of thought as it responds to the raw data of experience. As a walk poem, then, "An Ordinary Evening in New Haven" represents a radical alternative to Frost's parabolic modulation of the genre. For Stevens the walk provides not a narrative armature but an occasion, an experiential node out of which the poem's "never-ending meditation" flows. That occasion in turn shapes the vision of the poem, which finds motion or traversal to be the ultimate form of reality. The ephebe's walk is thus much more than a particular experience of a particular city; under the pressure of Stevens's imagination it becomes a source of authentic vision, a way of seeing the world in its essential integrity while recognizing that it, like the walker, remains caught up in motion. Poem, world, and walker all participate in the same fluid process, the same windy occasion. "An Ordinary Evening in New Haven" gives us a metaphysics of the walk, in which movement subsumes real and unreal, visible and invisible, poem and occasion. No American poem has entered more deeply into the kinetics of experience.

III

WILLIAM CARLOS WILLIAMS: THE WALK AS MUSIC

THE TWO MAJOR walk poems of William Carlos Williams, *Paterson* Book Two and "The Desert Music," represent a third distinctively American development of the genre. These poems treat the walk in a densely mimetic fashion, in contrast to the parabolic and meditative treatments of Frost and Stevens. In their effort to capture the precise transactions between self and environment, they focus with almost photographic clarity on the walker's perceptions, on the particular objects and impressions that enter his consciousness. More significantly perhaps, they register the exact movements of attention and understanding as he responds to what he sees and hears. Williams's walk poems are thus more thoroughly *transcriptive* than those of Frost and Stevens, more committed to the raw material of sense data in all its contingency and successiveness. Unlike Stevens, Williams openly courts "the journalism of subjects," since for him value lies in the particulars of experience themselves rather than the "perquisites of sanctity" they manifest. And unlike Frost, he avoids imposing a factitious narrative shape on the walk that would subordinate its fullness and variety to a sense of achieved wisdom.

As a result, however, his poems veer more dangerously close to the representational pole of journalism, a mode which we have seen can be antithetical to poetry, since the poem must distinguish itself from a mere record of facts if it is to legitimate itself as a work of art. In fact throughout his career Williams vigorously rejects purely mimetic theories of poetry, insisting that the poem is not "description nor an evocation of objects or situations . . . poetry does not tamper with the world but moves it—It affirms reality most powerfully and therefore, since reality needs no personal support but exists free from human action, as proven by science in the indestructibility of matter and of force, it creates a new object, a play, a dance which is not a mirror up to nature but—."[1] The incompleteness of this sentence is symptomatic of Williams's ongoing ambivalence with regard to representation. For all his protests that the poem exists as an autonomous object with its own form and energy, he at times gives equal emphasis to the importance of "transcription," the poet's capacity "to write down that which happens at that time— . . . To perfect the ability to record at the moment when the consciousness is enlarged by the sympathies and the unity of understanding which the imagination gives."[2] There is a real tension, then, between the mimetic or transcriptive function in Williams's poetics and the nonmimetic, dynamic quality of the poem as he describes it, a tension that finds its primary locus in Williams's concept of imagination as a "dynamizing" of experience through the power of naming.[3] Williams's most characteristic poems devote themselves to attaining a point of balance between, on the one hand, minute accuracy of observation and naming, and on the other a purely verbal energy that permits the poem to transcend its mimetic function and to stand apart as an independent structure or movement.

Clearly the walk affords Williams a special opportunity to unite the transcriptive and the dynamic. By combining bodily movement and observation of the world, it seems to offer a precise experiential correlative for the poem as Williams conceives it. Yet it is worth noting that he only turns to the walk as form and subject fairly late in his career, with one or two minor exceptions.[4] Williams's earlier "Objectivist" poems, such as the famous lyrics about the red wheel barrow, the cat climbing over the jam closet, the young sycamore, and many others, tend to take the form of perceptual snapshots, records of a single instant of attention. The dynamism in these poems comes from the movement of syntax and prosody as they scan the object in question. The poet as observer is seldom a bodily presence in the poems, since their aim is to present "the thing itself" with as little subjective interference as possible. There are, of course, many other early poems in which the observer's perspective is either implied (as in "By the road to the contagious hospital") or made an explicit element of the poem's structure (as in "The Young Housewife"); but even these poems tend to focus on the object of perception rather than the consciousness of the observer. The closest the early Williams comes to representing experience as a continuous interplay of mind and world is in some of the prose poems of *Kora in Hell,* whose "improvisational" texture permits them to weave more fluidly between internal and external phenomena.

It is primarily in his later poetry that Williams turns to a more sustained, cinematic mode of representation in which the observer's shifting perspective and consciousness are fully acknowledged and incorporated.[5] In effect the object of transcription shifts in these later poems from individual "things" to the experiential medium that contains them. Now objects are caught up in the flux of perception and movement; as a result they lose some of their hard-edged clarity and instead become participants in an ongoing dialogue between mind and world. *Paterson* Two and "The Desert Music" in particular set out to capture what M. L. Rosenthal calls "the music of awareness"; and indeed music is Williams's own favorite trope for the variable continuum of phenomenal reality.[6] By characterizing his experience of the world as a kind of music he is able to posit a deep continuity underlying the discrete sights and sounds he encounters, binding them into an aesthetic whole; and this wholeness can in turn be transferred to the poem, which by transcribing the music of time and place assumes a similar continuity. Such a musical form enables Williams to fulfill his desire, expressed early in his career, "to place a value upon experience and the objects of experience that would satisfy my sense of inclusiveness without redundancy"; and ultimately to reveal what he calls "the one-ness of experience."[7]

. . . . .

In his long poem *Paterson,* the first book of which appeared in 1946, Williams develops a flexible, carefully shaped verse form capable of registering the manifold shifts of attention and intensity within experience more clearly and graphically than had been previously possible in poetry. While much of the poem approaches its titular subject, the city of Paterson, New Jersey, from a panoptic point of view, seeing the place and its inhabitants as a mythological whole, Book Two, "Sunday in the Park," locates itself firmly within a specific landscape on a specific day. Everything that is seen and heard in the park is seen and heard by a consciousness made available to the reader through such devices as indirect discourse and lyric utterance. What separates *Paterson* Two from the normative walk poem as I have defined it is the fact that the walker whose sensibility mediates the world for us is an openly fictional creation. The poem's protagonist, Mr. Paterson, is an explicit personification of the city of Paterson, and hence he is a strangely double figure. He is both a kind of Stevensian giant, a figure like that of Major Man in Stevens's *Notes Toward a Supreme Fiction,* whose "body" is the geography of the city—

> Paterson lies in the valley under the Passaic Falls
> its spent waters forming the outline of his back. He
> lies on his right side, head near the thunder
> of the waters filling his dreams![8]

—and at the same time he is an individual *within* the landscape of the city, possessed of a surprisingly idiosyncratic life history:

> Twice a month Paterson receives
> communications from the Pope and Jacques
>   Barzun
> (Isocrates). His works

have been done into French
and Portuguese. And clerks in the post-
office ungum rare stamps from
his packages and steal them for their
childrens' albums   .

(p. 9)

These two versions of the "character" Paterson clearly cannot be reconciled; but it is the second that predominates in the poem. Indeed it is
difficult not to take Mr. Paterson as a fairly perfunctory mask for the
poet himself; like the poet, Paterson appears to be a doctor as well as a
man of letters.[9] Yet Williams insists on maintaining the persona at all
times, so that no matter how transparent a disguise we may find it to
be, we cannot ignore it.

For all its documentary roughness and randomness, then, *Paterson* is
a poem constructed around a central and audaciously realized fiction:
the fiction of "the city / the man, an identity" (p. 3). Why does Williams insist on fictionalizing the consciousness of a poem so committed
to the power of facts? One answer, surely, is that he remains suspicious
of more candid or confessional forms of self-dramatization: "Why even
speak of 'I,' he dreams, which / interests me almost not at all?" (p.
19). In a sense the figure of Mr. Paterson is another evasion of the first
person, a way of representing subjectivity without throwing the poem
under the shadow of the artistic ego. But another reason, one more
closely related to the high ambitions behind the writing of *Paterson,* is
that Williams wants to retain an omniscient, bardic perspective while at
the same time depicting the scene intimately, through the eyes of a single observer. Unwilling to sacrifice poetic authority in favor of experiential immediacy, he divides himself into Mr. Paterson, the persona
who walks through the landscape, and the impersonal maker who inter-
lards this walk with prose passages on everything from the history of
the city to economic theory, including extracts from letters obviously
written to Williams himself.

The poem thus manifests a continuous tension between a Wordsworthian portrayal of the self interacting with its environment, and a
Poundian effort to achieve a kind of panoptic inclusiveness, through
an ongoing collocation of diverse cultural and historical materials (although unlike Pound's *Cantos, Paterson* generally holds these materials
within a strongly local context). This tension between omniscience and
experience is perhaps most clearly displayed in the first section of
Book Two, in which the initial distinction between Paterson the walker
and Williams the poet keeps threatening to collapse. The many prose
passages interpolated throughout the walk might thus be seen as discursive wedges forcibly separating the represented consciousness of

the walker from the authorial perspective of Williams himself, who remains at a distance from immediate experience. Paradoxically, the prose passages attest to *Paterson* Two's status as a *poem*, a made object, rather than a mere transcript of experience.

Nonetheless the first section of Book Two emphasizes the primacy of direct experience through its use of the walk as an approach to the world. The book opens with a clear expression of the motivating impulse behind this walk:

> Outside
>
>   outside myself
>
>   there is a world,
>
> he rumbled, subject to my incursions
> —a world
>
>   (to me) at rest,
>
>   which I approach
>
> concretely—
>
>   (p. 43)

The very stepwise motion of the opening lines (which only later became a fixed pattern for Williams) evokes a gradual awakening to the presence of an external world. This world is both autonomous and subject to the walker's "incursions"; to quote a passage from *Spring and All*, it is "A world . . . sufficient to itself, removed from him (as it most certainly is) with which he has bitter and delicious relations and from which he is independent—moving at will from one thing to another—as he pleases, unbound—complete."[10] The sexual undertone of this passage ("bitter and delicious relations") becomes a central feature of *Paterson* Two. The walker moves freely about the park, "from one thing to another," yet all the while he is aware of the frustrating distance between himself and the world, a distance that no exploration can overcome. The walk thus becomes a kind of lovemaking that never achieves fulfillment, but maintains a constant level of desire and sensual arousal.

The lyric and meditative tone of this opening might lead us to assume that it is the poet's own utterance; but that assumption is quickly corrected by the phrase "he rumbled" (a portmanteau of "mumbled" and "rambled"?), which in effect places invisible quotation marks around the lines I have cited. Characteristically in this poem, apparently lyric speech is converted into direct discourse, so that the "I" which follows has to be assigned to a speaker other than the poet. But the boundary between the poet's voice and Mr. Paterson's is never clear, and the two often become indistinguishable. Even here the absence of quotation marks and other signals makes it difficult to tell precisely where the one voice leaves off and the other begins. Presumably it is the poet we hear speaking in the next lines:

> The scene's the Park
> upon the rock,
> female to the city

> —upon whose body Paterson instructs his thoughts
> (concretely)

Now the speaker's identity is clear if for no other reason than that he refers to Paterson in the third person. The lines that follow are also in the third person, and therefore grammatically constitute a distanced narration of Paterson's walk; but it is difficult not to take the next two lines,

> —late spring,
> a Sunday afternoon!

as a kind of indirect discourse, the exclamation mark reflecting the walker's own response to time, place, and weather. There is also an antiphonal effect, since the exclamation I have just quoted interrupts a verb clause that continues in the next line:

> —and goes by the footpath to the cliff (counting:
> the proof)

We have to look back to realize that the subject of "goes" is Paterson, since the short lines intervene. The sheer syntactical difficulty of this writing, which persists throughout the poem, is a function of the ambiguity of Paterson himself as a figure; the poem's uneasy wavering between first and third persons expresses Williams's uncertainty as to whether he himself or the personified city is the poem's true protagonist.

This ambiguity becomes more pronounced a few lines later, after a brief description of the many picnickers calling to each other, climbing the path, "pouring down! / For the flower of a day!" The passage that follows all but imperceptibly shifts in mode from narrative to lyric:

> Arrived breathless, after a hard climb he,
> looks back (beautiful but expensive!) to
> the pearl-grey towers! Re-turns
> and starts, possessive, through the trees,

> — that love,
> that is not, is not in those terms
> to which I'm still the positive

in spite of all;
the ground dry, — passive-possessive

(p. 44)

The first four lines are clearly in the third person, although the parenthetical phrase has the same quality of an indirect ejaculation that we saw in the lines "—late spring, / a Sunday afternoon!" But the next lines are evidently uttered by Paterson himself, and the lack of a clear transition further obscures the boundary between poet and protagonist. Taken as a whole, the passage enacts a movement from sensory experience to emotional response that may account for the grammatical shift from third to first person. Paterson's bodily interaction with the landscape, his hard climb, his view of the city, his possessive, almost sexual movement into the woods, gives rise to the reflection that follows. His love of the place has been stirred, but the place can give back only a negative love, a love "that is not"; he is himself "the positive," the actively desiring lover seeking some response from his beloved. (This love is further evoked on the next page, in the elliptical line "How do I love you? These!" Most striking here is Williams's substitution of pure deictic gesture for Barrett Browning's elaborate catalog; in effect he carries Stevens's use of the demonstrative in "An Ordinary Evening" a step further by eliding the noun altogether, simply pointing at a set of particulars that remain unnamed and so outside the realm of representation.)

The last line can be taken as an epitome of the poem's effort to fuse concrete imagery and abstract thought, "ideas" and "things." The ground is dry; this is simply an observation of fact. Yet it occasions a thought on the nature of the "love" that the place bears him: it is "passive-possessive," because while it does nothing to *show* its love for him—it is "dry," not wet and embracing—its ground still mutely possesses him. Whether this thought is Williams's or Paterson's is finally immaterial; in moments like this the two cannot be distinguished. What is important is the way the thought emerges from the walk, from the experience of the landscape. In its barely articulate struggle to express a difficult understanding, the passage is much closer to lyric than dramatic utterance. Much of the poem's strength lies precisely in its ability to combine such passionate lyricism with a careful enumeration of particulars.

Just such an enumeration follows, preceded by a word that recurs seven times in Book Two, serving as a sort of connective tissue linking the separate episodes, encounters, and observations of the walk—the word "Walking," followed by a dash. In effect this word stands in for a fuller narration of Paterson's movement in the park; rather than having to be told where he walks, at what pace, through what kind of terrain, we can simply infer that some movement has occurred. Moreover, the present participle refers to the action in a grammatically open-ended way, without specifying an agent, and so manages to avoid the whole problem of pronouns, while still invoking the experiential ground that unites the poem's particulars.

Here the word introduces a series of brief observations that together form a kind of cinematic montage, a train of images connected by the spatial logic of walking itself:

> Walking —
>
> Thickets gather about groups of squat sand-pine,
> all but from bare rock   .   .
>
> —a scattering of man-high cedars (sharp cones),
> antlered sumac   .
>
> —roots, for the most part, writhing
> upon the surface
> 　　　　　　(so close are we to ruin every
> day!)
> 　　　　searching the punk-dry rot

(p. 44)

These lines present an extraordinary mimesis of the very rhythm of perception. Rather than forming logically coherent structures, their syntax seems to follow the movement of the eye as it penetrates from surrounding thickets to inner trees to the underlying rock, or as it pauses for a moment to register the sharp cones on the cedars before moving on to the sumac. When the walker's eye drops to the ground, perception leads to another thought, whose different status is signaled by the use of parentheses. The rapid motion of consciousness is captured in the quick, terse phrases and the sudden shift to generalization, which disappears as quickly as it came. Syntax here becomes almost purely temporal rather than logical, a medium for graphing the momentary leaps and waves of attention as it moves through the world.

This kind of phenomenological exactitude represents only one pole in the poem, however. *Paterson* repeatedly moves away from such mimesis, towards a more abstract mode of utterance whose authority is underwritten by Williams's appropriation of history, science, and economics as part of his material. Indeed the next passage turns to a scientific account of the very action that had been rendered experientially in the previous lines. After another appearance of the word "Walking," we are given a dry textbook description of the ambulatory process, complete with a reference to an unseen diagram. This is followed by one of the "Cress" letters that return throughout Book Two, and then by two more prose passages, the first a short dialogue quoted from a novel, the second a journalistic account of a riot that took place in Paterson in 1880. All these prose passages have the effect of interrupting the walk from outside, since they cannot very well be a part of Mr. Paterson's own consciousness as he moves through the park. They thus establish a different kind of textual space, a space of authority rather than experience, of writing as an independent activity rather than as a representation of "things" and consciousness. Neither of these two spaces can truly be said to dominate the other; they simply alternate, each for a moment asserting its claim and then giving way to its opposite. Their ongoing competition reflects Williams's own uneasiness about the mode of representation proper to a long poem following in the wake of Pound's *Cantos*, Eliot's *Quartets*, and Stevens's *Notes Toward a Supreme Fiction*, all of them works that assume an oracular authority transcending the experiential. Williams wants to embrace experience more fully than his rivals do, but at the same time he recognizes that as a genre the long poem demands more totalizing forms of knowledge and assertion; the prose thus functions in part to raise the poem *above* the walk, into a more purely discursive realm later figured as the library of Book Three.

After this series of prose interpolations we return to the walk once more, this time for a more continuous account of Mr. Paterson's movement and consciousness:

> Signs everywhere of birds nesting, while
> in the air, slow, a crow zigzags
> with heavy wings before the wasp-thrusts
> of smaller birds circling about him
> that dive from above stabbing for his eyes

Walking—

> he leaves the path, finds hard going
> across-field, stubble and matted brambles
> seeming a pasture—but no pasture
> —old furrows, to say labor sweated or
> had sweated here   .
>
> > > > a flame,
>
> spent.

(pp. 46–47)

The first part might almost be a piece of eighteenth-century descriptive verse, with its relatively smooth hypotaxis; but here too the syntax mimes the flow of perception, as it moves from the nests to the crow and then to the smaller birds around him, ending with the sudden, shocking movement downward, towards the "eyes"—literally the crow's, although surely the violence of the perception is also in a sense stabbing at the spectator's eyes. "Walking" signals another transition, as the grammar shifts more firmly into third person narration. Once again we are given a clear graph of the mind's movement from external observation to internal reflection, as Mr. Paterson works his way across a tangled field, sees the rough growth, then speculates about the field's former state. His first thought is that it was a pasture, but he rejects this as he takes note of "old furrows," which show that the field had once been labored over. The fact having been established, there is a pause, followed by a more condensed, metaphorical thought about the nature of labor, a thought that evidently required more time and distance from the original perception before it could take shape.

The next passage presents us with one of the poem's most spectacular instances of an experiential moment giving rise to lyric meditation:

> The file-sharp grass   .
>
> When! from before his feet, half tripping,
> picking a way, there starts   .
>   a flight of empurpled wings!
> —invisibly created (their
> jackets dust-grey) from the dust kindled
> to sudden ardor!
>
>   They fly away, churring! until
> their strength spent they plunge
> to the coarse cover again and disappear
> —but leave, livening the mind, a flashing
> of wings and a churring song   .
>
> AND a grasshopper of red basalt, boot-long,
> tumbles from the core of his mind,
> a rubble-bank disintegrating beneath a
> tropic downpour
>
> Chapultepec! grasshopper hill!
>
> —a matt stone solicitously instructed
> to bear away some rumor
> of the living presence that has preceded
> it, out precedented in its breath   .
>
> These wings do not unfold for flight—
> no need!

the weight (to the hand) finding
a counter-weight or counter buoyancy
by the mind's wings   .

He is afraid! What then?

Before his feet, at each step, the flight
is renewed. A burst of wings, a quick
churring sound   :

      couriers to the ceremonial of love!

—aflame in flight!
     —aflame only in flight!
          No flesh but the caress!

He is led forward by their announcing wings.

                    (pp. 47–48)

As I have quoted it, the passage begins with a brief yet remarkably precise notation of "The file-sharp grass," which keenly evokes the rough, serrated surface of overgrown blades of grass. More importantly perhaps, the image establishes the trajectory of Mr. Paterson's gaze, so that the sudden explosion of the next lines seems to arise naturally out of the poem's perceptual field. Williams may well be guilty of overusing exclamation marks, but here the mark following the word "When" has a precise and characteristic function; it does not signal a spoken exclamation so much as a kind of jolt, a temporally punctual eruption flaring up in the midst of the walk much as the exclamation mark itself flares into the midst of the sentence. The flock of grasshoppers that spring up from their hiding place in the grass interrupt the relaxed rhythm of perception and reflection that governed the previous passage, and force a more intense and instantaneous awareness on Mr. Paterson, as conveyed by the jagged line breaks and the continued use of exclamation marks. This sudden obtrusion is subtly linked to the previous reflection on labor as "a flame, / spent" by means of the word "kindled," suggesting that the grasshoppers are themselves a kind of flame, a flame alive and present in the scene, not "spent." Mr. Paterson's attention has thus been turned from the barely visible furrows, which had become for him almost textual traces of a departed human presence, to the immediate life hidden under the "coarse cover" of the ground. This turn has been effected not by his own will, but by the assertive reality of the landscape thrusting itself upon his consciousness.

In a sense, then, the landscape actively participates in the walker's thought, impinging on it in a way that shapes both its form and content, just as Dr. Johnson says it should. The afterimage left by this momentary uprising—"a flashing of wings and a churring song"—germinates in Paterson's mind to set off a lyric meditation that takes as its central metaphor a Mayan sculpture in the shape of a grasshopper, the memory of which has obviously been summoned up by the actual grasshoppers. This sculpture is said to "tumble from the core of his mind," almost as though it had fallen onto the ground before him, to join the reality which called it forth (in fact we learn that the sculpture was found when a "tropic downpour" uncovered it where it lay buried in a rubble-bank). Having brought this artifact to mind, Mr. Paterson's thoughts turn to the miracle of art's embodiment of departed spirit, its ability to "bear away some rumor / of the living presence that has preceded / it." The sculpture thus serves as a counterimage to the furrows, which likewise point to a vanished human presence but with none of the infused spirituality that preserves or memorializes an originating mind.

Paterson's meditation becomes more rhapsodic and idealizing as he meets the inanimacy of the stone grasshopper with the sublime "counter buoyancy" of "the mind's wings." Yet as if in reaction to the excessiveness of this vision, there is a pause, after which we are told that "He is afraid!"—possibly of the reality and finality of death, which his glorification of the artifact's immortality has sought to repress. The ambiguous question "What then?" which may be dismissing either the optimistic vision of art or the fear itself, seems to leave Paterson's train of thought at an impasse; and it is therefore natural that his attention returns to the scene before him, to the actual grasshoppers which initiated the meditation. Now it is they who are transformed and idealized by Paterson's imagination, as each step sends them briefly into the air once more: "couriers to the ceremonial of love! / —aflame in flight! / aflame only in flight! / No flesh but the caress!" The rhetoric has reached a precarious yet powerful pitch, as the grasshoppers become visionary go-betweens in Mr. Paterson's courtship of the park, "female to the city"—a courtship in which any display of "flesh," of the living body of the place in all its forms, takes on the sexual intensity of a caress. The verse section ends with the calm yet majestic line "He is led forward by their announcing wings," evoking the image of a marriage procession.

After another passage from a "Cress" letter, Mr. Paterson's meditation on the sculpture is recapitulated. Now, however, there is a strange synthesis of actual and artifactual grasshoppers: we are told that the stone grasshopper "falls from an undermined bank / and—begins churring!" (p. 49). The sudden emergence of the living grasshoppers from the dirt becomes a metaphor for the emergence of the stone grasshopper into a kind of aesthetic life after having been lost, and by extension for the life of all art as it preserves the love of the mind that made it: "The stone lives, the flesh dies / —we know nothing of death." By giving the stone grasshopper properties of the living grasshoppers before his eyes, Paterson is able to overcome the threatening inanimacy of the sculpture, which had previously derailed his affirmative vision.

The experience of the landscape thus informs the meditation more profoundly than by mere associative stimulation. Initially the experience simply calls forth the *memory* of the stone grasshopper, a memory which sets off an independent train of thought that seems to founder and end in fear. Only after returning to the experience and viewing it more imaginatively is Paterson able to fuse it with the object of his meditation, and to end in a confident affirmation of the immortality of art. The sequence moves toward a more intimate bonding between immediate experience and meditative thought, in which thought does not move independently but remains in contact with the objects that aroused it. The poet cannot simply ignore external stimuli once they have fertilized his imagination; they remain constantly before him, and consequently he must find a way to give them an ongoing place in his thoughts. In its delicate interplay of real and remembered grasshoppers, this sequence shows with special clarity the reciprocal workings of experience and imagination as they are brought together within the temporal frame of the walk.

After another prose interpolation we are given the famous passage beginning "Without invention." As Louis Martz points out, the passage is an explicit response to Pound's Canto XLV, "With usura."[11] It thus belongs to *Paterson*'s Poundian or cosmic phase, although the vision it asserts is presented as an alternative to the timeless cultural tradition of the *Cantos*. The voice that utters these lines is not the voice of Mr. Paterson, of a bodily self located within a particular landscape, but rather of an impersonal poet pronouncing oracular and universal truths. Yet it moves from the relatively abstract language of its opening lines towards imagery derived from the landscape through which Mr. Paterson has been walking, so that although the walk itself has receded from view, its memory lingers, informing the rhetoric of the passage much as the real grasshoppers informed Mr. Paterson's meditation on the stone grasshopper:

> without invention
> nothing lies under the witch-hazel
> bush, the alder does not grow from among
> the hummocks margining the all
> but spent channel of the old swale,

the small foot-prints
of the mice under the overhanging
tufts of the bunch-grass will not
appear[.]

(p. 50)

Characteristically, Williams redefines invention to denote not a purely
mental activity but a perceptual one as well, reminding us of the
word's Latin etymology, with its root meaning "to come upon." Here,
then, Williams succeeds in uniting the experiential ground of the
poem with its more programmatic ambitions; invention is shown to be
a process wholly in keeping with Mr. Paterson's leisurely, attentive walk
in the park.

A transitional passage takes us from the large concerns of the meditation on invention towards a more descriptive mode by way of an image
from the earlier passage, of something left unnamed lying "under the
witch-hazel / bush":

Under the bush they lie protected
from the offending sun—
11 o'clock
            They seem to talk

—a park, devoted to pleasure : devoted to . grasshoppers!

(p. 50–51)

Paterson's walk now begins to focus more sustainedly on the other people in the park, whose presence comes to dominate his experience of
the place. This emphasis on others strikingly distinguishes Williams's
walks from those of Frost and Stevens; for Williams the world is always
social as well as phenomenal, and so the claims of other human beings
on one's attention must be acknowledged. We meet "3 colored girls, of
age!," then a white girl and her boyfriend lying indolently, discussing
her newly purchased bathing suit: "just / pants and a brassier." Mr.
Paterson is now not simply an observer but a voyeur as he watches the
couple lying "beneath / the sun in frank vulgarity," and reflects that
"among / the working classes SOME sort / of breakdown / has occurred." This last remark does not pretend to be genuine social analysis; it is simply the idle thought of a man walking in a park and eyeing
a particular couple with distaste.

As he continues to observe them, however, he begins to appreciate
their authenticity; he sees that they are "Not undignified," that their intimate talk has created "perfect domesticity" in the middle of a public
place, and that "their pitiful thoughts do meet / in the flesh." As if to
honor this achievement, Mr. Paterson returns to his earlier idealization

of the grasshoppers as "couriers to the ceremonial of love"; now he sees the couple

> surrounded
> by churring loves! Gay wings
> to bear them (in sleep)
>
> their thoughts alight,
> away
> .   .   among the grass

(p. 52)

The grasshoppers have become embodiments of the couple's "pitiful thoughts" alighting and disappearing at random. The man and woman are now seen to enact in human form the marriage that Mr. Paterson has sought with the place itself. Their initial tawdriness has been transformed, through sustained imaginative contact, into a vital part of the scene in all its mythic power.

Clearly the poem could go on like this for quite a long time. Each episode has had its own interest; precisely detailed natural and social observations have mingled with a vivid depiction of a mind responding imaginatively to the world before its eyes. Yet one of the major challenges of the walk poem is to bring a sense of unity to the disparate objects and moments that it represents. Although the repetition of the word "Walking" has created a tenuous formal unity (not unlike the repetition of the "Promenade" theme in Mussorgsky's *Pictures at an Exhibition*), it cannot begin to do the deeper work of unifying the walk thematically. This is a task Williams takes up in the last part of section I. As has been the case from the beginning of *Paterson*, his central agent of unification is sound; like Wordsworth, Williams finds in aural experience a means of healing the discontinuities and distances imposed by seeing. The careful enumeration of visual particulars thus gives way in the closing pages of the section to a more strenuous attempt to hear and evoke an underlying voice that can lend a sense of wholeness to Mr. Paterson's experience of the park—"as if to hear, / Hear hard, gets at an essential integrity."[12]

This work of hearing begins as Mr. Paterson ascends to the highest point of the park and turns his attention to the hordes of picnickers who keep arriving. His position at the lookout point now enables him to take in larger stretches of landscape, and so to attain a more comprehensive view of the park:

> And still the picnickers come on, now
> early afternoon, and scatter through the
> trees over the fenced-in acres   .

Voices!
multiple and inarticulate . voices
clattering loudly to the sun, to
the clouds. Voices!
assaulting the air gaily from all sides.

—among which the ear strains to catch
the movement of one voice among the rest
—a reed-like voice
of peculiar accent.

(p. 54)

Within this mass of voices, "multiple and inarticulate," Paterson strains to hear a single voice, "reed-like" and "of peculiar accent." On one level Mr. Paterson simply hears a particular voice which intrigues him, and which he struggles to discern above the babble. But surely the epithet "reed-like" is meant to evoke the image of Pan as well, of a nature god whose music arises from the landscape itself. In any case this single voice acts as a kind of continuo holding together all the others, giving Mr. Paterson's consciousness of the scene and its chaos a unifying center.

The sexual imagery of female park and male city (of which Mr. Paterson remains vestigially a personification) now returns, although the metaphor has modulated from courtship to physical lovemaking:

> Thus she finds what peace there is, reclines,
> before his approach, stroked
> by their clambering feet—for pleasure
> It is all for
> pleasure . their feet . aimlessly
> wandering

(pp. 54–55)

The passage moves uneasily between portraying Mr. Paterson as the singular lover—"his approach"—and seeing the crowd as a throng of lovers, but this difficulty can be resolved if we take the picnickers to be parts of Paterson's "body," administering individual caresses of which he is the ultimate origin. This returns us more forcefully to the man-city identification with which the poem began, an identification that endangers the experiential style of Book Two, since it verges on the allegorical. As if retreating from allegory, Williams moves us away from the mythological giant forms of city and landscape, and back to the lookout point where Mr. Paterson has been standing:

> Sunday in the park,
> limited by the escarpment, eastward; to

> the west abutting on the old road: recreation
> with a view! the binoculars chained
> to anchored stanchions along the east wall—
>   beyond which, a hawk
>   soars!
>
> —a trumpet sounds fitfully.
>
> (p. 55)

Seeing, here represented by the binoculars (which, significantly perhaps, are "chained"), again gives way to hearing, a sense directed toward continuity rather than discrete particulars. The same movement
occurs in the next passage:

> Stand at the rampart (use a metronome
> if your ear is deficient, one made in Hungary
> if you prefer)
> and look away north by east where the church
> spires still spend their wits against
> the sky   to the ball-park
> in the hollow with its minute figures running
> —beyond the gap where the river
> plunges into the narrow gorge, unseen
>
> and the imagination soars, as a voice
> beckons, a thundrous voice, endless
> —as sleep: the voice
> that has ineluctably called them—
>   that unmoving roar!
>
> (p. 55)

The reference to the metronome may seem puzzling, although evidently it is meant as a counterpart to the binoculars stationed at the
rampart. But why a metronome rather than, say, an ear trumpet? On
the one hand, it takes up the motif of counting which was first introduced on the opening page of Book Two ("counting: the proof"
[p. 43]); more importantly, it suggests that the hearing required of
us is not simply a matter of picking up sounds but of discerning a
music, a rhythm that underlies them. (His granting of permission to
use a metronome imported from Hungary may indicate that Williams
is not picky about what kind of rhythm we hear; a mazurka will do as
well as a foxtrot.) After describing the prospect, significantly in terms
of what remains "unseen," he turns to an image of voice once more,
although this voice is very different from the "reed-like voice" we
heard earlier. It is in fact the voice of the falls, "that unmoving roar,"
which was the central symbol of Book One. The difference between

seeing and hearing is again strongly operative here; where the visual
experience of the landscape included a soaring hawk, its distance
from the viewer marked by wide spacing, in listening to the falls it
is "the imagination" that "soars," participating more actively in the
scene.

And so it is the voice of the falls that provides the ground tone uniting the particulars of the walk: "—his voice, one among many (un-
heard) / moving under all" (p. 56). But this voice too remains a figure
for a more elusive and ubiquitous voice, a voice that inhabits Mr. Paterson's own voice as well:

> So during the early afternoon, from place
> to place he moves,
> his voice mingling with other voices
> —the voice in his voice
> opening his old throat, blowing out his lips,
> kindling his mind (more
> than his mind will kindle)
>
> —following the hikers.

(p. 56)

This passage is unique in that it gives a kind of synoptic overview of the
walk, as an ongoing movement "from place to place." Surprisingly, it
portrays Mr. Paterson as speaking in the course of the walk, although
the poem has recorded no literal speech of his, only the fitful motions
of his thought. Like Williams', his voice is not his alone, but acts as a vehicle for "*the* voice" (italics mine), presumably the voice of the falls but
more generally the voice of the place speaking through and in him,
"kindling his mind." By identifying it *as* a voice now, Williams confers a
kind of retroactive unity on the scattered sights and sounds of the
poem.

Having approached the poem's thematic center, Williams now takes
us to the literal center of the landscape:

> At last he comes to the idlers' favorite
> haunts, the picturesque summit, where
> the blue-stone (rust-red where exposed)
> has been faulted at various levels
> (ferns rife among the stones)
> into rough terraces and partly closed in
> dens of sweet grass, the ground gently sloping.
>
> Loiterers in groups straggle
> over the bare rock-table—scratched by their

boot-nails more than the glacier scratched
them—walking indifferent through
each other's privacy

—in any case,
the center of movement, the core of gaiety.

(p. 56)

The words "At last" inform us that we have arrived at the goal of the
walk, not in the sense of a place where some practical end has been accomplished, but simply a natural point of rest. Just as Paterson's walk
has found a temporal unity in the trope of voice, it finds a spatial unity
in its penetration to "the center of movement, the core of gaiety." This
center is not, like the lookout point, a place removed from the landscape and its inhabitants; although it is at the summit, it is densely
populated, and so within rather than above the "gaiety" of the Sunday
outings.

What Paterson sees in this center is a kind of timeless sexual or Di-
onysian energy, epitomized by an old Italian woman perhaps significantly named Mary, dancing gaily and exhorting others to join her:
"What a bunch of bums! Afraid somebody see / you? . / Blah! /*Escre-
menti*!" (p. 57). Like other female figures in *Paterson*, notably the First
Wife in Book One and Beautiful Thing in Book Three, Mary embodies
a primitive, almost Platonic beauty that transcends time and place,
although she is given a more specific historical identity than the other
avatars: she breathes "the air of the Midi / and the old cultures."[13]
She thus represents the persistence of both a European peasant tradition, further evoked in the next lines by a memory of an old Russian
peon drinking from a wineskin in a lost Eisenstein film, and an even
older Mediterranean culture of Bacchic ritual: "goatherd / and goat,
fertility the attack, drunk, / cleansed" (p. 58). This imagery is reinforced by an earlier description of a young man "sitting with his back
to the rock among / some ferns playing a guitar, dead pan" (p. 56).
The slightly odd separation of the last two words emphasizes the
pun, which picks up on the earlier hint in the phrase "reed-like voice";
despite the adjective, Pan clearly is *not* dead but alive and well and living in New Jersey. In the midst of a modern park infested by economic
pressures of various kinds, Paterson glimpses a true Arcadia based on
sheer bodily indulgence, and linked to an ancient but oft-repressed
strain of pagan worship: "This is the old, the very old, old upon old, /
The undying." This tableau acts as a visual counterpart to the music
that continues to sound through the remainder of the walk; it is the
cynosure that holds the park together, just as the music holds the walk
together.

The word "Walking" returns a last time, and the final movement of the section begins, as Mr. Paterson once more takes up a voyeuristic stance:

> Walking —
>
>> look down (from a ledge) into this grassy
>> den
>>> (somewhat removed from the traffic)
>>>> above whose brows
>>> a moon! where she lies sweating at his side:
>>>>> She stirs, distraught,
>>>> against him—wounded (drunk), moves
>>>> against him (a lump) desiring,
>>>> against him, bored   .
>
> (p. 59)

This may be the couple Mr. Paterson saw earlier, or it may be a different couple; in any case they again figure forth the male/female relationship of park and city, and of Mr. Paterson and the landscape through which he moves. Now however it is the male who is asleep and indifferent, and the female who actively desires. In her effort to arouse him she resorts to drastic measures:

>>>> —moving nearer
>>> she—lean as a goat—leans
>>> her lean belly to the man's backside
>>> toying with the clips of his
>>> suspenders   .
>>> —to which he adds his useless voice:
>>> until there moves in his sleep
>>> a music that is whole, unequivocal (in
>>> his sleep, sweating in his sleep—laboring
>>> against sleep, agasp!)
>>>> —and does not waken.
>
> (pp. 59–60)

The sound imagery returns now in explicitly musical form. In the terms of this episode, which like others is balanced between literal narrative and allegory, this music penetrates into our consciousness even when we are asleep, oblivious to the external world, because even then the world continues to act on us, attempting to waken us to its presence. To apprehend this music consciously is for Williams the chief task of poetry.

Music, the falls, and the "one voice" heard in the crowd all come together in the next passage, a climactic integration of the poem's sonic metaphors:

> Sees, alive (asleep)
>   —the fall's roar entering
> his sleep (to be fulfilled)
>   reborn
>
> in his sleep—scattered over the mountain
> severally .
>
>   —by which he woos her, severally.
>
> And the amnesic crowd (the scattered),
> called about — strains
> to catch the movement of one voice   .
>
>   hears,
>
> Pleasure! Pleasure!
>
>   —feels,
> half dismayed, the afternoon of complex
> voices its own—
>   and is relieved
>   (relived)
>
>   (p. 60)

This passage returns again to the figure of Paterson as a giant sleeping with his head beside the falls, whose "thoughts" are the people of the city. But more important than this mythic construct is the complexity of the sound depicted here. It originates in the roar of the falls, passes through Paterson's sleep and emerges in the picnickers scattered through the park, who themselves "strain . . . to catch the movement of one voice," just as Mr. Paterson had strained to hear the reed-like voice earlier. What the crowd hears is the sound of its own pleasure, "the afternoon of complex / voices its own." In taking the sound of the falls into themselves and emitting it again in the form of voices crying out in pleasure they are both "relieved" of the pressure of the falls, and "relived," revived. (The reference to relieving becomes literalized a moment later as we are told that "A cop is directing traffic . . . toward /the conveniences.") For the crowd, then, the summoning voice of the falls is answered through translation into pleasure; the process requires no heightened attention to the place itself, only unself-conscious abandonment to "gaiety."

For the poet, however, the task is more difficult. He must attend to the falls directly, to the voice of the place and to the particulars of place; and he must attempt to record that voice and those particulars:

                              oaks, choke-cherry,
          dogwoods, white and green, iron-wood :
          humped roots matted into the shallow soil
          —mostly gone: rock out-croppings
          polished by the feet of the picnickers:
          sweetbarked sassafras   .

          leaning from the rancid grease:
                                        deformity—

          —to be deciphered (a horn, a trumpet!)
          an elucidation by multiplicity,
          a corrosion, a parasitic curd, a clarion
          for belief, to be good dogs   :

     NO DOGS ALLOWED AT LARGE IN THIS PARK

                                                    (p. 61)

This closing passage, like so much of *Paterson*, alternates between images of beauty and degradation, wholeness and deformity. Both are
present within this landscape, for the park is not a true wilderness but
an urbanized parcel of "nature," contaminated by the vulgarity of modern culture. But the burden of the passage is to suggest what the poet's
obligation to such a place must be: to stay faithful both to the single
unifying voice or music—"(a horn, a trumpet!)"—which binds the
place, and to the endless particular details which compose it—"an elu-
cidation by multiplicity." Neither alone is sufficient; only by holding
them together can the poet simultaneously represent the unity and the
diversity of the place in which he walks.

     The last line of the section supplies a final ironic comment, suggest-
ing that the entire walk has been a kind of transgression (the Preface
at the beginning of Book One speaks of the poet as "just another dog
/ among a lot of dogs"[p. 3]). Yet despite the constricting forces of bu-
reaucracy, Mr. Paterson's walk has taken him freely from place to
place; he has seen, we feel, everything there is to see. Book Two is not
over, of course; "Sunday in the Park" continues through two more sections. But the next sections, while also located in the park, are more
tendentious and less experiential than the first: section II concerns itself primarily with a long sermon by an evangelist preaching in the
park, and with the economic and religious themes that his sermon
raises, while section III returns to the mythic space of the symbolic landscape, and works out its latent drama in powerful, nonmimetic terms.
It is only in section I that the casual, aimless experience of the walk is
evoked in all its miscellany and immediacy.[14]

     Section I of "Sunday in the Park" can thus stand apart as a separate
walk poem; and indeed several editors have recognized the internal

unity of the piece, printing it as a self-contained excerpt.[15] In its larger structure it moves from a precise transcription of individual moments of perception and reflection as they occur within the time of the walk, to a broader sense of the continuous voice or music that underlies all these moments and holds them together. The section achieves a delicate balance between concrete detail and the evocation of a female spirit of place whose presence lends a kind of erotic intensity to the walk. At the same time, however, we are constantly reminded of the epic ambitions of *Paterson* as a whole, largely by the many prose passages that interrupt the continuous flow of the walk. These passages, and the use of Mr. Paterson as a persona, firmly tie the section to the rest of the poem, subordinating its mimesis of experience to the larger symbolic scheme of the first four books. *Paterson* Two thus offers a clear instance of the tension between the walk poem and more canonical forms. Williams's *resistance* to the walk, and to the mode of experiential representation it brings with it, is a measure of his desire to write a poem that can stand above experience, surveying the landscape as a whole rather than as a series of points along the way. The figure of Paterson himself neatly expresses Williams's ambivalence, since he is both a surrogate for the poet walking in the world and responding to what he sees, and a totalizing trope for the city itself as viewed by an omniscient bard.

.　.　.　.　.

A more self-sufficient and integrated representation of the walk is achieved in Williams's late poem "The Desert Music," which I find to be one of the poet's most entirely successful and moving works. In this judgement I differ with such important Williams critics as Louis Martz and Thomas Whitaker, but concur with others like J. Hillis Miller and, most notably, Sherman Paul, who has devoted an entire book to the poem.[16] The issue of judgment is an important one for my interpretation, because I want to argue that the poem's success (which I take as a given) rests on the richness with which it represents the poet's experience, while moving outward from that experience with impressive ease to touch a generality of thought that finds its center once again in the trope of music. The disjunctive alternation of verse and prose and the hectoring tone that characterize much of *Paterson* are here quietly left behind; instead Williams creates a more seamless blending of the discursive and the experiential.

Interestingly, like "An Ordinary Evening in New Haven," "The Desert Music" was originally written for public recital, as part of Phi Beta Kappa ceremonies at Harvard.[17] Unlike Stevens, however, Williams does not attempt to unite the poem's public and private occasions; his walk takes place not in Cambridge but in Juárez, Mexico, across the border from El Paso. Although it was written to be spoken, it does not have the meditative smoothness of the "variable foot" poems Williams wrote in his last years, including the long "Of Asphodel, That Greeny Flower." Those poems have something of the feel of blank verse, or perhaps more nearly of Stevens's tercet poems; the relatively even measure creates the effect of a single continuous utterance. This is not true of "The Desert Music"; the poem's form is in fact much closer to the verse of *Paterson*, with its irregular spacing, variable rhythm and line length, and essentially mimetic values. But where the rapid formal mutations of *Paterson* tend to express tension or conflict between such elements as the literal and the figurative, particularity and generality, experience and authority, in "The Desert Music" they reflect smoother transitions *within* experience: movements between recorded speech, perception, and thought, or between different levels of aesthetic and emotional intensity.

The major reason for the poem's greater continuity when set beside *Paterson* lies in the fact that it is openly about the poet's own experience. Not only is the poem written in the first person, but the speaker is addressed by name at one point as "William Carlos Williams," definitively announcing Williams's emergence as the protagonist of his own poetry; it may be significant that the poem was written shortly after the completion of his autobiography. Because poet and protagonist are one, a natural continuity is possible between narrated experience and lyric reflection, in contrast to the awkward movements between first and third person in *Paterson.*

Like "An Ordinary Evening in New Haven," then, the poem is occasional in the deeper sense: the writing of the poem is perceived as a continuation of the experience represented in the poem, not a separate or secondary activity. The poem can move easily and naturally from narration to the lyric present, without any sense of disjunction. Perhaps the clearest illustration of this movement occurs near the end of the poem, as Williams reflects upon the power of music:

> the music! the
> *music* as when Casals struck
> and held a deep cello tone
> and I am speechless .[18]

The shift from the past tense of "held" to the present "I am," while noticeable, is not jarring, because present utterance and remembered experience seem so closely knit in this poem. The moment epitomizes the poem's ongoing effort to harmonize the figurative music of lyric speech and the literal music heard in Juárez. Sense experience and the writing of poetry fuse more completely here than they had in *Paterson*, through the overt mediation of the "I."

The experience recorded in "The Desert Music" was first sparely set down in prose form, in a paragraph of Williams's *Autobiography*:

> Juárez, across the bridge. Three cents the trip. *Sur le pont d'Avignon*—is all I could think of. The sparrows at night in the park—Bob [McAlmon] and his brothers, George and Alec and their wives—tequila at five cents a glass, a quail dinner and the Mexicans, the poor Indians—one huddled into a lump against the ironwork of the bridge at night—safe perhaps from both sides, incredibly compressed into a shapeless obstruction—asleep.[19]

The paragraph is a mere list of nouns; this is in fact precisely what distinguishes it from the poem, of which Williams says "The verb calls it into being" (p. 110). "The Desert Music" takes this collection of nouns, of sights, memories, and impressions, and supplies the missing verbs that can turn it into a complete "sentence," a dynamic whole. As Sherman Paul points out, even the crucial themes of music and the dance are latent here in the memory of the French song, which does not appear in the poem.[20] What the *Autobiography* passage documents is both the virtual presence of the poem in the experience—the presence, that is, of all the important images and even metaphors of the poem, along with a sense of their potential meaning—and its lack of articulation there. The writing of the poem becomes an unfolding, a spacing and "verbing" of what existed in a packed, compressed state in the experience itself, and in the journalistic notation of that experience.

The poem's structure is strikingly similar to that of another great poem of Williams's later years, "Burning the Christmas Greens." Like that poem, "The Desert Music" opens with a kind of flash-forward or prolepsis of the image on which the poem will come to rest.[21] In both poems the anticipatory opening strengthens the effect of closure decisively, by making the poem seem to come full circle. Surprise is sacrificed for a sense of completion. We might contrast this method with Frost's poems, in particular "The Wood-Pile," where only the title looks forward to the closing image; within the poem itself the woodpile seems to loom up entirely without warning. Williams prefers to prepare his reader for the poem's final image, so that it can be swiftly and effectively inserted into the stream of the poem's narrative without awkward pauses for description.

And so the poem begins where it ends, with a disturbing encounter in the dark, on the border between two countries:

　　　　—the dance begins: to end about a form
　　　　propped motionless—on the bridge
　　　　between Juárez and El Paso—unrecognizable
　　　　in the semi-dark

　　　　　　　　　　Wait!

　　　　The others waited while you inspected it,
　　　　on the very walk itself

　　　　　　　　　Is it alive?

　　　　　　　　　　　　　　—neither a head,
　　　　legs nor arms!

　　　　　　　It isn't a sack of rags someone
　　　　has abandoned here　　　.　　　torpid against
　　　　the flange of the supporting girder　　　　?

　　　　　　　　　　　an inhuman shapelessness,
　　　　knees hugged tight up into the belly

　　　　　　　Egg-shaped!

　　　　　　　　　　What a place to sleep!
　　　　on the International Boundary. Where else,
　　　　interjurisdictional, not to be disturbed?

　　　　　　　　　　　　　　　　　(pp. 273–74)

This shapeless human form, in its moving embodiment of minimal life
processes (although even its life remains in question here), demon-
strates for Williams more starkly than any image of sudden beauty the
power of the actual to seize us and force us into a relationship with the
world—a relationship that, despite the disturbing quality of this sight,
remains essentially aesthetic. For as the opening line tells us, this
strange object coincides with the final cadence of a "dance" that the
poem itself performs. The dance metaphor is strikingly visualized in
the very typography of the poem; lines and phrases move about on the
page with remarkable agility and freedom, though never arbitrarily.
Williams exploits the puns that connect prosody and dance through
such terms as "measure" and "foot" most memorably in the closing
lines of *Paterson* Five; but those puns are implicit here as well.

　　Rhetorically the poem dances among several different kinds of discourse: lyric, descriptive, transcriptive, narrative. This opening passage
includes all of these: there are brief snatches of speech that have been
(presumably) set down verbatim ("Wait!" "Is it alive?"); an extended
question which might at first seem also to be spoken, but whose more
writerly syntax quickly reveals it to be descriptive in function ("It isn't a

sack of rags someone / has abandoned here . torpid against / the flange of the supporting girder?"); straightforward narration ("The others waited while you inspected it"); and metaphorical reflection on the object ("an inhuman shapelessness"). Each of these modes is set off by typographical space, so that the transitions between them are clearly articulated; at the same time, however, Williams avoids conventional signals such as quotation marks, which would reduce the demand on the reader to "place" individual lines and phrases.

The opening passage of the poem, with its description of the sleeping derelict, is followed by a polemical discourse that at first seems wholly unrelated to what precedes it:

> How shall we get said what must be said?
>
> Only the poem.
>
> Only the counted poem, to an exact measure:
> to imitate, not to copy nature, not
> to copy nature
>
> NOT, prostrate, to copy nature
>   but a dance! to dance
> two and two with him—
>   sequestered there asleep,
>   right end up!
>
>   A music
> supersedes his composure, hallooing to us
> across a great distance   .   .
>
>   wakens the dance
> who blows upon his benumbed fingers!
>
>   (p. 274)

In his emphatic distinction between imitating and copying nature, Williams is elaborating a polemic that he has been carrying on at least since *Spring and All*, insisting once again on the dynamic nature of poetic representation, its status as action rather than picture. Hence the trope of dance is a fitting one for his conception of the poem. The trope seems peculiarly out of place, however, when Williams applies it to the figure of the sleeping man; for how can one "dance / two and two" with this shapeless lump? In effect the incongruity of its application calls attention to the essentially verbal nature of this dance; even a motionless, shapeless body can be caught up in it through the medium of words.

The trope of dance leads Williams to the even more central trope of music announced by the poem's title. Before the dance of the poem can

take place, a music must be heard; and this music comes from outside
the poem, "hallooing to us / across a great distance." Like the music
evoked at the end of *Paterson* Two, section I, this music is a unifying
force that can turn the agony of experience into an aesthetic whole:

> an agony of self-realization
> bound into a whole
> by that which surrounds us .
>
> (p. 275)

This is followed by a startlingly anguished first-person statement:

> I cannot escape
>
> I cannot vomit it up

In their forthright engagement of the lyric present, these lines express
the desperate compulsion behind Williams's sense of poetic vocation.
He cannot escape the music of "that which surrounds us," but neither
can he vomit it up; in terms of the alimentary metaphor, he must di-
gest it and make it into a poem (the Freudian identification of art and
feces may lurk in the background here):

> Only the poem!
>
> Only the made poem, the verb calls it
> into being.

The polemical digression as a whole states the poetic program behind
"The Desert Music." The poet must first hear a music that originates in
the world, in experience; he must "dance" to this music, taking it into
himself; and he must convert it into a "made poem," a poem energized
by the verb that "calls it into being." The poem is therefore more than
a simple account of experience; it is the trace of an action, of a dance
that has been prompted by an external music. The poet's walk
through the streets of Juárez literalizes this dynamic metaphor, providing a spatial and temporal frame for the poem's responsive dance as it
sets down the music of the desert and its inhabitants.

This music breaks into the poem most forcefully at three distinct moments, each a kind of unforeseen epiphany that seizes the poet's attention and makes him intensely conscious of an external world. Such
heightened attention is of course characteristic of Williams's poetry
generally; what makes "The Desert Music" unique is that we are given a
series of intense perceptual moments, along with the temporal continuum that unites them. In effect the poem provides a context for Williams's typical short lyrics, setting their flashes of heightened perception within the more ordinary consciousness out of which they emerge.
This gives the epiphanic moments a special force, since they contrast
so brilliantly with what surrounds them. But it also creates a formida-

ble aesthetic difficulty: if certain moments within experience are presented as intensely affective, this necessarily implies that the rest of the experience is comparatively diffuse. How then can one portray that interim experience in such a way as to convey its relative lack of intensity, and yet not succumb to the imitative fallacy and produce diffuse or boring poetry, mere filler or, in the vaudevillian term, "vamping"?

To some extent Williams cannot escape this dilemma; the poem does contain deliberately flat passages which seem designed to set off the more aesthetically charged moments. But they are managed so skillfully, prolonged only to the point at which we sense their lower energy level, that they do not damage our involvement in the poem. Moreover, in his very choice of setting Williams hits on a partial solution to the problem; he is essentially a tourist in Juárez, and the tourist's attitude of mild, detached interest in a foreign place brings a certain level of aesthetic awareness to even the connective passages. But it is only when the tourist's distanced observation of the exotic gives way to the poet's sudden, intimate apprehension of the familiar that the desert music makes itself heard. The encounters that genuinely move the poet are encounters with individuals as human beings, not as specimens of native culture. The desert music arises from the discovery of a common ground of humanity that connects the poet to others despite their foreignness.

The enigmatic human form on the bridge is the first such encounter in the poem, although as I have noted it is in fact a prolepsis of the poem's final moments, as Williams and his companions return across the bridge to El Paso. But in its placement at the beginning of the poem, the body stands as an emblem of the shocking obtrusion of the human in its barest state (one is reminded of the blind beggar in Wordsworth's *Prelude*, Book v); and after his digression on poetics, which is explicitly presented as an attempt to come to terms with such a sight, to "dance" with it, Williams returns briefly to the body itself:

> —it looks too small for a man.
> A woman. Or a very shriveled old man.
> Maybe dead. They probably inspect the place
> and will cart it away later   .
>
>   Heave it into the river.
> A good thing.

(p. 275)

These utterances are not attributed to particular speakers, and so they may reflect the callousness of Williams's companions rather than his own response; but the very act of recording these words can be seen as a defensive gesture, an attempt to deflect the disturbing implications of the sight by viewing it in purely pragmatic terms. In effect the poet has not truly begun to dance with the body, because he has not yet apprehended its music fully. That apprehension does not take place until the end of the poem, after Williams has experienced Juárez in all its sordid and touching detail.

With the next lines the poem moves back in time to give a kind of narrative prelude to the walk in Juárez:

> Leaving California to return east, the fertile desert
> > (were it to get water)
> surrounded us, a music of survival, subdued, distant, half
> > heard; we were engulfed
> by it as in the early evening, seeing the wind lift
> > and drive the sand, we
> passed Yuma. All night long, heading for El Paso to
> > meet our friend,
> we slept fitfully. Thinking of Paris, I waked to the tick
> > of the rails. The
> jagged desert   .
>
> > > > (p. 275)

These long lines, with their more continuous, prosaic rhythm, nicely capture the larger time-scale represented here, as distinct from the more microscopic time of the walk. The passage establishes both the circumstances behind the visit to Juárez, and the titular trope of the desert's music, a music emanating from the landscape itself in its mixture of barrenness and fertility. Like the human form on the bridge, the desert represents life in its most minimal state, yet nonetheless *alive*; Williams may be thinking of the longevity of seeds underground in arid areas, which when given water will blossom years after they were produced. The man on the bridge is like a human counterpart to these seeds; he is, after all, "egg-shaped."

A prolegomenon to the more detailed account of the walk itself follows, resuming the polemic of the earlier passage on imitating nature:

> > > —to tell
> > what subsequently I saw and what heard
>
> > > > —to place myself (in
> > my nature) beside nature
>
> > > —to imitate
> > nature (for to copy nature would be a
> > > shameful thing)
>
> > > I lay myself down:
>
> > > > (pp. 275–76)

This last phrase is especially noteworthy, given Williams's earlier resolution "NOT, prostrate, to copy nature." If prostration is associated with passive copying rather than active imitation, why must Williams lay himself down "to imitate nature"? This can hardly be an accidental inconsistency; rather, it reflects Williams's tacit recognition that the distinction between copying and imitating on which his polemic rests is not a stable one. Copying, in the sense of taking down, transcribing, is a necessary *part* of the poetic act, though only a part; and similarly, lying down may be a necessary prelude to the more active dance of the poem. Only after Williams has passively taken in the sights and sounds of the place, "what subsequently I saw and what heard," can he proceed to dance with them, dynamizing them into poetry. We should not insist on a strict temporal progression from copying to imitation, coordinated either with the poem's internal temporality or with the process of composition; in reality copying and imitating are continuously intertwined in the poem. But in laying himself down at the outset, Williams subtly alerts us that his announced rejection of copying is polemical, not absolute.

In fact the account of the walk begins with an extended passage of "copying" or transcription, as Williams records the speech of his hosts, his wife, and himself: "The Old Market's a good place to begin: / Let's cut through here—"; "I do / my drinking on the main drag"; "What color! Isn't it / wonderful!"; "What makes Texans so tall?"; "Texas rain they call it" (pp. 276–77). I have quoted selectively to give the flavor of this transcriptive mode; whether or not Williams has verbatim recall, he captures the cadences of ordinary speech with remarkable accuracy. But full quotation is unnecessary, because the passage is not thematically weighted; indeed it can be seen as one of the poem's first "vamping" segments, marking time between the walk's more aesthetically charged moments. As I have said, however, these passages have their own interest, as casual records of unpressured speech and miscellaneous observation (there is also a brief catalog of items in an Indian's shop: "dried peppers, onions, print goods, children's / clothing"). In their relaxed, uninflected notation they establish the ground tone out of which the brighter strains of music will fitfully emerge.

The first such emergence breaks abruptly into the midst of the tourists' conversation:

> There were four
>
> I saw only two
>
> They were looking
> right at you all the time   .
>
> Penny please! Give me penny please, mister.

Don't give them anything.

                                 . instinctively
one has already drawn one's naked
wrist away from those obscene fingers
as in the mind a vague apprehension speaks
and the music rouses   .

(p. 277)

The shift to narration and a more writerly diction signals the onset of a
newly aroused state of consciousness, as the poet is suddenly made
aware of a more importunate reality than that of the shops and their
goods. The involvement of the body itself is reflected in the usurpation
of the other senses by that of touch; the young beggar has literally
taken hold of Williams. The language with which he describes his
shocked sense of violation is curiously sexual—"naked," "obscene"—as
though looking forward to another central figure in the poem, that of
the stripper. We should note the play on the word "apprehension"
here, which at first seems to mean "anxiety"; but with the line "and the
music rouses" its meaning shifts to "hearing." Through the beggar
boy's clutching hands and speech, Williams faintly apprehends the
music for the first time.

His initial reaction, however, like that of his companions, is to recoil
in disgust:

Let's get in here.
a music! cut off as
the bar door closes behind us.

(p. 277)

The exclamation mark after "music" indicates that Williams is excited
by it, even as he escapes from it with his friends into the bar. When
they return to the street, that brief exposure to the music appears to
have left its mark on him; he begins to pay increasing attention to the
people and things around him. The transcribed bits of speech ("My
feet are beginning to ache me") now alternate with flashes of description, suggesting that Williams is half-listening, half-looking:

—three half-grown girls, one of them eating a
pomegranate. Laughing.

and the serious tourist,
man and wife, middle-aged, middle-western,
their arms loaded with loot, whispering
together—still looking for bargains   .

(p. 278)

Williams has begun to awaken to the reality of the place and its inhabitants, to break out of the closed sphere of his group and their sociable conversation, and to see what is immediately before him on the streets of Juárez.

This process of awakening continues when they enter a nightclub to have a drink, and inadvertently find themselves watching an aging stripper perform:

> Do you mean it? Wow! Look at her.
> You'd have to be
> pretty drunk to get any kick out of that.
> She's no Mexican. Some worn-out trouper from
> the States. Look at those breasts
>
> (p. 279)

Whether Williams himself speaks these lines or his companions do, they are set in sharp contrast with the lyrical description that follows:

> There is a fascination
> seeing her shake
> the beaded sequins from
> a string about her hips
>
> She gyrates but it's
> not what you think,
> one does not laugh
> to watch her belly.
>
> One is moved but not
> at the dull show. The
> guitarist yawns. She
> cannot even sing. She
>
> has about her painted
> hardihood a screen
> of pretty doves which
> flutter their wings.
>
> Her cold eyes perfunc-
> torily moan but do not
> smile. Yet they bill
> and coo by grace of
> a certain candor. She
>
> is heavy on her feet.
> That's good. She

bends forward leaning
on the table of the
balding man sitting
upright, alone, so that
everything hangs for-
ward.

(pp. 279–80)

The more regular rhythm and stanza form of this passage may be intended to mirror the presence within the walk of an art-experience, of
however low a sort. But it also signals another heightening of the
poet's own aesthetic consciousness. All the tawdry details of the spectacle fascinate him; most of all, he is moved by the woman herself, her
plain reality as it reveals itself behind the show's seamy trappings. The
fact that this is a strip tease is significant, for it is precisely the experience of seeing humanity naked, in its essential poverty and ugliness,
that rouses the music for Williams. His use of the pronoun "one" here,
as in the passage describing the beggar's fingers on his wrist, does not
express detachment; on the contrary, it indicates a degree of inward-
ness so great that the self becomes universal. Like Stevens's use of
"one," Williams's "one" suggests that the poet is talking to himself
alone, and that pronouns distinguishing between persons are therefore unnecessary.

The privacy of Williams's response to the stripper is confirmed when
he is asked, "What the hell / are you grinning / to yourself about?" His
reply returns to the theme of music; but now it is difficult to tell
whether the music invoked is literal or figurative:

> The music!
> I like her. She fits
>
> the music   .

(p. 280)

Because the stripper has been accompanied by musicians, this can be
taken simply as a reference to *their* music; but the reappearance of the
exclamation mark, and the deliberate setting off of the phrase "the
music" the second time, unmistakably connects this music with the metaphorical music heard earlier. Yet it is important to distinguish between the actual music of the nightclub and the metaphorical music of
the place as a whole, because the former is clearly denigrated in the
next passage:

> Why don't these Indians get over this nauseating
> prattle about their souls and their loves and sing
> us something else for a change?

```
This place is rank
with it.   She
at least knows she's
part of another tune,
knows her customers,
has the same
opinion of them as I
have.   That gives her
one up   .   one up
following the lying
music   .
```

(p. 280)

The vulgar and sentimental music of the nightclub, with its hypocritical glorifying of love in a crassly commercial context, has nothing to do with the music that Williams hears in the presence of the stripper. As he goes on to say, she belongs to a different music:

```
There is another music. The bright-colored candy
of her nakedness lifts her unexpectedly
to partake of its tune   .

                           Andromeda of those rocks,
the virgin of her mind        .        those unearthly
greens and reds

                           in her mockery of virtue
she becomes unaccountably virtuous   .
                           though she in no
way pretends it   .

Let's get out of this.
```

(pp. 280–81)

It is this other music that the stripper, by virtue of her nakedness, arouses. Her lack of hypocrisy, her evident disdain for her audience, gives her an aura of unaccountable virtue; Williams here begins that exploration of the virgin/whore antithesis which he is to develop more fully in *Paterson* Five. It is this "candor," echoed in the "candy" of her nakedness, that moves Williams. She too is a living creature stripped to her essence, unprotected by grace or beauty.

But as he leaves the nightclub with his friends, Williams is beset by doubts as to the authenticity of his response:

```
                           In the street it hit
me in the face as we started to walk again. Or
am I merely playing the poet? Do I merely invent
it out of whole cloth? I thought   .
```

What in the form of an old whore in
a cheap Mexican joint in Juárez, her bare
can waggling crazily can be
so refreshing to me, raise to my ear
so sweet a tune, built of such slime?

(p. 281)

The intensity of his self-questioning attests to Williams's horror of solipsistic projection, his fear that the music he hears may not originate outside of himself, but in his own poetic will. But as the passage shifts back into the regular stanzas used to describe the stripper, the question becomes rhetorical, acting as a reaffirmation of the music's authenticity. Though built of slime, the music is real, emanating from the woman herself, "her bare can waggling crazily."

The four-line stanzas continue, although now they serve as more "vamping," describing with detached precision the interior and occupants of the restaurant where the group is having dinner. As the meal begins, Williams is interrogated by a member of the party (presumably one of McAlmon's brothers):

So this is William
Carlos Williams, the poet   .

Floss and I had half consumed
our quartered hearts of lettuce before
we noticed the others hadn't touched theirs   .
You seem quite normal. Can you tell me? Why
does one want to write a poem?

Because it's there to be written.

Oh. A matter of inspiration then?

Of necessity.

Oh. But what sets it off?

I am that he whose brains
are scattered
aimlessly

(p. 282)

Following hard upon Williams's own self-questioning, this interrogation, however well-intentioned, cannot help but take on a challenging tone. Pressed to define himself and his activity, Williams finds his crisis of poethood revived; at the same time he is given an opportunity to articulate his beliefs, and so to reassure himself of his own sincerity. His answer to the question "Why does one want to write a poem?" is espe-

cially revealing, though possibly intended as a parody of Hilary's comment on climbing Everest. Unlike a mountain, of course, a poem is not
literally "there" until it has been written; yet Williams's answer implies
that the poem does have a kind of preexistence, that the writing of it
merely actualizes an already latent presence. Clearly in its unrealized
state the poem is to be identified with the music the poet hears in his
surroundings, a music that exists independently of him, but that can
only be preserved and communicated through the dance of the poem.
His reply to the question "But what sets it off?" seems more frivolous,
but in fact it gives a less aesthetic version of the dance trope: "I am that
he whose brains / are scattered / aimlessly." The passive construction
is significant, since the poet's brains are implicitly scattered *by* something—presumably by whatever it is that enables him to hear the music
to which the poem is a response.

Having taken leave of his hosts and set off with Flossie back toward
the border, Williams hears the music again, as he is accosted once
more by the young beggars:

> —and so, on the naked wrist, we feel again
> those insistent fingers   .
>
>   Penny please, mister.
> Penny please. Give me penny.
>
>   Here! now go away.
>
> —but the music, the music has reawakened
> as we leave the busier parts of the street
> and come again to the bridge in the semi-dark,
> pay our fee and begin again to cross   .
> seeing the lights along the mountain back of El
> Paso and pause to watch the boys calling out
> to us to throw more coins to them standing
> in the shallow water   .   so that's
> where the incentive lay, with the annoyance
> of those surprising fingers.
>
>   (pp. 282–83)

The fact that Williams gives the boy a penny this time is significant less
as an act of generosity than as an *acknowledgment* of the boy and his humanity. Williams is no longer, under the influence of his friends,
shielding himself from the insistent pressure of the place; having been
awakened by the stripper to the music of actuality, he can now respond
to the beggars as well and their insistent demands.

The music reawakens as the couple returns to the bridge; but Williams's doubts also revive, as he addresses himself mockingly:

So you're a poet?
a good thing to be got rid of—half drunk,
a free dinner under your belt, even though you
get typhoid—and to have met people you
can at least talk to .

             relief from that changeless, endless
inescapable and insistent music .

(p. 283)

The phrase "a good thing to be got rid of" identifies the poet with the lump on the bridge ("Heave it into the river. / A good thing"). As though fleeing from the demands of poethood, Williams now turns against the music as well; he appears thankful that his social evening has provided "relief" from its insistence.

But Williams's attempt to evade both his vocation and the music that calls him to it cannot be maintained; after a digression that returns contemptuously to the sentimentality of the literal music of Mexico, the poet is once more confronted with a sight that summons up the "other music":

                        What's that?

Oh, come on.

        But what's THAT?

                   the music! the
music as when Casals struck
and held a deep cello tone
and I am speechless .

(pp. 283–84)

The emphatic repetition of the phrase "the music," heightened by the use of italics, suggests that the music's "volume" has dramatically increased. Its initial effect is to render the poet "speechless," as he passively absorbs its influx. It is perhaps significant that the musician Williams invokes to provide an analogy for the music's power over him is a Spaniard; he thus counteracts his earlier dismissal of Spanish music as insufferably sentimental. In its depth and dark timbre the cello seems an instrument especially suited to stand for the ubiquitous, elemental music rising up from the desert and its inhabitants.

Having taken this music into himself speechlessly, Williams is at last ready to "dance" with the sight before him. Once again he describes the shapeless human form on the bridge, but now he does so in a powerful and moving lyric passage that records not only the object's appearance, but his own mind's effort to comprehend its mysterious affect:

> There it sat
> in the projecting angle of the bridge flange
> as I stood aghast and looked at it—
> in the half-light: shapeless or rather returned
> to its original shape, armless, legless,
> headless, packed like the pit of a fruit into
> that obscure corner—or
> a fish to swim against the stream—or
> a child in the womb prepared to imitate life,
> warding its life against
> a birth of awful promise. The music
> guards it, a mucus, a film that surrounds it,
> a benumbing ink that stains the
> sea of our minds—to hold us off—shed
> of a shape close as it can get to no shape,
> a music! a protecting music   .
>
> (p. 284)

In form this climactic passage abandons typographical shaping in favor of a more sustained and continuous versification that approaches the blank verse of Wordsworth; clearly then the "dance" it executes is not prosodic but imaginative. It is a kind of pas de deux in which the poet keeps turning to new tropes in an attempt to touch the sight in all its pathos. Interestingly the sequence of metaphors seems to follow an evolutionary pattern, from "the pit of a fruit" to "a fish" to "a child in the womb," as though Williams were progressively recognizing the creature's humanity. In its grotequely compressed state, and in the half-light on the bridge, the object cannot be known literally; we still do not know the creature's gender, whether it is alive or dead, young or old. But it is precisely this indeterminacy that allows it to become a powerful emblem for humanity at its most basic and vulnerable, "warding its life against / a birth of awful promise."

Williams now perceives the function of the music clearly; it is a protecting film or, in a spectacular anagrammatic pun that picks up the fetal imagery, "a mucus." This account may seem puzzling, since after all the music is *heard* not by the sleeping creature, but by Williams himself. But the identification between the two has in fact become complete; it is the poet whose oceanic mind is stained by the music's "benumbing ink." The music, the apprehension of its beauty, the possibility of an aesthetic response to the world in its very ugliness, is all that protects him from mortality, holding him off from its awful promise.

Recognizing at last that the music he hears is his own creation, though a creation that necessarily begins with an outer world, Williams can embrace his poethood with renewed fervor:

> I *am* a poet! I
> am. I am. I am a poet, I reaffirmed, ashamed

(p. 284)

The last word comes as a surprise; is Williams ashamed to have ever
doubted his vocation, or is he ashamed at the vocation itself, its precarious aestheticizing of human suffering? In any case the pride that is evident in his repeated and emphatic affirmation clearly outweighs the
avowed shame. In the next lines he again enters the lyric present, closing the temporal gap between the experience of the music and the moment of composition:

> Now the music volleys through as in
> a lonely moment I hear it. Now it is all
> about me. The dance! The verb detaches itself
> seeking to become articulate   .

We cannot tell if this "now" is the time of the visit to Juárez, or the
time of the writing of the poem. That distinction collapses as the poem
comes to an end. Phenomenal experience and the act of writing are
subsumed by the dance or "verb" that the poem articulates. Both are
part of a single dynamic process, unfolding in a continuous present.
Such a dynamic conception provides the means for fusing represented
experience and the medium of representation; both partake of the
same essential *activity*, an activity that spans the boundary between life
and art (it is perhaps significant that the poem's climactic moment occurs precisely on the border between two countries). Poem and experience are joined by the dance, the incessant movement of mind with
and against world that is Williams's version of Stevens's "force that traverses a shade."

The final lines of the poem openly express the pride that was implicit in Williams's reaffirmation of his poethood:

> And I could not help thinking
> of the wonders of the brain that
> hears that music and of our
> skill sometimes to record it.

(p. 284)

Interestingly, Williams here returns to the narrative past tense, locating
this "thought" in Juárez, as the poet gazes at the shape on the bridge.
Ultimately, it would seem, differences in time and place must be respected, since only through such particulars can the music make itself
heard. His earlier polemical attack on "copying," which was already
qualified by his declaration "I lay myself down," now is undermined
completely by the use of the word "record," with its suggestion that the

poem is finally a pure transcription. The poem as a whole has been far more than a record, of course; but much of its power has come from its dense journalistic texture, the authenticating presence of countless details, trivial utterances, and the like, all of which have served both as witnesses to the reality of the poet's experience and as foils to the music itself. This music has periodically broken through the surface of the poem, at moments of intense lyricism that move away from description and towards a kind of non-mimetic "dance" of the imagination. But only by faithfully transcribing the particulars of the experience has Williams been able to record both the music of the desert and his own imaginative dance, since the apprehension of that music has depended absolutely on the poet's attention to the world around him at its homeliest.

As a walk poem, then, "The Desert Music" represents a synthesis of "the journalism of subjects" and "the cry of its occasion." Like Stevens, Williams insists on the occasionality of the poem, its continuity with the experience it records; yet unlike him he represents that experience with journalistic accuracy. Representation and the spontaneous "cry" of lyric utterance are brought into harmony through the tropes of music and dance; the music of the real calls forth the dance of the poet's imagination, and both must be recorded in the poem. Few poems so thoroughly integrate the dynamic and receptive aspects of experience, as rooted in the basic physiological dualism between sensory influx and motor discharge. What Williams sees and hears in Juárez finds its way into the poem as the stimulus and accompaniment to the poem's own movement, its dance of words and of feeling. In this way the poem overcomes the split between representation and construction that polarizes much of *Paterson*. Where Book Two of that poem alternates between direct mimesis of Mr. Paterson's walk and a kind of collage technique that emphasizes the labor of composition, "The Desert Music" achieves a more reciprocal relation between the past of the walk and the present of the poem. It thus provides the ultimate fulfillment of Williams's early definition of art as "experience dynamized into reality."[22] The music of experience and the dance of the poem run side by side, not as separate elements, as in *Paterson*, but as the two faces of a single ongoing motion through and with the world.

IV

THEODORE ROETHKE AND ELIZABETH BISHOP:

THE WALK AS REVELATION ·

FROST, STEVENS, and Williams establish the three major versions of the walk in twentieth-century American poetry. Later poets work many variations on these three paradigms, sometimes combining them in different proportions, but they do not essentially go beyond the modes of representation that their predecessors develop. For all three, as I have suggested, the primary challenge is to find a way to affirm the immanent poetic value of ordinary life without writing journalism; to reconcile, that is, the demands of canonical art with the ephemerality of immediate experience. The walk provides a basis for such an attempt, because its formal structure seems to combine the closure of art with the openness and contingency of experience.

Yet in itself the representation of the walk cannot guarantee a poem's singularity and coherence, as my discussion of the case of Clare in the Introduction was meant to demonstrate. Further transformative strategies are needed, and Frost, Stevens, and Williams each explore one such possibility to its utmost. For Frost the walk becomes a parable whose value lies in its embodiment of wisdom or insight; it is therefore primarily cognitive in function, as his proleptic "we shall see" in "The Wood-Pile" suggests. For Stevens the walk serves as an occasion for a "never-ending meditation" whose value lies not in its arrival at a final insight but in its continual movement of qualification and refinement; its function can be described as reflective, since its object is thought itself rather than revealed truth. For Williams the walk gives the poet access to a phenomenal "music" that in turn stimulates the dance of the poem; its function is in the broadest sense aesthetic, directed toward the apprehension of a beauty or pathos conceived to be immanent in the world.

Each of these three ways of conferring poetic value on the walk has its followers in subsequent American poetry. Schematically speaking, their dominance is staggered over the past forty years, passing from the cognitive in the forties and early fifties to the aesthetic in the late fifties and sixties to the meditative in the seventies and eighties. In this chapter I will discuss two representative poets of the generation immediately following Frost, Stevens, and Williams. For these poets, as for

Frost, the aim of poetry is ultimately cognitive, and lies in the achievement of an understanding that goes beyond particular circumstances, although it may have its origin in them. To be sure, such younger poets as Theodore Roethke, Elizabeth Bishop, Robert Penn Warren, and Robert Lowell were not directly influenced by Frost in the way they were by more overtly modernist poets like Eliot, Crane, and Moore. But it is Frost who provides them with the clearest paradigm for the poetic fusion of experience and wisdom. These younger poets tend to resist the openly parabolic manner of Frost's work, however, its candid assumption of the authority of its own insights. The overt didacticism of Frost's later poetry is largely alien to them. They favor a more tentative relation to experience, and so are less willing to shape and select, more open to the random and the contingent. Yet while they generally distrust abstraction, they remain committed to the Horatian criterion of universal truth as the measure of a poem's success. They must thus find subtler ways to move from anecdotal particulars to large vision. Their solution is to represent truth in the form of revelation, as a kind of emergent property of phenomena themselves. In this way they can avoid the clear-cut narrative or teleological structure that Frost imposes on his walks, while nonetheless finding in the walk a means of access to universal truth that can lift the poem above the circumstantial and validate it as canonical art.

Such a strategy requires great tact and subtlety if the poem is to convince us that its revelation is genuinely immanent in the scene, not a projection on or extrapolation from it. I cannot deal with Warren or Lowell in detail here; let me simply sketch their respective approaches to this problem. More so than the other three, Warren is willing to deal directly in abstractions. Indeed he is notorious for his use of such explicit thematic terms as Truth, Fate, Dream—terms whose weight he deliberately augments through capitalization. At the same time, he remains conscientiously faithful to the particular circumstances of place, time, event, and perception that give rise to his apprehensions of the absolute. His well-known "Sunset Walk in Thaw-Time in Vermont" presents the speaker moving from the sudden, startling appearance of a partridge rushing through the boughs of a tree to a larger sense of time rushing by into "No-Time," and finally to a reassuring awareness of generational continuity, of "an immortality in the loving vigilance of death."[1] It thus proceeds from a particular phenomenon to an openly abstract insight into the nature of human time, a trajectory that much of his poetry follows. Although many of his landscape poems invoke the walk as occasion, their epiphanic nature prevents them from assuming a genuinely walklike form; as in the greater Romantic lyric, their speakers are usually static, as they take in and ponder a vision of what Warren calls "No-Time."[2]

Where Warren freely (and at times embarrassingly) uses abstract nouns, in Lowell the thematic burden is more often carried by adjectives; hence at the end of his "At the Mouth of the Hudson," after a detailed but neutral description of an industrial scene, he allows the landscape to reveal its full meaning in the single epithet "unforgivable."[3] By contrast, Roethke (at least in his middle poetry) and Bishop concertedly avoid abstract terms, preferring to let a sense of revelation emerge directly from the concrete images they evoke. They differ markedly, of course, in the tone and manner of their revelations, the one ecstatic and visionary, the other restrained and self-conscious. For both, however, the poem's achievement of closure depends on its ability to move naturally and smoothly from the particular phenomena of the walk to a moment of pure cognition that synthesizes the data of experience, producing an effect of revealed truth.

. . . . .

For Theodore Roethke, the locus of revelation lies in what the title of one poem calls "The Minimal": "the lives on a leaf: the little / Sleepers, numb nudgers in cold dimensions."[4] He often writes a kind of microscopic nature poetry, focused not on landscapes viewed in their entire sweep, but on the tiniest objects and forms of life that he can perceive: birds, insects, worms, dust, moss. Ultimately this insistence on the value of minimal entities derives from Blake's celebration of "minute particulars," like the famous "grain of sand." But Roethke's vision is more naturalistic; unlike Blake, he believes that poetry can be made entirely from such particulars, without the machinery of myth.

As I have suggested, however, his emphasis on smallness often takes on a visionary quality which subtly alters the status of the particulars he presents. Unlike Williams, Roethke seems interested in natural objects less for their absolute particularity than for their shared *qualities*—their smallness, their lack of self-consciousness, their innocence, and so on. They tend to become examples rather than entities in their own right, and so his descriptive poetry has a curiously doubled effect; on the one hand objects are carefully named, placed before us as concrete entities, yet on the other hand they are always on the verge of disappearing into purely conceptual categories. It is by means of this ambiguous placement of his natural images between percept and concept that Roethke is able to introduce thematic concerns into a poetry that often seems to remain at the level of description.[5]

Roethke's first volume, *Open House*, contains a number of poems that make use of a walker's perspective—"The Premonition," "The Light Comes Brighter," "The Coming of the Cold," for example—but the rather stiff formality of these poems keeps them from entering deeply into the walk as a mode of experience. It is worth noting that in the last two poems mentioned, Roethke does not use the first person but refers instead to "the walker," an abstraction that is symptomatic of the slightly distant manner of these early poems. But with his second book, *The Lost Son*, Roethke emerges as an original and almost shockingly self-revealing poet, obsessed with his own childhood, both in its pure joy and its primitive sexuality. In these poems he develops a strikingly idiosyncratic voice that clearly takes its cadence from children's singsong chanting.

Such a poem is "The Waking," a lyric that gives a brief, highly colored synopsis of a walk through a field, and provides an initial example of how Roethke represents experience as incipient revelation:

> I strolled across
> An open field;
> The sun was out;
> Heat was happy.
>
> This way! This way!
> The wren's throat shimmered,
> Either to other,
> The blossoms sang.
>
> The stones sang,
> The little ones did,
> And flowers jumped
> Like small goats.
>
> A ragged fringe
> Of daisies waved;
> I wasn't alone
> In a grove of apples.
>
> Far in the wood
> A nestling sighed;
> The dew loosened
> Its morning smells.
>
> I came where the river
> Ran over stones:
> My ears knew
> An early joy.
>
> And all the waters
> Of all the streams
> Sang in my veins
> That summer day.

(*Poems*, p. 49)

The short two-beat lines, while not as regular, inevitably call to mind the rhythms of children's rhymes. But more significant is the poem's attempt to evoke a childlike sense of immanence, of a world in which all things are playfellows. It would be somewhat inaccurate, I think, to call a line like "Heat was happy" a personification; it has neither the self-consciousness of metaphor nor the mediation of a recognizably human persona. Within the consciousness of the poem it appears simply to be a statement of fact. Yet the poem is not spoken by a child; this is true not merely because we know that it was not *written* by a child, but because the last two stanzas of the poem manifest an adult self-consciousness ("My ears knew / An early joy") and a more overt use of trope ("And all the waters / Of all the streams / Sang in my veins"). Clearly, then, the speaker's childish innocence is a fiction, as in Blake's *Songs of Innocence*; the poem is a forcible attempt to recapture a lost state of mind, in which natural objects take on a literal rather than figurative personhood. To be sure, one might question the success of this effort; there is something a little disingenuous about the speaker's repeated insistence on the landscape's vocalism ("The blossoms sang. // The stones sang"). Yet if we must finally doubt the authenticity of the speaker's childlike consciousness as it is represented to us, we cannot doubt the strength of his *desire* for such a consciousness; and it is this desire that gives the poem much of its visionary intensity. The very straining of the poem toward a state of Edenic communion with the landscape—a strain made visible in its rhetorical excesses—helps to give it a felt energy, an energy of desire rather than fulfillment.

Thus although "The Waking" belongs among Roethke's least abstract poems, in its emphatic adoption of a kind of consciousness associated with childhood it moves beyond mere description, and enters into an obliquely visionary space. The title is the clearest expression of the poem's apocalyptic thrust, implying that this walking has been a waking as well, presumably into a freshened mode of consciousness. The use of the article "the" is a subtle pointer away from experience and toward a more conceptual realm, in which waking is not a particular act but a poetic figure. (Significantly, Roethke later gave the title "The Waking" to one of his most beautiful poems, a villanelle that is quite openly universal in its language.)

One moment in which the poem moves closer to explicit generalization occurs in the fourth stanza, with the lines "I wasn't alone / In a grove of apples." The introduction of a negative construction enacts the logical gesture of contrast; the significance of Roethke's walk defines itself more clearly in being set against its opposite. But simply to say "I wasn't alone" would be too general a statement for a poem attempting to deal exclusively in natural images, and so he adds the modifying clause "In a grove of apples." The relation between the two is unclear, however; is he *in* a grove of apples, but not alone there? Or is he in a field *rather* than a grove of apples, and therefore not alone, because he can see more of the life in the landscape? I would tend to favor the latter reading, but the ambiguity helps Roethke to mitigate any hint of the didactic.

The poem's last two stanzas most openly display their cognitive leanings, their effort to convert immediate experience into a totalizing knowledge of the world. The slightly odd use of the verb "know" in the lines "My ears knew / An early joy" betrays this aim, although what is "known" here is not truth but joy, ordinarily an affective state. To *know* joy, however, suggests that it is not just an affect but a condition of the world (a status confirmed by the word "early," which can be taken to mean "unfallen"); hence it is perceived not by the heart but directly through the senses. His aim here as elsewhere is wholly to fuse sense perception and a more general level of understanding, not to see them as separate phases of consciousness. The last stanza fully acknowledges the universality of the knowledge achieved, through the repetition of "all": "And all the waters / Of all the streams / Sang in my veins / That summer day." The poet's walk has brought him to a point at which he finds himself in communion not simply with a particular landscape but with a revealed totality, here represented by Roethke's favorite trope of water as the element that binds the world into a whole.

We can perhaps most clearly appreciate the poem's visionary status by considering the nature of its perceptual images. These obviously lack the kind of specificity which gives Williams's images their striking immediacy. We sense that individual images—the wren's throat, the stones, the daisies—are not important in themselves, but only as points of departure for ecstatic vision. In this they resemble the natural objects in Blake's walk poem "With happiness stretchd across the hills."[6] But where in Blake's poem the transition from seeing a thistle to seeing an old man is clearly marked (as the juncture between "single" and "double vision"), Roethke blurs the boundary between natural and supernatural vision, through the medium of a revived childhood. Thus, where in Blake's poem we see an actual thistle with the image of an old man superimposed over it, in Roethke's poem we *see* very little. How does one visualize a synesthetic line such as "The stones sang?" Clearly we are not meant to; the poem works against such a literal-minded mode of reading. It does not want to draw sharp lines between literal and figurative, real and imaginary, since it is attempting to evoke a consciousness for which such distinctions do not exist. The price it pays for this evocation is a loss of sensual immediacy, that sense of particular phenomena pressing upon the mind from outside and forcing their way into the poem that Williams conveys. In "The Waking," phenomena exist in a hazy border state, reflecting both the poem's childlike perspective and Roethke's attraction to broad categories like joy, earliness, and totality, which tend to dissolve all minute particulars. He is unwilling to engage such abstractions directly, however; as Anthony Libby writes, contrasting him with Eliot, "Roethke wants us to feel the objects in his poem as he leads us to the visionary revelations he will not always articulate, or cannot articulate, lacking Eliot's precision with abstract language."[7]

Another walk poem from the same volume, "A Field of Light," conveys a stronger sense of particularity, in part because it is a longer, less strictly contained poem, with more room for description, and in part because it is not intent on recapturing the consciousness of childhood.[8] At the same time the poem does not evade abstraction as diligently as does "The Waking"; perhaps because it dramatizes a more mature psyche, it is able to incorporate more overtly thematic statements, although these are still couched in phenomenological terms. The poem is divided into three numbered sections, of which the first is the most purely descriptive:

> Came to lakes; came to dead water,
> Ponds with moss and leaves floating,
> Planks sunk in the sand.
>
> A log turned at the touch of a foot;
> A long weed floated upward;
> An eye tilted.
>
> > Small winds made
> > A chilly noise;
> > The softest cove
> > Cried for sound.
> >
> > Reached for a grape
> > And the leaves changed;
> > A stone's shape
> > Became a clam.
> >
> > A fine rain fell
> > On fat leaves;
> > I was there alone
> > In a watery drowse.

> (*Poems*, p. 59)

Here the speaker's unself-conscious absorption in the details of his walk is reflected in the elision of the "I" up until the last two lines of the section.[9] The first six lines are a deliberately flat account of things seen, or rather seen murkily; this imagery of stagnancy and viscosity is generally associated for Roethke with the inital formless state out of which life and form emerge. Perhaps signaling a shift to a clearer kind of perception, the poem moves into the more rhythmic stanza form of "The Waking," though with little of that poem's intense lyricism. The speaker's eye begins to pick out finer details: leaves change as he reaches toward them and sees them more closely; a stone turns out to be a clam; a fine rain shows itself against the leaves. The emergence of forms seems to precipitate the emergence of the "I" as well in the last two lines: "I was there alone / In a watery drowse." These lines should be contrasted with the lines from "The Waking": "I wasn't alone / In a grove of apples." Here the speaker has not yet achieved a sense of communion with the world around him; he remains solipsistically immersed in "a watery drowse," a state of formless preconsciousness in which the boundaries between self and world are not yet clear, although the very recognition of this state seems to presage its passing.

The second section moves into a more lyrical strain that features the "I" more prominently:

> Angel within me, I asked,
> Did I ever curse the sun?
> Speak and abide.

> Under, under the sheaves,
> Under the blackened leaves,
> Behind the green viscid trellis,
> In the deep grass at the edge of a field,
> Along the low ground dry only in August, —

> Was it dust I was kissing?
> A sigh came far.
> Alone, I kissed the skin of a stone;
> Marrow-soft, danced in the sand.

The opening interrogation hints that the speaker must undergo a kind of penance for an earlier withdrawal from the natural world, a penance that may be enacted in his ritual kissing of dust and stone. A series of prepositional clauses follow the poet downward in his search for the moist ground that is the source of plant life, a recurrent image in his poetry that ultimately stems from memories of his father's commercial greenhouse. But presumably the month is now August, since in the last four lines the ground is dry and dusty; the watery, formless state of selfless communion with which the poem began is giving way to a more differentiated sense of the world. But the final line of the section once more points to a blurring of boundaries; is it the poet who is "marrow-soft," or the sand in which he dances? The placement of the epithet joins the two, exemplifying the softening of hard edges that it referentially evokes.

The final section of the poem shows the poet achieving a heightened sense of "separateness," as reflected in the proliferation of short sentences in the first six lines:

> The dirt left my hand, visitor.
> I could feel the mare's nose.
> A path went walking.
> The sun glittered on a small rapids.
> Some morning thing came, beating its wings.
> The great elm filled with birds.

> Listen, love,
> The fat lark sang in the field;
> I touched the ground, the ground warmed by the killdeer,
> The salt laughed and the stones;
> The ferns had their ways, and the pulsing lizards,
> And the new plants, still awkward in their soil,
> The lovely diminuitives.
> I could watch! I could watch!
> I saw the separateness of all things!
> My heart lifted up with the great grasses;
> The weeds believed me, and the nesting birds.
> There were clouds making a rout of shapes crossing a windbreak of
> cedars,
> And a bee shaking drops from a rain-soaked honeysuckle.
> The worms were delighted as wrens.
> And I walked, I walked through the light air;
> I moved with the morning.

The first part, with its short sentences, is a montage of particular impressions, moving between such literal statements as "The sun glittered on a small rapids" and "The great elm filled with birds," and more metaphorical expressions: "The dirt left my hand, visitor," "A path went walking." All these phrases convey a rich sense of the walker's intimate involvement in the scene. By calling the dirt a "visitor" Roethke emphasizes both its autonomy and his temporary closeness to it; and similarly in personifying the path he projects his own movement on it, suggesting that he is as much carried along by the world as walking through it. Even the apparently straightforward line "I could feel the mare's nose" assumes a certain figurative complexity if we take the speaker to mean that simply in *looking* at the mare's nose he could feel it. The second, indented part of the section moves toward a more conjunctive vision of the landscape (subtly reinforced by the appearance of an undefined "love" to whom the poem is addressed); now different objects are brought together through parallel constructions in the lines "The salt laughed and the stones; / The ferns had their ways, and the pulsing lizards." All these objects are merged in the phrase "The lovely diminutives," another version of the category of "the minimal" for which Roethke has such passion.

The poem reaches a visionary climax with the blurted lines "I could watch! I could watch! / I saw the separateness of all things!" The double exclamation is virtually a Roethke trademark, occurring in most of the sequences in this and later volumes. Here it gives a kind of ecstatic force to what is in fact a curiously guarded statement, akin to Wordsworth's "I could wish my days to be / Bound each to each in natural piety." What Roethke *sees* in this moment of vision is not "all things" but their "separateness," which like "smallness" is a quality rather than an entity. He thus introduces another purely conceptual category into the poem in the guise of a perception. The use of the word "all," as in the last stanza of "The Waking," further reveals the cognitive status of this seeing, since it is directed toward an imagined totality not immediately accessible to the senses. Like Frost, he has moved from particular impressions to a more general insight; however, Roethke's insight is not embodied in a single emblematic image, but arises instead from the very diversity of particulars that the walk has encompassed.

To call Roethke's apprehension of separateness an "insight" may seem to give undue cognitive weight to what presents itself as a purely aesthetic intuition; yet there is a tone of finality in this declaration, however modest its content may be, that seems to give it the status of a genuine revelation. In part this sense of finality may be attributed to the ambiguity of the word "saw," which can be taken to mean either "perceived" or "recognized"; in one case the seeing is merely part of the continuing process of looking at the world, in the other it is a distinct epistemological event, in which separateness is not merely perceived but *revealed* to the poet. This second meaning is confirmed by the heightening of the poem's rhetoric immediately following the line "I saw the separateness of all things!" The speaker's heart is "lifted up with the great grasses," participating more actively in the landscape; and in a curious line we are told that "The weeds believed me, and the nesting birds." This is another example of the parallel construction we saw earlier, which in fact seems to work against a sense of "separateness" by grammatically conflating different objects. More striking is the use of the verb "believed"; what does it mean for weeds and birds to believe the poet, and what precisely do they believe? Evidently he has spoken to them, but we do not know what he has said; the poem gestures toward prophetic declamation, yet the content of that declamation remains elusive.

The poem ends by turning from such separate yet assimilable things as worms and wrens to the walker himself, whose movement arcs around and gathers together all the things he sees: "And I walked, I walked through the light air; / I moved with the morning." Like "The Waking," "A Field of Light" seems poised between an awareness of the "separateness of all things" and of their mutual participation in such general categories as smallness and indeed separateness itself.[10] Roethke does not want to use the landscape as a mere springboard for abstract assertion; but at the same time he feels the need for such assertion in order to lift the poem above sensory experience. Hence he must incorporate the *grammar* of insight into his poems, even when the poem seems a mere accounting of phenomena. As Kenneth Burke writes, "the constant reverberations about the edges of [Roethke's] images give the excitement of being on the edge of Revelation."[11] This courting of a revelation that shines through the concrete details of the poem is Roethke's solution to the problem of writing in an experiential mode while still maintaining contact with the sense of a larger truth that can only be expressed abstractly.

In his late poetry, by contrast, Roethke embraces abstraction uninhibitedly. This development can be explained in part by Roethke's open imitation in his final phase of Yeats, Eliot, and Stevens.[12] All of these poets are masters of aphorism, meditation, and other abstract modes. In consciously assimilating various elements of their styles into his later poems, Roethke makes room for a more open kind of thematic statement amid his customary natural imagery. Yet he remains committed to the particulars of experience, and so continues to lodge his abstract statements within accounts of the minutiae of time and place.

"A Walk in Late Summer," which appears in Roethke's penultimate volume, *Words for the Wind*, exhibits the aphoristic style the poet cultivated toward the end of his career, a style in which all his accumulated wisdom is compressed into a barrage of brief gnomic phrases. As the title indicates, however, the poem is rooted in the experience of a walk, and while this walk is not narrated as directly as the walk of "A Field of Light," it nevertheless provides the occasion and imagery for the poet's meditation on being and time. Here is the first section:

> A gull rides on the ripples of a dream,
> White upon white, slow-settling on a stone;
> Across my lawn the soft-backed creatures come;
> In the weak light they wander, each alone.

> Bring me the meek, for I would know their ways;
> I am a connoisseur of midnight eyes.
> The small! The small! I hear them singing clear
> On the long banks, in the soft summer air.
>
> (*Poems*, p. 143)

The poem quickly shifts from the gull, a specific creature, to categorical terms like "the soft-backed creatures," "the meek," and, predictably, "the small." The repeated exclamation again reinforces the word's visionary status; its referent remains unspecified beyond the pronoun "them." The catalogs of natural objects that gave a kind of referential solidity to the more general terms in "The Waking" and "A Field of Light" are dispensed with here; the poet moves immediately to the level of abstracted quality, indicating his new willingness to deal directly in conceptual language.

In the second section he enters decisively into a Yeatsian philosophical mode:

> What is there for the soul to understand?
> The slack face of the dismal pure inane?
> The wind dies down; my will dies with the wind,
> God's in that stone, or I am not a man!
> Body and soul transcend appearances
> Before the caving-in of all that is;
> I'm dying piecemeal, fervent in decay;
> My moments linger—that's eternity.

Although its language seems to leave the landscape behind, the passage in fact asserts the absolute dependence of understanding on the immediate conditions of time and place. "The dismal pure inane" is the realm of philosophical speculation untethered to concrete reality; against such a mode of thought, Roethke insists that the will is always informed by the wind. The dangers of this aphoristic manner become apparent with his bathetic declaration "God's in that stone, or I am not a man!"—a line that attempts to yoke the absolute and the particular too baldly. The section ends with a more persuasive assertion of the identity of the transient and the eternal, now framed in experiential rather than pantheistic terms.

The third section opens with another natural image: "A late rose ravages the casual eye, / A blaze of being on a central stem." I want to call particular attention to the odd use of the word "central" here; Roethke's strategy throughout the poem is to make the particulars of experience central rather than eccentric, agents of revelation rather than accidents of nature. Such an enterprise has its reward, since it allows the poet to find in the materials of experience tokens of universal truth. But in so doing he sacrifices precisely that quality of eccentricity, of randomness and excess, that gives richness and density to poetic representations of experience.

From the image of the rose he turns again to the theme of transience, ending with another image: "That dove's elaborate way of coming near / Reminds me I am dying with the year." Here the relation between the perceived object and the thought of which it "reminds" the poet is not at all clear; thought and perception seem to be juxtaposed rather than continuously joined. More explicitly than in his earlier poetry, natural imagery here serves Roethke as a pretext for meditation; yet at times we feel that the images are secondary, not essential to the thoughts they supposedly prompt.

The last section juxtaposes another image, that of a tree, with a final statement of the poet's temporal concerns:

> A tree arises on a central plain—
> It is no trick of change or chance of light.
> A tree all out of shape from wind and rain,
> A tree thinned by the wind obscures my sight.
> The long day dies; I walked the woods alone;
> Beyond the ridge two wood thrush sing as one.
> Being delights in being, and in time.
> The evening wraps me, steady as a flame.

Once more the word "central" carries the tree from the realm of experience to a more visionary dimension, in which the tree participates in a revelation of being and time. But again the tree's relationship to this revelation remains obscure; it does not become a transparent allegorical emblem (although clearly its windswept nature reflects the poet's sense of his own erosion by time). Like so many of Roethke's images, the tree is neither wholly symbolic nor wholly literal; the poet's insistence that "It is no trick of change or chance of light" seems to deny that the tree is an accident of nature or a mere phenomenon, but its revelatory quality remains at the level of, in Kenneth Burke's term, "reverberation." More apparent is the relation between the two wood thrush and the poem's concluding formulation, which takes us to new, Heideggerian heights of generality: "Being delights in being, and in time." Here Roethke's effort to distill philosophical truth from experience reaches its farthest limit; the aphorism represents a kind of ultimate statement which in its very abstraction threatens to implode into tautology. But the notion of delight keeps the line in touch with experience, since it is through the beauty of the beings around him that Roethke is reconciled with time and its effects on him. From this metaphysical height, the poem descends to its lovely closing line, which succeeds in gently combining theme and occasion: "The evening wraps me, steady as a flame." The image of the flame and its steadiness beautifully captures the notion of stability within transience expressed more abstractly in the line "My moments linger—that's eternity." Here at last experience and truth seem to be of a piece, not heterogenous elements laid side by side.

As compared to "The Waking" and "A Field of Light," "A Walk in Late Summer" contains remarkably little description, and what images it offers—the gull, the stone, the rose, the dove, the tree—all primarily serve as preludes to abstract thought. In such a poem the title takes on a special importance; as in "An Ordinary Evening in New Haven," it names the experiential context within which the poem's meditation must be understood, obviating the need for full internal representation.[13] Hence Roethke selects only a few details from his walk, placing them in such a way that they seem to conduct him to larger understandings. In "The Waking" and "A Field of Light," natural images hover on the edge of abstraction, but the general terms they imply are for the most part kept out of the poem. But with the didactic freedom of his later years, Roethke is able to link image and abstraction more explicitly. As a result, however, a poem like "A Walk in Late Summer" loses much of the volatile sense of a revelation immanent in the phenomenal world that the earlier poems convey. Now the poem can move freely between particulars and assertions of universal truth, and so the mode of understanding is less contingent on perception, more openly philosophical.

That sense of revelation returns in some of Roethke's very late poems, particularly the beautiful "North American Sequence," which takes up again the freer, more descriptive mode of "A Field of Light," though with a new meditative inflection. I quote a passage from the end of "The Far Field," the penultimate poem of the sequence:

> All finite things reveal infinitude:
> The mountain with its singular bright shade
> Like the blue shine on freshly frozen snow,
> The after-light upon ice-burdened pines;
> Odor of basswood on a mountain-slope,
> A scent beloved of bees;
> Silence of water upon a sunken tree:
> The pure serene of memory in one man,—
> A ripple widening from a single stone
> Winding around the waters of the world.
>
> (*Poems*, p. 195)

This simple catalog resonantly captures the fragile sense of infinitude, of a universal whole, that Roethke finds revealed in finite things. The last two lines remind us of the similarly totalizing allusion to "All the waters / Of all the world" in "The Waking." "A Far Field" is not a true walk poem, however; it does not represent experience and movement with the directness and specificity that characterize the genre. Roethke's stance in his very late poems tends to be more static and contemplative; he is not "mov[ing] with the morning," but is rather the still point around which all else moves. But in passages such as this one, his early faith that the minutest of particulars may reveal the universal finds a last expression. The difference between this passage and similar ones from earlier poems lies in the greater propositional directness of the line "All finite things reveal infinitude"; in effect by *announcing* the revelation, he no longer has to enact it verbally, through trope or through subtle conjunctions of the particular and the categorical. The poem's serenity is thus purchased at the price of the visionary energy that allows Roethke's earlier poems to vibrate on the borderline between perception and revelation.

. . . . .

Elizabeth Bishop approaches the representation of experience in a completely different way, although like Roethke she ultimately seeks a manifestation of what can only be called truth. She is famous for her cool, detached observation of fine details, her sad restraint, her lack of stridency. Unlike Warren and the later Roethke, she seems consciously to avoid the large terms of philosophical discourse, concentrating instead on the small-scale lyricism of place and appearance. Yet as most of her critics have pointed out, she is far more than a descriptive poet; her careful renderings of places and objects, which often seem miraculous in their precision, are invariably informed by a coherent and profound sense of what it means to live in a world that, in Stevens's great phrase, "is not our own and, much more, not ourselves" (*Palm*, p. 210). Revelation seems an overly emphatic term to apply to her quiet poetry; yet in her discreet way, Bishop is as concerned as other poets of her generation with the possibilities of human knowledge or vision.[14] For her as for Warren, Roethke, Lowell, and others, however, knowledge can only be had through direct experience of the world. More so than her male contemporaries, Bishop avoids overt moralizing or abstract proclamations, instead allowing her synthesizing vision to emerge silently from her minute observations. In her poetry the effort to fuse truth and experience, a project central to her generation as a whole, attains its purest realization.

"The End of March," which appears in her final volume *Geography III*, is Bishop's only true walk poem, although a number of her other poems bear a family resemblance to the genre, in particular "At the Fishhouses" and "The Moose." "The End of March" has a complete ease of manner, however, that goes beyond the poet's earlier relaxations of style. Its leisurely, incremental movement, its hesitant and scrupulously self-correcting attention to the landscape, and above all its lack of an obvious thematic center, some single highlighted image or event like Frost's wood-pile or her own moose, mark it as an unusually pure instance of the walk poem. Like other poems by Bishop, "The End of March" is capable of accommodating a higher degree of randomness, of the merely given material of experience in all its diversity and apparent inconsequentiality, than are poems by her immediate predecessors and contemporaries. Yet I want to argue that Bishop ultimately does seek the kind of thematic closure those poets bring to their works. By avoiding any explicit articulation of the truth that emerges from her walk, Bishop evades the tendentiousness that a poet like Warren at times displays; yet for all its matter-of-factness, its seeming insistence on presenting nothing more than the experience itself, "The End of March" is finally a teaching poem, instructing us in how to live and what to do.

As I have noted, the poem's style is unusually free for Bishop, who is sometimes, though rather inaccurately, viewed as a formalist. In this respect it differs from "The Moose," another poem about traveling through a landscape, but one which has a regular stanza and rhyme pattern. We might speculate, perhaps frivolously, that this difference has to do with the different modes of transportation in the two poems; "The Moose" is about a bus ride, a more contained, mediated form of locomotion, whereas "The End of March" has a loose, variable line that better captures the meandering rhythm of the walk. Beyond its prosodic openness, the poem displays a remarkable syntactic fluidity, creating the effect of a moment-by-moment unfolding that seems to follow the temporality of the walk itself with uncanny precision. It is worth noting that like all Bishop's poems, and unlike Roethke's or Warren's (but like Williams's), "The End of March" does not capitalize the first letter of each line—a small detail perhaps, but one that contributes to the dominant effect of fluidity.

The poem is divided into four uneven stanzas or verse paragraphs that block out the major movements of the walk. The first establishes the setting, climate, and emotional landscape that the poem will explore:

> It was cold and windy, scarcely the day
> to take a walk on that long beach.
> Everything was withdrawn as far as possible,
> indrawn: the tide far out, the ocean shrunken,
> seabirds in ones or twos.
> The rackety, icy, offshore wind

numbed our faces on one side;
disrupted the formation
of a lone flight of Canada geese;
and blew back the low, inaudible rollers
in upright, steely mist.[15]

Bishop's writing here is so effortless that one can easily overlook its mimetic mastery. With enormous skill and subtlety she combines a sense of an almost ontological withdrawal of entities into themselves with a precise accounting of particulars. The journalistic observation with which the poem opens—"It was cold and windy"—is in a sense the most important fact in the poem, governing all that follows and posing the essential problem that Bishop tries to solve: how can one take a walk when it is "scarcely the day / to take a walk"? How, that is, can one find aesthetic rewards in a hostile environment? More pertinently, how does one make a poem from an experience of cold and isolation?

The disruptive powers of this cold wind are made altogether palpable to us in this first section. One effect of the harsh weather is to force things and people deeper into themselves, in a kind of huddling movement: "Everything was withdrawn as far as possible, / indrawn." The substitution of "indrawn" for "withdrawn," almost as an afterthought, is the first of many such moments in the poem, and epitomizes its rhythm of tentative characterization and refinement. Again and again Bishop corrects or modifies her initial wording, as though feeling her way in the poem itself toward greater precision.[16] In this respect the poem has something in common with the self-qualifying style of "An Ordinary Evening in New Haven," although Bishop translates Stevens's richly figurative apposition into the homelier form of parenthetical speculation and belated epithets. Moreover, where Stevens's refinements take place at a highly conceptual level, Bishop remains wholly caught up with the empirical data of the walk, on the surface at least. In this case her replacement of "withdrawn" by "indrawn," substituting a more unusual word for an ordinary one, shifts us to a different perspective; we now identify with the entity drawing into itself rather than with the observer from whom it withdraws, and as a result the movement becomes a psychological rather than merely physical one.

Implicitly, then, the speaker is herself "indrawn," a fact confirmed when we consider the curious absence from the poem of any mention of her companions on the walk, presumably the two men named in the dedication, John Malcolm Brinnin and Bill Read. We only know that Bishop is not alone because she uses the first person plural: "numbed *our* faces." Yet clearly she *is* essentially alone, in part for the simple reason that no conversation is possible above the "rackety" wind. More profoundly, the harshness of the cold has the effect of isolating anyone exposed to it, as Bishop deftly suggests through the image of "seabirds in ones or twos." (This last image may also imply that the two men form a couple, leaving Bishop as the odd one out.) This strain of imagery is continued when we learn that the wind "disrupted the formation / of a lone flight of Canada geese"; again we can hardly avoid identifying this disrupted group with the walkers on the beach.

If the wind is a force that separates individuals and pushes them into themselves, it also causes the world itself to recede. There is, it seems, an "upright, steely mist" between the walkers and the landscape; the tide is "far out," the ocean itself "shrunken." The traditional source of sublimity has in effect dried up, rendering even more problematic the effort to find or make a poem here. (One might contrast this situation with that of Emily Dickinson's poem "I started Early — Took my Dog," in which the sea is depicted as a voracious lover, pursuing the speaker as she walks; it is only when she reaches a "Solid Town" that "The Sea withdrew."[17] Here of course the sea is withdrawn from the start, and so the possibility of such an intimate encounter is denied.)

In the second section or verse paragraph, however, sharp details begin to emerge from this recessive landscape, and the poet's sense of absence or withdrawal gives way to a kind of frustrated interest in the enigmatic particulars she encounters:

> The sky was darker than the water
> —*it* was the color of mutton-fat jade.
> Along the wet sand, in rubber boots, we followed
> a track of big dog-prints (so big
> they were more like lion-prints). Then we came on
> lengths and lengths, endless, of wet white string,
> looping up to the tide-line, down to the water,
> over and over. Finally they did end:
> a thick white snarl, man-size, awash,
> rising on every wave, a sodden ghost,
> falling back, sodden, giving up the ghost. . . .
> A kite string?—But no kite.

In this section we are given a fuller representation of the sequential movement of the walk; one observation is followed by another, and the very language of the passage embodies the temporal process of perception, approach and conjecture. The strange tone of the section is set by the opening lines: the fact that the sky is "darker than the water" suggests that things are somehow topsy-turvy, while the reference to the color of "mutton-fat jade" introduces a wildly incongruous image with vaguely unpleasant associations. Also strange is the ambiguity of "*it*" in the second line; we cannot tell with any certainty whether it refers to the sky or the sea. Indeed the italicizing, which is presumably meant to be helpful, actually *creates* the ambiguity, since without it we would naturally read "it" as referring to the sky, the subject of the preceding sentence; but the italics may be telling us to take the nearest noun as antecedent, which would be "water." This small difficulty, in itself perhaps inconsequential, adds to the dominant effect of opacity in this section, forcing us to stare at a simple word with all the bewilderment Bishop brings to the string on the beach.[18]

What initially characterizes both of the phenomena Bishop attends to in this section is their hyperbolic dimension; the dog-prints are "so big" they are "more like lion-prints" (another parenthetical refinement), and the string is "endless." Their very size and length, then, lends the prints and the string a surreal quality. They share other features as well: both are linear, leading the poet along the beach in a kind of mad quest; and both ultimately point to absences, the absent dog (or lion) and the absent kite. At this point it is difficult to avoid seeing Bishop in the role of a detective, following footprints, searching for clues, forming theories. And indeed like all detectives she eventually discovers a corpse: "a thick white snarl, man-size, awash." The eerie description of the snarl's movement in the water reinforces its resemblance to a dead body, while offering another brilliant instance of Bishop's mastery of repetition: "rising on every wave, a sodden ghost, / falling back, sodden, giving up the ghost." The image captures the ineffable sense of menace that invests the landscape, as though its reticence and opacity must inevitably lead to death.[19]

The third section strengthens the questlike nature of this walk by specifying its intended goal—a goal, however, that is never reached:

> I wanted to get as far as my proto-dream-house,
> my crypto-dream-house, that crooked box
> set up on pilings, shingled green,
> a sort of artichoke of a house, but greener
> (boiled with bicarbonate of soda?),
> protected from spring tides by a palisade
> of—are they railroad ties?
> (Many things about this place are dubious.)
> I'd like to retire there and do *nothing*,
> or nothing much, forever, in two bare rooms:
> look through binoculars, read boring books,
> old, long, long books, and write down useless notes,
> talk to myself, and, foggy days,
> watch the droplets slipping, heavy with light.
> At night, a *grog à l'américaine.*

I'd blaze it with a kitchen match
and lovely diaphanous blue flame
would waver, doubled in the window.
There must be a stove; there *is* a chimney,
askew, but braced with wires,
and electricity, possibly
—at least, at the back another wire
limply leashes the whole affair
to something off behind the dunes.
A light to read by—perfect! But—impossible.
And that day the wind was much too cold
even to get that far,
and of course the house was boarded up.

This haunting vision of literal withdrawal or retirement lies at the heart of the poem, and is clearly crucial to the walk's larger significance. Why is Bishop so attracted to this tiny, dilapidated house? In part the answer is simple: the house offers shelter from the cold wind. Even if the walkers cannot actually enter it, it serves as an emblem of protection, of warmth and quiet; hence Bishop's imagination leans toward it with almost bodily hunger. Less literally, of course, the house epitomizes the kind of withdrawal or "indrawal" evoked in the first section, a retreat from the violence of the outer world into a solipsistic space of pure reflection.

The section opens with what is perhaps the poem's most striking instance of self-correction, as Bishop substitutes the phrase "crypto-dream-house" for her initial "proto-dream-house." Like her replacement of "withdrawn" with "indrawn" in the first section, this doubling may at first appear to be an unnecessary redundancy, something any competent writer would delete; after all, if "crypto" is more accurate than "proto," why include both? Such a criticism misses the point entirely, of course, since what Bishop is interested in recording is precisely the movement of consciousness from one word to the other, a kind of mental analogue to the movement of walking. "Proto-dream-house" suggests an archetype or original, as though this house were the model for all the houses in Bishop's dreams. This is plausible in itself, but it fails to address the most salient feature of the house: its strangeness, its "dubiousness." "Crypto" moves us from the ideal or the archetypal to the enigmatic, and connects the house to those other puzzle pieces, the footprints and the string. Indeed this series of mysterious objects has something of the quality of a cryptogram or rebus, a kind of indecipherable picture writing. Bishop's playful questions about the house—"boiled with bicarbonate of soda?", "are they railroad ties?"—add to its cryptic nature; and as though acknowledging her own inability to give us positive information, she adds parenthetically that "Many things about this place are dubious."

In considering the phrase "crypto-dream-house," however, we must not overlook the hint that the house may be itself a crypt, thus taking us back to the string-corpse and the deathliness of the landscape.[20] The extraordinary fantasy of life in the house that follows does indeed seem a kind of death-in-life: "I'd like to retire there and do *nothing*." A purer expression of the death-drive could hardly be imagined. As though reacting against so total a nothingness, Bishop again corrects herself: "Or nothing much, forever, in two bare rooms." The insistence on *two* rooms preserves a certain minimal life instinct, since it makes possible movement and change. At the same time it introduces the obsessive imagery of doubleness that pervades this vision, a kind of objectified version of the verbal doublings we have already noted. The reference to binoculars continues the binary imagery, which reaches a climax in the image of the "diaphanous blue flame" that wavers, "doubled in the window." (We should also recall that Bishop has described this place as "dubious," a word etymologically connected to "double.") The image of the flame reflected in the window suggests that the doublings in the house all are forms of reflection, and that finally it is the house's inhabitant who is doubled by her own self-reflexive communication; she writes "useless notes" that only she will read, and talks to herself, reminding us that a solipsist always has two selves: the self who speaks and the self who listens.

In effect, then, Bishop is toying with the dream of being sealed into her own discourse; note that the books must be "boring," since otherwise they would establish a rival discourse. As it is they merely provide a kind of neutral material to be woven into her own text (compare the protagonist of Bishop's story "In Prison," who asks to be given "one very dull book to read, the duller the better," so that he "shall be able to experience with a free conscience the pleasure . . . of interpreting it not at all according to its own intent").[21] Such a sealing up is indeed cryptlike, and just as it shuts the self in, it shuts external reality out. Bishop's distance from the outside world is indicated by her need for binoculars, as well as by the fact that in looking at the window she sees only the droplets on the pane or the reflection of her flaming drink. Her motives for renouncing the world outside the house are plain, of course, as indicated in the opening line of the poem: "It was cold and windy." What starts as an instinctive withdrawal from her companions and from the weather becomes, in this fantasy, a full-fledged retreat into absolute isolation. (It is surely significant that Bishop compares the house to an artichoke, a vegetable whose armor of prickly leaves protects its soft center—a rather Moore-like image of self-fortification.) Such a retreat may be necessary to avoid the fate of the "sodden ghost," brutalized by the elements; but at the same time it produces its own kind of death, an entombment within the self.

Bishop's more practical concerns with stove, chimney, and electricity move her out of the fantasy and back to the present moment, in which she is forced to acknowledge the impossibility of her dream: "A light to read by—perfect! But—impossible." The life she envisions in the house is impossible not merely for practical reasons, but because so complete a withdrawal can occur only in death. Like the house, limply leashed "to something off behind the dunes," one is always connected to the world merely in existing; its cold wind can never be fully shut out. As Heidegger says in a passage I have quoted in my introduction, "its [Dasein's] primary kind of Being is such that it is always 'outside' alongside entities which it encounters and which belong to a world already discovered." Outsideness in this poem thus stands for our ineluctable placement in the world, and the impossibility of detaching ourselves from it. The last lines of the section surprise us by revealing that Bishop has not in fact even reached the house, that her description of it has been based on memory. Ironically it is the wind that keeps her from getting that far; in effect the wind's very power prohibits her finding shelter from it. The fact that the house is boarded up tells us that it is not a fit habitation, and by extension that the life Bishop has imagined there cannot be lived.

The fourth and final section returns us to the actual landscape, still cold and inhospitable, yet now less intractable to the imagination:

> On the way back our faces froze on the other side.
> The sun came out for just a minute.
> For just a minute, set in their bezels of sand,
> the drab, damp, scattered stones
> were multi-colored,
> and all those high enough threw out long shadows,
> individual shadows, then pulled them in again.
> They could have been teasing the lion sun,
> except that now he was behind them
> —a sun who'd walked the beach the last low tide,
> making those big, majestic paw-prints,
> who perhaps had batted a kite out of the sky to play with.

There is a satisfying and very Bishop-like symmetry in the freezing of the other side of their faces, emphasizing also the completion of the walk's circuit. ("The End of March" is a rare example of a walk poem that includes both the movement out and the movement back, thus framing the experience with special fullness.) The frustration of the thwarted quest for the artichoke-house is offset by an unexpected moment of radiance: "The sun came out for just a minute." Though tonelessly stated, this line in fact opens the possibility, heretofore denied, that the world can offer pleasure as well as pain. The brevity of this gift is emphasized by the repetition of the phrase "for just a minute"; unlike the enclosed, protected warmth of the house, this sunlight does not last "forever." Temporality, with its fluctuation, its transience, is a condition of life outside the house. Only in time can the gifts of the world be received, and then they can only be held for a minute.

Unlike the self-reflective flame of the poet's isolated ego, however, the sun's light reaches beyond itself, touching and transforming the entire landscape. The previously "drab" stones become "multi-colored" in the sun, revealing a diversity that had been hidden by the "steely mist" of the weather. The beautiful, resonant image of the stones throwing out and pulling in their shadows is both an accurately rendered observation and an unmistakable emblem for the poet's own act of mind in the poem; one could say that she too has thrown out a shadow in the form of her narcissistic fantasy, then pulled it in again in returning to the external world. A final example of self-revision comes with the sequence "long shadows, / individual shadows"; she might easily have written "long, individual shadows," but this would have lost both the effect of temporal process and the special emphasis on "individual," which is featured as a more difficult yet more precise term, and one that strengthens the relation between the stone's shadow and the individual's subjectivity casting itself upon the world. The image does not become an explicit trope, however, and it is a large part of Bishop's genius that she is able to imply so much without sacrificing the physical reality of the objects she describes.

In the last lines of the poem, Bishop does turn to overt trope, as her imagination finally works on her surroundings with spectacular results. It is instructive to note how discreetly she introduces the image of the lion sun by way of the stones' shadows, which she imagines as "teasing" the sun; although with characteristic scrupulosity she is forced to add that the sun is in fact *behind* them, and so cannot be the target of the shadows. Having entered the poem, however, the lion becomes the agent of closure, unifying all the scattered details that had previously seemed intransigently opaque. Harold Bloom has suggested, I think rightly, that this lion is to be associated with the lion of Juda in "An Ordinary Evening in New Haven."[22] That lion, we recall, must be transplanted to New Haven before he can participate fully in reality; only then will "the great cat stand potent in the sun." Bishop's cat *is* the sun, of course, and so necessarily an aspect of reality. Indeed, we can see her lion as fully exemplifying the kind of fiction making that Stevens's lion only symbolizes, a fiction making that begins with the poet's immediate surroundings. As opposed to the reflexive, isolated imagination locked in the house, endlessly reading and writing itself into dull books and useless notes, the lion represents the fertile interaction of imagination and reality, mind and world. It is just this mode of imaginative activity at which Bishop herself excels: the troping of given, factual matter into more humanly potent forms.

The walk thus comes to represent the very process of reimagining the world that lies at the heart of Bishop's poetics. Only *in* the world, exposed to its cold wind, seeing the enigmatic and sinister things it contains, can the mind find the material it needs to shape into poems. Shut off from the world, drawn into the self, no true creation is possible, only reflection. Bishop is under no illusions about the status of her fiction of the lion; it is a playful, highly self-conscious fabulation that does not pretend for a moment to be anything more.[23] Yet as a gesture, the projection of the lion is a way of regaining the world, a world that had itself withdrawn from the poet. Suddenly the baffling and deathly objects on the beach are domesticated, drawn into the fiction, made cheerful: it was the lion sun who made the "big, majestic pawprints, / who perhaps had batted a kite out of the sky to play with." (This doesn't explain what happened to the kite; presumably he ate it.) The trope provides a bridge between the poet's mind and the landscape, which had become estranged from each other through the alienating force of the cold wind.

At this point I must confess that when I first read "The End of March" many years ago, I found the ending vaguely repellent. It seemed to me too easy a gesture, too neat a tying up of the poem's threads (or strings); I felt that Bishop had broken faith with the very intransigence of the reality that the poem had so powerfully evoked, its *refusal* to be transformed or interpreted. Such a reaction is, I think, invited by the poem; but it now seems clear to me that the poem is larger, and can easily assimilate this kind of response into its own design. This lion does not have the half-phenomenal, half-visionary status of an image in a poem by Roethke, nor is he a parabolic emblem like Frost's wood-pile. Rather, what the lion reveals is simply the power that made him, the power of Bishop herself to assemble the fragments of experience into a fictive whole. Instead of withdrawing from the world, refusing to confront its cryptic surface, Bishop discovers the possibility of a kind of self-conscious fiction making that plays at explanation without really claiming to explain anything. It is in this marginal space, where brute reality and a playful, unassuming species of imagination come into contact (an area that perhaps has a topological affinity with the marginal space of the beach itself), that Bishop finally locates herself and her poetry.

"The End of March" is thus about the same broad issues explored by Stevens in "An Ordinary Evening in New Haven," yet Bishop's is not at all a meditative poem. Terms like "reality" and "imagination" never appear; she confines herself to a strict accounting of things seen and things imagined, one that never enters the realm of allegory.[24] One of the most striking characteristics of Bishop's poetry is its ability to suggest a kind of wisdom without resorting to aphorism or other kinds of abstract statement. As Harold Bloom has written, "[Bishop's] strength is cognitive, even analytical, and surpasses philosophy and psychoanalysis in its power to expose human truth."[25] The human truth exposed in "The End of March" has to do with our necessary placement in the world, and with the minimal yet finally redemptive ways in which we can imaginatively transform that world. This truth emerges most forcefully in the poem's closing lines, with the entrance of the lion sun, and his masterful assimilation of the incongruous items on the beach. The poem's ending thus takes on something of the impact of a genuine revelation, despite the lion's patently fictive status. What is revealed in the poem's closing lines is simply the poet's own fiction-making capacity, her ability to construct a trope that can unite and make sense of the objects on the beach.

Revelation thus becomes an intensely self-conscious affair in Bishop's hands, deeply aware of its own fragility and factitiousness; yet it is important to recognize that revelation *remains* a central element in her poetics. "The End of March"'s emphatic closing, with its pseudo-visionary manifestation, is a wry, slightly ironic, but ultimately earnest gesture that confronts the problem of making experience into poetry in essentially the way that Frost and Roethke do: by forcing experience to yield up truth. Bishop's walk in "The End of March" justifies its perpetuation as a poem because it *teaches* us, not in any narrow sense, but in the sense Frost intends when he speaks of a poem as a "clarification of life." Both clarification and revelation presume an ability to see *through* experience, into an order that remains beyond the flux of private perception and consciousness. Bishop's accomplishment, I think a great one, is to absorb into her poetry as much of the randomness, the opacity, the sheer intransigent reality of experience as possible without renouncing her hold on the truth beyond it. Poets like Roethke and Warren to varying degrees subordinate the record of their own experience to the more abstract insights they offer; but in Bishop the sense of lived experience remains primary. A poem like "The End of March" is so moving because the very modesty of its revelation seems a mark of its authenticity. She does not pretend to read the runes of nature, to achieve an insight into the ultimate nature of Being and Time; all she can offer us is a portent of the mind's own capacity, feeble and inconsequential as it may be, to reimagine the world in a more playful, responsive guise.

V

FRANK O'HARA AND GARY SNYDER:

THE WALK AS SAMPLE

FOR ALL ITS awareness of the world's opacity, Bishop's poetry continues to engage truth as a canonical criterion. A number of poets of the generation succeeding hers appear to abandon this criterion altogether; in what seems a radical departure from traditional notions of poetic value, they purify their poetry of all overtly thematic aspirations, confining themselves to the recording of experience entirely for its own sake. They thus deliberately invite questions about the status of their work: most obviously, is it poetry? Why should we read or, more importantly, reread a poem that offers us no wisdom, no large extrapolation from the contingencies of experience? How can such poems establish their own poetic standing?

Frank O'Hara and Gary Snyder are two of the most important practitioners of what might be called, following Robert Pinsky, a "nominalist" poetry.[1] Pinsky uses the term to designate the distrust of abstraction, and the accompanying belief that only particulars matter, that characterizes much American poetry of the later fifties and sixties; he sets it against more openly discursive kinds of poetry, in which ideas and concepts are forthrightly engaged (his own allegiance clearly being with this latter mode). For Pinsky the difficulty with a nominalist position is that it leads ultimately to silence, since, as he puts it, "every word is an abstraction or category, not a particular" (p. 5). But while Pinsky is surely right to claim that language is always in its essence an abstraction from the particulars of reality, the absoluteness of his position to some extent prevents him from recognizing distinctions in *degrees* of abstraction within language. Ultimately an awareness of such incremental distinctions is what governs the stylistic practice of poets like O'Hara and Snyder, not a naive faith in the ability of language to reproduce reality exactly.

At the same time it would be wrong to suggest that O'Hara and Snyder never write about ideas or abstractions; O'Hara has a poem called "Ode on Causality," for example, and Snyder regularly introduces concepts from Eastern philosophy into his poems. Their poetry explores a range of possible relationships to the utterly particular fabric of the world, and while both always maintain a strong connection with their own experience, their work varies considerably in the level of abstraction that it allows itself. But in many poems both poets go further toward a direct transcription of the world in its phenomenal aspect than have previous twentieth century poets (including Williams, with whom both have obvious affinities). Both O'Hara and Snyder frequently write about their walks, but they do so with a casualness, a lack of evident formal or thematic ambition, that places their walk poems at an extreme point on the representational continuum. They neither organize their walks around moments of revelation, nor take them as occasions for abstract reflection or rumination; instead they simply set down the facts of their experience as directly as possible, with little rhetorical adornment. They thus assert a more intimate identity between poetry and experience than have prior poets; implicitly, they seem to claim that the aesthetic value of their poems inheres wholly in the experiential occasions they record, that the poems are valuable because the walks themselves are valuable. In a rare moment of definitional candor, O'Hara writes that "Poetry is experience, often peculiar to the poet," an innocent-sounding but genuinely radical statement insofar as it asserts not just a connection but an *identity* between the two realms.[2]

Such an attitude, as we have seen already with Wordsworth and Clare, courts the diffusion of poetic value, since potentially *all* experience may be translated into poetry, and so no single poem can claim to be uniquely valuable. In considering O'Hara and Snyder, I want especially to inquire into the ways they succeed in surmounting this problem. How do they make each poem a unique artifact? And to what extent do their successful poems belie the notion that they are simply transcriptions, whose meaning and value stem entirely from what has been transcribed? The very unevenness of their work, perhaps inevitable given the radical nature of their aesthetic assumptions, allows us to measure the difference between their most "successful" poems (by which I mean those whose place in the canon has been established through anthologizing, commentary, and other institutional practices, unreliable though they may be), and poems that seem to succumb to the ephemerality of their occasions.

· · · · ·

In many ways, of course, Frank O'Hara and Gary Snyder are markedly different poets. Tone, imagery, range of allusion, and above all setting distinguish them decisively from each other; yet these differences all derive from differences in their subject matter, not in their poetic practice. O'Hara is the quintessential New York poet, and everything he writes is bathed in the ambience of Manhattan, not just its landscape and its inhabitants but its tone, its rhythm, its cultural density and diversity. Snyder, on the other hand, is a poet of, as he titles one volume, *The Back Country*, be it the northern California Sierras or the hills of Japan; his primary concern is with those parts of the world that have not been remade by human labors. The two poets therefore embody the familiar split between city and country that has been associated since classical times with different literary genres and attitudes.[3]

Yet across this split, O'Hara and Snyder share fundamental aesthetic assumptions. Both are unusually prolific poets, and in reading their work it is easy to see why. Poems for them do not constitute watersheds or momentous statements that can be made only once; they are part of the natural produce of living, the residue of their activity in the world. O'Hara, while working a full schedule as curator at the Museum of Modern Art, managed to write poems constantly, in the interstices of his daily tasks and dizzying social life. Many of his poems were of necessity dashed off, tossed casually in a drawer, and often completely forgotten. Their aesthetic status is therefore rather different from that of a poem labored over for months, assiduously revised, and published with fanfare. Because such poems participate so intimately in the ephemeral aspects of experience, they do not claim for themselves the permanence of classical art (although this is less true of O'Hara's more obviously ambitious works like *Second Avenue*, "In Memory of My Feelings," and the *Odes*). Yet despite O'Hara's cavalier attitude toward his own production, he clearly aspires to be an important, even a canonical poet; and so the occasional and improvisational nature of his work has to be reconciled with more traditional forms of closure capable of bestowing on individual poems a sense of singularity.

While somewhat less prolific, Snyder is similarly occasional in his output. Perhaps because his subject matter is less involved with cultural ephemera, his poems do not seem as tied to the moment, but they also are clearly written in the midst of worldly activities—physical labor, domestic duties, and so on. Both poets differ from writers like Warren and even Bishop in that the nature of their work—its volume, its tone, its loose form—tends to deny the momentousness of the represented experience. One may even come to feel that there is something essentially arbitrary about the way these poets select from the continuum of their experience particular segments to be made into poems. Because they generally avoid Romantic epiphanies and other forms of cognitive revelation favored by the previous generation of poets, their poems no longer claim to be held together and justified by the insights they contain. Instead their aesthetic implies that each poem is simply a random sample of experience, no more intrinsically poetic than some other occasion which didn't happen to be made into a poem.

Most of O'Hara's earlier poetry takes up an oblique relationship to his own experience, freely dropping names of friends, acquaintances, places, and the like, but weaving them into a disjunctive tapestry of wild images and mock-odelike rhetoric.[4] His characteristic "I do this, I do that" manner emerges in the later fifties, as he develops a more relaxed, idiomatic style capable of registering the details of ordinary experience without the transforming lens of surrealism.[5] Many of these poems describe things seen in the course of O'Hara's walks in New York, often during his lunch hour (hence most of them were published under the title *Lunch Poems*), and one can surmise from the poems themselves and from other indications in the poet's writing that this was a particularly vital mode of experience for him. Walking in a crowded city seems to have provided him with exactly the balance of solitude, motion, stimulation, change, and leisure that he needed for his poetry; the texture and rhythm of an urban walk corresponded closely to the texture and rhythm he sought for his poems.

What is perhaps most remarkable about O'Hara's walk poems is their insistence on coinciding absolutely with their occasions. Not only their habitual use of the present tense, but also their fluid, often ungrammatical language seems to cancel all distance between represented experience and representational text, as though the poem had come into being simultaneously with the walk itself. O'Hara playfully encourages such a view of the genesis of his poems in the blurb to his volume *Lunch Poems*:

> Often this poet, strolling through the noisy splintered glare of a Manhattan noon, has paused at a sample Olivetti to type up thirty or forty lines of ruminations, or pondering more deeply has withdrawn to a darkened ware- or fire-house, to limn his computed misunderstandings of the eternal questions of life, co-existence and depth, while never forgetting to eat Lunch his favorite meal.[6]

O'Hara here absurdly literalizes the coincidence of experience and composition implied by the use of the present tense in his walk poems. Obviously the poems were not actually typed up in the course of his walks; yet we can certainly speculate that many of them were composed not long after the experience they describe had occurred, since we know that O'Hara often wrote poems while at his desk in the Museum of Modern Art.[7] That the poet should strive to abolish even this small increment of temporal distance tells us a great deal about his conception of poetry, and its value for him. The poem must get as close to the headlong rush of life as possible, absorbing all the ephemeral details and occurrences that it can, approximating the spontaneity of film,

O'Hara's favorite medium. As James Breslin writes, "With their realistic precision and their swift, free, uncommitted movement, the lunch hour poems create the poetic self as a rapid, filmlike series of transparencies, open to experience, neutrally and indiscriminately taking it in."[8] To this end he must make the writing of poetry an activity inseparable from all the other activities his poems record.

This open, receptive attitude toward experience is not without its risks, however. O'Hara's poems are often beset by intuitions of loss or danger that seem to arise without warning from the flux of perception and feeling. Charles Altieri characterizes this aspect of his poetry well when he writes, "Coexisting with O'Hara's evident joy in a kaleidoscopic rush of details and encounters are frequent perceptions of a lurking anxiety ready to seize him if the flow of events should give it a moment's foothold."[9] In effect O'Hara's desire to assimilate all of experience as fully as possible leaves him especially vulnerable to such anxiety, which is almost continually present in his poems, sometimes as a faint undertone, sometimes as an enervating force that takes over the poem and drains it of its momentum. Yet it could be said that anxiety, for all its affective unpleasantness, is part of the secret of O'Hara's success in his "I do this, I do that" poems, exerting a kind of gravitational pull against which the poems must struggle in order to maintain their equable, ongoing immersion in the world. Without it the poems might seem too weightless, too blithely accepting; its presence insures that O'Hara acknowledge the dark side of experience as well as its effervescence.

"A Step Away From Them" is a breakthrough poem for O'Hara, in which he lays aside the surreal mannerisms and inflated rhetoric of his earlier work, and experiments with direct transcription:

> It's my lunch hour, so I go
> for a walk among the hum-colored
> cabs. First, down the sidewalk
> where laborers feed their dirty
> glistening torsos sandwiches
> and Coca-Cola, with yellow helmets
> on. They protect them from falling
> bricks, I guess. Then onto the
> avenue where skirts are flipping
> above heels and blow up over
> grates. The sun is hot, but the
> cabs stir up the air. I look
> at bargains in wristwatches. There
> are cats playing in sawdust.

On
to Times Square, where the sign
blows smoke over my head, and higher
the waterfall pours lightly. A
Negro stands in a doorway with a
toothpick, languorously agitating.
A blonde chorus girl clicks: he
smiles and rubs his chin. Everything
suddenly honks: it is 12:40 of
a Thursday.
Neon in daylight is a
great pleasure, as Edwin Denby would
write, as are light bulbs in daylight.
I stop for a cheeseburger at JULIET'S
CORNER. Giuletta Masina, wife of
Federico Fellini, *e bell' attrice.*
And chocolate malted. A lady in
foxes on such a day puts her poodle
in a cab.
There are several Puerto
Ricans on the avenue today, which
makes it beautiful and warm. First
Bunny died, then John Latouche,
then Jackson Pollock. But is the
earth as full as life was full, of them?
And one has eaten and one walks,
past the magazines with nudes
and the posters for BULLFIGHT and
the Manhattan Storage Warehouse,
which they'll soon tear down. I
used to think they had the Armory
Show there.
A glass of papaya juice
and back to work. My heart is in my
pocket, it is Poems by Pierre Reverdy.

(*Poems*, pp. 257–58)

Perhaps the first thing to notice about the poem is how much of O'Hara's characteristic voice has been muted. Gone are the exclamation points that liberally pepper his more discursive poems; the willful zaniness of imagery and phrase that we find elsewhere has been restrained as well. Yet by dampening his rhetorical energies, O'Hara invents the kind of poetry for which he is best remembered, a poetry wholly devoted to the flux of urban experience. To be sure, the very transcriptiveness of this poetry seems to some to call its aesthetic status into question; James Breslin, a sympathetic critic, cites "A Step Away From Them" as a poem which he read in the fifties and dismissed: "it was not that [it] was a *bad* poem; it was *no* poem."[10] But by the same token, its faith in its material and its courage in occupying so extreme a position has won for this and similar poems by O'Hara a special place in the contemporary canon. Although his walk poems have spawned more than a few imitations, most poets recognize that "A Step Away From Them" is not so much a viable model for further poems as it is a liberating *gesture*, a new validation of ordinary experience as potential poetry.

This is not to say, however, that the poem's value inheres entirely in its stance rather than its execution. It takes real skill to achieve the kind of transparency to experience displayed in "A Step Away From Them." While this transparency may not be the product of a rigorous Flaubertian art—like most of O'Hara's poems, "A Step Away From Them" was probably dashed off during working hours—it nevertheless can be analyzed minutely, and its various constituents pointed out. Most prominently, of course, there is the use of the present tense, a device encountered in a number of earlier walk poems: "The Country Walk," "An Evening Walk," "Good Hours," "An Ordinary Evening in New Haven," and *Paterson* Two, for example. Perhaps for some readers the device is disingenuous, a mannerism that can never create the presence it seems to announce; but used skillfully, as it is by O'Hara, the present tense has a purely deictic force that is hard to deny. Whether or not we credit the poem's claim to coincide with the walk it records, the representation becomes palpably more immediate, drawing us almost irresistibly into the temporality of the walk.

The present tense serves another important function in the poem, enforcing a sense of absolute successiveness, in which each moment follows the one before it with no evident subordination or narrative structuring. Because O'Hara denies himself a retrospective vantage from which the individual moments can be viewed as a spatialized whole, the poem takes on a strange temporal shallowness, evoking a rapt attention that never leaves the present moment of consciousness. Each sentence represents a new, isolated encounter with the world, and these encounters are connected by nothing more than their sequential ordering in the walk. The poem thus pursues the metonymic organization inherent in the walk as form to an extreme point, at which metaphor seems to disappear entirely, and continuity and contiguity become identical. O'Hara's guiding motto in this respect might be a line by one of his favorite poets, Walt Whitman: "The glories strung like beads on my smallest sights and hearings, on the walk in the street and the passage over the river."[11]

Given such an apparent looseness of form, lacking the metaphoric and thematic apparatus that traditionally unifies and justifies a poem, it becomes difficult to know on what grounds to praise "A Step Away From Them." Mere accuracy hardly seems a sufficient virtue to validate a work of art; fidelity to experience must be combined with an active sensibility that allows us to discern the aesthetic qualities of the experience itself, qualities that may then be transferred to the poem as well. Such a sensibility manifests itself throughout the poem, continuously registering the random perceptual pleasures and stray thoughts that O'Hara feels are worthy of memorializing, not so much for their documentary truth as for their various investments of feeling and desire.

The poem begins, like so many of O'Hara's poems, by announcing the time of day: "It's my lunch hour." Like the walk itself, the lunch hour provides a ready-made aesthetic frame; located between blocks of purposive activity, it defines a space of temporary freedom and leisure amid the demands of work. Within this indeterminate and unplanned space, O'Hara can wander at his ease, pursuing no fixed goal (other than lunch itself, of course), but simply enjoying the privilege of taking "a step away from them," presumably his fellow-workers. The close relation between lunch hour and walk as aesthetic containers is signaled by the logical preposition "so": "so I go / for a walk among the hum-colored / cabs." Going for a walk is clearly the best way to maximize the possibilities for undirected enjoyment that the lunch hour holds.

With the phrase "among the hum-colored cabs" a descriptive element first enters the poem, albeit a wry and at times almost parodic kind of description. For example, what does "hum-colored" mean? New York cabs are for the most part yellow, of course, and O'Hara does not need to remind us of this boring fact; his use of a more fanciful color term is therefore meant to supplement and modify our automatic assumption about the way cabs look. As to what precisely O'Hara has in mind by "hum-colored," there are several possibilities. The phrase may be meant as a synesthetic trope, suggesting that the color of the cabs corresponds in Baudelairean fashion to a humming sound, perhaps a sound made by the cabs themselves as they idle, perhaps the sound of bumblebees, which the cabs resemble both in their busy movement and their black-and-yellow coloring; on the other hand, the phrase may be meant to evoke the dull familiarity of the cabs, their "ho-hum" or "humdrum" character. The very use of so strange an epithet, of course, to some extent defamiliarizes the cabs, so that we begin to see them freshly even as we recall their ordinary appearance.

Another aspect of the poem's descriptiveness which should not be overlooked might be called its "generic" quality. There is a kind of pop art shorthand at work in the references to the laborers' "dirty glistening torsos" and "yellow helmets," and to the "skirts ... flipping above heels and blow[ing] up over grates." These clichéd synecdoches are popular culture's way of coding gender in its most extreme and sexual forms; and clearly O'Hara deploys them knowingly, with a kind of affectionate amusement at them. At the same time they signal his intensely erotic relation to the world through which he walks. People are reduced to sexy body parts, not I think in any insidiously dehumanizing way, but simply because that is how they are perceived by a man walking briskly through Manhattan on his lunch hour. O'Hara's overwhelmingly sexual sensibility registers everything as teasingly erotic, full of hedonistic potential. In part it is this sense of both possible and immediate pleasures available at every turn that makes the poem itself so pleasurable to read.

Another kind of sensual pleasure is evoked in the sentence "The sun is hot, but the / cabs stir up the air," subtly conveying a tension between heat, languor, stasis, and breeze, desire, motion—a tension particularly delightful to O'Hara, as Marjorie Perloff observes.[12] The image of the cabs returns in a leitmotivic fashion throughout the poem, and we must recall that O'Hara had initially described his walk as taking place "*among*" them (italics mine). While in themselves banal, they thus lend the poem a certain imagistic unity, almost as though they embodied the spirit of the place itself, the genius of the landscape in which the poet walks. Like the poet, the cabs are in constant motion, and so they nicely capture the poem's kinetic rhythm, its sense of things flashing by in an endless and random series, with no causal plot to connect them.

Just such a series of quick, snapshotlike images follows: bargains in wristwatches, cats playing in sawdust, the signs in Times Square with their silly special effects, the Negro in the doorway ogling a blonde chorus girl. It is difficult to know how to generalize about such a series; certain connections can be drawn, for example between the small-scale promotion of the wristwatches and the large-scale advertising of the billboards, but the essence of the series is its contingency. It is more than a mere list, however; O'Hara is careful to vary the rhythm of description, slowing down for the signs and even more for the man, thus suggesting different degrees of attentiveness. To dispose each sight neatly in a single line would produce something closer to a catalog than a transcript of experience; each item would be given the same weight as the rest, and so would lose its unique experiential flavor. O'Hara wants to preserve not only the particulars of the walk, but also the precise force with which they impinge on his consciousness.

This series of discrete perceptual moments is followed by a sentence
that overtly seeks to encompass the whole of the landscape: "Everything suddenly honks: it is 12:40 of a Thursday." "Everything" here evidently refers primarily to the cabs again; once more they function in
the poem as synecdoches for the place as a whole. The use of so inclusive a noun, however, suggests that "suddenly honks" must be taken in
a more than literal sense, evoking what Breslin calls "an unexpected
sense of unity."[13] All of the separate, scattered objects that surround
O'Hara are briefly conflated as the subject of the verb "honks," which
takes on an almost Heideggerian generality; indeed the line could be
taken as O'Hara's more whimsical version of Heidegger's statement
that "the world worlds." The honking is simply the collective action or
utterance of the world as O'Hara perceives it, a world that has suddenly coalesced for him at a particular moment: "12:40 of a Thursday."
His careful specifying of the time of day emphasizes the precarious
temporal status of this moment of totalization. If it is an epiphany, it is
one in which nothing is revealed, in which the world simply declares itself as present; in this respect it differs from moments of totalization in
Roethke, which tend to have a cognitive as well as aesthetic force. Yet
as Perloff notes, there is a vestigial radiance to the moment, as though
it kept a Romantic sublimity even while denying Romantic versions of
transcendence.[14]

With the next verse paragraph, the poem shifts into a less purely descriptive idiom, entering more deeply into the walker's consciousness
and admitting thoughts as well as perceptions onto the page. "Neon in
daylight is a great pleasure" is the poem's first general statement, and
although it clearly has an immediate referent in the phenomenality of
the walk, its grammar is not descriptive but assertive. Acknowledging
the shift in style, O'Hara immediately attributes this kind of statement
to the poet and critic Edwin Denby, as though trying to distance himself from even such minimally discursive language. Still, the observation is in keeping with what has gone before, especially in its emphasis
on pleasure; O'Hara is again communicating his aesthetic enjoyment
of the scene to us, letting the poem act as a medium for the perpetuation of his own fleeting perceptual delights. The images of neon and
light bulbs in daylight return to the kind of titillating tension between
opposites that we saw in the relation between heat and motion earlier;
it is this kind of faintly sexual energy, diffused through the very light
and air, that gives the poem its quality of alert, pleased excitement. (A
similar sense of pleasurable tension may be present in the cross-racial
desire of the black man for the blonde chorus girl, again a mixture of
conjunction and contrast; if the man in the doorway were white, some
of this tension would surely be lost.)

O'Hara's lunch, the only purely functional element of his walk, is casually tossed down in a line or two, occasioning another bit of free associative name-dropping:

> I stop for a cheeseburger at JULIET'S
> CORNER. Giulietta Masina, wife of
> Federico Fellini, *è bell' attrice.*
> And chocolate malted.

The brief intrusion of an Italian movie star into O'Hara's lunch, literally sandwiched between cheeseburger and malted, wonderfully captures the fugitive motions of his mind, steeped as it is in cultural trivia, while adding a chic European touch to what is otherwise a thoroughly American repast. As with the reference to Edwin Denby, the appearance of Giulietta Masina signals a movement of internalization, as O'Hara turns from the literal notation of things seen to a transcription of his own consciousness in the act of assimilating and playing with phenomena.

After another quick snapshot, which again picks up the cab imagery ("A lady in / foxes on such a day puts her poodle / in a cab"), and another appreciative glance at the passersby, who are now seen to participate in a larger aesthetic whole ("There are several Puerto / Ricans on the avenue today, which / makes it beautiful and warm"), O'Hara withdraws still further into his own thoughts, and for the first time the mood of the poem darkens:

> First
> Bunny died, then John Latouche,
> then Jackson Pollock. But is the
> earth as full as life was full, of them?

The startling impingement of death upon the poet's seemingly carefree walk is not prepared for by anything in the scene; unlike the references to Denby and Masina, the thought of O'Hara's dead friends does not seem to arise naturally from the phenomena he encounters. Like death itself, the thought simply interrupts what had been an entirely pleasurable experience. The thought's connection to the experience becomes clear, however, as O'Hara goes on to frame his question: "is the / earth as full as life was full, of them?" In the midst of his own experience of fullness, of the beauty and warmth created by the people on the street, O'Hara is reminded of people who are no longer there, people who once contributed to that fullness.

The thought thus comes almost as a chastisement for his unqualified pleasure in the world, a pleasure that necessarily excludes or represses death. James Breslin has skillfully analyzed the syntactical ambiguities in O'Hara's question (does it ask if the earth, where they are buried, is as full of them now as life was once full of them?, or if the world from which they have departed is as full now that they are dead?), and the way it inverts the cliché of people being "full of life."[15] But it is as gesture that the line is most significant; in effect O'Hara abruptly questions his own mood, allowing death to infiltrate his consciousness and darken his walk. One might ask why a poem that has devoted itself so exclusively to sensual pleasures should suddenly veer into a meditation, however brief, on mortality. To be sure, the relation between beauty and death has been a great theme of poetry from Keats to Stevens; yet I do not think it is quite correct to say, with Perloff, that the poem "has been moving all along to the central recognition of the affinity of life and death, to the perception that death is, as it was for Wallace Stevens, the mother of beauty."[16] This is to ascribe too deliberate a thematic intention to O'Hara, who was generally wary of what he called "the important utterance."[17] It would be more accurate to say that he includes the thought of death in the poem simply because it is part of the walk, and because to leave it out in the interests of consistency would be to falsify the variegated texture of experience itself. To insist that the thought of death is the poem's *meaning*, its "central recognition," is to unbalance its resolutely serial structure; the thought is merely one element of many, a moment of consciousness that exists side by side with all the other moments of consciousness represented in the poem.

Nonetheless, this remembrance of death cannot be easily dismissed, and it clearly affects the remainder of the poem. One prominent change that occurs after O'Hara thinks of his dead friends is a pronominal shift from "I" to "one": "And one has eaten and one walks." Evidently a certain distance between voice and self has been imposed by the thought of death, although I think Breslin slightly exaggerates this change when he suggests that O'Hara has become "a melancholy, anonymous 'one' who keeps moving but who merely seems to be going through the motions in a depressed, mechanical way."[18] "Melancholy" is too strong a word here; "pensive" might be better. In any case, an elegiac note has clearly entered the poem, as in the reference to the Manhattan Storage Warehouse, "which they'll soon tear down." Even the poet's slightly embarrassed confession that he "used to think they had the Armory / Show there" evokes an inevitable disillusionment that harmonizes with the newly dominant sense of transience. Significantly, the erotic element of the world has now been reduced from living bodies to "magazines with nudes," suggesting O'Hara's growing detachment from the scene. The aesthetic pleasures that had previously filled the walk have given way to a subtle awareness of time and its destructive effects.

THE WALK AS SAMPLE 185

Yet, as Breslin writes, "O'Hara's depression simply passes. The poem presents a rapid series of unconnected moments and any vestigial desire we may feel to spatialize the poem by viewing it as a conflict between feelings of presence and loss is thwarted by the way these issues are just dropped and by O'Hara's steadfast refusal to provide anything like a resolution at the end."[19] The poem closes cheerfully enough with a glass of papaya juice on the way back to work, ending with a final proper name: "My heart is in my pocket, it is poems by Pierre Reverdy." The first phrase, a deliberate parody of the clichés in which the heart is said to be "on my sleeve" or "in my throat," epitomizes O'Hara's metonymic portrayal of the self, in which feeling is defined in terms of objects rather than essence. Here O'Hara's "heart" has attached itself, perhaps in pleasurable anticipation, to the book of poems he carries in his pocket. The aesthetic thus reasserts itself at the end of "A Step Away From Them," though now in a literary rather than experiential form. It might be argued that by invoking Reverdy, O'Hara is taking refuge in art, having found experience too unreliable a source of pleasure (a surmise strengthened by the fact that he is returning to the Museum of Modern Art). The reference to a book of poems can also be taken as a gesture meant to certify the poetic status of the poem we have been reading, a way of setting the seal on its translation of experience into art. In any case, the line provides a firm but unemphatic kind of closure, turning as it does from the flux of perceptual experience to the spatial trope of the heart and the timeless realm of literature. As Breslin says, nothing has been resolved; the closure is not thematic, as in Roethke and Bishop. The last line is simply a kind of period, signaling that the walk is at an end, and that the poet must now return to literature and to work.

Yet if the poem's closure is essentially arbitrary, the impulse to find some spatial or dramatic form governing it still remains powerful. One may focus on the title, as both Breslin and Perloff do, and read it as a reflection both on O'Hara's relation to the world, which always remains at a slight distance, and on his relation to his dead friends, whose fate he must eventually share.[20] Such interpretations of the poem cannot be dismissed, and it is a large part of its accomplishment that it can be so suggestive while at the same time avoiding any insistent thematizing of its concerns. In the end, however, the poem cedes authority to experience. Few other walk poems seem so wholly open to the world in all its contingency, refusing to arrange or comment on it beyond setting down the unconnected thoughts it provokes. To experience the poem is in a real sense to experience the walk; the margins of text and occasion are so flush that the two can scarcely be distinguished.

"A Step Away From Them" is O'Hara's purest walk poem, the one most committed to what I've been calling serial structure, in which moments succeed one another without causal or discursive connections, and with little sense of climax or subordination. In his experimentation with the walk as a model for poetry, O'Hara follows roughly the same pattern as Wordsworth, though at a more accelerated pace. Having written a pure walk poem, O'Hara must surely have realized that the feat could not be successfully duplicated. Although he might go on taking walks during his lunch hour, walks which individually might have just as much claim to being recorded as the one immortalized in "A Step Away From Them," to go on writing such poems would be a kind of poetic suicide. As I argue in my introduction, the fundamental difference between poetry and experience is that, while experience may repeat itself incessantly without losing its interest, a poem must be absolutely singular. A poet like O'Hara, then, who asserts that "poetry *is* experience," (italics mine), faces a special challenge. How can he continue to generate poems from his daily experience—an experience which in its most aesthetically vibrant phase consists largely of walking in New York—without turning out the same poem over and over? If all experience is equally valuable, how does one select particular samples of it for representation?

Wordsworth's solution lies in the development of the notion of spots of time, moments of special intensity that organize the experience around them and give it meaning. Such a notion represents a retreat from the position that all experience is equally worthy of representation, a position implied by Wordsworth's earliest poetry; now experience is hierarchized, arranged into affective centers and connective tissue. A similar shift can be seen in O'Hara's next major walk poem, and indeed the most famous of all his poems, "The Day Lady Died." In form it closely resembles "A Step Away From Them"; yet I would argue that a fundamental change has occurred, one that alters not only the tone but the structure of the poem:

> It is 12:20 in New York a Friday
> three days after Bastille day, yes
> it is 1959 and I go get a shoeshine
> because I will get off the 4:19 in Easthampton
> at 7:15 and then go straight to dinner
> and I don't know the people who will feed me
>
> I walk up the muggy street beginning to sun
> and have a hamburger and a malted and buy
> an ugly NEW WORLD WRITING to see what the poets
> in Ghana are doing these days
>   I go on to the bank
> and Miss Stillwagon (first name Linda I once heard)

doesn't even look up my balance for once in her life
and in the GOLDEN GRIFFIN I get a little Verlaine
for Patsy with drawings by Bonnard although I do
think of Hesiod, trans. Richmond Lattimore or
Brendan Behan's new play or *Le Balcon* or *Les Nègres*
of Genet, but I don't, I stick with Verlaine
after practically going to sleep with quandariness

and for Mike I just stroll into the PARK LANE
Liquor Store and ask for a bottle of Strega and
then I go back where I came from to 6th Avenue
and the tobacconist in the Ziegfield Theatre and
casually ask for a carton of Gauloises and a carton
of Picayunes, and a NEW YORK POST with her face on it

and I am sweating a lot by now and thinking of
leaning on the john door in the 5 SPOT
while she whispered a song along the keyboard
to Mal Waldron and everyone and I stopped breathing

(Poems, p. 325)

The most striking difference between this poem and "A Step Away From Them" is the almost total absence of the aesthetic element that made the earlier poem so pleasurable to read. Unlike "A Step Away From Them," this poem contains very little of what could properly be called "description," that is, the verbal evocation of phenomena.[21] Virtually all the items set down in the poem are economic transactions rather than moments of perception. As a result the poem has none of the energy or exuberance, the almost sexual enjoyment of the world, that characterized "A Step Away From Them." The economic and the aesthetic are perennially at odds with one another, of course, and by focusing the greater portion of his poem so exclusively on acts of buying and selling, O'Hara effectively drains it of aesthetic interest. While not strictly speaking economic, the barrage of numerically precise times and dates presented in the first paragraph share in this quantification of experience. Note also that O'Hara's only relationship with his future hosts is not social or emotional but baldly pragmatic: they are "the people who will feed me," a strangely impersonal phrase. Art itself becomes a mere commodity; unlike the book of poems by Reverdy, in which the poet invested so much feeling that it became his "heart," the various books mentioned at the Golden Griffin are simply possible purchases whose literary qualities are not even hinted at. This lack of affective involvement is made explicit in the curious phrase "after practically going to sleep with quandariness," suggesting that the effort to make a choice based on aesthetic criteria only heightens O'Hara's boredom with experience.

But of course the realm of the aesthetic is powerfully embodied by the figure of Billie Holiday herself, who emerges at the end of the poem as its true subject. Clearly, then, O'Hara's suppression of aesthetic experience in the first twenty-five lines is deliberate, meant to throw into sharp relief the poem's final "spot of time," in which he remembers listening to Holiday sing in a nightclub. Like Williams in "The Desert Music," he gives over a large portion of the poem to an intentionally flat account of his actions that acts as a foil for a single moment of intense lyricism or music, here in the form of an involuntary memory (although O'Hara more resolutely empties this preparatory account of aesthetic interest than does Williams). The relation between the serial part of the poem and its final lines is therefore hierarchical rather than purely sequential; the memory of Holiday is intensely affective, where the previous lines were bored and mechanical, wholly lacking in the vitality that characterized O'Hara's walk in "A Step Away From Them."

Reading "The Day Lady Died" thus becomes a radically different experience from reading the earlier walk poem. We do not ride the crest of the poet's walk, absorbing each moment separately and then moving on to the next; because the tone and style of the poem is so uninflected and flat, we feel that the first twenty-five lines must simply be "gotten through," and that the aesthetic charge of the poem is only to be had at the end. The fact that the poem is unpunctuated, consisting of clauses loosely strung together by a series of "ands," contributes to the sense that the individual items registered in the poem do not constitute separate moments to be dwelt on for their particular pleasures but are instead mere pauses in the poet's dull round of tasks. O'Hara's emotional distance from the commodities he buys in the first part of the poem is underscored by the fact that they are all foreign, unlike Holiday, who is the poem's only authentic representative of American culture, and the only figure with whom the poet is emotionally engaged. (In this connection it may be significant that O'Hara specifies the date as "three days after Bastille day," perhaps suggesting an estrangement from time as well as place.)

"The Day Lady Died" is, of course, an elegy of sorts, and that fact largely accounts for the absence of the kind of delight in the physical scene that we find in "A Step Away From Them." Let me note in this connection that while the poem has generally been read as leading up to the discovery of Holiday's death, when O'Hara sees her face on the New York Post, it is equally possible that he *already* knows about her death when the poem begins. This would explain the numbed quality of the first part of the poem, since clearly the news depresses him; it would also put the entire poem under the shadow of its title. The day, with all its particulars of time and place, is meaningful only because it is the day Lady died; to defer the knowledge of that death until the end of the poem would be to limit the title's resonance too much. It is perhaps also noteworthy that O'Hara does not behave as though he were receiving a piece of tragic information at the end of the poem; there is no dramatized moment of discovery. Still, the question of whether he knows of her death from the start or learns of it only at the end cannot finally be resolved, and it is part of the poem's disturbing reticence that it refuses to clarify such matters.

"The Day Lady Died" thus expands on the elegiac element already present in "A Step Away From Them." But where the earlier poem maintained a light-footed poise above grief, letting the thought of death briefly interrupt the poet's walk without permitting it to overshadow his pleasures in observing the world, "The Day Lady Died" shows how grief can empty experience of its aesthetic charge, reducing it to a mere series of transactions. Once this happens, the poem can only justify its *own* aesthetic status through a representation of the object of grief, an object that concentrates within itself all the affective investment that has been lost from the world. Accordingly, the last lines of the poem offer a compressed but extraordinarily evocative account of a Holiday performance, as witnessed by O'Hara while "leaning against the john door at the 5 spot." The emotional power of her singing literally takes her audience's breath away: "she whispered a song along the keyboard / to Mal Waldron and everyone and I stopped breathing." The final line presents a special challenge to interpretation. To begin with, the syntactical place of "everyone" is ambiguous, since it can be grouped either with Mal Waldron as the indirect object of "whispered . . . to," or with "I" as the subject of "stopped breathing." This slipperiness allows O'Hara to remain set apart in his response, while nonetheless connecting him to a larger group of listeners who share his emotion. More significantly, perhaps, it is difficult in reading the last three words of the poem not to apply them to the poet in the *present*, as he buys the newspaper with Holiday's face on it. Strictly speaking, of course, this cannot legitimately be done, because the entire poem is in the present tense except for the closing memory. The stoppage of breath can only be taking place in the past, then, not in the present. Yet the inevitable confusion of temporal layers created by the last line is surely deliberate, since it leaves us with a sense that the present tense no longer exists, that the poem itself has been sucked into the memory of Holiday, as her death has sucked experience of its sensual immediacy. (O'Hara lays the ground for our confusion with the earlier line "I'm sweating a lot by now," suggesting a state of physical strain that might easily lead to loss of breath as well.)

O'Hara's habitual use of the present tense, which in "A Step Away From Them" reflected the poet's total engagement in the present moment of experience, thus gives way at the end of "The Day Lady Died" to a deathlike withdrawal of experience into the past. The knowledge of Holiday's death first empties and anesthetizes the present moment, leaving O'Hara to walk dully from bank to store, seeing none of the "glories strung like beads" that made up his earlier walk—and then cancels the present entirely. There is something self-consuming about O'Hara's walk, removing it as far from the immanent seriality of "A Step Away From Them" as possible. This turn from the earlier, looser mode is understandable; as I've suggested, simply to write more poems recording the haphazard thoughts and perceptions framed by his walks would work against the singularity demanded by poetry. Like Wordsworth, O'Hara realized that to continue representing one's ordinary experience in poetry requires the ability to give each poem a unique center, a "spot of time." In "The Day Lady Died," that center is provided by the memory with which the poem closes, a memory that retroactively justifies the preceding string of seemingly uninteresting particulars, while at the same time destroying any sense of present experience that the poem had previously conveyed.

O'Hara pays a price, then, for the poem's centered quality. While he gains a weight, an emotional intensity, that his more casual poems are unable to summon, he loses the attentiveness and pleasurable absorption in immediate experience that "A Step Away From Them" so wonderfully conveys. It is worth noting that "The Day Lady Died" is undoubtedly O'Hara's most securely canonized poem; clearly his effort to overcome the repetitiveness of journalistic representation, a repetitiveness that stands in opposition to the ideals of canonical art, has been well rewarded in this case. By subordinating the randomness of experience to a single charged moment, depicted as all-consuming, O'Hara is able to produce a poem that meets such canonical criteria as singularity, concentration, and unity, touching a kind of timelessness and making personal experience participate in the universal ("everyone and I").

As I've suggested, however, to do this he must sacrifice his innate aesthetic interest in the surface of the moment, in the flux of phenomena, and in the random succession of feelings and thoughts that make up experience. In later walk poems he returns to the less centered, more serial mode of "A Step Away From Them," ringing variations on its open and inclusive structure but not essentially altering it. To some extent he does succumb in these later poems to the threat of repetition; none of them are as successful and appealing as "A Step," largely because they are aware of themselves as versions of a paradigm rather than unique translations of experience. These poems are of interest largely in the way they show O'Hara gradually working toward a point at which the assumptions behind the genre collapse, and he is forced to abandon it completely.

The opening line of "Personal Poem" candidly acknowledges its place as a later entry in O'Hara's walk series: "Now when I walk around at lunchtime...." (*Poems*, p. 335). Such a line only makes sense coming *after* "A Step Away From Them" and "The Day Lady Died," since it implicitly contrasts itself with earlier lunchtime walks with which it assumes the reader to be familiar. "Personal Poem" clearly reworks some of the material of "A Step Away From Them," although it has a more social tone, centering as it does on a lunch with LeRoi Jones. The walk in the street is still represented, however, under the hot and humid weather conditions that seem perpetually present in O'Hara's New York:

> I walk through the luminous humidity
> passing the House of Seagram with its wet
> and its loungers and the construction to
> the left that closed the sidewalk if
> I ever get to be a construction worker
> I'd like to have a silver hat please

Many of the elements of "A Step Away From Them" are here, even including the construction workers and their fascinating hats. But "Personal Poem" lacks the precision with which the earlier poem records O'Hara's perceptions and responses to the scene; it has a more relaxed conversational quality that again may reflect the social nature of its occasion. Like "The Day Lady Died," the poem is unpunctuated, but rather than connecting separate clauses with "ands," it simply runs together phrases regardless of grammatical boundaries (as in the line ending "sidewalk if," where obviously the "if" signals the beginning of a new independent clause). The careful punctuation in "A Step Away From Them" contributes enormously to the poem's sense of sharply defined moments set side by side, not blurred together. Here that sense is lost; instead the poet's own voice, jokey and fey ("I'd like to have a silver hat please"), comes to the fore, blotting out the transparency to experience achieved in the earlier poem.

A later poem, "F. (Missive & Walk) I. #53," is a more successful blending of the conversational and the mimetic, one that also offers an especially revealing glimpse of O'Hara's ambivalence toward the flux of experience (the title places it in a series of mock-memos that

O'Hara sent to his friend Bill Berkson, under the general title "F.Y.I.," that is, "for your information"):

> I'm getting tired of not wearing underwear
> and then again I like it
>   strolling along
> feeling the wind blow softly on my genitals
> though I also like them encased in something
> firm, almost tight, like a projectile
>   at
> a streetcorner I stop and a lamppost is
> bending over the traffic pensively like a
> praying mantis, not lighting anything,
> just looking
>   who dropped that empty carton
> of cracker jacks I wonder I find the favor
> that's a good sign
>   it's the blue everyone
> is talking about an enormous cloud which hides
> the observatory blimp   when you
> ride on a 5th Avenue bus you hide on a 5th
> Avenue bus I mean compared to you walking
> don't hide   there you are trying
> to hide behind a fire hydrant   I'm
> not going to the Colisseum I'm going to
> the Russian Tea Room fooled you didn't I
> well   it is nicer in the Park
> with the pond and all that   okay
> lake   and bicyclists give you
> a feeling of being at leisure in the open
> air lazy and good-tempered   which is
> fairly unusual these days   I liked
> for instance   carrying my old Gautier book
> and *L'Ombra* over to LeRoi's the other
> pale afternoon through the crowds of 3rd
> Avenue and the ambulance and the drunk

(Poems, p. 420)

While more chatty than "A Step Away From Them," presumably because it is addressed to a friend (the poem was written after O'Hara had developed his credo of "Personism," which holds that a poem is not essentially different from a telephone call),[22] "F. (Missive & Walk) I. #53" has much of the earlier poem's responsiveness to immediate phenomenal experience. Like "Personal Poem," it is unpunctuated, but it makes effective use of spacing to convey syntactical and grammatical articulations, and so does not seem as deliberately slurred.

The poem opens with a much more literal version of O'Hara's sexual relationship to the world at large that we saw in "A Step Away From Them." His indecision about whether he prefers to go with or without underwear is an amusing but ultimately serious reflection on the nature of that relationship: is O'Hara to remain passively open to the world's caresses, letting "the wind blow softly on [his] genitals," or is he to assume a more aggressive yet more "encased" stance toward it, "like a projectile"? The poem appears to favor the former possibility; O'Hara is after all underwearless as the poem begins, and this fact is reflected in the way he casually registers such ordinary sights as the lamppost "bending over the traffic pensively like a / praying mantis," and the box of cracker jacks, which rewards his attention by letting him find the favor—"a good sign." The alternatives of "encasement" and openness return as the poet contrasts riding on the bus with walking in the street. The former, we are told, is a way of hiding from the world, whereas in the latter one is completely exposed; the image of "trying to hide behind a fire hydrant" is evidently meant to point up the absurdity of such an attempt.

After more breezy remarks about mood and weather, the poem ends with a memory of another walk that the poet claims to have enjoyed, "carrying my old Gautier book / and L'Ombra over to LeRoi's the other / pale afternoon through the crowds of 3rd / Avenue and the ambulance and the drunk." Again the walk is characterized by miscellaneous details, but now they have taken on an unmistakably ominous tone, particularly in the images of the ambulance and the drunk; these can be seen as negative versions of the earlier opposition between bus and walker, exposing the darker sides of both containment and openness. The drunk's vulnerability and the ambulance rider's proximity to death are equally horrifying alternatives, suggesting that there is finally no way to fend off the world's destructive aspect.

Why does the poem end on such a dark note, after having presented such an apparently lighthearted relationship to the world? I would suggest that O'Hara is forcing himself and us to recognize the dangers of the open attitude that he assumes at the beginning of the poem. By taking in everything, accepting all the particulars of the world into his poem and his consciousness, O'Hara must confront not only such pleasurable phenomena as the breeze on his genitals, the lamppost, the cracker jacks box with its favor, the Park "with the pond and all that," but also the city's ubiquitous signs of suffering and failure. Faced with such sights as "the ambulance and the drunk," which seem to enter the poem almost without O'Hara's conscious will, as though simply registering themselves on the page like photographic images, the poet may well wish himself to be "encased in something / firm, almost tight, like a projectile"; may wish that he were hiding on a bus rather than walking on the street. (There is a clear resemblance to Bishop's desire for shelter from the cold wind; unlike her, however, O'Hara does not openly represent and then reject this desire, instead allowing it to manifest itself more subliminally.)

Yet O'Hara does not show any affective response to these sights, for a very simple reason: the poem ends, with an abruptness emphasized by the lack of a period. That fact is *itself* the response. Having acknowledged the more threatening aspect of the world, the aspect that provokes withdrawal rather than acceptance, the poem cannot simply continue on its cheerful path. Its very closure thus becomes a form of "encasement," a way of shutting out a world that has grown too disturbing to be lovingly embraced. As in "The Day Lady Died," the poem ends with a kind of emotional vacuum that brings everything to a halt. Here, however, the ending seems genuinely unforeseen; O'Hara's walk remains untroubled until the last line, when it is suddenly ambushed by anxiety.[23] The poem is not a carefully controlled piece of emotional portraiture like "The Day Lady Died," but an attempt at a spontaneous and open representation of the world that goes curiously awry. Its ending thus seems more an abortion than a fulfillment, a cutting off of a process that has gotten out of the poet's hands. We are left feeling uneasy and unsatisfied, as though the poet, having promised us one kind of emotional experience, had abandoned us in the midst of another, less reassuring kind.

The final walk poem by O'Hara that I want to discuss can be viewed as his farewell to the genre, candidly expressing his ultimate recognition of the impossibility of making poetry and experience coincide. It is entitled, inaccurately enough, "Petite Poème en Prose," and begins with a rambling, macaronic meditation on the Provençal song "C'était un étranger." Only at line 13 do we learn that this train of thought has been occurring during a walk:

> cherishing these reflections as I walked along I came to a
>   garbage dump
> the poured concrete dome of which
> was covered with children's inscriptions
> the most interesting of which
> was "I ate you up"
> it was not a very interesting dump
> so I pursued my "course" of thought
> "tu es mon amour depuis. . ." oh no, not

that, and then "Ich fühle ein kleiner. . ."
unh unh
yet simply to walk, walk on, did not seem nearly enough for
    my rabid nerves
so I began to hum the Beer Barrel Polka
hopping and skipping along
in my scarf which came to my heels
and soon caught on a door knob

I was back in town!
what a relief!
I popped into the nearest movie house and saw two marvelous
    Westerns
but, alas! this is all I remember of the magnificent poem I
    made on my walk
why are you reading this poem anyway?

(Poems, p. 427)

The most notable difference between the language of this poem and that of previous walk poems by O'Hara is of course the use of the past tense. By accepting the inevitable distance that intervenes between experience and its poetic transcription, O'Hara implicitly acknowledges the falsity of his earlier present-tense poems as well, refusing to perpetuate their illusive assertion of a complete merging of poem and occasion.

Yet notice how once he gives up his insistence on the poem's direct participation in experience, all interest in the walk is lost as well. This becomes painfully clear in the passage on the garbage dump, in which it seems O'Hara is straining to recapture the kind of loving attention to ordinary objects that he shows in previous walk poems, to little avail. The verse is flatly end-stopped and lamely phrased, and the poet even goes so far as to admit that "it was not a very interesting dump." In effect the poem's entire mode of representation becomes ironic rather than aesthetic; particulars are not being recorded because they are uniquely worthy of preservation, but because they show the poet's disaffection from the scene, his *lack* of interest in it.

After sketching a frivolous "'course' of thought" that seems almost to parody the serious meditative concerns of earlier walk poets like Stevens and Williams, O'Hara concludes with an explicit and almost brutal rejection of the principles behind the walk poem: "but, alas! this is all I remember of the magnificent poem I made on my walk / why are you reading this poem anyway?" Once the poem acknowledges, in its use of the past tense, that it is being composed *after* the experience it records has taken place, then its reliance on the imperfect faculty of memory becomes evident. O'Hara frankly confesses that his memory of the walk is incomplete, that the poem itself is necessarily a mere fragment of the experience, not a full transcription. Perhaps more interesting than the foregrounding of memory, however, is his literalizing of the notion, implicit in earlier poems, that the poem is composed *during* the walk. We cannot be sure, of course, that the "magnificent poem" O'Hara claims to have made was really so magnificent, since he remembers so little of it. We do know, however, that this lost poem is not some imaginative composition bearing no relation to the walk itself, since what he does give us of the poem, the "this" of "this is all," is simply an account *of* the walk. O'Hara is thus ironically subverting his earlier claim that "poetry is experience" by showing that if so, and if all experience is conversely poetry, then the true poems are ephemeral, and the written versions are necessarily incomplete, dependent as they are on the poet's faulty memory.

Having questioned the poem's capacity to represent experience in anything but a highly mediated form, O'Hara proceeds in the final line to question, even more devastatingly, the very value of such representation: "why are you reading this poem anyway?" If the poem is incapable of preserving the true "magnificence" of experience, then it is worthless, a mere collection of private notations that can have no meaning to anyone other than the poet. O'Hara's blunt question to the reader thus establishes an absolute division between his experience and ours, a division the poem itself cannot possibly bridge. The ironic tone of this question reflects the poet's newly skeptical attitude towards poetry as a representational medium. He has moved from a faith in its ability to capture and preserve experience in all its aesthetic immediacy to an awareness of the inescapable distance that must intervene between any representation and its object. Once he has embraced this awareness, he cannot continue to write poems like "A Step Away From Them," "Personal Poem," and the others in that mode. The project of bringing poetry so close to experience that all distance vanishes must finally be abandoned, leaving in its place only various modes of irony.[24]

This internal critique of the walk poem does not, of course, invalidate O'Hara's earlier successes in the genre. "A Step Away From Them" is a wonderful poem, but much of its effect depends on its lack of self-consciousness regarding the illusion of immediacy that it creates. Once O'Hara brings an ironic formal awareness to the genre, there is no turning back, no regaining of that immediacy. Sadly, we cannot know what direction his poetry would have gone on to take, since his untimely death came shortly after "Petite Poème en Prose."

Whether or not he would have continued to write walk poems, his trajectory from "A Step Away From Them" to "Petite Poème en Prose" gives us a remarkably clear sense of the difficulties and contradictions latent in the genre. More than any other poet except Wordsworth, O'Hara makes us aware of the volatile half-life of the walk poem. Because it opposes itself to the very idea of poetry as an artistic medium distinct from experience, the walk poem ultimately threatens to destroy poetry from within; hence a poet who, like O'Hara, chooses to adopt the genre in its most radical form must eventually modify, and at last abandon it completely. In the meantime, however, he may create poems that are exhilarating precisely in their willingness to situate themselves so close to the borderline of poetry, to risk their very status as art objects in order to represent the immediate pleasures and anxieties of ordinary experience.

. . . . .

Gary Snyder does not explore the genre in as sustained and systematic a manner, but for him as for O'Hara it is a form that defines his whole poetic enterprise, and to which he keeps returning throughout his career.[25] Perhaps because his temperament is less restless and ironic, he does not feel compelled to keep pushing the walk poem away from an original simplicity until it finally self-destructs; instead he remains faithful to its basic outlines from the beginning of his career to its most recent phase. Each of his walk poems seeks the same kind of intimacy with and proximity to phenomenal experience that O'Hara most fully achieves in "A Step Away From Them." But unlike O'Hara, Snyder does not confine himself to one locale, one kind of landscape; and so his many walk poems are different precisely to the extent that the walks themselves are different. Where O'Hara's poems bring widely differing emotional and tonal inflections to an experience that remains phenomenally fairly constant, Snyder emphasizes the sheer physical variety of the world itself, a variety that offers a more objective basis for the poetics of transcription.

Because he concerns himself primarily with the natural world, the many kinds of cultural mediation that play so large a role in O'Hara's walks—names of artists and movie stars, remembered songs, clichés—do not enter into Snyder's walks. For Snyder a walk is a more purely physical process, in which the body interacts with and comes to know its environment; it is less a form of aesthetic play, as it is for O'Hara, than a kind of labor, though not in any narrowly economic sense. The physical, muscular engagement of self and world is at the center of Snyder's poetry, as he himself has acknowledged:

I've just recently come to realize that the rhythms of my poems follow the rhythm of the physical work I'm doing and life I'm leading at any given time—which makes the music in my head which creates the line.... "Riprap" is really a class of poems I wrote under the influence of the geology of the Sierra Nevada and the daily trail-crew work of picking up and placing granite stones in tight cobble patterns on hard slab....Walking, climbing, placing with the hands. I tried writing poems of tough, simple, short words, with the complexity far beneath the surface texture.[26]

One of Snyder's earliest walk poems, "Above Pate Valley," belongs to this group. Because his trail-clearing work is itself physical, the line between work and walk is blurred, not clearly defined as in "A Step Away From Them." Nonetheless, the poem devotes itself to the same kind of undirected activity and observation that characterizes O'Hara's walk poems:

> We finished clearing the last
> Section of trail by noon,
> High on the ridge-side
> Two thousand feet above the creek
> Reached the pass, went on
> Beyond the white pine groves,
> Granite shoulders, to a small
> Green meadow watered by the snow,
> Edged with Aspen—sun
> Straight high and blazing
> But the air was cool.
> Ate a cold fried trout in the
> Trembling shadows. I spied
> A glitter, and found a flake
> Black volcanic glass—obsidian—
> By a flower. Hands and knees
> Pushing the Bear grass, thousands
> Of arrowhead leavings over a
> Hundred yards. Not one good
> Head, just razor flakes
> On a hill snowed all but summer,
> A land of fat summer deer,
> They came to camp. On their
> Own trails. I followed my own
> Trail here. Picked up the cold-drill,
> Pick, singlejack, and sack
> Of dynamite.
> Ten thousand years.[27]

This poem does indeed exhibit the "tight cobble pattern" with which Snyder was so familiar in his trail crew work. The short lines and elliptical sentences themselves form a kind of trail, conducting the reader through the landscape, among its various objects, to the startlingly terse recognition of its temporal duration in the last line. Surprising as it is, this phrase has been carefully prepared for in the poem; note the fourth line, "Two thousand feet above the creek," and the reference to "thousands / Of arrowhead leavings." It could be said that units of a thousand, unlike hundreds, are not phenomenologically graspable, and therefore represent the point at which reality surmounts the measure of the human. This sense of spatial and numerical vastness is carried over into the realm of time at the end of the poem, rounding out the poem's consciousness of the earth's magnitude even in its most localized aspect.

But the poet's awareness of his own insignificance as set against both the temporal and spatial scale of the landscape is combined with an intimate sense of bodily presence: "Ate a cold fried trout," "I spied a glitter," "Hands and knees," "I followed my own / Trail here." He does not attempt to erase himself from the scene; his is not finally an antihumanist stance. The arrowhead leavings, after all, which have now become part of the landscape, were produced by other humans. His own activity is partly destructive, as the reference to the sack of dynamite makes clear, but he shows no signs of guilt; whatever scars he may leave on the land will be part of its history, like the arrowheads. His aim here, as in much of his poetry, is simply to situate the human in the larger context of geological time and space, without seeking to transcend his own experiential perspective. In this way he hopes to show how experience can begin to incorporate a respectful but not intimidated consciousness of the natural enormities that lie beyond its scope.

The walk provides an apt means to achieve this end, enabling the poet to focus on his own movements and perceptions, while continually reminding him that the world is larger than what he can perceive at any given moment, since each step brings something new into sight. Snyder magnifies this structural principle in his most ambitious work to date, the open-ended sequence *Mountains and Rivers Without End*, which he describes as dealing with "travel, the sense of journey in space that modern people have lost (it takes as long to go from Cedar Grove to the Bighorn Plateau in the Sierras as it does to cross American by train), and rise and fall of rock and water."[28] Each section of the poem (six of which have been published in chapbook form) follows the poet's movement through a different landscape, allowing themes and metaphors to emerge in time with his wandering. Sherman Paul writes of it, "Like the Chinese scroll that proposed this form, the poem is to be viewed not spatially but temporally, a view at a time, as on an actual walk."[29] But as its title admits, *Mountains and Rivers Without End* lacks the kind of innate closure that the walk poem generally exhibits; since it does not confine itself to a single journey, new sections can be generated as long as Snyder has new travels to draw on. For this reason it will probably always remain a work in progress, to be completed at last only by the poet's death.

The "sense of journey in space" that *Mountains and Rivers Without End* attempts to evoke is perhaps more intimately conveyed in those poems that focus on the poet's movement within a briefer span of time. While "Above Pate Valley" involves physical movement, it does not have the extended, rambling quality of later walk poems by Snyder, in which he tries to capture, not the "tight cobble pattern" of trail-clearing work, but the more open, aimless patterns made by walking for its own sake. Such a poem is "A Walk":

> Sunday the only day we don't work
> Mules farting around the meadow,
>> Murphy fishing,
> The tent flaps in the warm
> Early sun: I've eaten breakfast and I'll
>> take a walk
> To Benson Lake. Packed a lunch,
> Goodbye. Hopping on creekbed boulders
> Up the rock throat three miles
>> Piute Creek—
> In steep gorge glacier-slick rattlesnake country
> Jump, land by a pool, trout skitter,
> The clear sky. Deer tracks.
> Bad place by a falls, boulders big as houses,
> Lunch tied to a belt,
> I stemmed up a crack and almost fell
> But rolled out safe on a ledge
>> and ambled on.
> Quail chicks freeze underfoot, color of stone
> Then run cheep! away, hen quail fussing.
> Craggy west end of Benson Lake—after edging
> Past dark creek pools on a long white slope—
> Lookt down in the ice-black lake
>> lined with cliff
> From far above: deep shimmering trout.
> A lone duck in a gunsightpass
>> steep side hill

Through slide-aspen and talus, to the east end,
Down to grass, wading a wide smooth stream
Into camp. At last.
                    By the rusty three-year-
Ago left-behind cookstove
Of the old trail crew,
Stoppt and swam and ate my lunch.[30]

"A Walk" has been anthologized several times, as well as cited by a number of respected critics, so that in a purely institutional sense it has
achieved a kind of canonical stature. From a more intrinsic point of
view, how can a poem so deeply rooted in transient particulars claim
for itself the kind of permanence and universality associated with canonical art?

We might begin by noting that its title makes this claim even more
problematic. This is one of the only walk poems I've found that simply calls itself "A Walk," with no qualifying adjective or prepositional
phrase (such as "A Late Walk," "An Evening Walk," "A Walk After
Dark," "The Country Walk"). The implication of this lack of a modi-
fier, I would suggest, is that the walk described in the poem is absolutely particular; it is not a special *kind* of walk, one that could be taken
as representative of some larger category of walks, but just *a* walk, a
completely singular experience. By refusing to categorize his walk
either temporally or spatially in his title, Snyder bestows on it a certain
dignified opacity. It is not an example but a sample, a segment of the
continuum that does not pretend to represent anything beyond itself.

The poem begins, like "A Step Away From Them," by establishing
the time of the walk as distinct from the time of work. Snyder's time-
scale is larger than O'Hara's, since he is concerned with a day rather
than an hour, but like O'Hara's lunch hour this day is defined by its
lack of structure and necessity. The mules, which presumably act as
beasts of burden during the rest of the week, are "farting around the
meadow," a phrase which reduces to its crassest physical level the kind
of free wandering available within this open space of time. But Snyder
recognizes the poetic possibilities of this unstructured stretch of time,
that it is precisely *aesthetic* time, in which all moments are of equal
value rather than subservient to some pragmatic end. His decision to
take a walk can thus hardly be distinguished from his decision to write
a poem about the walk, since both acts take advantage of what might
be called the contained freedom of the sabbath, a freedom that gathers intensity and value from its very enclosure by work.[31]

The poem's grammar is of particular interest. Where "A Step Away
From Them" and other walk poems use the present tense throughout

in order to heighten the sense of immediacy, of the walk unfolding in precise tandem with the poem, Snyder is more flexible and slippery in his use of verb tense. While he begins with the present tense and its related tenses, present perfect and future ("The tent flaps in the warm / Early sun: I've eaten breakfast and I'll / take a walk"), he immediately shifts into the past tense with "Packed a lunch." From that point on the poem remains in the past tense more or less continuously, although there are several places where it reverts to the present: "Jump, land by a pool," "Quail chicks freeze underfoot." Snyder also uses present participles—"hopping," "edging"—and includes a number of phrases with no verbs at all, such as "A lone duck in a gunsight pass." This refusal to pin himself down grammatically can be seen in part as an effort to imitate the very fluidity of the walk itself, although it may also reflect Snyder's desire to avoid the implicit claims of the present tense, which we saw eventually led O'Hara to abandon it entirely. Snyder is quite willing to concede that the experience recorded in the poem occurred in the past, but at the same time he allows it to burst into the present at certain moments of perceptual or motor intensity, thus capturing the variable texture of the experience, with its peaks and planes, more accurately than he could by consistently employing a single tense.

Indeed much of the poem's effectiveness can be attributed to the suppleness with which it bends and stretches to fit the changing contours of the walk. Syntax as well as grammar is varied and often violated to catch the walk's shifting rhythms of motion, pause, and arrival. Perhaps what is most striking about the poem's mimesis of the walk is its deeply physical character; at every moment we are made aware of the centrality of the body, its priority over intelligence and even consciousness. The poem's language almost miraculously succeeds in tracking the bodily movements and postures that constitute the walk's essential armature. As an example, consider this passage: "In steep gorge glacier-slick rattlesnake country / Jump, land by a pool, trout skitter, / The clear sky. Deer tracks." These lines embody a three-phase process or movement. As the poet slowly negotiates a difficult landscape, the long string of adjectives, with their jagged consonantal clusters, slows the reader down as well. When he suddenly jumps, the abruptness of the action is evoked by the absence of a subject pronoun and by the use of the present tense, and is answered by the scattering motion of the trout, who have presumably been startled by his sudden arrival— the short, comma-linked clauses nicely capturing the quick rhythm of this chain of events. Finally he is still, absorbing visual phenomena like the sky reflected in the now empty pool and the tracks of deer who have come there to drink; their calm, motionless appearance is conveyed by simple noun phrases set off entirely without syntax, and punctuated not by commas, as in the previous line where a sense of causal continuity was needed, but by periods, which emphasize the separateness and autonomy of the objects named. The passage also provides a remarkably precise graph of the trajectory of the poet's gaze; the juxtaposition of "trout skitter" and "The clear sky" tells us that only after his eye has been caught by the sudden motion of the fish does Snyder notice the static reflection of the sky that appears after they are gone.

The poem abounds in such skillfully evocative language. Where O'Hara is most interested in his own sensibility as it registers and responds to the outer world, Snyder goes farther than any previous poet toward setting down the physical facts of the walk with almost photographic clarity. He deliberately suppresses all metaphorical and stylistic elaboration, instead writing in a kind of shorthand that nonetheless has great descriptive power. Much is conveyed by a simple phrase like "Lunch tied to a belt"; we are made conscious of the precariousness of Snyder's position, since he evidently needs both his hands to climb the "boulders big as houses." Typographical placement is also used to suggest physical movements; the indentation of the short phrase "and ambled on" after Snyder nearly falls suggests a pause for breath and reorientation, followed by a return to his previous jaunty pace.

Even punctuation contributes to the poem's mimesis, as in the lines "Quail chicks freeze underfoot, color of stone / Then run cheep! away, hen quail fussing." This passage bears a marked resemblance to the more extended passage on the grasshoppers in *Paterson* Two; like Williams, Snyder uses the exclamation point to signal the sudden, startling movement of creatures that had previously blended into the ground. But Snyder creates a more precise simulacrum of the perception in the very rhythm of the sentence, as the chicks' "cheep!" jumps up between "run" and "away" and so forces itself on our attention as a non-syntactical event possessing an almost phenomenal immediacy. Even so tiny a detail as the absence of punctuation after the phrase "color of stone" has a mimetic function, creating a subtle sense of pause that corresponds to the chicks' freezing underfoot.

All this is to suggest that Snyder's skillful manipulation of language succeeds in making his experience viscerally and sensually available to us. Few other writers are capable of description that seems so intimately connected to its referents. Although his association with the Beat movement may have gained him a reputation for improvisational sloppiness, Snyder is in fact a brilliant craftsman who knows exactly how to shape his sentences for maximum effect. Yet as my introductory discussion has meant to suggest, it is not enough simply to evoke the phenomenal content of a walk, however vividly. Such mimesis has its aesthetic value, but it does not suffice for a poem. What is needed is a sense of closure, of emotional fulfillment, that will make the poem seem a coherent whole, not a collection of descriptive fragments.

Such a sense gradually emerges in the last third of the poem, as Snyder arrives at the lake that has been the goal of his walk. An extraordinary tone of accomplishment begins to make itself felt, almost as though the walk had been transformed into a quest. This effect is again created through subtle uses of syntax and other formal elements, as in these lines: "Craggy west end of Benson Lake—after edging / Past dark creek pools on a long white slope—." Snyder departs here from strict chronological sequence in order to heighten the sense of arrival; by putting the creek pools and white slope into a subordinate clause defined as temporally prior to the initial noun clause, he makes the "craggy west end of Benson Lake" stand out in the sentence as an isolated formation toward which everything else strains.

As in other poems by Snyder, such as "Trail Crew Camp at Bear Valley" and "Mid-August at Sourdough Mountain Lookout," "A Walk" reaches a climax in a moment of literal perception that takes on a genuinely visionary quality[32]:

> Lookt down in the ice-black lake
> > lined with cliff
> From far above: deep shimmering trout.

This passage exhibits the same artful control of language displayed in previous lines. There is again the careful setting off of the object of perception as an independent grammatical unit, thus lending it an autonomy and immediacy it would lack if it were assimilated into a subject-verb-object structure. And Snyder again makes use of typography to suggest topography; the indenting of "lined with cliff" creates an open space that cannot help but evoke the space between Snyder and the lake. Beyond these mimetic elements of the passage, however, which do not contribute to any larger pattern that might serve to unify the poem as a whole, it is important to recognize that Snyder's view of the lake acts as a deeply satisfying fulfillment of an earlier moment in the poem. I have already discussed the phenomenological precision of the lines "Jump, land by a pool, trout skitter, / The clear sky"; they clearly stand in an antithetical relation to the later vision of the "deep shimmering trout." One of Snyder's characteristic themes is the dependence of vision on distance, on the watcher's ability to abstract himself from the scene. He deals with the theme more discursively, though using precisely the same images, in a passage from *Mountains and Rivers Without End*:

> a half iced-over lake, twelve thousand feet
>   its sterile boulder bank
> but filled with leaping trout:
>   reflections wobble in the
> mingling circles always spreading out
>   the crazy web of wavelets makes sense
>   seen from high above.[33]

In "A Walk" this point is not stated but embodied in the contrast between skittering and shimmering trout. When Snyder violently obtrudes on the landscape, landing by the pool with a thud, he frightens away the life in the scene; only when he stands high above the lake is he rewarded with a glimpse of "deep shimmering trout." Frustration at the elusiveness of this life (the trout acting almost as genius locii here) is replaced by a penetrating vision into the landscape's depths that makes up in clarity what it loses in proximity. What had seemed a furtive, skittering motion from close up reveals itself from above as a "shimmering," a kind of undulant iridescence, again suggesting that the perception of pattern and wholeness requires a certain distance. (The phonetic relation between "skitter" and "shimmer" adds to the effect, as the punctual, percussive "sk" and "t" sounds are replaced by the softer, more drawn-out "sh" and "m" sounds.)

This visionary moment is thus a kind of Wordsworthian epiphany, in which Snyder sees into the life of things; yet it is also a merely literal vision of the landscape in its bare reality. Snyder is often able to create such an epiphanic effect without departing from the particulars at hand, without broadening his scope to the universal. Unlike Roethke or Warren, he does not import abstractions to add weight to his experience; he relies entirely on the value of the experience in itself, its innate form and rhythm. As David Perkins writes in discussing another, similar poem of Snyder's, "The meaning of the poem lies essentially in the rhythm of the whole experience, an experience that moves through phases of difficulty, achievement, and satisfaction, a rhythm in which each phase has its goodness and gives meaning to the others."[34] Snyder's view of the lake from the cliff represents the poem's phase of achievement, since what is achieved is a vision denied him earlier. It is quite literally the high point of the poem; and it leads directly into the poem's closing phase, what Perkins calls the phase of satisfaction.

The final lines of the poem can be described as a long descent and relaxation, as Snyder moves down from the cliff, along a "steep side hill," to the lake:

> Through slide-aspen and talus, to the east end,
> Down to grass, wading a wide smooth stream
> Into camp. At last.

Again syntax mimes physical experience, as the series of prepositional clauses suggest a movement accelerating towards its goal. The last quoted line, for all its simplicity, carries an almost visceral sense of arrival and relief. Given the poem's general lack of expressive or emotive language, the minimal utterance "At last" has the effect of a deep sigh.[35] (We might recall Williams's use of the same words when Mr. Paterson reaches the summit of the mountain; although there they do not carry as much affective weight because they are not set off as a separate sentence.) If the vision of the lake from above was the poem's epiphany, Snyder's arrival at the camp marks the completion of his quest, the moment at which he can enjoy the rewards of his labor. Those rewards are spelled out in the poem's final lines:

> By the rusty three-year-
> Ago left-behind cookstove
> Of the old trail crew,
> Stoppt and swam and ate my lunch.

The abandoned cookstove clearly demands comparison with Frost's wood-pile; but where for Frost the object gathered a parabolic resonance that pushed it to the center of the poem, for Snyder it merely marks a place to stop where others have also stopped. The last line is beautifully prepared for by the long prepositional clause that precedes it; the elaborate hyphenated modifiers attached to the cookstove point up the plain monosyllables that describe Snyder's activity at the campsite. The complex historical grammar needed to explain the stove gives way to a paratactic string of discrete verbs, each constituting a pure, autonomous present. These acts—stopping, swimming, eating lunch—are so ordinary that they hardly seem to provide the kind of cadence normally expected of a poem. Yet as Perkins suggests, their value is determined by their place in a larger rhythm. Come upon after having read the entire poem, the closing line takes on a wonderful glow of simple dignity and consummation. It acts almost as the equivalent of the ritual feasting and lovemaking that comes at the end of chivalric quests. After all the poem's strenuous windings and amblings, it is fitting that it conclude with a moment of pure enjoyment, of the body fulfilling itself in the elemental pleasures of rest, water and food.

As in "A Step Away From Them," closure in "A Walk" is not thematic but experiential. Its wholeness is a function of the process it depicts, a process in which each moment is interesting for itself, but in which all of the individual moments cohere in a larger pattern. This pattern is simply the classic human one of anticipation, exertion, climax, and relaxation. It can hardly be called a literary pattern, since it is a rhythm fundamental to experience itself. Thus one cannot claim that Snyder imposes it on his material; it is rather exposed than imposed. This raises again the question of where the creative will is to be located in a poem so utterly committed to actual experience. As Perkins says (again of another poem), "Read superficially, this poem . . . may seem to be jottings, as in a diary, of which the poem makes little. The day is merely reported in a language that seems to lack density and resonance."[36] What makes the poem more than a diary entry is the depth of its involvement in the physical sensations and impressions of the walk. Ultimately Snyder, like O'Hara, subscribes to the American belief that experience is already a poem, and that the poet's task is simply to transcribe that poem, or some manageable fragment of it. But as I hope my analysis has begun to show, it is Snyder's verbal artistry that makes this transcription a poem in its own right, his ability to translate fleeting perceptions into a language possessed of an uncanny mimetic power. He moves further toward the impossible goal of making poetic language absolutely transparent to experience than any other poet of our time, while simultaneously bringing forward what Perkins calls the "rhythmic contour" of his experience, so that it takes on the formal beauty of classical art.

In their commitment to the direct, detailed rendering of their experience in all its particularity, without the kind of thematic infrastructure that normally enables a poem to assert its relation to universal truth, O'Hara and Snyder occupy a position at the outer limits of their art. It is a dangerous position, because it risks the loss of poetry's privileged status. If a poem need do nothing more than take down the innate poetry of experience, then it can easily become a second-order phenomenon, a mere simulacrum rather than an object in its own right. Snyder and O'Hara are willing to take this risk, however, at least in some of their poems. For each the walk serves as a convenient means to sample the ongoing continuum of experience, to represent its stray pleasures without claiming more for them than their phenomenal reality. While they differ in the kinds of pleasure they take— O'Hara's for the most part involving tension and desire, Snyder's involving labor and satisfaction—they both share Williams's sense of experience as a kind of music, an aesthetically charged medium with its own beauties and intensities. They differ from Williams, however, in their greater willingness simply to record that music, not to answer it with a dance of the imagination. Their walk poems do not claim the dynamic autonomy that Williams's do; they are more frankly mimetic, more designedly transparent. Yet even as they proclaim themselves mere samples of the daily, they achieve a permanence that seems at odds with such modesty of aim. By giving up the claim to universality that traditionally sets the poem apart from experience, they allow poem and walk to merge more fully; and it is just this fusion of language and experience, dependent as it is on consummate yet self-effacing verbal art and complete absorption in the world's particulars, that makes their best walk poems such unfailing sources of pleasure no matter how often we read them.

VI

A. R. AMMONS AND JOHN ASHBERY:

THE WALK AS THINKING

I F THE FIFTIES and sixties are in part marked by a reaction against various modes of abstraction, and a turn to a purified form of representation that claims for itself the status of sample rather than metaphor, the past twenty years have seen a pronounced shift back to what Robert Pinsky calls "the discursive aspect of poetry," an aspect that encompasses all the ways in which poems deal directly with ideas.[1] But where poets like Frost, Warren, and Roethke tend to represent wisdom as originating beyond the poet's own consciousness, more recent poets, most notably A. R. Ammons and John Ashbery, have insisted on the coextensiveness of consciousness and insight. For them understanding occurs not as a revelation of truth but as an ongoing process of thinking, a process not to be dissociated from experience as a whole. Their poems follow in the mode of Stevens' "An Ordinary Evening in New Haven," charting the incessant shifting and gliding movements of the poet's meditation as it comes into fitful contact with a reality beyond itself.

Ammons and Ashbery are thus poets of thinking, rather than poets of truth or wisdom. They are more concerned with rendering the *experience* of reflection, its rhythms and contours, than with delivering completed thoughts that can claim the status of truth. Discussing the "complex forms of contemporary discursiveness," Charles Altieri usefully analyzes "the opposition between thinking and thought," and traces the valorization of thinking as a central Romantic enterprise descending from Wordsworth and Shelley to Stevens. Altieri's prejudice against what he calls "the scenic imagination," however, leads him to dismiss the empirical situation of the poet-thinker: "instead of a self positioned in the world, the poetics of thinking explores a transpersonal self virtually coextensive with the world's existence *as* an object of concern."[2] By "object of concern," I take Altieri to mean an object of thought rather than perception; the "transpersonal self" of the poem is coextensive with the world in this sense because both are abstractions that exist solely in the language and "thinking" of the poem. In this chapter I want to emphasize the *persistence* of the world as an empirical reality that informs poetic meditation at its most profound. The walk, I would suggest, appeals to poets of thinking precisely because it enables them to anchor thought in the world, to provide the mind with a continuous yet ever-changing point of reference that can keep it from becoming sealed in its own discourse.

· · · · ·

The names of Ammons and Ashbery are commonly linked both on the basis of their shared penchant for a sophisticated form of meditative poetry and through Harold Bloom's impassioned advocacy of the two as contemporary figures of comparable "strength."[3] It hardly needs to be pointed out, however, that beyond their deployment of the meditative mode, they are in fact profoundly different poets. Indeed it might be said that they constitute in their very *difference* from each other discursive counterparts to the pair of poets examined in the previous chapter, Gary Snyder and Frank O'Hara. Like Snyder, Ammons is a poet of nature, in the sense that his poems center on natural phenomena, however strenuously they seek to translate those phenomena into the realm of the spirit.[4] Conversely, Ashbery is overwhelmingly preoccupied with the same ambience of cultural density, geographically epitomized by New York City, that provides the subject matter of his close friend Frank O'Hara. But where Snyder and O'Hara approach their respective realms primarily by means of mimesis or transcription, each setting down as directly as possible the phenomena that interest him, Ammons and Ashbery confront these same realms reflectively, taking them primarily as grounds against which to measure the workings of their own consciousnesses. They thus repeat the difference between nature and culture that separates Snyder and O'Hara, but in a far more introspective key. The external conditions they behold—for Ammons, unity in diversity, the struggle for survival, ineluctable causality; for Ashbery, ephemerality, disjunctiveness, flatness of surface—provide each with potent correlatives for the way consciousness opens onto reality.

Walking is a central motif in both men's work, in part because it offers a bodily analogue both to the movement of thinking and articulating in language, and to the larger flux of reality as it enters the senses.[5] It thus represents a meeting place of the discursive and the phenomenal, two elements whose coordination is a central project in their poetry. The analogy between discursiveness and walking has been most clearly stated by Robert Pinsky, whom I have already cited:

> Definitions of the term "discursive" tend to divide into two apparently contradictory senses. On the one hand, the word describes speech or writing which is wandering and disorganized; on the other, it can also mean "explanatory"—pointed, organized around a setting forth of material.

These opposites are reconciled by the radical sense of motion over terrain; the word signifies going through or going over one's subject. Whether digressively or directly, at a walk or at a run, the motion is on ground and by foot, putting its weight part by part onto the terrain to be covered.[6]

Similarly, the poet David Antin has written, "I can imagine my impulse to speak, to move through language to some formulation, to some new place as being like a kind of walk."[7] These statements show how pervasive the identification of discursive language and walking has been among recent poets. Both Ammons and Ashbery exploit this figurative identification by representing themselves as literally walking, thus giving a kind of experiential body to the discursive motions of their poems.

As I have suggested, however, the motion of the walk also functions for them as analogue to the motion of reality itself. Like Stevens, Ammons and Ashbery share a Heraclitean sense of reality and experience as incessantly flowing and becoming. This theme takes on a different inflection in each poet's work; Ammons tends to emphasize change, the ongoing transformation of spatial entities, whereas Ashbery represents process as a purely temporal succession of moments, in which no fixed object can be grasped. Thus where Ammons is generally able to find some principle of stability underlying the world's shifting appearances, Ashbery is more frustratingly trapped in the slipperiness of temporality. For both poets, however, motion is the dominant feature of the world, and both find a wide array of images for this motion: Ammons ends his long poem *Sphere* with a virtual litany of such images—gliding, sailing, riding a roller coaster—while Ashbery speaks in one poem of the "vehicular madness" of experience.[8] Unlike these images, however, which suggest an essentially passive relationship to the motion of time and world, the walk offers a measure of control, illusory perhaps but nonetheless important for the act of shaping the flux of experience into a poem. For both Ammons and Ashbery the walk becomes a vehicle for exploring the swifter, more evanescent motions each seeks to embody in his poetry.

A. R. Ammons occupies a privileged place in this study, since he is the poet who has reflected most explicitly on the symbiotic relation of poem and walk. I have already discussed his essay "A Poem is a Walk," in which he spells out the formal analogies between the two. I want here to focus on the ways in which his own poetic representations of the walk enable him to unite discursive thought and concrete perception, permitting them to flow almost imperceptibly into one another. The centrality of the walk to Ammons's formal and imaginative methods has been noted by several critics. Richard Howard, for example, writes that Ammons "is the poet of walking, and his is the topography of what one pair of legs can stride over, studies in *enjambment* indeed." Similarly, David Lehman calls him "one of poetry's great walkers, who composes while walking and whose poems keep to a peripatetic pace"; while John Hollander writes, "As a poet of nature he walks in the country accompanied by the moving shadow cast by the light of his own consciousness."[9] The fullest treatment of this motif in Ammons's poetry is by John Elder, who writes that "like Wordsworth, Ammons is a walker," and who recognizes the special role of the walk in his creation of "a balanced field of vision and reflection": "He is always conscious of walking through his own mind, and of the way the mental and terrestrial spheres express each other's particulars, as they spiral together through the unifying processes of poetry."[10] The insistence of this metaphor indicates how essential it is to Ammons's own conception of his poetry, which he has repeatedly described as having "the form of a motion."[11]

Yet the walk functions as more than metaphor in many of Ammons's poems, most notably his two masterpieces "Corsons Inlet" and "Saliences." Both these poems present themselves as meditations unfolding in the course of actual walks; and both seek to integrate the phenomenal data of the walk with its accompanying stream of thought. They use the walk to lend a formal unity to the formless flux of consciousness, to stake out beginning and ending points, and to establish a spatial ground for the poem's temporal wanderings. The physical walk thus plays an indispensable role in firming up and shaping the analogical, discursive "walking" that the poem enacts, enabling the poet to coordinate his inner processes with the real time of experience, and so to be simultaneously faithful to the limitations of particular circumstance and to the expansive possibilities of pure thought.

"Corsons Inlet" is a volatile balancing of these two conditions, alternating between tight contractions to perceived particulars and broadly general assertions. Ammons originally titled the poem "A Nature Walk," but while this certainly lays greater emphasis on the formal coincidence of poem and walk, it also tips the balance too far in the direction of a universal "Nature," and away from the restrictions of the local. In naming the poem after the place in which it is set, Ammons implicitly announces his fidelity to the particulars of his walk, his refusal to synthesize them into some larger conception that would replace or dissolve them. Indeed this refusal constitutes the central discursive gesture of the poem, a fact that accounts for a peculiar discordance between its style and theme. Over and over Ammons tells us that he has "reached no conclusions," committed no "humbling of reality to precept," "perceived nothing completely"; yet he does so in a tone of calm authority and certitude that seems radically at odds with his meaning.[12] One might say that the grammar of statement in the poem clashes with the more fluid kind of syntax associated with the walk itself, so that we are being given both a representation of consciousness in flux and a series of firm claims retrospectively imposed on that flux. The poem's strength lies in its ability to balance this didactic mode of assertion with evocations of a more genuinely open consciousness caught up in the becoming of experience.

The poem opens with a straightforward narration of the walk in its purely external aspect:

> I went for a walk over the dunes again this morning
> to the sea,
> then turned right along
>   the surf
>
>   rounded a naked headland
>   and returned
>   along the inlet shore:
>
>   it was muggy sunny, the wind from the sea steady and high,
> crisp in the running sand,
>   some breakthroughs of sun
> but after a bit
>
> continuous overcast:[13]

Ammons's language here is at its most mimetic, reminiscent of Williams and Snyder in its alignment of topography and typography. The shape and rhythm of the poem both work to capture the experiential contours of the walk; as David Lehman writes: "Such poems as the frequently anthologized 'Corsons Inlet' feature a more rambling gait, uneven lines with jagged edges that suggest a grammar of space; the poet constantly shifts his margins in an effort to set up antiphonal patterns apposite for 'a walk over the dunes' beside 'the inlet's cutting edge.' "[14] Ammons makes subtle use of spacing here and throughout the poem to convey not only spatial forms, like that of the headland, but also temporal rhythms, as in the contrast between "some breakthroughs of sun," slightly indented to suggest its intermittent character, and "continuous overcast," which is set off on the page in a way that seems to mime the condition of linear stasis it describes. This kind of mimesis, however, is somewhat foreign to Ammons, who does not share Snyder's willingness to let his experience embody its own meaning. These opening lines must therefore be seen as a deliberately restrained prologue, in which the merely physical aspect of the walk is laid out so as to establish the ground of the poem's discursive utterances. It is essential to the poem's procedure that it *begin* with the physical experience, since this provides the necessary frame for its assertions, locating them temporally and spatially and so reminding us of their provisional, circumstantial character.

Unlike O'Hara, Ammons sets his walk in the past tense, thus acknowledging the inevitable gap that intervenes between occasion and composition. This gap becomes palpable in the course of the poem, since its discursive assertions are all cast in the present tense, and so are sharply differentiated from its mimesis of the walk as an event in the past. This grammatical difference creates a problem for the reader, however; are we to interpret the poem's thought-content as taking shape *after* the walk, during the act of composition? Or does the poet's thought unfold in the course of the walk itself? At first Ammons maintains the temporal separation between walk and thought, as if meditating on an experience that had already taken place; but as the poem continues this division is slowly blurred, until walk and reflection become virtually indistinguishable.

The structure of the poem as a whole may thus be described as a gradual convergence of seeing and thinking, perception and reflection, two modes of consciousness that are at first kept rigorously distinct:

> the walk liberating, I was released from forms,
> from the perpendiculars,
>   straight lines, blocks, boxes, binds
> of thought
> into the hues, shadings, rises, flowing bends and blends
>   of sight:

Here Ammons insists that his walk is *not* contaminated by the rigid forms of thought, but is given over entirely to the subtle continuities of perception. A firm opposition is thus established between thought, with its sharp, angular schemata (imitated in the very sound of the words "blocks, boxes"), and sight, with its "flowing bends and blends," its apprehension of curve and gradation. Yet while Ammons is clearly valorizing the flowing contours of perception, his compartmentalizing of thought and sight in fact *exemplifies* the "blocks and boxes" of thought, a contradiction that the poem must wrestle to overcome.

While persuasive at first, the opposition between thought and sight turns out to be dangerously constricting as the poem proceeds, since it presents as mutually exclusive aspects of experience that the poet ultimately hopes to unite. While the passage ends with a colon, suggesting that it will be followed by some illustration of the "flowing bends and blends of sight," it in fact gives way to a more blatant instance of "thought," that is, abstract statement, though now framed in terms taken directly from the landscape of the walk:

> I allow myself eddies of meaning:
> yield to a direction of significance
> running
> like a stream through the geography of my work:
>   you can find
> in my sayings
>   swerves of action
>   like the inlet's cutting edge:
>   there are dunes of motion,
> organizations of grass, white sandy paths of remembrance
> in the overall wandering of mirroring mind:
>
> but Overall is beyond me: is the sum of these events
> I cannot draw, the ledger I cannot keep, the accounting
> beyond the account:

This conversion of the landscape into a metaphor for the poem represents an overly facile solution to the problem of mediating between sense experience and thought; the notion of "mirroring mind," which recurs throughout Ammons's work (see his poem "Reflective") is here given too literal a realization. Note especially the use of the familiar allegorical "of" construction ("white sandy paths of remembrance"), which has the effect of denying the empirical reality of its first term.[15] This allegorizing of the landscape is, I think, an inevitable outcome of Ammons's overly rigid distinction between perception and thought at the outset of the poem. Like Stevens in "An Ordinary Evening in New Haven," Ammons begins with a static polarity that forces him to commit crude reductions in his effort to bridge the poles. This passage is thus the equivalent of canto II of "An Ordinary Evening," in which Stevens internalizes New Haven too fully, rendering it "an impalpable town." Like Stevens, Ammons must blur his initial polarity if he is to arrive at a subtle and nuanced account of experience. Accordingly, as the poem proceeds, a more fluid relationship between the literal details of the landscape and the poet's meditation on his own consciousness begins to emerge, in which the landscape does not act as a mere emblem of mind, but rather provides the means by which mind measures its own uncertainties and fluctuations.

The poem's central assertion, as I have said, is its denial of totalization, of the possibility of achieving an "Overall" understanding. All that the poet can do is to enumerate or record, one by one, the separate "events" of both mind and nature as they occur, without seeking to amass them into a larger configuration. Yet the very denial of such a synthesis itself constitutes an act of synthetic thought, an attempt to generalize at the most all-encompassing level. Throughout his work Ammons weds this insatiable penchant for generality with a nominalist distrust of all general concepts; as a result his poetry must keep in constant motion, oscillating between provisional efforts to theorize about the cosmos and adamant returns to the hard data of experience.

Such a return to the immediate circumstances of the walk takes place in the next lines:

> in nature there are few sharp lines: there are areas of
> primrose
>   more or less dispersed;
> disorderly orders of bayberry; between the rows
> of dunes,
> irregular swamps of reeds,
> though not reeds alone, but grass, bayberry, yarrow, all . . .
> predominantly reeds:

The passage begins with another general assertion, but thereafter shifts to an account of particulars—somewhat disorientingly, since we are abruptly brought from the level of "nature" as a whole to the localized landscape of the poem without any evident transition. In cataloging the different forms of vegetation he sees, Ammons now adopts in his own language the kind of self-modifying looseness that he didactically invokes in the discursive portions of the poem. At first calling attention to the "irregular swamps of reeds," he at once feels compelled to point out that these contain "not reeds alone, but grass, bayberry, yarrow, all. . . ." He trails off because he knows he can never adequately account for the multifarious particulars of the scene, that he will always be guilty of some degree of oversimplification. The "all" thus stands as a gesture toward the many organisms he has had to omit from his catalog; and it is followed by a new formulation that returns to his initial reduction, but this time acknowledges its inadequacy: "*predominantly* reeds" (italics mine). The three lines nicely illustrate the essential trajectory of Ammons's thought, as he moves from a too singular account of the world ("reeds") to a futile effort to represent its full complexity and multiplicity ("though not reeds alone"), finally coming back to his first account with a new awareness of its partial nature ("predominantly reeds"). They thus begin to offer an antidote to the stark mind/ world dualism that led Ammons to allegorize the landscape in the previous passage. Now the poet is able to represent mind and world simultaneously, not by subordinating one as vehicle to the other as tenor, but by depicting mind in the process of grasping world in all its complexity. Seeing and thinking have begun to coalesce.

In the next lines Ammons returns to the assertive mode that runs throughout the poem, alternating with more tentative, exploratory passages:

> I have reached no conclusions, have erected no boundaries,
> shutting out and shutting in, separating inside
>
>> from outside: I have
>> drawn no lines:
>> as
>
> manifold events of sand
> change the dune's shape that will not be the same shape
> tomorrow,
>
> so I am willing to go along, to accept
> the becoming
> thought, to stake off no beginnings or ends, establish
>> no walls:

Ammons's claim that he has not separated "inside / from outside" stands in direct contradiction to the various dualisms we have already observed in the poem. Yet if Ammons's poem never quite behaves the way he keeps insisting it does, it nonetheless manifests a genuine tendency toward "the becoming / thought," in its less assertive passages at least. The ever-shifting shapes of dunes are his central emblem of mind in motion, an image that will be stunningly developed in "Saliences." A more relevant image of mental process for our purposes comes in his claim to be "willing to go along," in which the literal and analogical dimensions of the walk merge, as they have been implicitly merging throughout the poem. In Ammons's own words (from "A Poem is a Walk"), the walk is "an externalization of an interior seeking" (p. 16), representing with physical immediacy the restless wanderings of a mind that is rarely content to stand still. The problem with the poem up to this point is that Ammons has spent too much time striking a pose, and not enough time "going along," an imbalance that he will shortly begin to remedy.

The notion of transition as "soft," impossible to fix at a given place or moment, is elaborated in another descriptive passage:

> by transitions the land falls from grassy dunes to creek
> to undercreek: but there are no lines, though
>> change in that transition is clear

as any sharpness: but "sharpness" spread out,
allowed to occur over a wider range
than mental lines can keep:

This again conveys the poet's vision of change as minutely incremental, too gradual to be assimilated to "mental lines." The landscape
is no longer merely a metaphor for the poet's consciousness; although
this image of natural transition clearly has relevance to what Ammons
calls "the becoming thought," it also retains its integrity as a view of the
landscape. Indeed this passage itself serves as a transition to the
poem's central exploration of the place and its inhabitants, as Ammons leaves behind his posturing and gives us an extended representation of mind caught up in the becoming of world:

the moon was full last night: today, low tide was low:
black shoals of mussels exposed to the risk
of air
and, earlier, of sun,
waved in and out with the waterline, waterline inexact,
caught always in the event of change:
a young mottled gull stood free on the shoals
and ate
to vomiting: another gull, squawking possession, cracked a crab,
picked out the entrails, swallowed the soft-shelled legs, a ruddy
turnstone running in to snatch leftover bits:

risk is full: every living thing in
siege: the demand is life, to keep life: the small
white blacklegged egret, how beautiful, quietly stalks and spears
the shallows, darts to shore
to stab—what? I couldn't
see against the black mudflats—a frightened
fiddler crab?

In this brilliant passage, sight and thought are at last fully united. We
are no longer conscious of any gap between the experience of the walk
and the meditation that it prompts; the verb tenses waver between past
("a young mottled gull stood free") and present ("white blacklegged
egret . . . quietly stalks"), suggesting that Ammons is no longer intent
on separating occasion and composition. Most importantly, the poem
is no longer alternating, as in its opening passages, between two extremes of discourse, one a detached, flat reportage of external phenomena, the other a rather strident assertion of the poet's own nomi-
nalism. Now exactly rendered perceptions are blended with a flexible
meditation that always maintains contact with the world through which

the poet walks. As in the central sections of "An Ordinary Evening in New Haven," where Stevens carefully measures the mutual impingements of mind and reality, Ammons here succeeds in representing the fluid interminglings of thought and perception, now seen as interdependent rather than mutually exclusive. Like Stevens, then, Ammons moves toward the notion of "a visibility of thought," a state in which seeing and thinking can no longer be differentiated, as they had been in the poem's opening lines.

Much of the power of this passage lies in its adoption of what Linda Orr calls "an imitative language," one that stands in sharp contrast to the language of assertion that has previously dominated the poem. As Orr points out, "Sentences in poems-of-process must be doubling back all the time, qualifying, contradicting. . . . The poet must be alert to any tendencies for rest and sweep the words up again."[16] In this respect the language of this passage most resembles that of Bishop's "The End of March," with its incessant qualifications and questionings of its own perceptions. But Ammons is more intent on interpreting what he sees than Bishop; hence he is constantly broadening out from particular phenomena to larger ideas of order. Unlike its earlier assertions of a general stance, however, the poem's conceptual language now remains firmly tied to the minute particulars of the walk, representing the poet's moment-to-moment effort at making sense of the landscape before him.

The most prominent feature of this landscape is expressed by the recurrent term "risk," which evokes both the terror and the exhilaration of natural freedom. Throughout the passage Ammons expresses a simultaneous awareness of the aesthetic dimension of the scene and the savage struggle for life that underlies it. This doubleness is epitomized in the first line: "the moon was full last night: today, low tide was low." Full moon and low tide can both be seen as aesthetic phenomena, each permitting a human spectator to *see* more than is normally visible. But in the next line this aesthetic bonus is revealed as a terrible danger to the creatures who inhabit the shore: "black shoals of mussels exposed to the risk / of air / and, earlier, of sun." Suddenly we are made aware of the helplessness of creatures for whom air and sun are not pleasures but threats.

Yet having acknowledged this darker aspect of the scene, Ammons cannot help continuing to dwell on its beauty, as in the lovely line "waved in and out with the waterline, waterline inexact," which seems to embody, in its undulating rhythm and evocative use of repetition, the motions it describes, like the line in which Bishop describes the wet string rising and falling in the water. But the next line again underscores the predicament of the mussels, while translating it into an exis-

tential condition: "caught always in the event of change." Change itself
is the source of both beauty and terror here, combining freedom and
risk in one violent spectacle. The brilliant description of the feeding
birds does not seek to pass judgment on the predators, but sees their
activity as deeply natural, if also deeply frightening. Responding to the
sight, the poet again takes refuge in generalization: "risk is full: every
living thing in / siege: the demand is life, to keep life." The key word
here is "full," which takes us back to the full moon, and implies that
what seems destructive is in fact a form of plenitude, the fullness of life
desperately holding on to itself, even if it be at the expense of other
life.[17]

The next lines offer a particularly fine rendering of the concurrent
beauty and savagery of nature. Ammons has to interrupt his description of the "small white black-legged egret" to exclaim "how beautiful,"
then goes on to tell of how it "quietly stalks and spears / the shallows."
What follows is a striking instance of the way Ammons cues the poem's
syntax to the phenomenological time of the walk: the egret "darts to
shore / to stab—what? I couldn't / see against the black mudflats—a
frightened / fiddler crab?" The torsions of the sentence create the effect that it is unfolding simultaneously with the perceptions it describes, a device we have seen in Williams, Bishop, and Snyder as well.
This temporalizing of syntax is an important element in Ammons's
style, since it permits him to give a verbal form not only to the flux of
phenomena but to "the becoming thought." Just as important here is
the poet's acknowledgment of his own limited perspective; he does not
have a godlike vantage on the scene—"Overall is beyond me"—but can
only see according to his position at any given moment. He is willing
to speculate about what he cannot see, however, and his surmise is in
no way less harsh than the realities he has witnessed: he is careful to
specify that his hypothetical fiddler crab is "frightened."

From the terror of "every living thing in siege," the poet has but to
turn his head to observe a different spectacle, one with less baleful implications:

> the news to my left over the dunes and
> reeds and bayberry clumps was
> fall: thousands of tree swallows
> gathering for flight:
> an order held
> in constant change: a congregation
> rich with entropy: nevertheless, separable, noticeable
> as one event,
> not chaos: preparations for

flight from winter,
cheet, cheet, cheet, cheet, wings rifling the green clumps,
beaks
at the bayberries
  a perception full of wind, flight, curve,
  sound:
  the possibility of rule as the sum of rulelessness:
the "field" of action
with moving, incalculable center:

Here again perception modulates into thought all but imperceptibly, in part with the aid of Ammons's beloved colon, which helps to enforce the sense of continual forward motion that all his poems try to embody. Now rather than the vision of nature as an ongoing struggle for life in which every creature must work for itself, he beholds a more delicately balanced picture of "order held / in constant change." For all its multiplicity, the gathering of swallows coheres into a single phenomenon, "a congregation / rich with entropy." That last phrase resembles the earlier "risk is full" in its insistence on the plenitude made possible by change and disorder. The syntax of this passage consists not of a shifting hypotaxis imitating the temporality of particular events, as in the previous passage, but of a looser paratactic sequence of clauses held together only by colons. It thus approximates the state of order in multiplicity embodied by the swallows, in which individual entities form a larger whole not by virtue of any specific transactions among them, like the predatorial transactions of egret and fiddler crab, but simply through their contiguity, their copresence in a shared space.

Still describing the swallows, Ammons gives us a vivid series of close-ups that emphasize the restlessness of this pseudo-organism: "wings rifling the green clumps, / beaks / at the bayberries." The word "full" returns once more in the phrase "a perception full of wind, flight, curve, / sound," again evoking a condition of maximal activity, in which too many things are occurring at once to be perceived completely. Clearly this condition is an exhilarating one for Ammons, suggesting "the possibility of rule as the sum of rulelessness: / the 'field' of action / with moving, incalculable center."[18] It could be said that the poem's own "moving, incalculable center" lies somewhere between these two alternative visions of natural process and change, the predatorial, Darwinian vision of "every living thing in siege" and the more harmonious "congregation / rich with entropy" of the swallows. That moving center is in fact simply the poet's own body, as his use of the coordinate "to my left" suggests. Rather than locating the phenomena he describes in objective spatial terms, he acknowledges the central place of the body and the perceiving self in balancing different aspects of the environment. His walk thus becomes a vehicle for achieving a kind of equilibrium between the news to the right and "the news to [the] left," the harsh and the harmonious possibilities of life. Ultimately Ammons's Thoreauvian temperament inclines him to see order rather than struggle as the dominant principle in nature; thus it may be significant that he turns *from* the predators *to* the swallows. Spatially the two are symmetrically balanced, but temporally the second replaces the first, allowing the poet to move toward a final affirmative vision of an order that transcends individual struggle.

From the swallows, with their evocation of a "soft" order, shapeless but unified, the poet's gaze narrows to discrete objects with definite forms:

> in the smaller view, order tight with shape:
> blue tiny flowers on a leafless weed: carapace of crab:
> snail shell:
>> pulsations of order
>> in the bellies of minnows: orders swallowed,
> broken down, transferred through membranes
> to strengthen larger orders: but in the large view, no
> lines or changeless shapes: the working in and out, together
> and against, of millions of events: this,
>>> so that I make
>>> no form of
>>> formlessness:

Ammons here acknowledges that nature offers countless instances of hard-edged form—flowers, shells, organisms—but insists that phenomenologically these represent details in a larger picture that contains no "lines or changeless shapes." The very act of turning his gaze to small, formally perfect items may relieve the poet of the burden of comprehending the "millions of events" constantly working together; but that relief can only be momentary, since his primary commitment remains with "the large view," the difficult vision of process and multiplicity microcosmically represented by the swallows.

Reflecting further on the large view, Ammons now chooses to characterize it with a rather surprising word, "serenity":

> orders as summaries, as outcomes of actions override
>> or in some way result, not predictably (seeing me gain
> the top of a dune,
> the swallows

could take flight—some other fields of bayberry
     could enter fall
     berryless) and there is serenity:

     no arranged terror: no forcing of image, plan,
or thought:
no propaganda, no humbling of reality to precept:

terror pervades but is not arranged, all possibilities
of escape open: no route shut, except in
     the sudden loss of all routes:

The very absence of a controlling will, the poet argues, creates a sense
of peace, despite the ongoing struggle he had earlier depicted. Terror
is a pervasive force here, he concedes, but it "is not arranged," and
hence not evil. He takes comfort in the knowledge that "all possibilities / of escape [are] open" (what possibilities of escape for the hap-
less mussels, we might ask), that "no route [is] shut, except / in the
sudden loss of all routes." The last phrase, evidently a reference to
death, seems a fairly drastic qualification of the sense of freedom and
serenity being evoked here; yet after all it is a mark of Ammons's willingness to "accept the becoming thought," even if it leads him back to
the darker vision of "every living thing in siege" that he has been working to overturn.

The poem's closing lines shift back into the rhetoric of assertion
that had been abandoned in the middle section:

     I see narrow orders, limited tightness, but will
not run to that easy victory:
     still around the looser, wider forces work:
     I will try
        to fasten into order enlarging grasps of disorder, widening
scope, but enjoying the freedom that
Scope eludes my grasp, that there is no finality of vision,
that I have perceived nothing completely,
     that tomorrow a new walk is a new walk.

Once again the poet gives us a statement of policy, though now oriented toward the future rather than the past, and so less self-congratu-
latory in tone. Ammons's use of capitalization to distinguish between vision in process ("scope") and a totalizing perspective ("Scope") is perhaps overly subtle, but the contrast is clear nonetheless. If the preceding lines are a little too comfortably abstract, however, the final line
beautifully returns us to the poem's generative occasion, and gives us a
formulation at once concise and concrete: "tomorrow a new walk is a

new walk." This is I think deeply satisfying both in its air of cadential firmness and in its implicit denial of closure. For once the poem's paradoxical conjunction of authority and provisionality does not seem contradictory, perhaps because the line refers beyond itself to experience. In reminding us that the poem's meditation has been framed by a particular walk, Ammons locates its categorical claims in time and space, and so softens their authority. These are my thoughts today, he tells us; tomorrow I will change my mind. We should recall at this point that the poem's first line announced, "I went for a walk over the dunes *again* this morning" (italics mine), implying that this walk is already one of a potentially open-ended series, and should not be taken as in any way definitive or unique. Ammons does not claim that this particular walk, like Frost's walk in "The Wood-Pile," for example, deserves to be singled out from the poet's experience because it has yielded a special insight; tomorrow's walk will be equally valuable in the thoughts that it occasions.

Taken by itself, this closing line may seem a striking but ultimately empty declaration, paying lip service to a principle it cannot truly observe. After all, "Corsons Inlet" is a poem fully conscious of its centrality to the poet's oeuvre; it is not by accident that it has become the most anthologized of Ammons's poems, for its rhetoric aims at the very "finality of vision" whose possibility it denies. Remarkably enough, however, Ammons chose to take his last line literally: the next day he went for another walk, and wrote another poem about it.[19] He thus confronted, more squarely and explicitly than any other poet I have so far discussed, a problem central to the mode of representation that the walk poem exemplifies, the problem of repetition. If "tomorrow a new walk is a new walk," that is, if all experience is equally valuable, equally fresh, can one simply go on writing poem after poem based on walk after walk? Surely at a certain point sameness will overcome newness, and monotony will set in. We have seen how Frank O'Hara wrestled with this danger, ultimately destroying the very grounds on which his walk poems are based out of a restless urge to move on. But Ammons is not as restlessly innovative as O'Hara, although in a subtle way he may be the more daring of the two. For he takes up the challenge of repetition with unprecedented directness, writing a second poem the day after his great manifesto was composed, and taking as his occasion another walk in precisely the same setting.

That poem, "Saliences," while less immediately accessible, is for a number of reasons a better poem than "Corsons Inlet." It does not contain the manifesto-like rhetoric that to my mind mars certain portions of the earlier poem ("I have drawn / no lines"); instead it feels its way more tentatively towards insight. In a sense, then, "Corsons Inlet" can be described as the prescription of which "Saliences" is the enactment. Rather than obsessively *telling* us that it will "accept the becoming thought," it simply does so. In its narrower, more linear format, the poem seems to embody pure mental process, a sharply focused flow of consciousness directing itself at an outer scene, while retaining a strong sense of its own interiority. Its language, as David Kalstone has demonstrated, is a remarkable effort to embody "a whirl of motion, self merging with the outer world. . . . The rhythm, the short lines and relentless alternation of noun and participle practically blot out differences between actions of mind and nature."[20] Where the language of "Corsons Inlet" is leisurely, taking its time to look the landscape over and draw out all its implications, "Saliences" is rapid and concentrated; as Harold Bloom puts it, the poem "punches itself along with an overwhelming vigor, showing its exuberance by ramming through every blocking particular."[21]

All these characterizations of the poem's language, however, must be qualified by a recognition that "Saliences" is structurally divided into two very different parts, the division being explicitly marked by an asterisk. These two parts correspond to two separate writing occasions, both occurring on the same day.[22] Stylistically, the first part is far more tumultuous, tracing the poet's rapt contemplation of the dunes in their constant metamorphoses, both festive and fearful:

> Consistencies rise
> and ride
> the mind down
> hard routes
>   walled
> with no outlet and so
> to open a variable geography,
>   proliferate
> possibility, here
> is this dune fest
>   releasing mind feeding out,
> gathering clusters,
> fields of order in disorder,
> where choice
> can make beginnings,
>   turns,
>   reversals,
> where straight line
> and air-hard thought
> can meet

> unarranged disorder,
>   dissolve
> before the one event that
> creates present time
> in the multi-variable
>   scope:[23]

As in "Corsons Inlet," Ammons here celebrates the power of natural process to counteract "consistencies," to "open a variable geography" and allow the mind to "make beginnings, / turns, / reversals." Once again the landscape offers an image of the mind in motion, although now, as Kalstone points out, the two can hardly be distinguished grammatically; hence neither is subordinated as vehicle to the other's tenor. What is most striking about this section of the poem is its insistence on *presence*, both spatial and temporal. This is reflected in its barrage of present participles and gerundives, which continues to the end of the section, and in its evocation of "the one event that / creates present time," a phrase reminiscent of the phrase "caught always in the event of change" in "Corsons Inlet." An equally strong sense of spatial presence is created by the use of such demonstrative pronouns as "here" and "this": "here / is this dune fest." Indeed if one did not know that these lines, like all Ammons's poems, were composed at the typewriter, one might easily assume that they had been scribbled in a notebook as the poet stood amidst the dunes. In any case, the poem's fictional presentation of its own utterance is more important than the literal circumstances of its composition; and in this first section of "Saliences," Ammons appears eager to bring himself and his poem as close to the flurrying events of dune and wind as he possibly can through the resources of language.

Another feature that distinguishes "Saliences" from "Corsons Inlet" is the relative lack of prominence of the first-person pronoun, which only enters in the second part of the poem. As Kalstone notes, "an elaborate syntax keeps the 'I' from making assertions in any ordinary way."[24] Thus the poem suppresses the kind of self-aggrandizing claims that are scattered throughout "Corsons Inlet" ("I have reached no conclusions," "I make / no form of / formlessness"), instead preferring to articulate its themes through a more difficult process of meditative discovery. The abstract "mind" substitutes in the opening lines for "I," perhaps because it is better suited to illustrate the movements of "feeding out" and "gathering" on which the poem centers. But it is important to note that the lack of an "I" here does not constitute an effort to transcend or escape the self; as in "An Ordinary Evening in New Haven," the absence of the first person in fact signals a more radical subjectivity, in which the self becomes the very ground of discourse rather than a mere grammatical element.

The next part of the first section explores one variable in "the multi-variable / scope":

> a variable of wind
> among the dunes,
> making variables
> of position and direction and sound
> of every reed leaf
> and bloom,
> running streams of sand,
> winding, rising, at a depression
> falling out into deltas,
> weathering shells with blast,
> striking hiss into clumps of grass,
> against bayberry leaves,
>   lifting
> the spider from footing to footing
> hard across the dry even crust
> toward the surf:
> wind, a variable, soft wind, hard
> steady wind, wind
> shaped and kept in the
> bent of trees,
> the prevailing dipping seaward
> of reeds,
> the kept and erased sandcrab trails:
> wind, the variable to the gull's flight,
> how and where he drops the clam
> and the way he heads in, running to loft:
> wind, from the sea, high surf
> and cool weather;
> from the land, a lessened breakage
> and the land's heat:
> wind alone as a variable,
> as a factor in millions of events,
> leaves no two moments
>   on the dunes the same:

As in canto XII of "An Ordinary Evening," the wind here acts as an emblem of pure process, a "force that traverses a shade," sweeping together all the particulars of the scene in its violent motion. The passage brilliantly conveys the wind's restlessness and power in its insistent repetitions and drumlike sequence of present participles; the phrase "striking hiss into clumps of grass" is a particularly felicitous example of Ammons's gift for onomatopoeia. Although the wind thrusts itself on the poet's attention through its pervasive influence, it enables him to catalog all the other elements of the scene as well: reeds, dunes, trees, gulls. It thus epitomizes what Ammons means by "salience," namely any element or feature in the field of perception that obtrudes itself, allowing it to be grasped as an entity. On this point I must take issue with Bloom, who tells us that "Saliences etymologically are out-leapings, 'mind feeding out,' not taking in perceptions but turning its violent energies out into the field of action."[26] Whatever the word's etymology may be, it is Ammons's usage that matters; and while Bloom quotes the phrase "mind feeding out," he does not cite the next words, "gathering clusters." These perceptual clusters, it seems to me, are what Ammons means by saliences, not the "violent energies" of pure mind.

Indeed it is the role of these saliences precisely to *defeat* the autonomous energies of mind, to force mind to change in accordance with external forces, as the next lines make clear:

> keep
> free to these events,
> bend to these
> changing weathers:
>
> multiple as sand, events of sense
> alter old dunes
> of mind,
> release new channels of flow,
> free materials
> to new forms:
> wind alone as a variable
> takes this neck of dunes
> out of calculation's reach:
> come out of the hard
> routes and ruts,
> pour over the walls
> of previous assessments: turn to
> the open,
> the unexpected, to new saliences of feature.

Shifting into the imperative mode, Ammons now adopts a more didactic manner, although again the absence of the first-person pronoun keeps these lines from taking on the assertive tone of "Corson's Inlet." Indeed we do not know whether the imperatives are directed to the reader or the poet himself; both seem equally likely. What sets this passage apart from similar passages in the previous poem is precisely the notion of salience, a notion that gives the poet a firmer means of relating external and internal change than the metaphorical "of" (which nonetheless briefly reappears in the phrase "old dunes of mind"). Saliences are phenomena that one cannot help noticing; they thus force the mind to admit new objects, to break out of the "hard / routes and ruts" of its "previous assessments." By staying open to the world, the mind will always find stimuli for change; it is only when the mind remains trapped in itself, "walled / with no outlet," that it stagnates.

The first section of the poem features change raised to an almost apocalyptic pitch, in which "no two moments [are] the same." The sense of dizzying proximity to the "dune fest," of being fully caught up in the interplay of wind and landscape, keeps the poet from apprehending any principle of constancy other than change itself. While this vision has its liberating aspect, "free[ing] materials / to new forms," it is ultimately too thoroughgoing an abandonment of identity and wholeness for Ammons. In the second section, written after some time had passed, he attempts to redress the balance, laying emphasis on the larger constancy that underlies the frenetic change of the first section:

> The reassurance is
> that through change
> continuities sinuously work,
> cause and effect
>   without alarm,
> gradual shadings out or in,
> motions that full
>   with time
> do not surprise, no
> abrupt leap or burst: possibility,
> with meaningful development
> of circumstance:

The word "reassurance" indicates how disturbing the violent change depicted in the first section really is to Ammons, however much he may have seemed to welcome it. A new calm prevails, one that seems to bespeak a greater distance from the events being described.

Recollection in tranquility is the dominant tone of this second section, which next moves into the past tense and a more conventionally narrative grammar:

> when I went back to the dunes today,
>   saliences,
> congruent to memory,
> spread firmingly across my sight:
> the narrow white path
> rose and dropped over
> grassy rises toward the sea:
> sheets of reeds,
> tasseling now near fall,
> filled the hollows
> with shapes of ponds or lakes:
> bayberry, darker, made wandering
> chains of clumps, sometimes pouring
> into heads, like stopped water:

The poet no longer depicts himself as present in the scene; his spatial and temporal separation from it now permits him to perceive it in a calmer, larger view. For the first time the "I" enters the poem, suggesting that self and world are no longer caught up and blurred together by the wind as actual and grammatical agent, but have regained their sharp-edged autonomy. Particular objects stand out with a clarity they lacked in the previous passage, where they entered only as indexes of the wind's power. The volatile flux of the first section gives way to a sense of solidity and permanence: "saliences, / congruent to memory, / spread firmingly across my sight." A crucial change has taken place in the notion of saliences; where in the previous section they represented the obtrusion of new phenomena, here they are "congruent to memory"; that is, they are phenomena that give a firmness to sight precisely through their *familiarity.* Fortunately we share the poet's memory, that is if we have read "Corsons Inlet," since the sights he remembers from his previous walk in this landscape are all recorded in his previous poem. Thus we too feel a pleasant sense of recognition as we encounter the reeds and bayberry once more; for us as for Ammons they are reassuringly solid and familiar, signs that we know where we are.

Ammons's reprising of the cast of characters from "Corsons Inlet" continues in the next passage, as constancy is again emphasized:

> much seemed
> constant, to be looked
> forward to, expected:
> from the top of a dune rise,
> look of ocean salience: in
>   the hollow,

> where a runlet
>   makes in
> at full tide and fills a bowl,
> extravagance of pink periwinkle
> along the grassy edge,
> and a blue, bunchy weed, deep blue,
> deep into the mind the dark blue
>   constant:
> minnows left high in the tide-deserted pocket,
>   fiddler crabs
> bringing up gray pellets of drying sand,
> disappearing from air's faster events
> at any close approach:
> certain things and habits
>   recognizable as
> having lasted through the night:

The beauty of this passage lies in the ease with which it integrates a purely aesthetic appreciation of phenomena with a more reflective awareness of what it means for these things to have "lasted through the night." Rather than focusing sharply on each object and observing its particular functions, as he had in "Corsons Inlet," the poet's gaze flits about the scene more lightly, touching each thing once as if to confirm its presence and then moving on. There are occasional pauses to savor details, as in the lovely lines on the "blue, bunchy weed": "deep into the mind the dark blue / constant." Evidently these are the "blue tiny flowers on a leafless weed" of "Corsons Inlet"; but now they have taken on a deep, penetrating blueness that can only be the result of their constancy, as they rouse an answering memory in the mind. Once more I must differ with Bloom, whose more visionary bent leads him, I think, to distort Ammons's phenomenal acuity; he says of the lines on the blue flower: "[Ammons] finds himself now in an astonishing equilibrium with the particulars, containing them in his own mind by reimagining them there."[26] But it is memory rather than imagination that gives these flowers their resonance for Ammons; because he had seen them the day before, he perceives them now not merely as being but as *continuing*.

Not everything continues, however, as we learn in the next lines:

> though what change in
> a day's doing!
> desertions of swallows
>   that yesterday
> ravaged air, bush, reed, attention

in gatherings wide as this neck of dunes:
now, not a sound
or shadow, no trace of memory, no remnant
   explanation:
summations of permanence!

The swallows, so prominent a part of "Corsons Inlet," have flown away. This single departure, although it is one the poet himself had anticipated when he wrote of their "preparations for flight," rends a hole in the fabric of constancy that the previous lines have woven. In effect the very *absence* of the swallows becomes a salience more obtrusive than the familiar "look of ocean salience" in the previous lines. The poet's effort to counter the changes wrought by the wind in the first half of the poem by focusing instead on continuities is thus brought up short, as he is forced to acknowledge that loss or departure has decisively altered the face of the landscape, however much still remains intact.

This recognition precipitates the poem's magnificent close, in which a still larger vision of constancy is achieved:

where not a single single thing endures,
the overall reassures,
deaths and flights,
shifts and sudden assaults claiming
limited orders,
the separate particles:
earth brings to grief
much in an hour that sang, leaped, swirled,
yet keeps a round
   quiet turning,
beyond loss or gain,
beyond concern for the separate reach.

Ammons's scope has widened now to include the earth as a whole, the "Overall" that he had insisted was beyond him in "Corsons Inlet." From this perspective, all "shifts and sudden assaults" are incidental to the "round, / quiet turning" that encloses them. At this farthest remove, in which the poet assumes the vantage of an astronaut, the "separate particles" no longer show up as anything more than motes. This sense of reassuring quietude and constancy has thus been purchased at the price of the intimate, phenomenal involvement with the landscape evidenced in the poem's previous lines. The poet cannot simultaneously maintain contact with the particulars of the scene and with the greater whole that includes them; he can only oscillate between these mutually exclusive perspectives.

The poem as a whole executes a gradual tracking movement from close-up to long shot. In the first half, the poet is so near to the landscape that all separation is lost, and he becomes another dune at the mercy of the wind. In the second half, he keeps enough distance to make out the separate forms clearly, to let the salient features of the landscape emerge and be recognized. But the absence of the swallows impels him to back away still farther, until all particular losses are dissolved in a "summation of permanence." The mobility of perspective that is a central feature of the walk is thus converted by Ammons into a structural and thematic principle: "Saliences" dramatizes an effort to find the proper distance from which to view the world. Ultimately, of course, the poem underwrites the necessity of movement itself, since each perspective must sacrifice one "salience" or aspect of reality in favor of another. Only by remaining in continual motion can the observer perceive the world's minute, flurrying changes in appearances, its solid but transitory objects, and the permanent whole that encompasses them by turns.

The poem thus *incorporates* motion or mobility far more fully than does "Corsons Inlet," which invokes motion as a didactic concept without wholly giving itself over to motion as a poetic principle. Between them the two poems display the full range of possible relationships between thinking and seeing: "Corsons Inlet" is more leisurely, allowing individual thoughts to emerge naturally from particular phenomena, and binding them into a whole by means of a programmatic rhetoric that insists on the impossibility of wholeness; while "Saliences" announces its theme from the outset, pursuing it in a more sustained way as it finds various embodiments in the landscape. Both poems, however, insist on the interdependence of thinking and perceiving; the virtue of particulars for Ammons lies precisely in their ability to become saliences, impingements that alter the mind's direction, insuring that thought, like the world, remains constantly changing, constantly moving. The two poems are vivid illustrations of the worldliness of thinking, of the mind's inability to separate itself from external events and phenomena. That two such utterly different yet masterful poems could be written on successive days, about walks in the same landscape, is the ultimate testimony to Ammons's faith in change, his knowledge that "tomorrow a new walk is a new walk."

. . . . .

Unlike Ammons, John Ashbery is not a poet greatly given to description, in the sense of the verbal representation of external objects or phenomena. Critics have tended to emphasize the detachment of his poetry from all external referents; thus Robert Pinsky writes that Ashbery's language "comes closer than one might have thought possible to being, itself, a nominalistic particular: pure, referring to nothing else, unique."[27] And Paul Breslin argues that "Ashbery's poetry seldom connects itself unequivocally to any external occasion or context."[28] Many similar statements could be adduced; indeed a consensus seems to have formed among most readers that Ashbery's poetry is entirely self-referential, to be admired or censured as such. Yet Ashbery himself, in statements and interviews, has consistently emphasized the mimetic function of his work, its effort to transcribe the experience of consciousness itself at its most elusive. Thus in a statement for the encyclopedia *Contemporary Poets of the English Language* he claims that his poetry presents "an individual consciousness confronting or confronted by a world of external phenomena. The work is a very complex but, I hope, clear and concrete transcript of the impressions left by these phenomena on that consciousness."[29] Ashbery's emphasis here on the role played by a world external to consciousness is especially revealing, since it is just such externality that most critics find lacking in his work.

Equally significant is the notion of the poem as transcript, which allies Ashbery with such worldly poets as O'Hara and Snyder. He reinforces this mimetic or transcriptive view of his work in various interviews, claiming that it is "a mimesis of how experience comes to me," and that his poems are "about the experience of experience. . . . [T]he particular occasion is of lesser interest to me than the way a happening or experience filters through to me. . . . I'm trying to set down a generalized transcript of what's really going on in our minds all day long."[30] Perhaps the most literal version of this transcriptive poetics is suggested by a method of composition Ashbery reports having experimented with: "I waste a lot of time before writing by going for long walks—and occasionally I would take this pocket tape recorder along, fish it out of my pocket and mutter something into it."[31] This sounds suspiciously similar to O'Hara's more playful account on the back cover of *Lunch Poems* of how in the course of his walks he would pause "at a sample Olivetti to type up thirty or forty lines of ruminations"; both poets seem intent on abolishing the gap between occasion and composition completely, allowing the poem to emerge simultaneously with the experience that gives rise to it.

Ashbery differs from O'Hara, however, in that his focus is less on the particular occasion than on what he calls "the experience of experience," a deeply reflexive sense of how phenomena enter the mind and impinge on its workings. Thus his poetry offers not a representation of particular phenomena, like O'Hara's, but what David Lehman calls "a new mimesis, with consciousness itself as the model."[32] By shifting his attention from the surface of the world to the surface of the mind, Ashbery in effect reinvents mimesis, making of it a remarkably supple instrument for registering the fluid and at times ungraspable movements of thought as they are deflected by external phenomena. Many of the difficult features of his work, then, its tortuous syntax, its half-realized images, its disjunctive transitions, are intended to reflect the way consciousness is forever being distracted by the world. Discursive clarity and organization presuppose an ability to shut out irrelevancies, to remain wholly tied to the matter at hand. For Ashbery such single-mindedness is impossible; the world is always intruding, interrupting, forcing itself upon the mind. Yet by the same token Ashbery is unable to give himself over to the outside world entirely, as O'Hara and Snyder do; new phenomena are continually setting off new trains of thought that demand to be followed, until they too are derailed by irrelevant intrusions.

Ashbery's poetry is thus deeply occasional in nature, despite its apparent "refusal of occasion."[33] For Ashbery as for Stevens, an occasion is not a subject for representation, but the experiential context of which the poem is itself a part. The poem cannot escape this context, as much as it may wish to, because occasions always shape the thought and language that they generate. In this sense, even the least referential of Ashbery's poems can be called "the cry of its occasion." But as Breslin notes, the poems vary widely in the degree to which they explicitly represent their occasions, and one may agree with him in finding Ashbery's best poems to be those that most fully display their "anchorage in experience."[34] In those poems the tension between the autonomous workings of mind and the impingements of world and occasion create a felt energy that the less overtly mimetic poems often lack (although these latter have their own compensatory virtues). Such poems seek a balance between the particularity of a given occasion and the more generalized "experience of experience" Ashbery wants to set down. Thus the represented occasion is not valuable in itself, as it might be for O'Hara or Snyder, but only insofar as it manifests the qualities of all experience: its shapelessness, fluidity, transience. Ultimately Ashbery's great subject is human time, a medium which tends to dissolve all occasions in pure successiveness; hence the particular occasion in his poem is always extremely volatile, to be glimpsed only in the act of vanishing into the past. But the very act of trying to hold on to an occasion, to find a foothold in the flux, allows Ashbery to make that flux more palpable to us, as it continually sweeps us past any stable reference point.

Perhaps Ashbery's most sustained and heroic attempt to keep his hold on a particular occasion comes in a dazzling poem from *Self-Por-*

trait in a Convex Mirror entitled "Grand Galop," which documents what
John Hollander calls "a great walk through urban dreck."[35] Here he
bravely confronts the flux of phenomena assailing him on the streets
of the city, and tries desperately to assimilate and somehow redeem
that flux in all its trashiness. Unlike his friend Frank O'Hara, he is tem-
peramentally incapable of a purely aesthetic glorification of the city;
his eye is trained to pick out banalities rather than beauties. The poem
owes much to "An Ordinary Evening in New Haven," but Ashbery is
far more fixated on the unassimilable debris of urban existence than
Stevens, who is able to move with impressive ease from New Haven
to Juda. Indeed the ancestral poem "Grand Galop" most insistently
echoes is "The Waste Land," although Ashbery rejects Eliot's impersonal, Tiresian stance and instead presents himself as a walker helplessly trapped in time and space, unable to escape the million bits of
information that swarm about him as he walks:

> All things seem mention of themselves
> And the names which stem from them branch out to other referents.
> Hugely, spring exists again. The weigela does its dusty thing
> In fire-hammered air. And garbage cans are heaved against
> The railing as the tulips yawn and crack open and fall apart.
> And today is Monday. Today's lunch is: Spanish omelet, lettuce and
>   tomato salad,
> Jello, milk and cookies. Tomorrow's: sloppy joe on bun,
> Scalloped corn, stewed tomatoes, rice pudding and milk.[36]

David Kalstone comments that this passage represents "the end of the
line for Whitman's famous catalogues," and indeed "Grand Galop" is
preoccupied with the problem of inclusion, of how much raw data poetry can comfortably absorb.[37] If one of the primary impulses behind
the walk poem is simply to transcribe what one sees, to "mention" as
much as possible, then such an impulse would appear to be derailed
when "All things seem mention of *themselves*" (italics mine). Ashbery
characteristically sees everything as already placed in quotation marks,
which leaves him with the problem of how to select particular "things"
for honorable mention. (The seemingly arbitrary "mention" of the
weigela may be taken as an instance of the kind of referential "branch-
ing" Ashbery describes; in itself a weigela is simply a kind of flower, but
in a context that includes images of spring, dust, fire, and waste it becomes difficult not to hear in the word an echo of *The Waste Land*'s
own allusion to the Rhinemaidens's "Weialala leia.")

  The easy continuity between language and experience on which the
walk poem has generally depended is thus ironized by Ashbery; it is
not that words are things, but that things are already words, already
caught up in culture and semiosis.[38] Hence any effort to reproduce ex-

perience verbally becomes a highly self-conscious affair; Ashbery's phrasing veers between parodic mannerisms ("Hugely, spring exists again," "The weigela does its dusty thing") and the deadpan banality of the institutional lunch menus. We should recall that O'Hara titled his best-known volume *Lunch Poems,* and often lists the contents of his mid-day meal for our delectation. Surely, then, Ashbery is deliberately if affectionately subverting his friend's sense that a given day can be defined and evoked through such particulars. "Today is Monday": the phrase could easily appear in an O'Hara poem, but Ashbery's emphasis is not on the special mix of sights, smells, and feelings that set the day apart, but rather on its dull predictability, the way that the various items offered for lunch have all been offered countless times before, are in fact more name than nourishment. Indeed it is probably no accident that the foods listed share a certain thickly homogeneous consistency—sloppy joe, scalloped corn, rice pudding. Such imagery recurs throughout the poem, as though to imply that experience itself partakes of this viscous, undifferentiated texture, halfway between liquid and solid, flux and paralysis.[39] From this perspective, the poem's very title takes on a new resonance; might it not be misread as "Grand Glop"?[40]

From this opening gambit, in which Ashbery tries out and immediately undermines the possibilities of pure denotation, a straightforward naming of phenomena, the poem moves into a more characteristically elusive and abstract style, purged of specificity yet still attached to the world:

> The names we stole don't remove us:
> We have moved on a little ahead of them
> And now it is time to wait again.
> Only waiting, the waiting: what fills up the time between?
> It is another kind of wait, waiting for the wait to be ended.
> Nothing takes up its fair share of time,
> The wait is built into the things just coming into their own.
> Nothing is partially incomplete, but the wait
> Invests everything like a climate.
> What time of day is it?
> Does anything matter?
> Yes, for you must wait to see what it is really like,
> This event rounding the corner
> Which will be unlike anything else and really
> Cause no surprise: it's too ample.

It is the more slippery, less lumpy medium of time itself that now concerns Ashbery, yet for him time cannot finally be separated from "things," the world in its concreteness. The passage presents a number of typically Ashberyan difficulties; is the stealing of names alluded to in the first line, for example, an act of naming or unnaming? In a sense, the ironic cataloging that opens the poem does both, by showing how readily names can become detached from their referents. In any case, this strategy turns out to have been largely ineffective, if its purpose was to "remove" us from the messy flux of language and experience. Irony can only take us so far ahead, then we must wait for something gloppy to contaminate us once more, prompting new evasive maneuvers. Seen this way, poetry becomes a constant effort to take in and purge the matter of living, a kind of verbal digestion that must continually renew itself by feeding on ever more unappetizing lunches.

The motif of waiting that figures so prominently here is thus in part simply an aspect of the digestive cycle as it operates on experience. But the wait takes other forms as well; there is the sheer tedium of "waiting for the wait to be ended," a wait with no object in mind other than its own completion. And there is the wait that is "built into the things just coming into their own," a more enigmatic kind of wait that seems connected to the poet's perpetual frustration in the face of the object-world. Ashbery frequently evokes this sense of an unrealized potential in things, a suspicion that they are holding back their essence from us until an assigned moment of disclosure arrives.[41] It is not that the world is "partially incomplete," that some crucial piece is missing that, once supplied, will cause the whole to emerge in perfect clarity. Rather, incompleteness is diffused throughout all particular objects: "the wait invests everything like a climate." A major theme both here and elsewhere in Ashbery is that appearances seem to promise more than they deliver; yet Ashbery is eternally hopeful, forever willing to wait for things to come into their own. For all the sameness and frustrating incompletion of the world, then, it *does* matter what time of day it is; the names, dates, lunches, all the particulars of experience count not in themselves, but in their potential participation in the nameless "event rounding the corner," the endlessly deferred amplitude or fullness of time whose advent will "cause no surprise," but will make all things seem much more than mention of themselves.

As its title suggests, the poem moves at a galloping pace far removed from the quiet, measured gait of "An Ordinary Evening in New Haven." David Kalstone perceptively remarks that "Grand Galop" "is almost literally an attempt to keep the poem's accounting powers even with the pace of inner and outer events," an attempt which "naturally ... doesn't succeed."[42] Hence the poem's jerky, abrupt transitions, in which the poet's attention is repeatedly jolted back toward the world. Each of the poem's seven verse paragraphs opens with the intrusion of some external stimulus, triggering a meditation that gradually wanders away from its occasion, until at last a new object forces itself on the poet. It is through this frustrating cycle of interruption and renewed meditation that Ashbery tries to keep up with both inner and outer events; and if he fails, as Kalstone suggests, it is because the two streams never quite converge, are always deflecting one another. Ashbery's profound distrust of the kind of "accounting" that O'Hara keeps is another reason his poem never seems able to keep abreast of the flux; defensive irony intervenes whenever he finds himself drawn too close to the O'Hara "I do this I do that" mode. As a result "Grand Galop" performs what Breslin aptly calls a "dance of approach and avoidance," constantly flirting with particulars, yet always pulling back from them in disgust.[43]

Such a recoil occurs most explicitly at the opening of the second paragraph:

> Water
> Drops from an air conditioner
> On those who pass underneath. It's one of the sights of our town.
> Puaagh. Vomit. Puaaaaagh. More vomit. One who comes
> Walking dog on leash is distant to say how all this
> Changes the minute to an hour, the hour
> To the times of day, days to months, those easy-to-grasp entities,
> And the months to seasons, which are far other, foreign
> To our concept of time. Better the months—
> They are almost persons—than these abstractions
> That sift like marble dust across the unfinished works of the studio
> Aging everything into a characterization of itself.

Where the first paragraph began with an air of dull acceptance, even of the awful lunches, this one opens with a decisive rejection of the world, as signaled by the literal return of the lunch. We might recall Williams's declaration "I cannot vomit it up" in "The Desert Music," which expresses the impossibility for him of keeping the world at a distance. For Ashbery such distance is all too easy to achieve; the real difficulty comes in keeping experience down once it's been swallowed. Vomit is, of course, another version of glop, the half-digested sludge of experience; what triggers this violent reaction against it seems to be once more a recognition of the nature of human time. The water drops, however banally realistic they seem, inevitably call to mind Ashbery's earlier masterpiece "Clepsydra," in which the image of a water clock embodies the empty repetition and discontinuity of time in its smallest increments, the passing of moments or drops. The mystery of how such moments, in themselves seemingly bodiless, accumulate into the significant divisions of days, months, seasons, is at the heart of

"Grand Galop," which remains constantly aware of the stupefying gap between the present moment of experience and the abstractions of time past. The perspective of the "One who comes / Walking dog on leash," a perspective implied throughout the poem, is wholly caught up in the flux of the present; yet the walker knows that the present moment too will eventually become "little more than a feature . . . Out of the dimly remembered whole," that the large, dusty months age "everything into a characterization of itself," draining the past of detail and immediacy. The difference between the similarly reflexive phrases "characterization of itself" and "mention of themselves" is crucial: the latter suggests an occurrence in time, the former a blurred, generalized picture completely lacking in temporality. The two words thus epitomize the difference between direct experience and long-term memory, each of which is in its way equally dissatisfying.

The second paragraph ends with another vague reference to a possible moment of redemption and amplitude "Under the smiling expanse of the sky." These proleptic visions of ultimate triumph are frequent in Ashbery, yet usually ring hollow; they serve more as gesture or cadence than as thought or assertion. His true subject is the perplexity of the present, which reasserts itself at the opening of the third paragraph, this time in an auditory form:

> The dog barks, the caravan passes on.
> The words had a sort of bloom on them
> But were weightless, carrying past what was being said.
> "A nice time," you think, "to go out:
> The early night is cool, but not
> Too anything. People parading with their pets
> Past lawns and vacant lots, as though these too were somehow
>   imponderables
> Before going home to the decency of one's private life
> Shut up behind doors, which is nobody's business.
> It does matter a little to the others
> But only because it makes them realize how far their respect
> Has brought them. No one would dare to intrude.
> It is a night like many another
> With the sky now a bit impatient for today to be over
> Like a bored salesgirl shifting from foot to stockinged foot."

Ashbery's poetry is always exceptionally open to various kinds of "noise," in this case another literal stimulus returning the poet to his immediate occasion. The image of the caravan, which recurs later in the poem, is another characteristic trope for the flux of experience;

significantly, Ashbery pictures the world as moving by in procession while he himself remains stationary. This almost Einsteinian reversal of the walk's usual vector betrays the profound sense of passivity that informs Ashbery's vision of experience, rendering him incapable of the kind of active, quasi-sexual participation in the world that we have seen in poets like Williams, Snyder, O'Hara, and even in some respects Stevens. Ashbery always seems to be standing still amid the tides of phenomena: "Like a rainstorm, he said, the braided colors / Wash over me and are no help."[44] Once again language itself is assimilated to this flux; although words have a "bloom," a tactile, aesthetic sheathing they share with such things as weigelas and tulips, they too are "weightless," insubstantial, mere signs or mentions swept past any stable referent.

Amid this vision of time, language, and experience as ineluctably slippery and fluid, Ashbery gives us a comically explicit mise-en-scène, setting the poem in its occasion with deliberate clumsiness, as though to mock the very impulse toward the occasional. Ashbery often plays with the conventions of quotation by incorporating long passages that seem pointlessly set off from the rest of the poem. Here the quotation marks satirize the mimetic distinction between stream of consciousness and a more articulated level of thought that can be presented as direct discourse. Naturally this latter level turns out to be thoroughly banal, at least at the outset. The notion that a thought might take the form of a proposition like "A nice time to go out" represents the kind of absurd simplification of inner life that Ashbery is always eager to expose. Yet he rarely descends into pure parody; here, as elsewhere, he maintains a delicate balance between lampoon and earnestness. As the "quotation" continues, it loses its overt banality and becomes a quiet reflection on such middle-class values as privacy and decency, before circling back to parody with another echo of "The Waste Land." Despite its flaunted artifice, however, the passage does serve the primary mimetic function of establishing time, place, and occasion, providing the poem with an experiential base from which to depart. If the poem lacked such a base, it would lose much of its complicated texture; like "An Ordinary Evening in New Haven," "Grand Galop" grows out of its simultaneous distrust of and reliance on representation. Ashbery needs the walk, the dog, the air conditioner, if only to introduce the noise of experience into what might otherwise be too quietly solipsistic a poem.

Having established the walk as occasion, the poem now moves into its central meditation on the walk as experience:

> These khaki undershorts hung out on lines,
> The wind billowing among them, are we never to make a statement?
> And certain buildings we always pass which are never mentioned—

It's getting out of hand.
As long as one has some sense that each thing knows its place
All is well, but with the arrival and departure
Of each new one overlapping so intensely in the semi-darkness
It's a bit mad. Too bad, I mean, that getting to know each just for a
    fleeting second
Must be replaced by imperfect knowledge of the featureless whole,
Like some pocket history of the world, so general
As to constitute a sob or wail unrelated
To any attempt at definition. And the minor eras
Take on an importance out of all proportion to the story
For it can no longer unwind, but must be kept on hand
Indefinitely, like a first-aid kit no one ever uses
Or a word in the dictionary that no one will ever look up.

The opening of this passage may again be seen as a parody of both "Waste Land" imagery and a certain kind of Imagist rhetoric that links utterly specific phenomena with generalized emotional responses (as in Stein's "Pigeons on the grass, alas," itself a parody). But the question is, I think, sincere, and might be paraphrased: what kind of statement can be large enough, inclusive enough, to take account of these under-shorts *and* everything else of comparable specificity? The next lines develop this dilemma further while simultaneously returning us to the poem's opening statement. If all things are mention of themselves, then everything has always already been mentioned merely in existing, and we need say nothing. This possibility, which Ashbery describes at the opening of *Three Poems* as "leav[ing] all out," relieves the poet of the burden of denotation, yet does nothing to diminish the frustrating recalcitrance of things.[45] Once he chooses to "put it all down," however, to "mention" everything he sees, to write a poem of inclusion, he is faced with the even more frustrating difficulty of exhausting or saturating the field of experience. Where does one draw the line? Even Whitman's catalogs are selections, not inventories, and hence incomplete. Ashbery's gnawing sense that all things matter equally leads him ultimately to reject description and denotation, which are necessarily selective. There will always be "certain buildings" that go unmentioned, and so the whole project of inclusion is doomed from the start.[46]

Yet the alternative, in which things mention themselves and so are self-sufficient, is also undermined by the necessity of motion, flux, walking: "As long as one has some sense that each thing knows its place / All is well, but with the arrival and departure / Of each new one overlapping so intensely in the semi-darkness / It's a bit mad." One can perhaps take it on faith that things have an autonomous existence so long as one is standing still; but seeing them in rapid succession seems to reduce them all to transient phenomena, tantalizingly close yet utterly inaccessible. Experience becomes hallucinogenic, a mad rush of appearances that cannot be stopped and held in mind. The consequence is that direct perception of the particular must always give way to abstraction, an "imperfect knowledge of the featureless whole." The fluidity of time hardens into a static, lifeless object, a "pocket history of the world," a first-aid kit, a dictionary. All of these images share a timeless ontology radically incompatible with the fluid nature of experience, and so they all merge into a "sob or wail" too general to tell us anything about our lives. This wail is very different from the Stevensian "cry of its occasion," which is rooted in the present; instead it expresses the pathos of never being able to stay in the moment, of having always to move toward the generality of history.

This inevitable hardening of the flux as it gets processed by the mind is cleverly captured by an image that also takes us back to the various forms of glop encountered earlier in the poem:

> The custard is setting; meanwhile
> I not only have my own history to worry about
> But am forced to fret over insufficient details related to large
> Unfinished concepts that can never bring themselves to the point
> Of being, with or without my help, if any were forthcoming.

The custard is always setting, this poem tells us; indeed the perpetual frustration of our experience lies precisely in its being forever caught between liquid and solid states. Thus our details are always insufficient and our concepts never finished; we can remain neither wholly in the present nor wholly out of it. Being and becoming contaminate one another to create the thick pudding in which we live and walk. Where a poet like Ammons is able to find a harmonious equilibrium between motion and permanence by playing different aspects of nature against one another, Ashbery's reality is less differentiated; for him conditions tend to average out to an unsatisfying uniformity ("I cannot explain the action of leveling, / Why it should all boil down to one / Uniform substance"[47]). He cannot duplicate Ammons's rapid and exhilarating shifts of perspective, in part because his element is time and not space. Thus his experience of the world, like O'Hara's, is characterized by sheer succession, rather than Ammonsian change, which presupposes a constant object like the dunes. Unsurprisingly, then, Ashbery's poetry is more deeply anxious, less able to strike satisfying balances and make ringing affirmations. Fulfillment in Ashbery is always proleptic, never actual.

The difficulty of achieving any sense of fulfillment or arrival within a temporality of pure succession is the central theme of the fourth paragraph, which resumes many of the concerns already taken up in the poem. Indeed it should be noted that Ashbery's "Grand Galop" takes him over the same ground a number of times; each of the verse paragraphs can be seen as a repetition, with refinements and variations, of the previous one, so that the poem can hardly be said to "go" anywhere. In this too it can be seen to follow in the footsteps of Stevens, whose "never-ending meditation" in "An Ordinary Evening" keeps rehearsing the same dialectic with ever finer subtlety of nuance. Ashbery remains more deeply mired in circumstance, however, which leads to his dominant experience of paralysis:

> It is just the movement of the caravan away
> Into an abstract night, with no
> Precise goal in view, and indeed not caring,
> That distributes this pause. Why be in a hurry
> To speed away in the opposite direction, toward the other end
>   of infinity?
> For things can harden meaningfully in the moment of indecision.
> I cannot decide in which direction to walk
> But this doesn't matter to me, and I might as well
> Decide to climb a mountain (it looks almost flat)
> As decide to go home
> Or to a bar or restaurant or to the home
> Of some friend as charming and ineffectual as I am
> Because these pauses are supposed to be life
> And they sink steel needles deep into the pores, as though to say
> There is no use trying to escape
> And it is all here anyway. And their steep, slippery sides defy
> Any notion of continuity.

Once more the caravan serves as an image of the slow-moving flux pursuing its course from the immediacy of the present to the abstraction of history. The peculiar phrase "distributes this pause," which appears as a consequence of the caravan's movement, suggests that the condition of pause is not momentary but diffused throughout experience, just as "the wait invests everything like a climate." The pause differs subtly from the wait, however, in that it is not oriented toward a future moment of projected transformation. Ashbery has begun to withdraw his earlier faith in an apocalyptic "event" yet to come; he questions the desire to "speed away" from the present, "toward the other end of infinity," and instead suggests that the present, for all its confusion, may itself be capable of illumination: "For things can harden meaningfully in the moment of indecision." Again meaning or knowledge and solidification are equated, but now they no longer seem to entail a dissolving of the moment within larger units of time. It is the very indecisiveness of the moment that causes it to "harden meaningfully," as though the pause opened up by this temporary paralysis allowed "things" a more adequate kind of being than does purpose and motion.

Yet what the "moment of indecision" appears to reveal is again simply the stultifying equivalence of particulars, their essential sameness. Like the lunches, the various options the poet considers all blend into a homogenous paste; even the mountain he fancifully thinks of climbing "looks almost flat." Place becomes irrelevant when one's true habitat is the moment, which always looks the same. The Beckett-like, bleakly reductive vision of time that follows, with its sardonic remark that "these pauses are supposed to be life," represents a willed disillusionment that verges on masochism, as the image of the steel needles in the pores horribly suggests. This powerful yet agonizing strain of negative insight in Ashbery (epitomized by the dark wisdom of Parmagianino in "Self-Portrait in a Convex Mirror") is usually answered by a renewed sense of possibility. Such a sense is readmitted to the poem after a brief excursus on history ("the lackluster, disorganized kind without dates"), introduced by a Stevensian "and yet":

> What precisely is it
> About the time of day it is, the weather, that causes people to note it
>   painstakingly in their diaries
> For them to read who shall come after?
> Surely it is because the ray of light
> Or gloom striking you this moment is hope
> In all its mature, matronly form, taking all things into account
> And reapportioning them according to size
> So that if one can't say that this is the natural way
> It should have happened, at least one can have no cause for complaint
> Which is the same thing as having reached the end, wise
> In that expectation and enhanced by its fulfillment, or the absence of it.

The question with which this passage begins lies at the heart of the very impulse to represent experience that issues in the walk poem, as well as in more prosaic forms like the diary and journal. Why, if all moments and all places are equally confining and opaque, should it matter what time of day it is or what the weather is like? Why should such items be recorded at all? Ashbery's own ambivalence toward journalistic representation is clear throughout the poem, which nevertheless announces at the start that "Today is Monday." If the particulars of time, place, and circumstance were really irrelevant, "Grand Galop" would

not continue to dwell on them, however ironically. Yet Ashbery firmly
rejects any notion of the epiphanic, any sense that one moment may
possess a deeper value than another. Even O'Hara and Snyder, for all
their apparent insistence on the status of their poems as mere samples
of the daily, maintain a residual sense of epiphany, if only in the phenomenal form of taxis honking and trout shimmering. But Ashbery's
radical stance toward experience forces him to assert that all particulars are fundamentally the same, while recognizing that they matter to
us nevertheless.

Unsurprisingly, it is hope, which is never quite dead in Ashbery, that
gives the moment its aura, makes it worthy of recording. In the first
paragraph, hope consists of waiting for an endlessly deferred "event"
that will transform experience. The possibility of such a transformation
is what makes "things" like the time of day matter. But here, Ashbery
seems to have finally abandoned this proleptic faith, instead presenting each moment as having already "reached the end." A new quietism
replaces his earlier apocalyptic anticipation, although his acceptance
of the present is wryly qualified: "So that if one can't say that this is the
natural way / It should have happened, at least one can have no cause
for complaint." "Hope," then, in its "mature, matronly form," simply
means taking what one is given as if it were an end or outcome,
whether it appear as "fulfillment, or the absence of it." The paragraph
closes with a brief protest and a briefer quelling of it:

> But we say, it cannot come to any such end
> As long as we are left around with no place to go.
> And yet it has ended, and the thing we have fulfilled we have become.

This rapid dialectic almost caricatures the poem's central tension between a sense of present experience as paralysis and as fulfillment. The
latter seems momentarily to have won out, but the victory is a precariously semantic one. Ashbery is really trying to justify his continued attachment to the particulars of time and place, despite his profound suspicion that they make no difference; but while the notion that each
moment constitutes an "end" seems to give stability to the self, it can
do so only by bracketing the world, whose shapeless flux constantly
threatens such stability. The very vagueness of such words as "it" and
"thing," always a frustrating feature of Ashbery's style, contributes to
the amorphous sense of an experience from which all particularity has
been drained.

Ashbery has thus reached an impasse, at which the present can be
rescued only at the cost of the thick flux of experience with which the
poem has been so preoccupied. From this point on, less and less effort
is made to include that flux in all its specificity; the poem gradually

loses its attachment to an occasion, and becomes a more free-floating meditation. Such a break may be inevitable, given Ashbery's ambivalence toward representation, yet I think it fair to say that the poem suffers a subsequent lessening of pressure and momentum. Much of its previous energy derives from the resistance or friction created by the immediacy of the world; once that friction starts to disappear, the poem cools down. Like "An Ordinary Evening in New Haven," "Grand Galop" moves from a direct engagement with its occasion to a more detached and autonomous series of reflections, thus embodying the very movement from immediate experience to abstract knowledge that the poem itself has repeatedly lamented.[48]

The newly hermetic nature of Ashbery's meditation in the fifth and sixth paragraphs is reflected by the way it pursues a more sustained line of thought, without the constant interruptions from outside that shaped the poem's earlier musings. The fifth paragraph ponders the relation between "the impulse of morning" and a sense of "still-perfect possibility" that insulates the self from all damage, sardonically concluding that "Morning is for sissies like you / But the real trials, the ones that separate the men from the boys, come later." The long sixth paragraph winds its way along a more serpentine path that begins with an evocation of Oregon as an alternative, quasi-pastoral landscape ("One whiffs just a slight odor of madness in the air"), returns to the here and now of April in the city, with its own indefinable sense of potential, then concludes with a fascinating meditation on the relation between poetic tradition (as personified by Wyatt and Surrey) and the "gorgeous raw material" of both experience and language. As always, Ashbery is most interested in how trash gets assimilated or included; poetic innovation turns out to consist, reductively, in the ability to pick up what previous poets discarded, such as "the word 'cock' or some other, brother and sister words." The inclusion of four-letter words may seem like a weak form of poetic originality, but it corresponds directly to the various sordid items included earlier in the poem: unappetizing lunches, vomit, undershorts. Ashbery's chief worry is that such detritus may be all that past poets have left unused, and that trash, both physical and verbal, cannot suffice as a basis for new poetry: "There is a note of desperation in one's voice, pleading for them."

Clearly the poem has by now moved rather far from its external occasion; indeed the movement is a fairly typical one for Ashbery, from the pressures of experience to the internal claims of poetry itself. In the final paragraph the poem returns to experience, but this time from the perspective not of a literal walk but of an allegorical quest, thus permitting a broader view than the poem's earlier focus on the moment had allowed:

> Ask a hog what is happening. Go on. Ask him.
> The road just seems to vanish
> And not that far in the distance, either. The horizon must have been
>   moved up.
> So it is that by limping carefully
> From one day to the next, one approaches a worn, round stone tower
> Crouching low in the hollow of a gully
> With no door or window but a lot of old license plates
> Tacked up over a slit too narrow for a wrist to pass through
> And a sign: "Van Camp's Pork and Beans."
> From then on in: *angst*-colored skies, emotional withdrawals
> As the whole business starts to frighten even you,
> Its originator and promoter.

The ghost of "The Waste Land," fitfully present throughout "Grand Galop," now gives way to one of its own ghostly ancestors, "Childe Roland to the Dark Tower Came." While Roland finds success where he looks for failure, however, Ashbery discovers only more of the same. The walk through urban dreck has been transmuted into a mock-heroic quest, but this simply means a change in scenery and props: a hog in place of a dog, etc. And when the "end" that the poem has been working so hard to conceive amid the endlessness of experience finally comes into sight, it turns out to be as infested with trash and glop as everything else; indeed the pork and beans almost certainly comes from the lunch menu for Wednesday, after Tuesday's sloppy joe on bun. The shift in perspective from "today" to the longer passage "from one day to the next" thus fails to reveal a cleaner, more heroic landscape in which direction and purpose become visible, only a mockery of a goal that cannot even be penetrated. That this goal is simply personal death, robbed of all aesthetic dignity, seems to be corroborated by the earlier image of the road vanishing "not that far in the distance," as well as by the implied slaughter and canning of the hog encountered at the beginning of the paragraph. It is no surprise, then, that the sight is met with *angst* and withdrawal, despite the fact that the quester seems to have "promoted" it himself by continuing on his way.

Perhaps the most natural response to fearful anticipation is nostalgia; and so the poet thinks back wistfully to his high school graduation, reflecting on both its distance and the continuities that link him to it: "I still have a sweater and one or two other things I had then." Wordsworthian memories of lost immediacy follow, though with a characteristically comic inflection:

> It seems only yesterday that we saw
> The movie with the cows in it
> And turned to one at your side, who burped

As morning saw a new garnet-and-pea-green order propose
Itself out of the endless bathos, like science-fiction lumps.

"The movie with the cows in it" is evidently a metonymy for a mode of experience directed unreflectively toward the world and its objects, as the cow's immediate appearance "at your side" would seem to confirm. Such experience may always be essentially pastoral, since it presupposes a harmonious relationship between self and landscape; even here, though, the cows are afflicted by digestive problems, suggesting that experience never goes down easily. And morning's "garnet-and-pea-green-order," for all its Arcadian verdancy, arises from "endless bathos, like science-fiction lumps," an image that seems, with its subliminal evocation of lumpy pea soup, vaguely reminiscent of all the earlier forms of glop that the poem has explored. In short, however he may idealize it, Ashbery can never wholly purify experience of those qualities that make it so frustrating a source of nourishment: its lack of shape, differentiation, definition, solidity.

The poem ends with a moving attempt to balance the remembered potentiality of the past against the paralysis of the present and the blankness of the future:

Impossible not to be moved by the tiny number
Those people wore, indicating they should be raised to this or
    that power.
But now we are at Cape Fear and the overland trail
Is impassable, and a dense curtain of mist hangs over the sea.

The image of the "tiny number / Those people wore," while fanciful, beautifully conveys the sense of untapped "power" endemic in youth, and represents the last and perhaps the purest version of that faith in possibility that has persisted fitfully throughout the poem as counter-song to its bleaker but more persuasive recognitions. This possibility is located, however, in an inaccessible past; the present remains paralyzed by fear, unable to move ahead or to see beyond itself. It is worth noting that even this barren allegorical landscape is informed by cultural trash: "Cape Fear" is the Bunyanesque title of a 1962 B-movie.[49] Thus even the consciousness of death, which I take to be the subject here, cannot entirely abstract experience from its referential surround; a final "mention" intrudes, tying the emptiness of universal dread back to a specific historical and cultural context, the world of movie theaters and cafeterias in which the poem began. But the ambivalent sense of motion attributed both to the walk and to the flux through which it moves has at last definitively stalled: "the overland trail / Is impassable." The "Grand Galop" of the poem can only come to rest through an evocation of ultimate stoppage, that is, of death.

Like some of O'Hara's walk poems, then, "Grand Galop" does not
so much achieve closure as it aborts itself. The poem starts out cheerfully enough, wading through the glop of experience with a measure
of disgust but a certain fascination as well. The sticky, confining nature
of the present offers little room for movement, yet Ashbery manages to
maintain a guarded faith in possibility, clinging precariously to his
sense that time, place, weather, and objects *do* somehow matter, can
continue to provide materials for poetry. But his profound distrust of
representation, together with his inherent disposition to see external
circumstances as dully homogenous, leads him to move further and further away from the poem's original occasion, toward the kind of "imperfect knowledge of the featureless whole" that he sees as the inevitable successor to immediate experience. From such a larger, historical
perspective, the apparent endlessness of experience is quickly revealed
to be sharply limited; death looms up as a "dense curtain of mist," at
once impenetrable and unavoidable. While mist may seem to share
some of the thick liquidity of experience, it is in fact altogether different, wholly devoid of substance where glop is lumpy and semisolid. It
thus represents a frightening alternative to the frustrations of the flux,
as does the sea, a traditional metaphor for the annihilation of linear
time in death.

Ashbery thus fails to muster any of the comforts that reassure Ammons and allow him to achieve a firm sense of closure. The shift in perspective of the final paragraph does not lead to a resolution of anxiety,
as in "Saliences," only to new anxieties. Given its relentless refusal of
closure, resolution, or consolation, one might legitimately wonder
whether the poem succeeds in offering any kind of pleasure or satisfaction to the reader; yet the fact remains that it is, for me at least, a wonderfully pleasurable poem. For all its suspicion of mimesis, it ultimately
offers a picture of ordinary experience that is at once analytically profound and convincingly particularized. That this picture is overwhelmingly negative in its emphasis on frustration, disgust, paralysis, and anxiety cannot finally undermine its sheer representational exuberance, an
exuberance accurately captured by the tempo-marking of the title. The
pathos and despair of experience as Ashbery portrays it is offset by the
pleasure of getting it down for all to see. Unlike O'Hara or Snyder, he
does not claim that his poem's value inheres in the value of the experience it commemorates; rather, it is precisely in the *gap* between the
frustrations of experience and the energy of the poem that its worth
can be located.

For all their differences in setting, theme, and affect, Ammons and
Ashbery are both poets in whom experience of the world and reflection on that experience converge. What sets their walk poems apart is

the remarkable suppleness with which they incorporate discursive, abstract thought within the phenomenal texture of the walks. They neither invoke the walk as a frame for independent meditation, like Rousseau, Schiller, and others, nor do they limit themselves to a transcription of external phenomena; instead thinking and perception are calibrated with each other exactly, so that we are made constantly aware of their profound interdependence. "Corsons Inlet," "Saliences," and "Grand Galop" all root the meditative motions of "An Ordinary Evening in New Haven" more firmly in particular perceptions; where Stevens avoids the direct representation of phenomena in order to keep his thoughts free to pursue their own course, Ammons and Ashbery insist that thought can never be dissociated from the particulars or saliences that give rise to it. Unlike Stevens, who portrays himself as "a strong mind in a weak neighborhood," Ammons and Ashbery emphasize the strength of the world itself to shape and direct the mind. For them the value of the walk lies precisely in its power to disrupt thought, to keep the mind new, to manifest the world as the inescapable and intrusive ground against which all thinking takes place. Their poems represent the give and take of mind and world with unprecedented clarity and precision.

CONCLUSION

THE WALK AND THE WORLD

THE CENTRAL QUESTION I have attempted to answer in this study is how walks, transient occasions, can be made into poems, permanent objects. Schematically speaking I have examined three strategies for effecting such a transformation, which I have named the cognitive, the meditative, and the aesthetic. Frost, Roethke, and Bishop all represent the walk as a way of access to truth or wisdom, to an understanding that transcends experience while taking its origin there. Stevens, Ammons, and Ashbery instead emphasize the continuous, unending *process* of thought as it negotiates the world, never arriving at a definitive point of rest but demonstrating rather the coextensiveness of mental motion and the motion of reality. Williams, O'Hara, and Snyder approach the walk aesthetically, as a phenomenal continuum that directly engages the walker's sensibility and body through its sensuous particulars. It goes without saying that within each of these groups the poets display all sorts of fundamental differences; but my emphasis has fallen on the way they each gravitate toward one or the other of the three basic approaches to representing experience that I have outlined. What these three approaches share is a sense that the fundamental object of the walk is simply the world; not, that is, some particular segment of the world, such as a specific place or category of places, but the world itself, conceived as the very horizon of experience. The walk transcends its own contingent, occasional character by disclosing a totality that extends beyond the walker's perceptual limits. It is this nonphenomenal apprehension of the world that ultimately allows the walk to assume the permanence of a poem.

I want to conclude this study by considering another poem by John Ashbery that explicitly meditates on the way an ephemeral occasion like a walk can be recovered and rendered permanent through just such a disclosure of worldhood. This poem, "The Thief of Poetry" (from *Houseboat Days*, the volume immediately following *Self-Portrait*), seems to take up the same themes of flux and transience that Ashbery explores in "Grand Galop"; yet it moves toward a sense of the possible recovery of the occasion that balances and ultimately negates the evanescence of linear time. In its moving vision of an imaginative transmutation of experience into a more permanent form, the poem expresses the desire that lies at the heart of the walk poem—the desire to keep what we have lived.

In its very form "The Thief of Poetry" emphasizes the attenuation of experience by time. Where "Grand Galop" is expansive and inclusive, willing to take in whatever stray thoughts and phenomena come its way, "The Thief of Poetry" is thin and ascetic, though still able to register a few trivial particulars:

> To you
> my friend who
> was in this
>
> street once
> were on it
> getting
>
> in with it
> getting on with it
> though
>
> only passing by
> a smell of hamburgers
> that day
>
> an old mattress
> and a box spring
> as it
>
> darkened
> filling the empty
> rumble
>
> of a street
> in decay of time
> it fell out that
>
> there was no
> remaining
> whether out of a wish
>
> to be moving on
> or frustrated
> willingness to stay
>
> here to stand
> still
> the moment
>
> had other plans
> and now in this
> jungle of darkness

> the future still makes plans
> O ready to go
> Conceive of your plight
>
> more integrally
> the snow
> that day
>
> buried all but the most obtuse
> only the most generalized
> survives [1]

In its narrow, concentrated flow of brief phrases, the poem is visually reminiscent of "Saliences"; but where Ammons's poem mimes in its short lines a continuous mental process cognate with that of wind and dune, Ashbery's language is more elliptical, reflecting the way past experience is eroded and fragmented by time. Time, indeed, is surely the identity of the "Thief of Poetry" named in the title; as in O'Hara's "Petite Poème en Prose," Ashbery is acknowledging the impossibility of holding on to the latent poetry of experience in anything but fragmentary form. The poem differs from "Grand Galop" most significantly in that it does not represent its occasion as a present occurrence pressing upon the mind, but as a hazy memory. The very phrase "that day," which acts almost as the poem's refrain, emphasizes its distance from the speaker, its inaccessibility. All that remains of the poet's remembered walk are a few stray impressions: a smell of hamburgers, an old mattress, the darkening street. These particulars, like the lunches and garbage at the opening of "Grand Galop," themselves manifest a heightened sense of transience; they are all on their way to oblivion. Yet as in "Grand Galop," a curious urgency makes itself felt, a desire to hold on to the moment in all its poverty. It is not that this occasion, this walk, holds some special value for the poet, whether aesthetic or cognitive; it simply exemplifies the way all occasions are lost "in decay of time." We cannot remain in the moment, whether we want to or not; our own desires are finally irrelevant in the face of time's "other plans." Moreover, once the occasion has passed we can retain almost nothing of it in our memories, for the "snow" of amnesia insures that "only the most generalized survives"; as in "Grand Galop," immediate experience gives way to blunt, obtuse generalities, "a pocket history of the world" drained of all particularity.

Thus the particular occasion, the "day" the poem keeps naming, must inevitably fade from memory:

> Now
> no one remembers
> the day you walked a certain distance

> along the beach
> and then
> walked back
>
> it seems
> in your tracks
> because it
>
> was ending
> for the first time

The chief interpretive difficulty here is determining the antecedent of "because": either the day is forgotten because it has ended, or the "you" turns back in his tracks because the light is failing. More peculiar but less ambiguous is the phrase "for the first time," which looks forward to the day's mysterious "second / beginning" in the poem's final movement. For now, however, it seems that the day is irretrievably lost, although we must note the paradox of *asserting* that an occasion has been forgotten when the very act of doing so memorializes it.

Up to this point the poem has offered an overwhelmingly temporal vision of experience in which time drowns space, and with it any sense of unity or worldhood. But a different conception of experience now emerges, one that is less relentlessly self-consuming:

> yes but now
>
> is another way of
> spreading out
> toward the end
>
> the linear style
> is discarded
> though this is
>
> not realized for centuries
> meanwhile
> another way of living had come and gone
>
> leaving its width
> behind
> now the tall cedars
>
> had become locked into
> the plan
> so that everywhere
>
> you looked
> was burning
> inferential

interior space
not for colonies
but already closed

turned in on itself
its back
as beautiful as the sea

where you go up
and say the word
eminence
to yourself

The opening "yes but" signals a decisive turn in the poem's representation of experience, as Ashbery moves from the forgotten walk to
the evocation of a change that is characteristically portrayed as historical, although in fact it takes place entirely within the consciousness of the poem itself. "The linear style is discarded": experience is
no longer conceived as a narrow succession of moments, each replac-
ing the one before, but as a "spreading out," a wider accumulation that
has room for "the tall cedars" and the other objects that had previously been swallowed up by the flux of time. Significantly, the walk's
setting is now described in terms of natural objects rather than urban
ephemera, implying that longevity has supplanted transience as the
salient feature of the landscape. Moreover the world is now three-
dimensional rather than linear, possessed of width and height as well
as length. This new spatiality makes itself felt not only as extension
but as interiority: "so that everywhere / you looked / was burning /
inferential / interior space." The existence of this space can only be inferred, since it is closed, inaccessible, "not for colonies"; yet the very
act of making such an inference, of imagining a depth within the phenomenal world that cannot be entered and inhabited, confers a new
beauty and spaciousness on it. This depth is assimilated to the sea,
which is no longer "the line of ocean" that earlier symbolized the triumph of linear time over space, but a spatial totality cognate with the
world itself.

This new sense of the world's infinite extension is gathered in the
single word "eminence," a word that again suggests height and depth
as well as a kind of majesty. Significantly, the word enters as a speech
act occurring within the frame of the walk, rather than as part of a
detached description of it; experience and language are beginning
to merge into a Stevensian cry of the occasion. The emergent fullness and grandeur of the world acts as a counterbalance to the thin-
ness of the moment, and so provides a means to recover what time has
stolen:

all was lived in
had been lived in

was coming to an end
again
in the featureless present

that was expanding to
cloister it
this just a little too

comic parable
and so insure the second
beginning

of that day seen against the street
of whichever way
you walked and talked

knowing not knowing
the thing that was describing you
and not knowing

your taller
well somehow more informed
bearing

as you wind down
only a second
it did matter

you come back so seldom
but it's all right
the way of staying

you started comes back
procession into the fire
into the sky

the dream you lost
firm in its day
reassured and remembered

The syntax at the beginning of this passage is too elliptical to reconstruct completely, but it seems to recapitulate the movement from
lived experience to "the featureless present" that drowns all particulars. The new "way of living" that had made itself felt, in which the
world reveals its full dimensions, seems about to disappear or at least
be "cloister[ed]" by time; hence the "parable" has become uncomforta-

bly "comic," as it yields again to the plans of the moment. (Ashbery's ambulatory parable differs from those of Frost not only in being comic rather than tragic, but in its lack of a firm narrative shape beyond the elusively shifting nature of recollected experience.)

Yet it is just this expansion of the present that seems to "insure" that the lost occasion can finally be recovered. The logic implied by that verb remains elusive, but there can be no doubt that, having ended for the first time, the occasion is now evincing a "second beginning"; somehow the walk is being repeated, relived, despite the fact that it was previously lost in the snows of time. Now, however, the walk is different, less desultory and transient, as reflected in the walker's "taller / well somehow more informed / bearing." Evidently the walker has taken on some of the "eminence," the vertical extension, earlier ascribed to the cedars. More importantly, his bearing is more "informed," presumably by the larger awareness of the world that intervenes between the day's first ending and its second beginning. By passing *through* the width and eminence of a nonlinear apprehension of the world, the forgotten walk takes on a new clarity and permanence. It is no longer an ephemeral experience of such transient phenomena as cooking smells and old mattresses; the occasion has retroactively assumed the largeness and unity of its world.

A possible source of this difference is identified in the strange lines "knowing not knowing / the thing that was describing you." In its second incarnation, the walk is evidently accompanied by a description *of* the walk; yet it is a description oddly detached from any authorial consciousness, being ascribed rather to a mysterious "thing." Ashbery deliberately refuses to depict the recovery of the occasion as a specifically poetic act, the memorialization of a lost day through verbal representation. Representation or description plays a central role in this repetition, but not as a conscious act on the part of the "you"; rather, the "you" is vaguely aware of *being described,* that is, of being the object rather than the agent of representation. The source of this description remains unspecified, however, except by the peculiarly impersonal term "thing."

Why does Ashbery so muddle the relationship between occasion and representation? Unlike Proust, he does not claim that lost time can be recaptured through an act of writing; this repetition of the past is curiously passive. Yet a process of "describing" does occur, in however indeterminate a form. I would suggest that what allows the occasion to be recovered is simply the recognition that it is *already* a poem. Characteristically for Ashbery, this means recognizing the textual nature of experience, as he also does at the beginning of "Grand Galop": "All things seem mention of themselves." Such a recognition takes priority over any secondary act of representation, such as the act of writing a poem *about* the occasion. By positing a kind of invisible descriptive agency or "thing," Ashbery redefines the occasion as both text and experience; in effect he learns to read his walk instead of simply taking it. If the walk is itself a poem rather than a transient occasion, then it is no longer hopelessly lost. The redefinition gives it a new value and importance— "it did matter"—while permitting the "you" to "come back," to revisit "that day" and live it again. The convergence of walk and poem thus constitutes a "way of staying" within the occasion, counteracting the poem's earlier assertion that "there was no remaining."

To understand fully how the nature of the occasion has changed, we have to recall the stages through which it passes. The poem falls into three parts: first, the original occasion in all its transience, swallowed up by linear time and buried in forgetfulness; second, the negation of linear time through a new consciousness of space, of the world as extension and depth; and third, the recovery or repetition of the occasion in a more permanent, heightened form. Clearly the intervention of the second phase is vital to the poem's ultimate recovery of the stolen day. In effect the linearity of temporal experience has to be united with the more totalizing awareness of the world as space before the occasion can become a poem; in the terms developed by Frederic Jameson and discussed in my Introduction (pp. 17–18), realism and romance must be fused, or at least conjoined. Once such a conjunction is achieved, the forgotten walk on the street or on the beach (the very setting remains indeterminate) can be kept, held, and remembered.

The occasion thus manifests a double movement, a "procession into the fire" of transience and "into the sky" (or "eminence") of a more lasting form. Ashbery here succeeds, as he does not in "Grand Galop," in combating the flux of temporality and achieving a precarious stability amid transience. Where the earlier poem ends in paralysis, "The Thief of Poetry" concludes with a confident, even triumphant affirmation: "the dream you lost / firm in its day / reassured and remembered." The dream of the walk, its volatile sense of a world full of oceanic depth and beauty and eminence, keeps the walk itself firmly in the poet's memory. It is no longer a hazy cluster of half-remembered sensations; under the synthesizing pressure of his imagination it has become a poem. This poem may be stolen by the thief of all poetry, the decay of time, but so long as it can be remembered it can be recovered. While the act of transcribing or writing down the occasion externalizes it and makes it available to others, that act is finally secondary to the essential act of imagination that finds in the particulars of the walk a way of apprehending the world as a whole. By giving his walk a unifying center, a solid core of vision, the poet allows it to be held by the mind, where earlier it flowed through consciousness like water.

"The Thief of Poetry" is thus a revision of the American doctrine that experience is already a poem. What Ashbery recognizes is that experience is not *necessarily* a poem; it can be a purely linear succession of transient phenomena forever disappearing into the past, leaving behind only faint traces and blurred outlines. But that oppressive conception of experience governed by time—associated with what I have called an imagery of glop in "Grand Galop"—can under the right circumstances give way to a different mode of consciousness in which space drowns the hum of time, and in which the contingency of the walk discloses the totality of the world. In their different ways all the walk poems I have examined in this study direct themselves toward the world. In one poem the world may look like a frozen swamp, in another like New Haven, in another like a windy beach, in another like Manhattan, but in each case the walker achieves a fitful sense of the world as a virtual whole that exceeds his perceptual limits. Whether that world is conceived as opaque or transparent, tragic or comic, transient or permanent, its presence as the condition of our being is a primary fact that demands acknowledgment. To write a poem about a walk is one way of acknowledging the world while recognizing that our knowledge of it is contingent and piecemeal. More than other poetic forms, the walk poem allows the poet to reflect directly on what it means to live in a world visible only in glimpses, continually beckoning us to go further and see more, but never showing itself as a whole. Such wholeness may only be inferred, not perceived; and the making of that inference, however momentary and provisional, is what finally enables a walk to become a poem.

EPILOGUE

SOME FURTHER WALKS

IN THIS BRIEF epilogue I want to survey quickly some of the many walk poems that fall outside the scope of my main argument. For purposes of organization I will break down the poems mentioned into a series of fairly makeshift groupings. What I hope will emerge is not an orderly taxonomy but a sense of the richness and diversity of the genre as it has been practiced over the centuries, and especially over the last one. Almost every conceivable kind of poem has been written about a walk; the very constancy with which the subject has been taken up by poets who otherwise have nothing in common attests to its compelling status as a paradigm for poetic experience. (I cannot deal here with the many prose accounts of walks in essays, journals, novels, and so on; those interested in the subject should consult Jeffrey Robinson's *The Walk: Notes on a Romantic Image*, especially the short but useful bibliographical essay.)

Paterson Two has provided one example of a walk embedded within a long poem, a device that has been common at least since Cowper's *The Task* and Wordsworth's *Prelude* and *Excursion*. Perhaps one reason that the walk appears so often in post-Romantic long poems is that it can serve as a meeting place of narrative and lyric energies. As epic and romance gradually cease to be viable generic models for the long poem, poets look for ways to represent extended experience without the linear pressure of traditional narrative plot. Among the long poems that contain walks or passages of walking, some of the most notable are Goethe's *Faust* (the "Oster Spaziergang"), Tennyson's *In Memoriam* (especially sections 95, 100, and 102) and *Maud*, Whitman's "Song of Myself," Eliot's *Four Quartets*, Crane's *The Bridge*, Robert Penn Warren's *Audubon*, W. D. Snodgrass's "Heart's Needle," Allen Ginsberg's "Kaddish," John Hollander's "From the Ramble," Galway Kinnell's *The Book of Nightmares*, Adrienne Rich's "Twenty-one Love Poems," James McMichael's *Four Good Things*, Alfred Corn's "A Call in the Midst of a Crowd," and Leslie Scalapino's *way*.

In poems of middle length, the walk often fills a different function, serving not as an embedded interlude but as a framing device. Such poems may depart completely from the walk once they are underway, pursuing independent meditations that make no reference to the scene, although as in the greater Romantic lyric they generally return to it at the end. The most famous instance is probably Eliot's "The

Love Song of J. Alfred Prufrock," which begins with a walk through "winding streets of insidious intent," then shifts into a more associative kind of consciousness. Other poems that use the walk to frame a meditation include Conrad Aiken's "The Walk in the Garden," W. H. Auden's "A Walk after Dark," Delmore Schwartz's "Calmly We Walk through This April's Day," Randall Jarrell's "The Soldier Walks Under the Trees of the University," Kenneth Koch's "The Departure from Hydra," A. R. Ammons's "Easter Morning," James Merrill's "An Urban Convalescence," Robert Bly's "A Meditation on Philosophy," Galway Kinnell's "The Seekonk Woods," Adrienne Rich's "A Walk by the Charles," Robert Hass's "Old Dominion," and John Morgan's "While the Pope and the President Meet at the Fairbanks Airport, the Poet Takes a Walk." Philip Levine's recent poem "A Walk with Tom Jefferson" uses the walk as a frame for a rambling conversation with an old black auto worker.

Walk poems that emphasize description rather than meditation can be most conveniently divided according to setting. The urban walk poem has become a genre unto itself, especially when set in O'Hara's Manhattan. Charles Reznikoff and Edwin Denby both anticipate O'Hara in their numerous poems recording moments of perceptual intensity on the sidewalks of New York; Reznikoff writes in the brief, freely lineated strophes associated with Objectivism, while Denby prefers the sonnet and other stanzaic forms. Other city walk poems include Carl Rakoski's "Manhattan, 1975," Robert Lowell's "Bright Day in Boston," Grace Paley's "On Mother's Day," Kenneth Koch's "Taking a Walk with You," Thom Gunn's "Iron Landscapes (and the Statue of Liberty)," Donald Petersen's "Walking Along the Hudson," W. S. Merwin's "The Way to the River" and "Coming Back in the Spring," Galway Kinnell's "The Avenue Bearing the Initial of Christ into the New World," Ron Padgett's "16 November 1964" and "Strawberries in Mexico," Alfred Corn's "To the End of the Pier," Donald Revell's "The More Lustrous," Tom Disch's "The Argument Resumed; or, Up through Tribeca," Michael Pettit's "Sunday Stroll," David St. John's "The Avenues," and David Lehman's "Shake the Superflux!"

New York walk poems have also been written from a non-native perspective, as in Federico Garcia Lorca's "The Poet in New York" and Ernesto Cardenal's "Trip to New York." Ancestors to this American genre can be found in such London walk poems as John Gay's *Trivia*, Charles Jenner's *The Town Eclogues*, Samuel Johnson's "London," William Blake's "London," and T. S. Eliot's "Rhapsody on a Windy Night," James Thomson's nightmare vision "The City of the Dreadful Night," and perhaps more directly in the Parisian walk poems of Charles Baudelaire's *Tableaux Parisiens* and Guillaume Apollinaire's "Zone."

City walk poems written by Americans abroad include Allen Ginsberg's "One Morning I Took a Walk in China," James Merrill's "Walks in Rome," and Adrienne Rich's "The Tourist and the Town." A final variation on the urban walk poem is the shopping poem, most famously exemplified by Randall Jarrell's "Next Day" (with its unforgettable first line "Moving from Cheer to Joy, from Joy to All") and by Ginsberg's "A Supermarket in California."

Unsurprisingly, walk poems set in rural landscapes are quite different in style and theme from city walks, as we have seen already in comparing O'Hara with Snyder and Ammons with Ashbery. Within the general category of country walks, different landscapes impose their own moods and visions. Most prevalent, almost to the point of cliché, is the beach walk, whose distinguished pedigree in American poetry reaches back to Whitman's "Sea-drift" poems, and even further back in English poetry to an anonymous eighteenth-century poem with the formidable title "An Evening's Reflection on the Universe, in a Walk on the Seashore." Twentieth-century instances, in addition to Bishop's "The End of March" and Ammons's "Corsons Inlet," include Dylan Thomas's "Poem in October," Robert Creeley's "Myself," John Logan's "Big Sur: Partington Cove," Sylvia Plath's "Bercke-Plage," Marge Piercy's "Sand Roads," Linda Pastan's "A Walk Before Breakfast," William Matthews's "A Walk," Douglas Crase's "Sagg Beach," John Morgan's "The Beach Walk at Port Townsend, WA," and Brad Leithauser's "Along Lake Michigan." A closely related subgenre is the river walk poem, exemplified by Auden's "As I walked out one evening," Patrick Kavanagh's "Canal Bank Walk," R. P. Blackmur's "River-Walk," and by James Applewhite's recent book *River Writing: An Eno Journal*, which consists entirely of poems based on his runs beside the Eno River. (In recent years the run poem has become an infrequent but visible variant of the walk poem, as evidenced by Richard Wilbur's "Running" and Dave Smith's "Rainy Day: Last Run." I would only point out that the essentially aesthetic disposition of the walk is to some degree cancelled by the purposive nature of the run; even when one isn't trying to get anywhere, the act of running is defined as labor rather than leisure. For this reason I doubt that the run poem will ever supplant the walk poem in centrality. You can tell that I'm no runner.)

When the rural walk does not have a body of water to contemplate, Ishmael-like, its emphasis falls on the more general relation between walker and landscape, which in contemporary poetry is often one of alienation. This may be especially true of those poems set in open fields; the bareness of the field creates a starker sense of the separation between walker and world. The earliest field walk poem is probably Henry Vaughan's "I walk'd the other day," which finds in the blankness of a winter landscape a correlative for the speaker's spiritual poverty. Another walk poem by Vaughan, "Regeneration," follows a more progressive movement, in which the diversity and profusion of the landscape gradually revives the walker's spirits and allows him to pray to "die before his death," presumably by losing his identity in God and nature. Successors to both these kinds of landscape-experience, alienation and immersion, can be found in later pastoral walks such as D. H. Lawrence's "The Wild Common," Robert Lowell's "Last Walk?," Richard Wilbur's "In a Field," James Dickey's "The Strength of Fields," James Wright's "Depressed by a Book of Bad Poetry, I Walk toward an Unused Pasture and Invite the Insects to Join Me," Galway Kinnell's "A Walk in the Country," Robert Bly's "After Long Busyness," Thomas Kinsella's "A Country Walk," Mark Strand's "Taking a Walk with You" and "Keeping Things Whole" (with its famous declaration of alienation, "In a field / I am the absence / of field"), James Tate's "Intimidations of an Autobiography," Stephen Dunn's "Walking the Marshland," Nancy Willard's "Walking Poem," Margaret Gibson's "Long Walks in the Afternoon," and Kenneth McClane's "Sloane's Woods." A slightly different relation to landscape appears in poems that follow a more strenuous path up hills or mountains; the muscular involvement seems to allow a greater sensual intimacy to emerge as well, as we saw in the case of Snyder's "A Walk." Other climb poems include James Schuyler's "The Walk," Gerald Stern's "Climbing this Hill Again," Charles Tomlinson's "Hill Walk," Reg Saner's "Long's Peak Trail," and John Morgan's "The Third Walk: McKinley Park Hotel to Mt. Healy Overlook."

A further category of descriptive walk poems consists of those characterized less by setting than by time, season, or weather. Thus we have snow walks, like Samuel Johnson's "The Winter Walk," and more recently Kenneth Rexroth's "Leda Hidden," Robert Bly's "A Walk," John Hollander's "Effet de Neige," Allen Grossman's "A Snowy Walk," Alfred Corn's "A Village Walk Under Snow," and Edward Hirsch's "Dawn Walk"; autumnal walks, like John Greenleaf Whittier's "Last Walk in Autumn," Robert Penn Warren's "Last Walk of Season," James Wright's "Late November in a Field," Robert Bly's "A Long Walk Before the Snows Began," Philip Whalen's "The First Day of November," Alvin Feinman's "November Sunday Morning," and J. D. McClatchy's "Late Autumn Walk"; sunset walks, like William Cullen Bryant's "A Walk at Sunset" and Robert Penn Warren's "Sunset Walk at Thawtime in Vermont"; and night walks, like Thomas Kinsella's "Nightwalker," Dave Smith's "Night-Walk, Montrose, Pennsylvania," Reg Saner's "Hiking at Night," and John Morgan's "Walking Past Midnight."

Another group of poems treats walking less as experiential fact than as a metaphor to be explored with varying degrees of fancifulness.

Richard Wilbur's poem "Walking to Sleep" describes a walk taken in the mind to ease the transition from waking to sleep. Other poems that turn the walk into a kind of allegory include Denise Levertov's "A Walk through the Notebooks" and "Stepping Westward," and W. D. Snodgrass's "These Trees Stand," with its brave refrain "Snodgrass is walking through the universe." John Hollander is the contemporary master of the ambulatory parable; in poems like "One of Our Walks," "Some Walks with You," "On the Trail," "The Way We Walk Now," "A View of the Ruins," and "A Find," he makes walking into a potent trope for the movement of understanding in all its complexity, agility, and frustration.

The final subgenre I will note is the marginal but interesting one of walk poems written from the point of view of dogs. I know of three examples: Lawrence Ferlinghetti's "The dog trots freely," Denise Levertov's "Overland to the Islands," and Thom Gunn's "Yoko" (Williams also plays with the canine perspective in *Paterson*). The dog's walk may well represent the purest form of the open, inquisitive, mobile relation to the world that the walk poem tries to capture. Unfortunately dogs don't write poems, and so poets have to do it for them. This slightly absurd effort to transcribe a completely nonverbal experience is in keeping with at least one major aim of the walk poem as a genre: to put phenomena into words so directly and accurately that the words disappear, and the reader is *there*, on the street or in the field.

NOTES

INTRODUCTION
A WALK IS A POEM, A POEM IS A WALK

1. Babette Deutsch, *Potable Gold* (New York: W. W. Norton, 1929), p. 21. Deutsch's analogy can be contrasted with Paul Valery's more famous assertion that poetry is to prose what dancing is to walking ("Poetry and Abstract Thought," in *Paul Valery. An Anthology*, ed. James R. Lawler [Princeton: Princeton University Press, 1977]). But Valery's definition of walking makes it clear that he regards it as a purely utilitarian activity: "Walking, like prose, has a definite aim. It is an act directed at something we wish to reach" (p. 154). What Deutsch describes as the experience of walking for its own sake is thus a humbler version of Valery's dance, "a system of actions whose end is in themselves."

2. A. R. Ammons, "A Poem Is a Walk," *Epoch* (Fall 1968): pp. 116–17.

3. Many statements could be cited, but the loci classici are in Emerson's "The Poet," where he speaks of "the mind's faith that the poems are a corrupt version of some text in nature with which they ought to be made to tally" (*Essays and Lectures*, ed. Joel Porte [New York: Library of America, 1983], p. 459), and in Whitman's first "Preface," when he says of the character and manners of the common American people that "these too are unrhymed poetry" (*Leaves of Grass*, ed. Sculley Bradley and Harold Blodgett [New York: Norton, 1973], p. 712). Similar statements in Stevens, Williams, and more recent poets could also be adduced.

4. The most extreme versions of this project are to be found not in poetry but in certain films by Andy Warhol that deliberately court a Zen-like tedium in their effort to reproduce long stretches of uneventful experience. His novel *a* is the ultimate literary expression of this aesthetic, comprising an unedited transcription (by a secretary, not Warhol himself) of a tape recording of everything his friend Ondine did during a single day. Warhol himself apparently never read the book.

5. M. H. Abrams, "Structure and Style in the Greater Romantic Lyric," in his *The Correspondent Breeze* (New York: Norton, 1984), pp. 76–77. Another closely related Romantic genre is defined by Theodore Ziolkowski in his book *The Classical German Elegy* (Princeton: Princeton University Press, 1980). For Ziolkowski this genre is most purely exemplified by Schiller's "Der Spaziergang" ("The Walk"); it differs from the English and American walk poem in that the poet's path leads him up a mountain from which he commands a sweeping prospect, thus occasioning a more extended and independent meditation (what Ziolkowski terms the poem's "meditative core") than the walk poem generally contains. In this respect the German elegy bears a closer resemblance to the greater Romantic lyric, which also moves away from description and toward sustained meditation.

6. Abrams, "Structure and Style," p. 103.

7. Ibid. Abrams earlier cites Coleridge's use of the *ouroboros* or snake with its tail in its mouth as an emblem for the deliberate spatializing of temporal succession that is the basic principle of poetic closure in the greater Romantic lyric (pp. 81–82).

8. *The Rambler*, No. 5, in *Samuel Johnson: Rasselas, Poems, and Selected Prose*, ed. Bertrand H. Bronson (New York: Holt, Rinehart and Winston, 1952), p. 75.

9. Calvin Bedient, *Eight Contemporary Poets* (New York: Oxford University Press, 1974), p. 129.

10. Jacques Derrida has analyzed the primacy of this metaphor in Western philosophy, in a series of lectures at Yale University (Spring 1982).

11. Significantly, perhaps, when Socrates begins his philosophical discussion with Phaedrus he sits down under a tree. To continue walking might have invited precisely the sort of distraction from pure dialectics that Samuel Johnson recommends. For an excellent discussion of the role of the walk in this dialogue, see Charles L. Griswold, *Self-Knowledge in Plato's "Phaedrus"* (New Haven: Yale University Press, 1986), pp. 33–36.

12. See especially the second "Promenade," in which Rousseau recounts being knocked unconscious by a Great Dane.

13. Jeffrey Robinson, *The Walk: Notes on a Romantic Image* (Norman: University of Oklahoma Press, 1989), p. 4. This book appeared after my own had been drafted, and while I have attempted to incorporate a few of its many insights in my introduction, I have not been able to acknowledge it as fully as I would like to.

14. John Elder, *Imagining the Earth* (Urbana: University of Illinois Press, 1985), p. 93.

15. The best-known statements of this conception are probably Frost's essay "The Figure a Poem Makes" ("Like a piece of ice on a hot stove the poem must ride on its own melting" [in *Selected Prose of Robert Frost*, ed. Edward Connery Lathem (New York: Holt, Rinehart and Winston, 1966), p. 20]) and Stevens's poem "Of Modern Poetry" ("The poem of the mind in the act of finding / What will suffice" [in Wallace Stevens, *The Palm at the End of the Mind*, ed. Holly Stevens (New York: Alfred A. Knopf, 1972), p. 174]).

16. Charles Olson, "Projective Verse," in *The Poetics of the New American Poetry*, ed. Donald Allen and Warren Tallman (New York: Grove Press, 1973), pp. 147–58.

17. See David Perkins's section on "Syntax as Kinesis" in his *A History of Modern Poetry: Modernism and After* (Cambridge: Harvard University Press, 1987), pp. 494–97.

18. Metaphorical uses of the walk by Black Mountain poets include Olson's statement that "a poem . . . ain't dreamt until it walks" ("A Foot Is to Kick With," *Human Universe* [New York: Grove Press, 1967], p. 80); Robert Duncan's assertion that the language and prosody of Olson's *Maximus* is "no more difficult than walking" (Allen, *Poetics of the New American Poetry*, p. 187); and Robert Creeley's declaration that one "must walk / all the things of life about which one talked" (*A Day Book* [New York: Scribner's, 1972], p. 28).

19. Paul Breslin points out how "with Olson's rejection of a world of discrete objects for one of fluid process came a rejection of symbolism, allegory, and

perhaps of mimesis altogether" (*The Psycho-Political Muse: American Poetry since the Fifties* [Chicago: University of Chicago Press, 1987], p. 188).

20. Williams's *Paterson* offers a richer instance of this tension between the omniscient and the experiential; see my analysis in Chapter Three. The passage in *Maximus* that most directly involves walking is significantly a literal attempt to survey a section of Gloucester on foot, by counting off paces between landmarks—e.g., "125 paces Grove Street /fr E end of Oak Grove cemetery" (Charles Olson, *The Maximus Poems* [Berkeley: University of California Press, 1983], p. 150). Here walking is explicitly placed in the service of the kind of panoptic knowledge Olson assumes throughout the poem; in this respect it might be compared with Pound's trope of *periplum*, a voyage made to map a coastline. Both Pound and Olson seek a fusion of process and panopsis, one that necessarily denies the experiential nature of process.

21. Charles Altieri, *Self and Sensibility in Contemporary American Poetry* (Cambridge: Cambridge University Press, 1984), pp. 10–11.

22. James Wright, *Collected Poems* (Middletown: Wesleyan University Press, 1972), p. 114.

23. Charles Olson, "Proprioception," in Allen, *Poetics of the New American Poetry*, p. 182.

24. Thus William Stafford titles a poem and volume *Things That Happen Where There Aren't Any People* (Brockport: BOA Editions, 1980); and Robert Bly echoes the phrase in the opening lines of his poem "Four Ways of Knowledge": "So many things happen /when no one is watching" (*The Man in the Black Coat Turns* [New York: Dial, 1981], p. 51).

25. Wallace Stevens, *Opus Posthumous* (New York: Alfred A. Knopf, 1957), p. 167.

26. Martin Heidegger, *Being and Time*, trans. John Macquarrie and Edward Robinson (New York: Harper and Row, 1962), p. 89.

27. Frederic Jameson, *The Political Unconscious* (Ithaca: Cornell University Press, 1981), p. 112.

28. John Vernon, for example, in *Poetry and the Body* (Urbana: University of Illinois Press, 1979), offers a lyrical account of how the poem functions as the meeting place of body and world, mobilizing the energies and desires of the body through the dancelike torsions of speech.

29. "Poetry and Abstract Thought," pp. 145–47.

30. Tony Hiss, "Experiencing Places—i," *The New Yorker*, June 22, 1987, p. 53.

31. An interesting parallel to Hiss's account of simultaneous perception can be found in James Gleick's popular book *Chaos* (New York: Viking Penguin, 1987), in which physicist Mitchell Feigenbaum's walks lead him to reflect on the way we understand and process complex, "nonlinear" phenomena (see p. 163).

32. John Crowe Ransom, *The World's Body* (New York: Scribner's, 1938); see especially the chapters "Poetry: A Note on Ontology" and "The Mimetic Principle."

33. Alfred Kazin, *The Open Street* (New York: Reynal and Hitchcock, 1948), p. 22. Interestingly, Kazin chose not to include this essay in *A Walker in the City*,

perhaps because the book takes the form of a past-tense memoir, while *The Open Street* is written in the lyric present, in keeping with its Whitmanian title.

34. Robinson, *The Walk*, p. 49.

35. Wallace Stevens, *The Palm at the End of the Mind* (New York: Alfred A. Knopf, 1971), p. 338.

36. Jonathan Culler, *Structuralist Poetics* (Ithaca: Cornell University Press, 1975), pp. 164–68.

37. Ludwig Wittgenstein, *Philosophical Investigations*, trans. G.E.M. Anscombe (New York: Macmillan, 1953), p. 197e.

38. Ibid., p. 189e.

39. James Merrill, "On 'Yannina': An Interview with David Kalstone," in his *Recitative* (Berkeley: North Point, 1986), p. 23.

40. Ammons, "A Poem Is a Walk," p. 117.

41. Paul Fussell, Jr., suggests that "the pleasures of meter are essentially physical and as intimately connected with the rhythmic quality of man's total experience as the similarly alternating and recurring phenomena of breathing, walking, or lovemaking" (*Poetic Meter and Poetic Form* [New York: Random House, 1965], p. 6).

42. Barbara Herrnstein Smith, *Poetic Closure* (Chicago: University of Chicago Press, 1968), pp. 124–25.

43. Olson, "Projective Verse," pp. 154–55.

44. John Hollander, *Rhyme's Reason* (New Haven: Yale University Press, 1981), pp. 29–30.

45. Charles Baudelaire, title essay in *The Painter of Modern Life and Other Essays*, trans. Jonathan Mayne (London: Da Capo, 1964), p. 13.

46. My use of the term "canon" throughout this book is meant to invoke the notion of permanence as a poetic ideal that informs the actual production of poetry; I am thus not primarily concerned with the canon as a historically determined institution that sorts and ranks poems, although inevitably the two senses will overlap.

47. William Wordsworth, *The Complete Poems*, vol. 1, ed. John O. Hayden (New Haven: Yale University Press, 1981), pp. 114, 116.

48. A sampling of titles: "Recollections after an Evening Walk," "Recollections after a Ramble," "Sunday Walks," "Sabbath Walks," "Wanderings in June," "Careless Rambles," "Walks in the Woods," "Winter's Walk," "A Walk in the Forest," "The Morning Walk."

49. Alastair Fowler, *Kinds of Literature* (Cambridge, Mass.: Harvard University Press, 1982), p. 191.

50. Jeffrey Robinson has some interesting remarks on the way the walk itself tends to absorb and combine different genres:

> When I walk, my mind does not flow like a stream. More literary than that, it works in mixed genres: at times autobiography, polemic, natural description, dialogue, essay, even treatise, story. Sometimes it seems a genre that keeps resisting genre. . . .
>
> This vulnerability of the walker might transform into the vulnerability of the writer to the mixing of genres.

Just as the walk is a quintessentially Romantic image, so the mixing of genres produces a quintessentially Romantic metagenre, what Friedrich Schlegel calls *Mischgedicht* [mixed poem]. (*The Walk*, p. 4)

51. I quote from the translation by E. A. Speiser in *The Anchor Bible: Genesis* (Garden City: Doubleday, 1964), p. 21.

52. *Selected Poetry of Edmund Spenser*, ed. William Nelson (New York: Modern Library, 1964), p. 573.

53. John Milton, *Complete Poems and Major Prose*, ed. Merritt Y. Hughes (Indianapolis: Odyssey, 1957), pp. 69–70.

54. Ibid., ll. 65–70.

55. Andrew Marvell, *The Complete Poems* (Harmondsworth: Penguin, 1972), p. 87.

56. *Grongar Hill*, ed. Richard C. Boys (Baltimore: Johns Hopkins University Press, 1941), p. 14.

57. See the account of the poem's stages by Richard C. Boys in his edition of *Grongar Hill*, pp. 45–67.

58. See Fowler's discussion of how satire "catalyzes generic mixture" (*Kinds of Literature*, p. 188). Other satirical walk poems include Donne's *Satire* 1 and Rochester's bawdy "A Ramble in St. James' Park."

59. John Gay, *Poetry and Prose*, vol. 1, ed. Vinton A. Dearing and Charles E. Beckworth (Oxford: Clarendon Press, 1974), p. 135.

60. *The Complete Poetical Works of William Cowper*, ed. H. S. Milford (London: Oxford University Press, 1913), p. 221.

61. Interestingly, passages of the poem were revised from an even earlier work, "The Vale of Esthwaite," which was written in the octosyllabics of "L'Allegro" and "Grongar Hill"; Wordsworth transposed them into the iambic pentameter couplets he uses in "An Evening Walk." The fullest reading of the poem to date is given by Alan Liu in his recent *Wordsworth: The Sense of History* (Stanford: Stanford University Press, 1989). Liu makes subtle points about the conventions of the picturesque in the poem and their relation to the economic history of the Lake District.

62. Wordsworth, *The Complete Poems*, p. 87.

63. See John Elder's discussion of the centrality of the walk in *The Prelude* in *Imagining the Earth*, pp. 93–115; and Jeffrey Robinson's discussion of Wordsworth's walks, in *The Walk*, pp. 18–28. Robinson writes of Wordsworth that "For more than half a century of his poetry the walk characterizes his entry into experience" (p. 25).

64. *The Complete Poetry and Prose of William Blake*, ed. David V. Erdman (Garden City: Anchor Press, 1982), pp. 720–22.

65. Whitman, *Leaves of Grass*, p. 150.

CHAPTER ONE
ROBERT FROST: THE WALK AS PARABLE

1. See *Selected Letters of Robert Frost*, ed. Lawrence Thompson (New York: Holt, Rinehart and Winston, 1964), pp. 182, 278.

2. "The Figure a Poem Makes," in *Selected Prose of Robert Frost*, ed. Edward Connery Lathem (New York: Holt Rinehart and Winston, 1966), pp. 18–20. Henceforth cited in text as *Prose*.

3. Robert Frost, *The Poetry of Robert Frost* (New York: Holt, Rinehart and Winston, 1969), p. 8. Henceforth cited in text as *Poetry*.

4. Richard Poirier, *Robert Frost: The Work of Knowing* (New York: Oxford University Press, 1977), p. 89. Poirier has some interesting remarks on the relation between "extra-vagance" and Frost's walk poems: "Wandering beyond boundaries of a household or a field is, in Frost, often the enactment of any search for possibilities greater than those already domesticated. His many poems of walking are thus poems of 'extravagance' in the most pedestrian sense while also being about the need, and advisability, of poetic 'extravagance'" (p. 89). In discussing "The Wood-Pile" Poirier contrasts the poem with "Tintern Abbey" and "Dejection," claiming that "it is more random in its structuring and has none of the demarcations of the descriptive-reflective mode," and adducing as an alternative paradigm Ammons's series of analogies in his "A Poem Is a Walk," *Epoch* (Fall 1968): pp. 138–39.

5. Poirier, *Robert Frost*, pp. 141–42.

6. See, for example, Robert Narveson, "On Frost's 'The Wood-Pile,'" *English Journal* 57 (1968): pp. 39–40; Marie Borroff, "Robert Frost's New Testament: The Uses of Simplicity," in *Robert Frost*, ed. Harold Bloom (New York: Chelsea House, 1986), p. 78; and Poirier, *Robert Frost*, p. 143.

7. Nathaniel Hawthorne, *The Blithedale Romance* (New York: Norton, 1978), pp. 195–96. Frost may also be recalling a passage at the beginning of Chapter Two, in which Coverdale compares his faded memory of Blithedale's cheery fire to "the merest phosphoric glimmer, like that which exudes, rather than shines, from damp fragments of decayed trees, deluding the benighted wanderer through the forest" (p. 9). He then calls this glimmer a "chill mockery of a fire," a phrase that clearly anticipates "The Wood-Pile"'s closing lines.

8. *Shelley's Poetry and Prose*, ed. Donald Reiman (New York: Norton, 1977), p. 103.

9. Poirier, *Robert Frost*, p. 139.

10. Ibid., p. 144.

11. T. S. Eliot, *The Complete Poems and Plays* (New York: Harcourt Brace and World, 1952), p. 5.

12. The increasing prominence of star imagery in Frost's later poetry is noted by John T. Ogilvie in "From Woods to Stars: A Pattern of Imagery in Robert Frost's Poetry," *South Atlantic Quarterly* 57 (1959): pp. 64–76.

13. Poirier is severely critical of what he calls the poem's "self-conscious and self-cuddling mode" (*Robert Frost*, p. 100), and feels that it has been overpraised; but I think he fails to see the function of the poem's admittedly cloying rhetoric, which is to prepare our palate for the cold draught that awaits us.

14. A well-known remark of Frost's may be apposite here: "I like to leave my toys lying around where people will fall forward over them in the dark. *Forward*, you understand, *and* in the dark." This joke can be taken as an accurate description of the movement of "Directive," particularly since it is we, not the poet, who do the falling.

15. We might compare it with "Hyla Brook," another watery embodiment of the reality principle, though of a less lofty and original kind.

CHAPTER TWO
WALLACE STEVENS: THE WALK AS OCCASION

1. I have perhaps illicitly combined two versions of this anecdote to produce what to my mind sounds most authentic, as well as most suggestive. The first and better-known version appears in Lawrance Thompson's biography *Robert Frost: The Years of Triumph, 1915–1938* (New York: Holt, Rinehart and Winston, 1970), p. 666: "On this occasion [in Feb. 1940 at Key West; Thompson was present], Stevens teased RF by saying, 'Your trouble, Robert, is that you write poems about—*things.*' RF replied, 'Your trouble, Wallace, is that you write poems about—*bric-a-brac.*' " The other version was reported by Frost himself in his interview with Richard Poirier (*Paris Review* 6 [Summer–Fall 1960]: p. 99): "Once he [Stevens] said to me, 'You write on subjects.' And I said, 'You write on bric-a-brac.' And when he sent me his next book he'd written 'S'more bric-a-brac' in it." It seems to me that Thompson probably caught the slight tone of animosity well enough, whether or not the words "Your trouble is" were actually spoken; but I feel sure that Frost would have been likely to remember the actual substance of Stevens's charge more accurately. In any case, "subjects" seems a far more subtle and characteristic term for Stevens to have used than "things."

2. Helen Vendler, *On Extended Wings: The Longer Poems of Wallace Stevens* (Cambridge: Harvard University Press, 1969), pp. 231, 234.

3. The circumstances of the poem's composition are reported in Peter Brazeau, *Parts of a World: Wallace Stevens Remembered* (New York: Random House, 1983), p. 175. Charles Berger notes the connection with canto XII in his *Forms of Farewell: The Late Poetry of Wallace Stevens* (Madison: University of Wisconsin Press, 1985), p. 95.

4. Brazeau, *Parts of a World*, p. 175.

5. As Joseph Riddell puts it, "There are always flickerings of New Haven in the poet's ideas, the place itself and the associations it inspires" (in *The Clairvoyant Eye* [Baton Rouge: Louisiana State University Press, 1965], pp. 256–57).

6. Brazeau, *Parts of a World*, p. 131.

7. Harold Bloom, *Wallace Stevens: The Poems of Our Climate* (Ithaca: Cornell University Press, 1977), p. 306. John Hollander has a wonderful prose poem called "Asylum Avenue," which meditates on the more familiar walk Stevens took every day to his Hartford office, finding in it much the same vision of reciprocal motion that informs "An Ordinary Evening": "Here is a region through which you move, yet which moves through you as you make your *paseo*" (*In Time and Place* [Baltimore: Johns Hopkins University Press, 1986], p. 97). The poem ends with a pun that wittily plays on Stevens's habit of composing while walking: "It would be a way of getting to work."

8. Wallace Stevens, *The Palm at the End of the Mind*, ed. Holly Stevens (New York: Alfred A. Knopf, 1972), p. 331. Henceforth cited in text as *Palm.*

9. Stevens had played in a similar way on the ambiguity of the word "vul-

gate" in *Notes Toward a Supreme Fiction,* "It Must Change," (IX): "The poem goes from the poet's gibberish to / The gibberish of the vulgate and back again" (*Palm,* p. 222). Here the vulgate is explicitly set against the more rarefied language of poetry, thus linking it with the vernacular rather than Latin. At the end of the canto he seems to reiterate this opposition, but in a way that playfully undermines it: the poet tries "To compound the imagination's Latin with / The lingua franca et jocundissima." The lines enact this compounding or confusing of dialects by speaking *of* each *in* the other.

10. Commentators like to point out that Stevens authorized a drastically shortened, eleven-canto version of the poem that was read at the Connecticut Academy and later appeared in his British *Selected Poems,* citing this as evidence of the poem's arbitrary form; see Berger, *Forms of Farewell,* p. 103. I myself resist the notion that Stevens saw this abridgment as simply another version of the poem, equally valid and complete, since I believe the poem in its original form does in fact manifest a continuity that does not admit of such reduction. In his full and stimulating reading of the poem, Harold Bloom makes the unfortunate error of assuming that the shorter version was the original, which Stevens then expanded. This leads him to consider the sections that appear only in the full-length version as interpolated "commentary," a view that fails to do justice to the poem's sustained meditative movement. Eleanor Cook cites definitive evidence that the poem was originally written in its longer version in her essay "Directions in Reading Wallace Stevens: Up, Down, Across," in *Lyric Poetry: Beyond New Criticism,* ed. Chaviva Hošek and Patricia Parker (Ithaca: Cornell University Press, 1985), p. 301, n. 5. According to Stevens's own account, he made the abridgment by reading the poem to his wife Elsie, and discarding the cantos which prompted her to cover her eyes and moan, "They're not going to understand this"; see Joan Richardson, *Wallace Stevens: The Later Years* (New York: William Morrow, 1988), p. 356.

11. Charles Berger refers to the poem's "gliding measure," relating it to its "thematic principle of non-catastrophic endings" (*Forms of Farewell,* p. 103). On Stevens's use of apposition, see Frank Doggett, "Wallace Stevens' Later Poetry," *ELH* 25 (June 1958): p. 146: "in apposition the poet seems to deliberate about his original concept. He appears to reconsider it by seeking an equivalent in another and another version, continuously altered yet presented as though it were the same."

12. Freud first develops these terms in his essay "Formulations Regarding the Two Principles in Mental Functioning" (reprinted in the volume *General Psychological Theory,* ed. Philip Rieff [New York: Collier Books, 1963], pp. 21–28). In his own comment on the poem, Stevens appears to emphasize the reality principle at the expense of the pleasure principle: "Here my interest is to try to get as close to the ordinary, the commonplace and the ugly as it is possible for a poet to get. It is not a question of grim reality but of plain reality. The object is of course to purge oneself of anything false" (*Letters of Wallace Stevens,* ed. Holly Stevens [New York: Alfred A. Knopf, 1966], p. 636). This emphasis is not surprising, however, given the poem's initial orientation toward reality, and its occasional nature. Certainly in comparison with other long poems by Stevens the reality principle is a more dominant element here.

13. Vendler notes how "the confrontation of the present is insisted on" in "Credences of Summer" and "The Auroras of Autumn" through the repeated use of "this" and "here" (*On Extended Wings*, p. 231).

14. Bloom, *Wallace Stevens*, pp. 311–12.

15. Vendler, *On Extended Wings*, pp. 301–2.

16. See especially the final canto of *Notes*, where Stevens addresses the world as "Fat girl, terrestrial, my summer, my night" (*Palm*, p. 232). In her essay on "An Ordinary Evening" ("Up, Down, Across"), Eleanor Cook cites a moving prose passage from Stevens's piece on John Crowe Ransom that expresses a similar strain of fierce longing: "One turns with something like ferocity towards a land that one loves, to which one is really and essentially native, to demand that it surrender, reveal, that in itself which one loves." (*Opus Posthumous* [New York: Alfred A. Knopf, 1956], p. 260).

17. The crucial phrase "love of the real" occurs also in Emerson's "Experience," an essay very much in the background of "An Ordinary Evening in New Haven": "Our love of the real draws us to permanence, but health of body consists of circulation, and sanity of mind in variety or facility of association. We need change of objects" (*Essays and Lectures*, ed. Joel Porte [New York: Library of America, 1983], p. 476).

18. Whitman, *Leaves of Grass*, ed. Sculley Bradley and Harold Blodgett (New York: Norton, 1973), p. 148.

19. Ibid., p. 165.

20. Ibid., p. 64. The allusion to the Palestinian kingdom of Judah (eccentrically spelled by Stevens, perhaps to emphasize the revisionary movement) takes us back to the biblical trope latent in the phrase "the vulgate of experience" in canto I; the Hebrew lion must be translated into a more vernacular form before he can inhabit New Haven. Further biblical references appear in the poem: to the burning bush in canto XVII, and to Ecclesiastes in canto XIX. More generally the poem abounds in religious imagery, suggesting that a large part of its effort, as in this canto, is to bring the religious sublime down to the level of New Haven and the real, through an ongoing process of translation. (Certainly one reason Stevens chooses to set the poem in New Haven, apart from his familiarity with it, is the resonance of its name; in *Notes* he plays on the words "heaven-haven" [*Palm*, p. 224], and that play is implicit throughout this poem as well. See Eleanor Cook's reading of the poem as an anti-apocalypse in "Up, Down, Across.")

21. These definitions are taken from Charlton T. Lewis, *Elementary Latin Dictionary* (Oxford: Clarendon Press, 1891).

22. Bloom, *Wallace Stevens*, p. 320–21.

23. John Ashbery, *Self-Portrait in a Convex Mirror* (New York: Viking Penguin, 1975), p. 78.

24. Bloom, *Wallace Stevens*, pp. 321–22.

25. Vendler, *On Extended Wings*, pp. 234–35.

26. "These lines epitomize the closing gesture so often favored by Stevens: a descent, or a reduction, to power" (Berger, *Forms of Farewell*, p. 109).

27. Eleanor Cook calls "An Ordinary Evening" a "poem of acrossness," emphasizing horizontal rather than vertical movement ("Up, Down, Across," p. 307).

CHAPTER THREE
WILLIAM CARLOS WILLIAMS: THE WALK AS MUSIC

1. William Carlos Williams, *Spring and All,* in *Imaginations* (New York: New Directions, 1970), p. 150.

2. Ibid., p. 120. The word "transcription" appears on p. 105.

3. See J. Hillis Miller's lucid account of this theory in *The Linguistic Moment* (Princeton: Princeton University Press, 1985), pp. 376–77.

4. Williams's early poem "Promenade" (in *The Collected Earlier Poems* [New York: New Directions, 1951], p. 132) is an interesting failure that tries to literalize the idea of the poem as "transcription" by presenting the walk as a dramatic monologue addressed to the poet's "mind": "Well, mind, here we have / our little son beside us: / a little diversion before breakfast!" This device draws attention to its own artifice and so makes the poem seem farther from rather than closer to the experience it records. Another early walk poem is "Morning" (*Collected Earlier Poems*, p. 393), which presents a fluid picture of a lower-class neighborhood, but avoids any direct representation of the walker as a presence in the scene; various stratagems are employed to keep even the first-person pronoun out of the poem.

5. The mode of *Paterson* is partly anticipated in Williams's early quest poem "The Wanderer," a few lines of which he quotes in Book Two. The highly charged Romantic rhetoric of that poem prevents it from taking on the factual density of *Paterson*, however.

6. M. L. Rosenthal, *Poetry and the Common Life* (New York: Oxford University Press, 1974), p. 38.

7. Williams, *Spring and All,* pp. 116, 107.

8. William Carlos Williams, *Paterson* (New York: New Directions, 1963), p. 6. All further page numbers will be given in the text.

9. Williams himself supports this identification when he says, speaking of Book Two, "If I as an artist had separated myself from the scene, it would be a defeat. But I have not. I have made myself part of the scene" (quoted in Benjamin Sankey, *A Companion to William Carlos Williams' "Paterson"* [Berkeley: University of California Press, 1971], p. 71).

10. Williams, *Spring and All,* p. 121.

11. Louis L. Martz, "The Unicorn in *Paterson,*" reprinted in *William Carlos Williams: A Collection of Critical Essays,* ed. J. Hillis Miller (Englewood Cliffs: Prentice Hall, 1966), p. 81.

12. "An Ordinary Evening in New Haven," canto XIII.

13. Jeffrey Walker discusses this passage as an example of the way Williams is forced to violate his programmatic emphasis on the local and the native through "appeals to non-native symbolic codes," thus joining Pound in the American poetic quest for a "sacerdotal authority" drawn from outside American cultural experience (*Bardic Ethos and the American Epic Poem* [Baton Rouge: Louisiana State University Press, 1989], p. 47). This passage would then be another instance of the tension between experiential representation and bardic authority that I have located in the alternation between verse and prose, although here the two elements are more subtly calibrated.

14. Marjorie Perloff has questioned the "openness" of the section, claiming

that it is "essentially pre-planned. The poet strolling through the park ostensibly records what he sees, observes, thinks, remembers, but in fact no detail is admitted into the space of the poem that does not relate to the central marriage-divorce tension that is the theme of the book" (*The Poetics of Indeterminacy* [Princeton: Princeton University Press, 1981], p. 151). While Perloff is right to emphasize the thematic pressures brought to bear on the poem, she seems to me to miss its genuinely random, contingent texture. What she really objects to, I think, are its mimetic aims, which keep it from attaining the improvisational freedom of *Kora in Hell* and other early works. It is a different kind of freedom that Williams seeks here, a freedom to know the world rather than to construct a text.

15. In Charles Tomlinson's edition of Williams's *Selected Poems* (New York: New Directions, 1985), for example, Book Two, section I is the only section of the poem excerpted in full. The first edition of *The Norton Anthology of American Literature* also reprints this section and no others.

16. In a review of the volume in which "The Desert Music" appeared, Martz writes of it, "I cannot make this poem work: the fragments will not form the 'dance' that the poet announces" (*Yale Review* 44 [Winter 1955]; reprinted in *William Carlos Williams: The Critical Heritage*, ed. Charles Doyle [London: Routledge and Kegan Paul, 1980], p. 282). In his *William Carlos Williams* (New York: Twayne, 1968), Thomas Whitaker says of "The Desert Music" that "the dramatized up-cadence is precarious, and the poem itself somewhat too insistent" (p. 153). But J. Hillis Miller in *Poets of Reality* (Cambridge: Harvard University Press, 1966) classes the poem with *Paterson* Five and "Asphodel, That Greeny Flower" as a late masterpiece. Sherman Paul's *The Music of Survival: A Biography of a Poem by William Carlos Williams* (Urbana: University of Illinois Press, 1968), is the most sustained appreciation of the poem. Paul sets it fully in the context of Williams's entire oeuvre, and relates it to such biographical matters as the poet's recent heart attack and his friendship with Robert McAlmon.

17. See Paul, *The Music of Survival*, pp. 1–2.

18. William Carlos Williams, *The Collected Poems*, vol. 2, ed. Christopher MacGowan (New York: New Directions, 1988), pp. 283–84. Subsequent page citations will be given in the text.

19. *The Autobiography of William Carlos Williams* (New York: New Directions, 1951), pp. 388–89.

20. Paul, *The Music of Survival*, p. 64.

21. It is possible that the lump on the bridge is encountered twice, once going into Juárez and once coming out. But I follow Paul in taking the opening description to be a displacement of the encounter that occurs at the end of the poem. The surprise in Williams's cry of "What's THAT?" when he sees the body there suggests that he is viewing it for the first time.

22. Williams, *Spring and All*, p. 134.

CHAPTER FOUR
THEODORE ROETHKE AND ELIZABETH BISHOP: THE WALK AS REVELATION

1. Robert Penn Warren, *Selected Poems, 1923–1975* (New York: Random House, 1976), p. 76.

2. See, for example, "Last Walk of Season," "Have You Ever Eaten Stars?" and "Why Have I Wandered the Asphalt of Midnight?" all in Robert Penn Warren, *New and Selected Poems, 1923–1985* (New York: Random House, 1985). Laurence Lieberman characterizes Warren's typical walk poem well in his essay "The Glacier's Offspring: A Reading of Robert Penn Warren's New Poetry" (*American Poetry Review* 10, no. 2 [March–April 1981]: p. 6):

> At seventy-five, Robert Penn Warren has lost none of his lifelong zest for strenuous nature hikes. In his new book of poems, *Being Here*, Warren's many excursions through woods, up hillside, across beach and rocky shoreline, run a gamut from sheer relish in the physical exertion—with lapses of muscle to explore a wealth of sensory perceptions—to profound meditations on the nature of Time and "Pure Being." By a succession of happy accidents, Warren's cross-country rambles lead him to encounters with living or non-living *beings* that amazingly mirror a profile of the author himself. His incandescent moments of recognition of each of his secret kin in nature submerges him in trance . . .; the noise and bustle of nature are frozen, momentarily . . .; and his spirit soars into a dimension of pure silence and motionlessness, a haven outside time.

3. Robert Lowell, *Selected Poems*, rev. ed. (New York: Farrar, Straus and Giroux, 1977), p. 104.

4. *The Collected Poems of Theodore Roethke* (Garden City: Anchor, 1975), p. 48. Henceforth cited in text as *Poems*.

5. Kenneth Burke recognizes this ambiguity when he writes, "Though Roethke has dealt always with very concrete things, there is a sense in which these very concretions are abstractions" ("The Vegetal Radicalism of Theodore Roethke," in *Language as Symbolic Action* [Berkeley: University of California Press, 1966], p. 280).

6. *The Complete Poetry and Prose of William Blake*, rev. ed., ed. David V. Erdman (Garden City: Anchor, 1982), pp. 720–22.

7. Anthony Libby, *Mythologies of Nothing* (Urbana: University of Illinois Press, 1984), p. 105.

8. The poem is in fact part of a long ongoing sequence that begins with "The Lost Son" and spans three volumes; all the individual poems in this sequence can be read as separate pieces, however, as well as stages in a psychological journey, and so I will discuss "A Field of Light" without reference to the entire sequence.

9. See Libby, *Mythologies of Nothing*, p. 114.

10. "The end of 'A Field of Light' announces a perception of 'the separateness of all things,' but carries an overriding sense of union" (ibid., p. 111).

11. Burke, "The Vegetal Radicalism of Theodore Roethke," p. 279.

12. For an excellent discussion of Roethke's late "imitations" of his modernist precursors, see Denis Donoghue, *Connoisseurs of Chaos*, 2nd ed. (New York: Columbia University Press, 1984), pp. 216–45.

13. Compare Auden's "A Walk After Dark" (*Selected Poems*, ed. Edward Mendelson [New York: Vintage, 1979], pp. 188–89); there too the walk is invoked

as a frame by the title, without entering organically into the poem, which is primarily a meditation on age and history.

14. This concern emerges most openly at the end of Bishop's great poem "At the Fishhouses," with its Frostian image of "cold dark deep and absolutely clear" water that "is like what we imagine knowledge to be." (Elizabeth Bishop, *The Complete Poems 1927–1979* [New York: Farrar, Straus and Giroux, 1983], pp. 65–66).

15. Ibid., p. 179.

16. See the excellent discussion of this aspect of Bishop's style by Jane Shore, "Elizabeth Bishop: The Art of Changing Your Mind," *Ploughshares* 5, no. 1 (1979): pp. 178–91.

17. *The Complete Poems of Emily Dickinson,* ed. Thomas H. Johnson (Boston: Little Brown, 1955), pp. 254–55. One of the most striking aspects of Bishop's poem, and perhaps part of the reason it can so effortlessly evoke the universal without leaving the particular, is the density of its allusive background; as I hope my notes will show, it unobtrusively transumes the entire American Romantic tradition, chiefly through the power of its images alone.

18. In his excellent discussion of the poem's use of echo and allusion, J. D. McClatchy points out that the reference to "mutton-fat jade" picks up on the proverbial saying about March that lurks in the background of the poem: "In like a lion, out like a lamb." McClatchy links this allusion with the Easter season, the paschal lamb, the lion-sun/Son, and even the kite's cross-shaped frame, while wisely concluding that these motifs "wait in the wings of the poem, but never . . . make enough of an appearance to merit much notice. Bishop is telling another kind of story" (*White Paper* [New York: Columbia University Press, 1989], p. 58).

19. This passage is uncannily reminiscent of the strange lines in Whitman's "As I Ebb'd with the Ocean of Life," another beach-walk poem, that describe the poet's own death: "See, from my dead lips the ooze exuding at last, / See, the prismatic colors glistening and rolling" (*Leaves of Grass*, ed. Sculley Bradley and Harold Blodgett [New York: Norton, 1973] p. 256). Whitman also refers to the debris on the beach as "little corpses."

20. Dickinson may again be in the background here, specifically the haunting image of the "House that seemed / A Swelling of the Ground" (712, "Because I could not stop for death," in *The Complete Poems*). McClatchy also cites 486, "I was the slightest in the House," as a possible source (*White Paper*, p. 63).

21. Elizabeth Bishop, *The Collected Prose* (New York: Farrar Straus Giroux, 1984), pp. 189–88. Another story, "The Sea and Its Shore" (pp. 171–80), seems unmistakably to be in the background of "The End of March" as well; it involves a beachcomber who dwells in a tiny shack, and who spends his time piecing together enigmatic fragments of text—bits of newspapers and books gathered on the beach—and trying to make coherent stories out of them. This is of course what Bishop is trying to do with the string and footprints, and what she finally succeeds in doing at the end of the poem. See McClatchy's discussion of both stories' relation to the poem (*White Paper*, pp. 64–65).

22. Harold Bloom, "Foreword," in *Elizabeth Bishop and Her Art*, ed. Lloyd Schwartz and Sybil P. Estess (Ann Arbor: University of Michigan Press, 1983),

p. xi. Whether or not Bishop's use of the lion is intended as a direct allusion to Stevens, it seems clear to me that "An Ordinary Evening in New Haven" is the crucial precursor poem for "The End of March" (compare also canto II of Stevens's poem, with its solipsistic imagery of "transparent dwellings of the self," with Bishop's vision of the house in the third section). Both poems ultimately recognize the inescapable place of fiction making in the human accommodation to reality, yet both insist also that these fictions must remain intimately rooted *in* reality. Where Bishop's poem differs most obviously from Stevens's poem is in its anecdotal style; unlike him, she does not "skip the journalism of subjects," but employs such journalism in order to illustrate the *specific* ways in which imagination can operate on reality. As a result her exemplary fiction, that of the lion sun, does not seems as exalted as Stevens's lion of Juda; in effect she claims less for the imagination because her realistic narrative mode forces her to accept its limits in a way that Stevens's meditative style does not. It might be said, then, that Bishop uses a Frostian mode (the beach house is reminiscent of "Directive") to illustrate a Stevensian movement; she is not content, as Frost is, with the cold, lofty contemplation of decay, but responds, as Stevens would, with a compensating fiction. The other precursor poem in Stevens, of course, is "The Auroras of Autumn," which this poem evokes in both its setting and its movement toward reconciliation. See McClatchy's full and persuasive account of the poem's indebtedness to Stevens (*White Paper*, pp. 69–74).

23. The trope's function is well-described by Bonnie Costello when she writes, "Such personification gives us no shelter from or power over the whims of nature, but makes them seem less predatory, precluding other more terrifying myths. Bishop cannot escape into this comprehensive myth, but she can make reference to it in a moment of fear. The lion-sun . . . does not change experience, but releases us from terror" ("Vision and Mastery in Elizabeth Bishop," *Twentieth Century Literature* 28, no. 4 [1982]: p. 368).

24. What Helen Vendler says of "The Moose" may be applied to "The End of March" as well: "[it] is such a purely linear poem, following as it does the journey of the bus, that an effort of will is required to gaze at it whole. The immediacy of each separate section . . . blots out what has gone before. But the temptation—felt when the poem is contemplated entire—to say something global, something almost allegorical, suggests that something in the sequence is more than purely arbitrary" ("Domestication, Domesticity, and the Otherworldly," in *Elizabeth Bishop and Her Art*, p. 47). Allegorical reading is a temptation in "The End of March" as well; yet Vendler's careful language, with its qualifications and refusals to specify ("something," "almost," etc.), steers clear of claiming "The Moose" to be an allegorical poem, just as I would avoid calling "The End of March" an allegory. The very elusiveness of the "something" in both poems that creates a sense of "global" meaning and "more than purely arbitrary" design is a tribute to Bishop's skill in cleaving so closely to experience that we are unable to say precisely how a major truth has been revealed in the process.

25. Bloom, "Foreword," p. x.

CHAPTER FIVE
FRANK O'HARA AND GARY SNYDER: THE WALK AS SAMPLE

1. Robert Pinsky, *The Situation of Poetry* (Princeton: Princeton University Press, 1976), pp. 4–5, 56–57, et passim.

2. From "On and About Kenneth Koch: A Counter Rebuttal," in *Standing Still and Walking in New York*, ed. Donald Allen (Bolinas: Four Seasons, 1975), p. 62. See also O'Hara's statement for *The New American Poetry*, ed. Donald Allen (New York: Grove, 1960), p. 419: "I am mainly preoccupied with the world as I experience it. . . . What is happening to me, allowing for lies and exaggerations which I try to avoid, goes into my poems. I don't think my experiences are clarified or made beautiful for myself or anyone else, they are just there in whatever form I can find them."

3. Charles Altieri has a useful discussion of the role of the city in O'Hara's poetry: "In the city, as in O'Hara's ontology, interesting and engaging details are continually becoming present. Yet not only do these momentary apparitions promise no underlying significance or meanings to be interpreted, they actually resist any attempt on our part to know them better" ("The Significance of Frank O'Hara," *Iowa Review* 4 [Winter 1973]; p. 93). By contrast, because of its grounding in natural landscapes, Snyder's poetry lacks this pervasive sense of transience and reticence, instead participating more fully in the phenomena it records through physical processes like labor and eating.

4. The most interesting example is his long poem *Second Avenue*, a densely surrealistic and virtually opaque poem that nonetheless insists on its connection to localized experience; of it O'Hara wrote, "everything in it either happened to me or I felt happening (saw, imagined) on Second Avenue" ("Notes on *Second Avenue*," in *Standing Still and Walking in New York*, pp. 39–40). It is thus a kind of cubist walk poem, opening the way for his later, purer experiments with the genre.

5. The phrase "I do this, I do that" comes from his poem "Getting Up Ahead of Someone," in *The Collected Poems of Frank O'Hara*, ed. Donald Allen (New York: Alfred A. Knopf, 1971), p. 341. Henceforth cited in text as *Poems*.

6. Frank O'Hara, *Lunch Poems* (San Francisco: City Lights, 1964), back cover.

7. See Marjorie Perloff, *Frank O'Hara: Poet Among Painters* (Austin: University of Texas, 1977), pp. 76–77.

8. James Breslin, *From Modern to Contemporary* (Chicago: Chicago University Press, 1984), p. 223.

9. Altieri, "The Significance of Frank O'Hara," p. 94.

10. Breslin, *From Modern to Contemporary*, p. xiii.

11. "Crossing Brooklyn Ferry," in Walt Whitman, *Leaves of Grass*, ed. Sculley Bradley and Harold Blodgett (New York: Norton, 1973), p. 160.

12. Marjorie Perloff, "Poetry Chronicle 1970–71," *Contemporary Literature* 14 (Winter 1973): p. 100.

13. Breslin, *From Modern to Contemporary*, p. 218.

14. Perloff, "Poetry Chronicle," p. 100.

15. Breslin, *From Modern to Contemporary*, pp. 218–19.

16. Perloff, "Poetry Chronicle," p. 101.

17. "An Interview with Frank O'Hara," in *Standing Still and Walking in New York*, p. 13.

18. Breslin, *From Modern to Contemporary*, p. 219.

19. Ibid.

20. Ibid., 218; Perloff, "Poetry Chronicle," p. 101.

21. Contrary to my view of the poem, Robert Pinsky cites "The Day Lady Died" as an example of poetic description, and goes on to connect it with the Wordsworthian tradition: "These addresses, malteds and proper names are O'Hara's version of 'nature poetry'" (*Situation of Poetry*, p. 102). It seems to me, however, that the poem lacks the element of sensual participation that characterizes true description; "notation" might be a more accurate term for the way particulars are recorded here.

22. "Personism: A Manifesto," in *Standing Still and Walking in New York*, p. 110. Interestingly, this, the most theoretical of O'Hara's statements on his own work, is itself a walk poem of sorts: "it [the 'Manifesto'] was a little diary of my thoughts, after lunch with LeRoi walking back to work, about the poem I turned out to be just about to write ('Personal Poem')" (Ibid., p. 114).

23. We may be reminded of a similar moment in "Song of Myself," when Whitman, after enthusiastically identifying himself with every kind of experience, finds himself drawn to scenes of greater and greater suffering, until he finally cries out "Enough! enough! enough!" (*Leaves of Grass*, p. 72). His gesture of breaking off does not, however, lead him to abandon the poem; he quickly finds energy and confidence to continue, unlike O'Hara.

24. One of O'Hara's most faithful poetic disciples, Ron Padgett, has pursued the application of postmodern irony to the walk poem in two poems clearly aware of their debt to O'Hara, "16 November 1964" and "Strawberries in Mexico" (in *Great Balls of Fire* [Chicago: Holt, Rinehart and Winston, 1969]). Each poem parodies the mannerisms and assumptions of O'Hara's typical walk poems in a way that exposes their conventionality. In the first the poet puts together a poem by writing down phrases he encounters on his walk in a small notebook; the resulting poem bears no resemblance to the transcribed phrases, thus exaggerating the inevitable gap between the representation and its occasion. The second heightens O'Hara's libidinous pleasure in the world to the point of mania, as the poet describes smokestacks as "beautiful" and garbage as "pretty." While the poems are intended as affectionate tributes to O'Hara, their effect is to further ironize the mode of representation he developed in "A Step Away From Them" and other poems.

25. Examples include "Elk Trails" and "Hills of Home" (early poems reprinted in his most recent volume, *Left Out in the Rain* [Berkeley: North Point, 1986]), "Trail Crew Camp at Bear Valley, 9000 Feet. Northern Sierra—White Bone and Threads of Snowmelt Water," in *The Back Country* (New York: New Directions, 1968), "The Bed in the Sky," in *Regarding Wave* (New York: New Directions, 1970), "Walking Home From *The Duchess of Malfi*," in *Turtle Island* (New York: New Directions, 1974), and "Berry Territory," "River in the Valley," "Walking Through Myoshin-Ji," and "Walked Two Days in Snow, Then It Cleared for Five," all in *Axe Handles* (Berkeley: North Point, 1983). Snyder's most recent

walk poem, "Walking the New York Bedrock Alive in the Sea of Information" (reprinted in *Best American Poetry 1988*, ed. John Ashbery [New York: Collier, 1988], p. 175), takes him into O'Hara's territory, but as the title suggests Snyder treats this setting as just another natural landscape, perhaps more exotic than the Sierras but equally organic: "New York like a sea anemone /Wide and waving in the Sea of Economy."

26. From Snyder's statement for Allen, *The New American Poetry*, pp. 420–21.

27. Gary Snyder, *Riprap and Cold Mountain Poems* (San Francisco: Four Seasons Foundation, 1966), p. 15.

28. Allen, *The New American Poetry*, p. 121.

29. Sherman Paul, *In Search of the Primitive* (Baton Rouge: Louisiana State University Press, 1986), p. 286.

30. Snyder, *The Back Country*, p. 11.

31. Sherman Paul writes that the poem exemplifies "the disciplined *play* Snyder puts against *work*" (*In Search of the Primitive*, p. 252).

32. David Perkins and Alan Williamson have both analyzed "Trail Crew Camp" along lines parallel to mine in discussing "A Walk"; see Perkins's *A History of Modern Poetry: Modernism and After* (Cambridge, Mass.: Harvard University Press, 1987), pp. 586–87, and Williamson's *Introspection in Contemporary Poetry* (Cambridge: Harvard University Press, 1984), pp. 71–73. Both critics discern a larger pattern in this poem which bears a striking similarity to the pattern of "A Walk," a movement from effortful passage to lofty vision to relaxed, sensual enjoyment.

33. Gary Snyder, *Six Sections From Mountains and Rivers Without End* (Bolinas: Four Seasons Foundation, 1979), p. 3. Charles Molesworth in his book *Gary Snyder's Vision: Poetry and the Real Work* (Columbia: University of Missouri Press, 1983) notes the connection between this passage and "A Walk," commenting "the whole section is about abstraction, in the sense of experiential moments connecting with one another to reveal a pattern that is not immediately apparent" (p. 115).

34. Perkins, *A History of Modern Poetry*, p. 586.

35. Charles Altieri notes the structural significance of the phrase, the way it "demands that the reader see some kind of completion in the concluding details" (*Enlarging the Temple* [Lewisburg: Bucknell University Press, 1979], p. 134).

36. Perkins, *A History of Modern Poetry*, p. 587.

CHAPTER SIX
A. R. AMMONS AND JOHN ASHBERY: THE WALK AS THINKING

1. Robert Pinsky, *The Situation of Poetry* (Princeton: Princeton University Press, 1976), p. 134.

2. Charles Altieri, *Self and Sensibility in Contemporary American Poetry* (Cambridge: Cambridge University Press, 1984), p. 104.

3. David Perkins, for example, in his *A History of Modern Poetry: Modernism and After* (Cambridge, Mass.: Harvard University Press, 1987), titles one chapter "Meditations of the Solitary Mind: John Ashbery and A. R. Ammons." Harold

Bloom's most extended commentary on the two poets is to be found in his *Figures of Capable Imagination* (New York: Seabury, 1976), along with an important earlier essay on Ammons in *The Ringers in the Tower* (Chicago: University of Chicago Press, 1971).

4. Ammons is apparently aware of, and probably admires, Snyder's work, as evidenced by a passing reference in section 24 of his long poem *Sphere* to the title of his fellow poet's volume *Regarding Wave.*

5. Denis Donoghue compares the two poets as walkers, first evoking a tradition of Romantic walks beside the sea of which Ammons is an heir, then noting Ashbery's urban variation on it: "Ashbery's poems belong to this Romantic or post-Romantic tradition, even though his walks are not as marine as Ammons's. His beaches are more often city streets" (*Reading America* [Berkeley: University of California Press, 1987], p. 303).

6. Pinsky, *The Situation of Poetry*, p. 134.

7. Quoted in Sherman Paul, *In Search of the Primitive* (Baton Rouge: Louisiana State University Press, 1986), p. 53.

8. A. R. Ammons, *Sphere* (New York: Norton, 1974), p. 79; "No Way of Knowing," in John Ashbery, *Self-Portrait in a Convex Mirror* (New York: Viking Penguin, 1975), p. 56.

9. The three quotes all appear in the collection of essays *A. R. Ammons*, ed. Harold Bloom (New York: Chelsea House, 1986), pp. 54, 256, and 258.

10. John Elder, *Imagining the Earth* (Urbana: University of Illinois Press, 1985), p. 137.

11. The phrase "the form of a motion," which is taken from William Carlos Williams's short poem "The Wind Increases," is the subtitle of Ammons's long poem *Sphere.* See also Ammons's poem "Untelling," quoted by Richard Howard in his *Alone with America*, enlarged ed. (New York: Atheneum, 1980), p. 56.

12. Robert Pinsky notes the tension between the poem's "tentative, doubting quality" and its "assertive, proscriptive tone" (*The Situation of Poetry*, p. 151). Pinsky uses this conflict as the basis for a relatively negative assessment of the entire poem; but I think he misses the way the poem itself struggles to resolve the conflict, succeeding beautifully in its middle section.

13. A. R. Ammons, *Selected Poems*, expanded ed. (New York: Norton, 1986), p. 43.

14. Bloom, *A. R. Ammons*, p. 245.

15. Linda Orr also expresses uneasiness with the poem's "repeated use of metaphor created by the *of* prepositional phrase" (ibid., p. 141).

16. Ibid., p. 245.

17. This passage may owe something to the chapter on "Spring" in *Walden*: "I love to see that Nature is so rife with life that myriads can afford to be sacrificed and suffered to prey on one another; that tender organizations can be so serenely squashed out of existence like pulp,—tadpoles which herons gobble up, and tortoises and toads run over in the road; and that sometimes it has rained flesh and blood! With the liability to accident, we must see how little account is to be made of it" (*Walden* [New York: Norton, 1966], p. 210).

18. The phrase "'field' of action" is almost certainly a conscious allusion to Charles Olson's notion of composition by field, a method Ammons could be

said to enlist in the service of more mimetic aims. William Carlos Williams, under Olson's influence, entitled a late essay "The Poem as Field of Action."

19. I am assuming that the clear indications given in the course of "Saliences" that it is composed on the day following the walk of "Corsons Inlet" are accurate; Ammons tells us, for example, that the swallows which had been so much in evidence the previous day have now departed.

20. *A. R. Ammons*, ed. Bloom, p. 110.

21. Ibid., p. 20. This is from Harold Bloom's first essay on Ammons, "When You Consider the Radiance," which he reprints as the "Introduction" to his volume of essays on the poet. It is characteristic of Bloom's reading both of this poem and of Ammons's work as a whole (indeed of all Romantic and post-Romantic poetry) that he views the particulars as obstacles rather than aids to the poet's imagination; his insistence on Ammons's effort to transcend the given substance of the natural world leads him to misread the poem rather seriously, as I will go on to show.

22. The poet was kind enough to show me the original typescript of the poem, which clearly reveals that it was composed in two sections (they were originally numbered I and II), and at separate times, although both are dated on the same day.

23. Ammons, *Selected Poems*, p. 47.

24. Bloom, *A. R. Ammons*, p. 110.

25. Ibid., p. 20.

26. Ibid. p. 22.

27. Pinsky, *The Situation of Poetry*, p. 80.

28. Paul Breslin, *The Psycho-Political Muse* (Chicago: University of Chicago Press, 1987), p. 215.

29. In *Contemporary Poets of the English Language*, ed. Rosalie Murphy (London: St. James Press, 1970), p. 33.

30. Interview with Louis Osti, *Confrontation* 9 (Fall 1974): p. 87; A. L. Poulin Jr., "The Experience of Experience: A Conversation with John Ashbery," *The Michigan Quarterly Review* 20 (1981): p. 245.

31. Interview with Janet Bloom and Robert Losada, *New York Quarterly* 9 (Winter 1972): p. 13.

32. *Beyond Amazement: New Essays on John Ashbery*, ed. David Lehman (Ithaca: Cornell University Press, 1980), p. 118. See also Charles Altieri's comment that Ashbery's poetry moves toward "a more complete mimesis" (*Self and Sensibility*, p. 137).

33. Breslin, *The Psycho-Political Muse*, p. 219.

34. Ibid., p. 234.

35. In *John Ashbery*, ed. Harold Bloom (New York: Chelsea House, 1985), p. 208.

36. Ashbery, *Self-Portrait in a Convex Mirror*, p. 14.

37. David Kalstone, *Five Temperaments* (New York: Oxford University Press, 1977), p. 194.

38. Stevens too describes New Haven's dilapidate appearances as "Words, lines, not meanings, not communications"; but Ashbery is more keenly aware of the cultural network that turns "things" into words or signs.

39. See Breslin's description of bourgeois experience as an "undifferenti-ated expanse . . . which becomes, in one's skeptical moments, a vast featureless plain on which no destination looks worth a pilgrimage" (*The Psycho-Political Muse*, p. 216).

40. This pun is, I think, reinforced by the repetition of the "lop" phoneme in "sloppy joe" and "scalloped corn."

41. This echoes Stevens's theme of the "venerable holding-in" of appear-ances, but in a less celebratory key.

42. Kalstone, *Five Temperaments*, p. 194.

43. Breslin, *The Psycho-Political Muse*, p. 226.

44. "Worsening Situation," in Ashbery, *Self-Portrait in a Convex Mirror*, p. 3.

45. John Ashbery, *Three Poems* (New York: Viking Penguin, 1972), p. 3.

46. Ashbery addresses this problem most explicitly in a passage from his long poem "The Skaters" (*Rivers and Mountains* [New York: Holt, Rinehart and Winston, 1966], p. 38):

> Labels on bottles
> And all kinds of discarded objects that ought to be described.
> But can one ever be sure of which ones?
> Isn't this a death-trap, wanting to put too much in
> So the floor sags, as under the weight of a piano, or a piano-legged girl,
> And the whole house of cards comes dinning down around one's ears!

47. Ashbery, *Self-Portrait in a Convex Mirror*, p. 71.

48. Ashbery describes this movement quite precisely in *Three Poems*: "we must register our appraisal of the moving world that is around us, but our song is leading us on now, farther and farther into that wilderness and away from the shrouded but familiar forms that were its first inspiration" (pp. 109–10).

49. The film is a very dark thriller about an ex-convict (Robert Mitchum) set on revenge against a lawyer (Gregory Peck) who testified against him. The con-vict stalks the lawyer and his family, eventually raping the wife and attacking the daughter in the swampy Florida vacation area that gives the film its title. Its unusually oppressive and morbid atmosphere may have appealed to Ashbery.

CONCLUSION
THE WALK AND THE WORLD

1. John Ashbery, *Houseboat Days* (New York: Viking Penguin, 1977), p. 54.

INDEX